P

Genius and the Mind

Genius and the Mind

Studies of Creativity and Temperament

Edited by
ANDREW STEPTOE

*Department of Psychology,
St George's Hospital Medical School, University of London*

Oxford   New York   Tokyo
OXFORD UNIVERSITY PRESS
1998

Oxford University Press, Great Clarendon Street, Oxford OX2 6DP

Oxford New York

Athens Auckland Bangkok Bogota Bombay Buenos Aires Calcutta
Cape Town Chennai Dar es Salaam Delhi Florence Hong Kong Istanbul
Karachi Kuala Lumpur Madrid Melbourne Mexico City Mumbai
Nairobi Paris São Paolo Singapore Taipei Tokyo Toronto Warsaw

and associated companies in
Berlin Ibadan

Oxford is a trade mark of Oxford University Press

Published in the United States
by Oxford University Press, Inc., New York

© Oxford University Press, 1998

A catalogue record for this book is available from the British Library

Library of Congress Cataloging in Publication Data
Genius and the mind : studies of creativity and temperament in the
historical record / edited by Andrew Steptoe.
Includes bibliographical references and index.
1. Genius.   2. Creative ability.   3. Nature and nurture.
4. Genius and mental illness.   5. Gifted persons–Case studies.
I. Steptoe, Andrew.
BF412.G435 1998   153.3'5–dc21   97-51708

ISBN 0 19 852373 4 (Hbk)

Typeset by Jayvee, Trivandrum, India
Printed in Great Britain by
Bookcraft (Bath) Ltd
Midsomer Norton, Avon

Foreword

Roy Porter, Professor of the Social History of Medicine, Wellcome Institute, London

I have always been wary of attempts to generalize about genius. That comes in large measure from being a historian. For one thing, study of the past shows that geniuses have appeared in all shapes and sizes, at all times and places; no patterns stand up and hit you in the face. There have been child prodigies, like Mozart, whereas other creative people, like Charles Darwin, were thought pretty stupid when they were young. Some have burnt themselves out fast; others, like Picasso, were to sustain their originality over immensely long careers. Some have excelled in mathematics, others in music, in playing cricket, or conducting orchestras or diplomacy. There seems to be no common denominator except uncommonness. We all know giftedness when we see it, but (the historical sceptic in me queries), is there much more that can be said than that?

History also indicates how many different explanations have been offered over the centuries to account for the phenomenon. Even Graeco-Roman antiquity had at least three major doctrines competing for attention, the 'divine fire' or 'God's touch' idea, the notion that creativity was the product of the melancholy humour, and of course the Muses. At other times, hereditarian theories have had their day, forerunners to the contemporary genetic outlooks which are discussed in this book. In context of the old conundrum—are geniuses born or made, is it nature or nurture?—the importance of early training, environment and conditioning has often been stressed. Others still see geniuses as quintessential outsiders, original perhaps through sheer incapacity to be, behave, or think normally. Birth-order theorists have sought to bring outsiderhood within an environmental model.

Eighteenth-century theorists, for their part, returning to the etymological roots of genius (*gigno*: I bring forth), often posited that geniuses had 'organic' minds rather than the 'mechanical' understandings ordinary people possessed. Romanticism then looked to some plastic power of imagination; a century later, IQ studies would be introduced; and throughout this century, as this book amply shows, psychologists have remained preoccupied by the daunting explanatory problems posed by exceptional talent. Doubtless, in the coming century, neurological theories will become more prominent once brain-scanning techniques are perfected; and genetic engineering and the cloning of geniuses will point to possible solutions—and certainly new problems. When theories proliferate, I was taught, suspicions ought to be raised.

As a historian, I'm also uncomfortably aware of the dangers involved in trying to diagnose genius, and the abuses which have followed from such practices. For one thing, as Andrew Steptoe remarks in his 'Introduction', a lot of third-rate history has been done in the name of the wilder sorts of quasi-Freudian psychohistory. All too often this has followed a circular argument—speculating on the basis of adult achievements what *must* have happened in childhood, and then, in the light of that hypothesized childhood, explaining the accomplishments of adulthood. Worse than this, theories about genius, and especially creativity in its relations to madness, have had stigmatizing applications. Many psychiatrists of the latter decades of the nineteenth century—Cesaro Lombroso in Italy and Theophilus Hyslop in Britain, to mention just two—pursuing the convergence between madness and genius, concluded that geniuses were invariably specimens of psychopathology (though not that all mad people were geniuses). For that reason poets and artists might be deemed fit for the madhouse and the arts be deemed degenerate. It is possible that some exceptionally talented individuals—John Clare or Robert Schumann for example—ended up tragically spending time—in Clare's case, most of his life—locked away in asylums in deference to such menacing beliefs. Only sixty years ago the Nazis were staging exhibitions of 'Degenerate Art', with a view to cultural cleansing.

And yet, despite all these *caveats*, as a historian I cannot help being fascinated by genius. I may not be able to understand it, but I cannot ignore the fact that geniuses have been historically prominent and have, in various ways, changed the course of history. That is most striking, of course, in science and the arts. Newtonian science would doubtless have come about in due course without Newton, but that doesn't diminish the breathtaking originality of the Cambridge professor's achievement. And without Shakespeare no one (certainly not Francis Bacon) would ever have written Shakespeare, and the course of English literature would have been unfathomably different. In other fields too genius has shone and mattered. One doesn't have to subscribe to some crude 'great man' theory of history to believe that there was something very special about Socrates and Christ, Freud or Gandhi. Any theory of genius which is exclusively preoccupied with cognitive dimensions and fails to take wider aspects of personality into account can hardly get to grips with the essentials.

Hence it was with pleasant expectation that I plunged into this collection. Most of the essays are more or less psychological in disciplinary orientation; but if this historian sometimes balks at the psychologist's methods (that penchant for scores and quantification, redoubled in these days of computer power), the rigour of the testing of hypotheses in these essays comes as a breath of fresh air. The richness of the biographical investigations in the pages below cannot fail to intrigue.

Genius is so singular that no single discipline can have a monopoly upon its investigation. The psychological essays which follow will be of great interest to readers from the range of the social sciences and the humanities. If our understanding of genius is to advance, there must be a meeting of minds from across the disciplines. Often, as with the discussion below of Lord Byron as Romantic and manic depressive, or the analysis of Vasari's *Lives of the artists*, that multidisciplinary approach is palpably being realized.

Contents

Contributors

Robert S. Albert, *Pitzer College, Claremont, CA 91711, USA.*

Vincent J. Cassandro, *University of California, Davis, California 95616-8686, USA.*

Gordon Claridge, *Magdalen College, Oxford OX1 4AU, UK.*

Mihaly Csikszentmihalyi, *Department of Psychology, The University of Chicago, 5848 South University Avenue, Chicago, Illinois 60637, USA.*

K. Anders Ericsson, *Department of Psychology, Florida State University, Tallahassee, FL 32306-1270, USA.*

Michael J. A. Howe, *Department of Psychology, Washington Singer Laboratory, University of Exeter, EX4 4QG, UK.*

Kay Redfield Jamison, *Affective Disorders Unit, Department of Psychiatry and Behavioral Sciences, John Hopkins University School of Medicine, 600 North Wolfe Street, Baltimore, MD 21287-7381, USA.*

Andreas C. Lehmann, *Department of Psychology, Florida State University, Tallahassee, FL 32306-1270, USA.*

David T. Lykken, *Department of Psychology, Elliott Hall, University of Minnesota, Minneapolis, MN 55455-0344, USA.*

Dean Keith Simonton, *Department of Psychology, University of California, Davis, California 95616-8686, USA.*

Andrew Steptoe, *Department of Psychology, St George's Hospital Medical School, Cranmer Terrace, London SW17 ORE, UK.*

Kathleen A. Taylor, *University of California, Davis, California 95616-8686, USA.*

Figures facing chapter openings

CHARLOTTE BRONTË

CHAPTER 1

Exceptional creativity and the psychological sciences

Andrew Steptoe

Introduction

PSYCHOLOGY is a relatively young intellectual discipline, but since the earliest phases there has been a strong interest in exceptional creativity. An extensive research literature has built up concerning the cognitive processes underlying creativity in the arts, sciences, and other domains. Studies from the clinical perspective have explored associations between creativity and disorders of temperament, while social scientists have identified important factors in the cultural milieu that influence the recognition and nurturing of artistic and scientific creativity. Much of this research is naturally focused on exceptional achievement in the present day, due to the strong desire to understand and foster giftedness in children. The aim of this book is rather different. It is an attempt to apply modern knowledge of the social, emotional, and biological factors that influence behaviour to the topic of exceptional creativity in the historical record. The purpose is to illustrate the ways in which contemporary research in the psychological sciences can deepen our understanding of the creativity, and the mental processes of those individuals in the past who might be described as geniuses.

Intellectual enquiry into the factors stimulating the creativity of exceptional people in the past is not novel. Francis Galton's work on hereditary genius, Sigmund Freud's study of Leonardo da Vinci, and Catherine Cox's computation of the intelligence of '300 geniuses', show some of the methods that have been applied to the historical record. Different authorities have construed creativity in a bewildering assortment of ways. It has been seen as a response to divine inspiration, an off-shoot of skilled craftsmanship, a manifestation of psychosexual disturbance, an inevitable product of genetically-determined abilities, a social construct, and as a response to deep emotional distress. There are important reasons why such diverse views have flourished. We are at a rather early stage in our understanding of the processes governing any original or innovative thoughts and actions, let alone the few creative products that have stood the test of time. Equally significantly, we lack the systematic data on writers, painters, musicians, or scientists of the past that would allow critical tests of competing hypotheses to be made. Caution is therefore needed in drawing inferences about the factors related to creativity in historical figures. On the other hand, there are innovative ways in which the known factors about the lives of geniuses, their creative products, and their utterances on ordinary aspects of life, can be used to further the debate. Several new and exciting approaches are described in this book.

Writing from a psychological perspective about genius and creativity was dominated in the first half of this century by psychodynamic thinking, rather than by experimental psychology and the behavioural sciences. Psychohistory and 'psychobiography' came to be identified with the application of psychoanalysis to the study of historical figures (Friedlander 1978). After Freud himself, famous examples are Clark's (1933) book on Abraham Lincoln, and Langer's (1972) work on Hitler, written during World War II at the behest of the US Government. Biographers in this tradition relied on the techniques of psychoanalysis, stressing the influence of early life and psychosexual experience, the significance of unconscious processes, and the interpretation of minor details or incidents. The prestige of the analytic movement was so great that it allowed Hitschmann (1956) to assert that 'Only an analyst is competent and qualified to write the biographies of great men'.

Unfortunately, the dominance of psychoanalysis has given the application of psychology to historical figures a bad name. Historians and literary scholars were swift to expose psychoanalytic biographies as limited and erroneous in their knowledge of their subjects (Runyan 1982). More general charges have also been made, such as over-emphasis on the significance of particular occurrences (eventism), reductionism in explaining behaviour in terms of internal psychological factors without taking the social and cultural context into account, and the trivialization of creativity as a product of early psychosexual experience or neurosis (Anderson 1978; Stone 1981). As psychoanalysis has waned as a valued approach to the understanding of human experience, so too has psychobiography been discredited.

There are alternative approaches. Runyan (1982) argued vigorously for a definition of psychobiography as the 'use of any explicit or formal psychological theory in biography'. One might, from this perspective, recommend biographical studies based on social learning theory, attributional theory, personal construct theory, or another perspective. However, as Howe (1997) has pointed out, enterprises of this kind may risk the same problems that beset psychoanalytic biographies. The dominant psychological theories of human behaviour have developed immeasurably over the past forty years. Psychological studies of historical figures that are tightly based on particular theoretical orientations may date in the same way as psychodynamic accounts.

A different perspective is taken in this book. It is not so much concerned with the application of theory, as with the use of knowledge from the psychological sciences in helping to understand genius. This psychological knowledge derives from experimentation and observation, but is not confined to a particular theory. Thus contributors draw on domains such as behavioural genetics, the psychology of skill acquisition, developmental and educational psychology, and on clinical observations for mental health research. Space has prevented all aspects of psychological research being represented. There is a vigorous research agenda on the cognitive psychology of creativity (Ward *et al.* 1997) and considerable interest in analogies with artificial intelligence

(Boden 1990) that are not touched upon here. Miller (1996) has recently developed an interesting thesis concerning the role of visual imagery that is not considered either. But one feature that does unify the chapters of this book is that knowledge acquired about psychological and social processes in general is applied to exceptional individuals or to groups of very creative people. The geniuses discussed here are seen as examples of broader processes, and not as unique phenomena outside the comprehension of psychological research. They are of course extreme cases, in as much as their works have enhanced life and culture, but they can still be understood within the general framework of behavioural development and psychological experience that is common to much of the human race.

The basic elements

The first group of chapters set the scene by presenting the major influences on creativity and exceptional achievement: genetics (Chapter 2 by David Lykken), the social world (Chapter 3 by Mihaly Csikszentmihalyi), and training and skill acquisition (Chapter 4 by Andreas Lehmann and Anders Ericsson).

Lykken has been in the forefront of the explosion of behavioural genetic research that has occurred over the past fifteen years. He is a member of the research group at the University of Minnesota that has been at the centre of research in this field, studying cohorts of identical and fraternal twins, and a rare cohort of twins separated early in life and reared apart. The notion that genetic factors contribute to individual differences in human behaviour and achievement was frowned on for many years, following the excesses of the Eugenics movement and the devastating consequences of beliefs in racial purity in Nazi Germany. Investigations of genetic factors were seen as endorsing an elitist and authoritarian view of human society. However, the intellectual climate has changed, due both to the advances in molecular genetics and the growing awareness of the contributions made by genetic research to understanding medical and developmental problems. Behavioural genetics has itself become highly sophisticated in its methods and in the interpretation of data (Plomin *et al.* 1997). In Chapter 2, Lykken outlines these advances and discusses their application to genius. As he points out, the question is no longer whether genetic or environmental factors determine behaviour, but how they interact. It is extremely unlikely that there is such a thing as a 'poetry gene' or a 'music gene', since complex human behaviours typically have a polygenic basis. Lykken describes the concept of emergenesis, an extreme form of epistasis, in which a unique combination of genes may lead to qualitative shifts in capacity or ability (Lykken 1982; Lykken *et al.* 1992). Such abilities are not inherited in a simple fashion. Genetic factors are likely to contribute not only to specific abilities, but also to traits such as persistence, the capacity to concentrate for extended periods, and curiosity about certain types of stimulation. These properties may in turn affect the individual's response to educational stimulation and tuition. The result is a complex interplay between inherited traits and environmental factors, in which genetics may underpin exposure to nurturing social and physical experiences.

A complementary perspective on creativity and achievement is provided by Mihaly Csikszentmihalyi (Chapter 3) in his discussion of the sociocultural dimension. Csikszentmihalyi has been prominent in the investigation of talent in early life, and in studying the relationship between optimal experiences, 'flow' and inventiveness (Csikszentmihalyi *et al.* 1993; Csikszentmihalyi 1996). In this chapter, he reminds us that exceptional ability is not a property of the individual in isolation, but depends on social recognition and appreciation. There is a complicated interchange between the person, the domain of activity in which he or she works, be it painting, science or fiction writing, and the social organization of that domain. This is best understood within a 'systems' perspective of interaction and feedback. Csikszentmihalyi argues that it is the 'gatekeepers' of that domain who determine what is creative and what is not. This is most obvious in technical areas such as mathematics, the sciences and certain types of philosophy, where the nature of problems and the validity of discoveries or solutions can only be properly understood by a small cohort of specialists. It is necessary for most of us to take on trust the fact, for example, that the Indian mathematician Srinivasa Ramanujan discussed by Robert Albert in Chapter 6 was a genius, since it requires advanced mathematical training to understand his field of activity.

But gatekeepers also operate in domains that are more accessible to the general public. There are few absolute standards of achievement, except perhaps in clearly competitive domains such as sports or chess. The consensus that Claude Monet was a greater master of French impressionism than Gustave Caillebotte, or that Charlotte Brontë was a superior novelist to Elizabeth Gaskell, is not so much a reflection of concrete differences in technical abilities or imagination, but in taste and understanding. Tastes are moulded by the specialists in a domain who help us to comprehend the subtleties of skill and innovation, and by exposure to the work itself. The roster of genius in any field of endeavour is not fixed, but changes over time. Franz Schubert was virtually unknown outside a small circle in nineteenth century Vienna, but he now ranks among the greatest of classical music composers. Anton Mesmer was regarded as a charlatan in his own time, yet was later recognized as a pioneer in the understanding of psychological processes (Ellenberger 1970). One interesting consequence of the argument developed by Csikszentmihalyi is that the rarity of exceptional achievement may not be due only to limitations in genetic variability or human potential, but also to the inability of cultures to respond to innovation and new ideas. His chapter also introduces a number of the themes concerning the personal characteristics of creative individuals that are elaborated in later sections of the book.

The third basic strand is training and experience, and these are addressed by Andreas Lehmann and Anders Ericsson in Chapter 4. There has been a spate of interest in the role of practice in the development of expert performance over recent years, stimulated in large part by the work of Ericsson and his colleagues (Ericsson *et al.* 1993; Ericsson 1996; Ericsson and Lehmann 1996). In a number of domains, it has been shown that elite performers have engaged in substantially more deliberate practice than their less competent peers, and have frequently begun to work at their skills from an earlier age. Reliable information about practice is difficult enough to obtain from contemporary individuals, since the evidence is typically shrouded in the memories of childhood. Longitudinal studies of people assessed as children, and then asked retrospectively to judge their experience from an adult standpoint, have shown major discrepancies between actual experience and adult recollection (Henry *et al.* 1994). Lehmann and Ericsson attempt something even more difficult in their chapter, by evaluating the development of expert performance in the historical record. Their chosen field is music, particularly piano playing. They use an innovative method of comparing key-board virtuosi of different eras, from J. S. Bach to the present time. Their analyses suggest that the acquisition of instrumental performance skills has accelerated over the past two hundred and fifty years. At the highest levels, the musical prodigies of the twentieth century have obtained levels of expertise at much earlier ages than did the prodigies of the past.

Lehmann and Ericsson also emphasize the interplay between individual skills and technology. The construction of instruments has changed gradually over many decades, and these developments have made easier certain types of performance: the invention of valves on brass instruments is a striking example. At the same time, modifications in instruments have challenged players to attempt greater feats of virtuosity, thereby stimulating new instrumental techniques.

It might be argued that technical skill in public performance has little to do with creativity and genius. But music is a domain in which performance and composition have always been very closely linked. With rare exceptions, composers of the past were performers who wrote music for their own use. Their own abilities not only determined the instruments for which they preferred to write, but the nature of the music itself. As performances became more expert and consistent, so the music could develop in complexity. Exceptional performers have in turn inspired composers as in the cases of the clarinettist Anton Stadler and Mozart, Brahms and the violinist Joszef Joachim, and William Walton and the viola player Lionel Tertis. Each composer matched his compositions to the expertise and strengths of the performer. Similar associations between technical skill and creativity can be seen in other forms of expression that have emerged from a craft base, such as painting and photography. In the performance arts (theatre, film, opera), there is no doubt that the skills of performers both inspire creators, and extend the imaginative possibilities of the medium.

Development and experience

Chapters 5–7 discuss the influence of early life and adult experience on the temperament and inventiveness of exceptional individuals. Michael Howe is an influential contemporary champion of the integration of psychology and biography (Howe 1997), and has made a particular study of the role of early experience and childhood (Howe 1990; Howe and Griffey 1995). In Chapter 5, he contrasts the childhood and adolescence of four nineteenth century Englishmen whose adult lives were characterized by great achievements: the social scientist and political philosopher J. S. Mill, Charles

Darwin, the physicist Michael Faraday and George Stephenson, railway engineer extraordinary. The childhoods and early lives of these individuals could hardly have been more different, ranging from intensive systematic instruction for Mill, to Stephenson's life which was so impoverished that he could not even read and write until adulthood. Howe argues that each man's experience suited him for his later achievements, by allowing him to develop appropriate skills which were not just intellectual but social. The ways in which Faraday and Stephenson overcame early disadvantages are particularly striking, and show how determination and intensely focused interest create educational opportunities out of the most unpromising situations.

A more specific comparison of two individuals who were both exceptionally able but differed in their inventiveness is provided by Robert Albert in Chapter 6. Albert has made a lifetime study of mathematical giftedness in children, how early talent can be nurtured, and the ways in which career choices are made (Albert 1990, 1994). Here he applies this knowledge to the investigation into the background of lives of Srinivasa Ramanujan and G. H. Hardy. Ramanujan was an extraordinary individual who emerged from an obscure background in southern India to become one of the most original mathematicians of the twentieth century. During his short life, he developed ideas in the theory of numbers and other mathematical fields that are still being puzzled over and applied in the present day. For some years he worked with G. H. Hardy, the quintessential Cambridge don whose achievements in mathematics were great without having that additional spark. An exploration of the background of these two shows the ways in which social factors and family interests help to mould abilities in early life. Albert places great emphasis on the identification of giftedness, acknowledging (as does Csikszentmihalyi) the ways in which the individual and domain interact.

Albert also considers the personalities of Ramanujan and Hardy. Instead of deriving generalized inferences from the historical material in an arbitrary fashion, he assess the evidence within the framework of a standardized personality test. This has two advantages in the study of exceptional individuals of the past. Firstly, the biographer's estimations of personality are not swayed by striking but unrepresentative features, since the information has to be assessed systematically across the entire range of personal characteristics. Secondly, standardized assessments make possible comparisons with other groups who have been administered the same tests, so that direct contrasts can be made with other sectors of the population. In Chapter 6, Albert shows that Hardy and his co-worker John Littlewood had personality profiles that very much accord with those of gifted young mathematicians and scientists of the present day. Ramanujan on the other hand showed a distinctive profile much closer to that of people of achievement outside the physical sciences. He had more of the artist in him, and this may have allowed him to make the creative leaps of the imagination that set his mathematics apart from others.

In Chapter 7, I discuss the life of Wolfgang Amadeus Mozart. Mozart has been the subject of a vast range of literature, and a number of biographies have been written with a psychological orientation (for example Hildesheimer 1983; Solomon 1995). My own research on Mozart started from a cultural and historical perspective, with an interest in the social context of his work and the background to his Italian operas (Steptoe 1981, 1982). However, when writing about his life, I have inevitably found myself drawing on the literature in the psychological sciences (Steptoe 1990).

I relate three themes in Mozart's life to the research literature in psychology and psychiatry. The first is the recognition and development of exceptional ability, and the transition to adult creativity. Mozart was an almost textbook child prodigy, stimulated by his ambitious father and leading a life that was extraordinary rich in terms of cultural and musical experience, but emotionally limited by insulation within his family group. Like many prodigies, he found the transition from childhood to mature success very difficult, involving as it did a severance of the family relationships that had sustained his early life. I relate Mozart's experience during this phase of his life with the psychological literature on the development of exceptionally talented people. The second theme is that of emotional stress and resilience. Mozart suffered a catalogue of stressful experiences during his adult life that might have completely overwhelmed many people. Yet his creative output seldom faltered, and he maintained a remarkable work load. I draw on the research literature relating stressful life events to health in order to understand his experience, and delineate the social and emotional resources that enabled him to cope effectively. His personal resources included the positive self-image he acquired in his childhood, and a fundamental confidence in his abilities and the value of his work. At an interpersonal level, he drew both on support from family and friends, and also on the belief systems of the Enlightenment era to which he subscribed.

The third theme of the chapter is Mozart's psychological temperament. We are fortunate that he wrote a series of vivid letters to family and friends throughout his life, and these give some insight into his views of the world. In Chapter 7, I use an innovative quantitative technique developed by Martin Seligman from the University of Pennsylvania and Christopher Peterson from the University of Michigan for the assessment of the 'cognitive style' underlying optimistic and depressive dispositions. This allows a more objective measurement of Mozart's outlook on life and reactions to events than can be obtained from simply surveying the correspondence. The results highlight the optimistic temperament that helped Mozart tolerate the manifold difficulties of his life.

Quantitative analysis of creative work

Chapter 8 is by Dean Simonton from the University of California at Davis, and his colleagues Kathleen Taylor and Vincent Cassandro. Simonton is a prolific writer on psychology, creativity, and history, and has ably surveyed these fields in a number of books (Simonton 1984, 1990, 1994). He is a champion of 'historiometric' methods, involving the application of quantitative statistics to historical figures and their activities. This approach has been made possible by the massive increase in personal computing power that has taken place over the past thirty years. This has allowed complex trends in data to be uncovered that are not visible to impressionistic inspection. Other investigators have also grasped the benefits of computers for assessing phenomena such as innovative content in the paintings of past masters (Martindale 1986), and the relationship between birth order and adherence to radical opinions (Sulloway 1996). Simonton has been particularly concerned with the growth and diminution of creative activities across the life span, and has developed a model of career trajectories to account for these patterns (Simonton 1997).

Statistical methods are generally applied to populations rather than individuals. However, in Chapter 8, these techniques are used to investigate the work of the greatest and most influential of playwrights, William Shakespeare. Simonton and his colleagues look for statistical regularities in the content of Shakespeare's plays and sonnets, so as to understand what facets make them particularly striking or memorable. This involves concepts such as aesthetic success and categories of word imagery. The findings in Chapter 8 disguise a huge amount of detailed quantification of verse rhythms, endings, and word use. The authors draw on psychological theories concerning imagery, form and content to drive the investigation. They find trends over Shakespeare's life in the themes that occupy his plays, related in part to historical events and in part to his own career trajectory. Associations between the imagery of the plays and their aesthetic success also emerge. In the sonnets as well, both style and content emerge as factors influencing quality.

This approach to one of the greatest geniuses of literature may meet with opposition. Academics and readers with a background in the humanities often find the statistical method distasteful, believing it to be reductionist, shredding the delicate fabric of exquisite poetry into bland categories. The response to the results sometimes resembles a common reaction to scientific psychology in general—the findings are obvious, so the work need never have been done. However, humans have an almost unlimited capacity rapidly to regard as 'obvious', phenomena of which they were hitherto ignorant (Nisbett and Ross 1980). The fact that statistical methods sometimes endorse commonly held beliefs should perhaps reinforce our confidence that they are working in the right direction. The advantage of this method is that conclusions are based on testable, reproducible formulations, and that general rules can begin to be derived from a secure base.

Temperament and creativity

The last three chapters of this book tackle in various ways the perennially fascinating issue of creativity, temperament, and mental health. This topic has been a theme in Western thought from the earliest times, and opinions have veered right across the spectrum from complete acceptance to rejection of the notion that certain types of artistic creativity are intimately linked with disorders of temperament (Murray 1989). Sir Peter Medawar, for example, dismissed the connection between genius and insanity as a 'gothic illusion'. Over recent decades, views have been based less on impressions than on systematic evaluations of large numbers of creative individuals using standardized methods (for example Post 1994; Ludwig 1995). Chapters 9, 10, and 11 illustrate some of the methods that can be used to tease out these inter-relationships.

Kay Jamison is a Professor of Psychiatry at Johns Hopkins University School of Medicine, and an international authority on manic-depressive disorders (Goodwin and Jamison 1990). She has been particularly interested in the relationship between artistic creativity and manic-depressive illness, and has discussed the evidence extensively in her book *Touched with fire* (Jamison 1993). Unusually for a professional in the field of mental health, she has been disarmingly frank about her own experience of manic depression, and in her autobiography has vividly described the exuberance of thought and imagination associated with mania (Jamison 1996). In Chapter 9, she explains the role of manic-depressive dispositions in the life and poetry of George, Lord Byron. Byron was an extraordinary individual who charismatically cut a swathe through early nineteenth century high society, just as his poetry virtually defined the era of romanticism. Jamison shows how his life was driven by violent mood swings from passionate excess and energy to abject melancholy. His painful self-awareness of his own turbulent temperament led to an insight into human nature that stimulated the most moving poetry. There is little doubt about the hereditary component to Byron's mood disorder, but his genius was not shared by his relatives. Perhaps only his daughter Ada, a pioneer in mechanical computation and co-worker of Charles Babbage, showed any of his generous creative capacity.

The theme of literary creation and mental illness is approached from a different perspective by Gordon Claridge in Chapter 10. Claridge is an authority on personality and psychiatric disorder, and has been particularly concerned with personality traits related to schizophrenia (Claridge 1985, 1997). He points out that although the notion of a link between creativity and madness is long established, the present intellectual climate in mental health research is perhaps less sympathetic than it has been in the past. Twenty years ago, serious mental illnesses were thought by many to be caused by social or inter-personal factors. In the current era of genetic studies, brain imaging and neurochemical investigation, the case for organic dysfunctions in schizophrenia is very strong. This perhaps weakens the apparent similarities between the bizarre novelty of schizophrenic thought and genuine creativity. On the other hand, evidence for traits of schizotypy, or dimensions of unusual cognitive processes that run through the population, is growing. Hence the distinction between mental illness and disturbed normality is less clear cut.

Claridge has previously collaborated with two literary scholars to consider the formal psychiatric status of ten writers known to have had serious mental problems, including John Clare, William Cowper, and Virginia Woolf (Claridge *et al.* 1990). In this chapter, he explores the use of a computer-based diagnostic protocol, in which the clinical and behavioural characteristics of the individual are entered in a systematic fashion. These data are then scored by algorithms that produce psychiatric diagnoses based on contemporary schemes, such as those developed by the American Psychiatric Association. This chapter further illustrates the strength of non-anecdotal approaches to the characterization of creative individuals. A particular concern is whether these creative writers have disorders of an affective or manic-depressive type (as argued by Jamison), or whether their conditions can be described as schizophrenic.

The results are interesting and relatively consistent, in showing schizophrenia in its various forms to be the predominant diagnosis. It is, however, notable that in some cases, such as the Victorian connoisseur and social commentator John Ruskin, there is wide disagreement between diagnostic schemes. Claridge relates these findings to the recent developments in the psychology of schizotypy, and argues that both manic or affective elements, and schizophrenic features, may be relevant to creativity. The former may provide the energy and colour to new work, while the latter stimulates the innovative associations between different areas that characterize much artistic, and possibly even scientific, thought.

The last chapter is rather different in orientation, although once again it involves the systematic abstraction and analysis of material from the historical record. In this chapter, I address the issue of temperament and creativity in the artists of the Italian Renaissance, including Michelangelo, Leonardo de Vinci, Raphael, and Titian. Of course, the information available about these individuals is much more scanty and unreliable than the evidence that survives concerning more recent artists. However, we are fortunate that they were the subjects of the first comprehensive biographical survey in the arts, that 'Bible' of the Italian Renaissance, Giorgio Vasari's *Lives of the painters, sculptors and architects*. This book was published in 1550 with a revised and expanded edition in 1568, and is a major source of knowledge about the Renaissance. The book includes information about the personalities and behaviour of the artists along with descriptions of their works. It is this material that was extracted for the content analysis described in Chapter 11. The approach is a deliberate attempt to go beyond anecdote, and develop a database against which hypotheses can be tested.

I began by asking the question of whether an analysis of the personality characteristics of the artists described by Vasari would give insight into the issue of temperament and creativity. However, it soon became clear that although the analysis was straightforward enough, interpretation was more problematic. Vasari was a biographer with an agenda. He was intent on establishing painting and sculpture, activities associated at that time with a plebeian craft base, as liberal arts. He also wanted artists themselves to be recognized as professionals with training and special expertise, thereby endowing them with the dignity that would allow them to consort with merchants, lawyers, and other professionals. In the terms outlined by Csikszentmihalyi in Chapter 3, Vasari was intent on establishing the parameters of the 'field' within the domain of the visual arts.

It might be supposed therefore that he would not wish the great artists to be perceived as unruly and tempestuous, but as men and women of distinction and sophistication. The data for these analyses are therefore filtered by an individual with a strong investment in a particular point of view. This must inevitably limit the conclusions that can be drawn.

One might object that Vasari's work is an inappropriate subject for such analyses. However, his book is unique in its breadth and influence. No other sources from the era come close to Vasari in providing relevant data. The experience of studying his work reinforces for me the concern that is shared by other contributors to this book, that the evidence from the historical record is seldom first hand. We as scientists, and the biographers and commentators on whom so much material is based, make decisions about the selection of evidence that are not always explicit. Part of the challenge for psychologists is to develop protocols that are transparent and open to the working of other researchers in the future.

Conclusions

My hope is that readers of this book will discover that contemporary psychological science has much to offer in deepening our understanding of genius in the arts and sciences. By examining the lives and works of exceptional individuals in the context of general (perhaps universal) psychological processes, we may go some way towards demystifying creativity. Our aim is not, however, to undermine the achievements of the extraordinary people studied in this book. Rather it is to enrich our experience of their works, while at the same time coming closer to comprehending the nature of human potential.

References

Albert, R. S. (1990). Identity, experiences, and career choice among the exceptionally gifted and eminent. In *Theories of creativity* (ed. M. A. Runco, and R. S. Albert), pp. 13–34. Sage Publications, Newbury Park, CA.

——(1994). The achievement of eminence: A longitudinal study of exceptionally gifted boys and their families. In *Beyond Terman: contemporary longitudinal studies of giftedness and talent* (ed. R. F. Subotnik and K. D. Arnold), pp. 282–315. Ablex Publishing Corp, Norwood, NJ.

Anderson, T. H. (1978). Becoming sane with psychobiography. *The Historian*, **41**, 1–20.

Boden, M. A. (1990). *The creative mind: myths and mechanisms*. Weidenfeld and Nicolson, London.

Claridge, G. (1985). *Origins of mental illness*. Blackwell, Oxford.

——(ed.) (1997). *Schizotypy: implications for illness and health*. Oxford University Press, Oxford.

——, Pryor, R., and Watkins, G. (1990). *Sounds from the bell jar: ten psychotic authors*. Macmillan, London.

Clark, L. P. (1933). *Lincoln: a psychobiography*. Scribner's, New York.

Csikszentmihalyi, M. (1996). *Creativity: flow and the psychology of discovery and invention*. HarperCollins, New York.

——, Rathunde, K., and Whalen, S. (1993). *Talented teenagers: the roots of success and failure*. Cambridge University Press, New York.

Ellenberger, H. F. (1970). *The discovery of the unconscious*. Allan Lane, London.

Ericsson, K. A. (ed.) (1996). *The road to excellence: the acquisition of expert performance in the arts, sciences, sports, and games*. Erlbaum, Mahwah, NJ.

——, and Lehmann, A. C. (1996). Expert and exceptional performance: evidence for maximal adaptations to task constraints. *Annual Review of Psychology*, **47**, 273–305.

Ericsson, K. A., Krampe, R. T., and Tesch-Römer, C. (1993). The role of deliberate practise in the acquisition of expert performance. *Psychological Review*, **100**, 363–406.

Friedlander, S. (1978). *History and psychoanalysis*. Holmes and Meier, New York.

Goodwin, F. K., and Jamison, K. R. (1990). *Manic-depressive illness*. Oxford University Press, New York.

Henry, B., Moffitt, T. E., Caspi, A., Langley, J., and Silva, P. A. (1994). On the 'Remembrance of things past': a longitudinal evaluation of the retrospective method. *Psychological Assessment*, **6**, 92–101.

Hildesheimer, W. (1983). *Mozart*. J. M. Dent, London.

Hitschmann, E. (1956). Some psychoanalytic aspects of biography. *International Journal of Psychoanalysis*, **37**, 265–9.

Howe, M. J. A. (1990). *The origins of exceptional abilities*. Blackwell, Oxford.

——(1997). Beyond psychobiography: Towards more effective synthesis of psychology and biography. *British Journal of Psychology*, **88**, 235–48.

——, and Griffey, H. (1995). *Give your child a better start: how to encourage early learning*. Penguin, London.

Jamison, K. R. (1993). *Touched with fire*. Free Press, New York.

——(1996). *An unquiet mind*. Picador, London.

Langer, W. C. (1972). *The mind of Adolf Hitler*. Basic Books, New York.

Ludwig, A. M. (1995). *The price of greatness*. Guilford Press, New York.

Lykken, D. T. (1982). Research with twins: the concept of emergenesis. *Psychophysiology*, **19**, 361–73.

——, Bouchard, T. J., McGue, M., and Tellegen, A. (1992). Emergenesis: genetic traits that do not run in families. *American Psychologist*, **47**, 1565–77.

Martindale, C. (1986). The evolution of Italian painting: a quantitative investigation of trends in style and content from the late Gothic to the Rococo period. *Leonardo*, **19**, 217–22.

Miller, A. I. (1996). *Insights of genius: imagery and creativity in science and art*. Springer-Verlag, New York.

Murray, P. (ed.) (1989). *Genius: the history of an idea*. Blackwell, Oxford.

Nisbett, R. E. and Ross, L. (1980). *Human inference: strategies and shortcomings of social judgement*. Prentice-Hall, Englewood Cliffs, NJ.

Plomin, R., DeFries, J. C., McClearn, G. E., and Rutter, M. (1997). *Behavioral genetics*. W. H. Freeman, New York.

Post, F. (1994). Creativity and psychopathology: a study of 291 world-famous men. *British Journal of Psychiatry*, **305**, 1198–202.

Runyan, W. M. (1982). *Life histories and psychobiography: explorations in theory and method*. Oxford University Press, New york.

Simonton, D. K. (1984). *Genius, creativity and leadership*. Harvard University Press, Cambridge, MA.

——(1990). *Psychology, science, and history: an introduction to historiometry*. Yale University Press, New Haven.

——(1994). *Greatness: who makes history and why*. Guilford Press, New York.

——(1997). Creative productivity: a predictive and explanatory model of career trajectories and landmarks. *Psychological Review*, **104**, 66–89.

Solomon, M. (1995). *Mozart: a life*. Hutchinson, London.

Steptoe, A. (1981). The sources of *Così fan tutte*: a reappraisal. *Music and Letters*, **62**, 281–94.

——(1982). Mozart, Joseph II and social sensitivity. *The Music Review*, **43**, 109–20.

——(1990). Mozart as an individual. In *The Mozart compendium.* (ed. H. C. Robbins Landon), pp. 102–131. Thames and Hudson, London.

Stone, L. (1981). *The past and the present.* Routledge & Kegan Paul, London.

Sulloway, F. J. (1996). *Born to rebel: birth order, family dynamics, and creative lives.* Pantheon Books, New York.

Ward, T. S., Smith, S. M., and Vaid, J. (ed.) (1997). *Creative thought: an investigation of conceptual structures and processes.* American Psychological Association, Washington, DC.

RICHARD FEYNMAN

CHAPTER 2

The genetics of genius

David T. Lykken

Since each individual produced by the sexual process contains a unique set of genes, very exceptional combinations of genes are unlikely to appear twice even within the same family. So if genius is to any extent hereditary, it winks on and off through the gene pool in a way that would be difficult to measure or predict. Like Sisyphus rolling his boulder up to the top of the hill only to have it tumble down again, the human gene pool creates hereditary genius in many ways in many places only to have it come apart in the next generation. (E. O. Wilson 1978)

Psychologists once thought, simplistically, that genius was nothing more than high general intelligence, the capacity measured by the *intelligence quotient* or IQ. IQ scores of 140 and above, attained by perhaps four in every thousand youngsters, were classified as in the 'genius range'. Stanford University's Lewis Terman, who was responsible for revising and standardizing the first individually-administered IQ test, the Stanford-Binet, identified some 1500 gifted children with IQs in this range and Terman's gifted group have now been followed through to middle age. Most of them have led relatively successful lives but none of them, so far as I am aware, would be classified as geniuses today.

At the other end of the IQ scale, a rare few of retarded or autistic persons, known as *savants*, can quickly specify the day of the week on which any date in history fell or, although unable to read music, can play on the piano any composition after just a single hearing. These highly specialized abilities seem all the more remarkable in people whose general intelligence may be so low that they are dependent on others for their care and sustenance. Autistic savants are not geniuses either, of course, but these remarkable people seem to me to illustrate an important fact about the structure of mind.

Autism and the modular brain

Autism was first described in 1944 and is extremely variable in its manifestations. Some autists seem to be profoundly retarded and never develop language. Others, often labelled Asperger's syndrome, have normal or superior IQs. One common theme in autism is an extraordinary lack of social motivation and social intelligence. Most autistic children are unresponsive to people, even to their mothers, and dislike being held or

Portions of this chapter were modified, with permission, from: Lykken *et al.* (1992) and from Lykken (1995).

fondled. Unlike normal children, they do not seem to see other members of their species as especially interesting, to be studied and imitated. This may explain why even high-level autists tend to be slow in language development and why, in spite of sometimes high general intelligence, they remain insensitive to social cues. Asperger children seem to be unable to identify with other persons and therefore unable to anticipate how others will react to what they do. Another rare congenital abnormality, Williams' syndrome, presents the antithesis of autism. Children with Williams' syndrome are verbally and socially precocious, they 'often appear exceptionally self-possessed, articulate, and witty, and only gradually is their mental deficit borne in on one' (Sacks 1995, p. 223).

A normal child has an innate fear of snakes and spiders, a reaction not shown to guns or electric sockets although the latter are more dangerous. Evolutionary psychologists point out that human toddlers back in the Pleistocene who instinctively avoided snakes and spiders were somewhat more likely in consequence to live to maturity and to become our ancestors. Since natural selection works slowly, such a reaction to electric sockets has not yet evolved. In a similar way, it was adaptive for ancestral infants to be fascinated by their mother's faces, to recognize an affinity with other creatures like themselves, to study and imitate them. This special-purpose 'mental module' facilitated learning language and the other skills required for social living. It would appear that this social-intelligence module is well-developed in Williams' syndrome, in spite of low general intelligence, but poorly developed in Asperger's syndrome even when general intelligence is normal.

Retarded or autistic savants seem to indicate the existence of other special-purpose modules that are capable of efficient functioning even in the presence of a low IQ. Neurologist Oliver Sacks describes some of these prodigies, such as Jedediah Buxton, a simple-minded labourer, who was a prodigious calculator. 'When asked what would be the cost of shoeing a horse with 140 nails if the price was one farthing for the first nail, then doubled for each remaining nail, he arrived at the figure of 725 958 096 074 907 868 531 656 993 638 851 106 pounds, 2 shillings and 8 pence.' (Sacks 1995, p. 191). When asked to square this number, he produced the 78-digit answer after ten weeks during which he did his work, held conversations, lived his life, while his astonishing calculating engine continued to grind away at the problem. A savant studied by Sacks personally could recite the entire nine volumes of Grove's 1954 *Dictionary of music and musicians* which had been read to him once by his father.

'Blind Tom', a slave child, was born in the 1850s nearly blind and he was unable to speak until age five or six, yet from the age of four, 'seated at the piano, he would play beautiful tunes, his little hands having already taken possession of the keys, and his wonderful ears of any combination of notes they had once heard' (Sacks 1995, p. 189). Tested at the age of 11 by musicologists, who played two entirely new compositions for him 13 and 20 pages in length, Tom 'reproduced them perfectly and with the least apparent effort'. Like Mozart, Tom could perform on the piano with his back to the keyboard and his hands inverted. It is important to understand that the gifts of these autistic prodigies seem to go far beyond extraordinary rote memory. Leslie Lemke, a modern 'Blind Tom', who also is congenitally blind and retarded, 'is as renowned for his improvisational powers as for his incredible musical memory. Lemke catches the style of any composer, from Bach to Bartok, after a single hearing, and can thereafter play any piece or improvise, effortlessly, in that style'. (Sacks 1995, p. 224).

Sacks also describes artistic prodigies such as Nadia, who 'suddenly started drawing at the age of three and a half, rendering horses, and later a variety of subjects, in a way that psychologists considered 'not possible'. Her drawings, they felt, were qualitatively different from those of other children; she had a sense of space, an ability to depict appearances and shadows, a sense of perspective such as the most gifted normal child might only develop at three times her age'. (Sacks 1995, p. 194). Stephen, a profoundly autistic child, was consigned at age four to a London school for the developmentally disabled. When he was five, Stephen began drawing, primarily cars and sometimes 'wickedly clever' caricatures of his teachers. At age seven, he began to specialize in drawing buildings, such as St Paul's Cathedral 'and other London landmarks, in tremendous detail, when other children his age were just drawing stick figures. It was the sophistication of his drawings, their mastery of line and perspective, that amazed me—and these were all there when he was seven'. (Sacks 1995, p. 199). Steven could draw from memory a complex scene (for example a construction site) viewed only for a few seconds but he also had an intuitive grasp for artistic and architectural style. Repeated drawings from memory of Sacks' house over the period of a year varied considerably in detail but not at all in style. Similar repeated renderings of Matisse paintings varied also, proving that he was not 'merely' faithfully copying a vivid visual memory but, rather, that he was improvising à la Matisse.

Examples like these have led psychologists to postulate the existence of numerous special intelligences which are seen in these savant cases in especially stark relief against a background of general intellectual poverty. It is of great importance to realize that such savant-like talents can also co-exist with high intelligence and in the absence of autism. The young concert pianist Evgeny Kissin, described as 'the most phenomenal prodigy of our time' (Solomon 1996, p. 113), spontaneously sang at the age of 11 months an entire Bach fugue that his older sister had been practising. At 30 months 'Genya sat down at the old Bechstein on which his mother taught and picked out with one finger some of the tunes he had been singing. The next day, he did the same again, and on the third day he played with both hands, using all his fingers . . . Chopin's *ballades* he would play with those little hands, as well as Beethoven sonatas and Liszt rhapsodies' (Solomon 1996, p. 115). The literary genius, Vladimir Nabokov, possessed 'a prodigious calculating gift, but this disappeared suddenly and completely, he wrote, following a high fever, with delirium, at the age of seven' (Sacks 1995, p. 226). The intellectually normal Chinese artist, Yani, displayed her artistic powers as early as did Nadia or Stephen and Sacks describes another gifted young man, now doing fundamental research in chemistry, who could read fluently and with comprehension at age two or repeat and even harmonize with any melody at the same age, and who did remarkable drawings with perspective at age three. Thus, it does not seem to be the case that savant-like gifts result from the conscription of all intellectual resources in the service of a single function.

This idea of a modular intelligence contrasts with the view of the brain as merely a general-purpose computer, the power of which can be assessed just by a single number, the IQ. Yet general intelligence is both real and important. Its role may be like that of the conductor of an orchestra in which the brass, percussion, strings, and wood-winds are the special-purpose modules. Like the best orchestral conductors, the computer-intelligence knows all of the parts but cannot play the flute as well as the flautist can; the conductor's function is to evaluate and to coordinate.

There is a useful analogy between the domains of mental and physical talent. Each Olympic sport makes different demands on different muscle groups, reaction times, gross or fine motor coordination, and so on. Because of their different genetic endowment, it is unlikely that any world-class distance runner could have become instead a world-class sprinter or weight-lifter or gymnast. Yet all world-class athletes have an unusual degree of general athletic ability. That is, if we were to construct a series of special tests designed to tap each athlete's special abilities, it is likely that the scores on all these tests would intercorrelate positively—would form what is called a 'positive manifold', both for the mixed group of world-class athletes and also for people in general.

Similarly, if we were to develop special tests for each of the several varieties of savant, tests designed to quantify their remarkable special abilities, we can be confident that, when administered to a sample of the general population, scores on these tests also would form a positive manifold. Good tonal memory would tend to go with good visual and conceptual memory as well as with the ability for mental computation. Retarded savants are remarkable not just because of a particular gift but also because of the absence of the related gifts that normally go with it.

Every acknowledged human genius seems to have had at least a good general intelligence *together with* an assortment of other gifts or attributes which, in combination, led to the extraordinary achievements that are the ultimate basis for classification into this special category. One of the ingredients in the recipe for genius, and which I believe may be as essential as general intelligence, is an exceptional degree of mental energy, permitting protracted periods of intensely focused concentration on the project in hand. The amount of energy required, for example to become a world-class classical musician is described in Chapter 4 by Andreas Lehmann and Anders Ericsson. Our question in this chapter has to do with the origins of these interacting attributes. Is it true that 'genius must be born and never can be taught', as Dryden claimed? Or, can genius be achieved? Is genius something that a doting parent can 'thrust upon' an otherwise ordinary child?

First, however, we need to address the curious fact that there are many people, including social scientists, even some geneticists—highly educated people who ought to know better—who believe that the human nervous system, unlike that of any other mammal, is unaffected by the same heritable variation that is obvious in the body's morphology. It follows from this postulate of *radical environmentalism*[1] that every

---

[1] Although radical environmentalism often is adopted for political or ideological reasons, 'radical' in this context is used in the sense of 'extreme'.

normal human infant, however distinctive in size, shape, and appearance, must arrive equipped with a brain that is essentially identical in structure and capacity with every other new brain, just as all new Macintosh computers are essentially identical when they arrive from the factory. Whatever differences in intellect, interests, character, or personality are to be found later in the adult must, in this view, be attributable solely to differences in subsequent experience or programming.

Radical environmentalism

During the middle half of the twentieth century, most social scientists and many intellectuals came to 'hold these truths to be self-evident, that all men are created equal . . .' and to interpret this fine phrase to mean biological equality. The fact is, however, that Jefferson modelled this first sentence of the American *Declaration of Independence* after the language of the constitution that had just been drafted for the state of Virginia. That document read like this: 'That all men are born equally free and independent and have certain inherent rights . . .' Jefferson kept the music but changed the words slightly for rhetorical effect. No practical man of that period would have given credence to the notion that all humans are biologically equal.

Charles Darwin (1809–82) was a scientist and scientists have to be practical people because they study the world of nature rather than the mistier realm of philosophy. Darwin knew that the offspring tend to resemble the parents. The great controversy over Darwin's *Origin of species and . . . the descent of man* was not about whether people's physiognomy and character tended to reflect their ancestry; like the invention of the wheel, the origins of that idea date back to prehistory. Animal breeders well knew that temperament, as well as running speed in horses or milk production in cows, reflected the animal's parentage and every dog fancier was aware that terriers were aggressive and sheep dogs inclined to herd things and that these behavioural traits tended to breed true.

Throughout most of human history, people have assumed that the same thing is true of our species, that smart parents tend to have smart children, and that the offspring of athletes tend to enjoy sports. But certain European philosophers have entertained the notion, following John Locke (1632–1704), that the minds of human babies begin as identical blank slates to be written on solely by experience. One important radical environmentalist was the British philosopher John Stuart Mill (1806–73), a contemporary of Darwin.

John Stuart Mill

Mill was the eldest child of James Mill, a brilliant Scots historian and philosopher, and James educated his firstborn son in an intensive manner described by Michael Howe in Chapter 5. Little John Stuart was reading by the age of three, he was reading Greek at five, and by the age of eight he had read all of Herodotus and all of Plato's Dialogues in the original. It is perhaps not surprising that, in his later life, Mill was inclined to attribute his own intellectual achievements to that extraordinary and intensive early training. What Mill failed to take into account, however, was that he had benefited, not only from his father's determined and ambitious educational efforts, but also from having received a half-helping of his brilliant father's genes.

It was not until the twentieth century, however, that large numbers of intellectuals took up radical environmentalism as an article of faith. They arrived at this common delusion from different starting points and for a variety of reasons.

Marxism

Karl Marx wanted to refute the prevailing assumption that the existing class structure of society was somehow preordained by God or human nature. Lamarck's (1744–1829) belief that acquired characteristics might be passed along genetically from parent to child provided what appeared to be a mechanism for achieving a new world order and became a part of neo-Marxist dogma. The Marxist scientists who still lead the attack on what they regard as the hereditarian heresy are too sophisticated to espouse Lamarckian ideas, but they cling to the egalitarian dream because they cannot imagine achieving the greatest good for the greatest number unless that dream is true.[2]

Liberalism

Political liberals, too, were concerned about the evils of oppression, both political and economic, and they believed that the achievements of the privileged classes were largely a consequence of that privilege rather than of some innate superiority. They reacted especially against Herbert Spencer's (1820–1903) *Social Darwinism* and his claim that the structure of Victorian society reflected the 'survival of the fittest', the workings of a natural law which we cannot change and with which we should not tamper. Upper class white males took for granted the genetic superiority of their race and gender and considered their dominant social position to be a birthright. The liberals believed, quite reasonably, that, with better living conditions and equivalent education, many children from the lower classes could excel in life's race over many scions of the aristocracy.

Anthropology and Margaret Mead

American cultural anthropology, led by Franz Boas (1858–1942), 'declared war on the idea that differences in culture derived from differences in innate capacity' (Degler

---

[2] For a sophisticated modern assertion of the Marxist opposition to 'biological determinism' see Lewontin *et al.* (1984).

1991, p. 62). By 1915, Alfred Kroeber, one of Boas' leading students, was asserting that, 'heredity cannot be allowed to have acted any part in history' (Degler 1991, p. 84). This position was most clearly articulated by another Boas disciple, Margaret Mead, whom he sent as a graduate student to the South Pacific with the aim of demonstrating that adolescence was less stormy and stressful in Samoa than in the United States because of cultural differences and, in particular, because of the greater sexual freedom allegedly enjoyed by young Samoans. Mead's (1928) book, *Coming of age in Samoa*, the most widely read anthropological treatise ever published, propelled her into the front rank of social thinkers and her views were strongly stated and widely influential. In her book *Male and female*, Mead explicitly asserted the radical environmentalist credo: 'Learned behaviors have replaced the biologically given ones' (Mead 1949, p. 216).

Part of the impetus for Mead's work throughout her distinguished career was her conviction that prevailing assumptions about psychological sex differences were mistaken and that cultural stereotypes, rather than innate genetic factors, play an important (she would say a decisive) role. We now know that Mead's Samoan research was superficial and that her conclusions were based largely upon innocent deceptions practised upon her by her young female Samoan informants (Freeman 1992). On the other hand, there is no doubt that there are marked differences in sexual attitudes and practices across human cultures and Mead was assuredly correct in insisting upon both the malleability of human culture and the important role that the culture plays in affecting human behaviour. Her mistake, it seems to me, was in conflating human culture, which is relatively easy to change, with human nature, which is not.

Behaviourism

The middle half of the twentieth century was the heyday of behaviourism and many behaviourists tended to be radical environmentalists. The founder of the movement, J. B. Watson, is famous for his claim:

Give me a dozen healthy infants, well formed, and my own specified world to bring them up in and I'll guarantee to take any one at random and train him to become any type of specialist I might select—doctor, lawyer, artist, merchant-chief, and, yes, even beggar-man and thief, regardless of his talents, penchants, tendencies, abilities, vocations, and the race of his ancestors (Watson 1924, p. 128).

Nearly sixty years after Watson, the geneticist, Richard Lewontin, made an even more extravagant claim:

Our genetic endowments confer a plasticity of psychic and physical development, so that in the course of our lives, from conception to death, each of us, irrespective of race, class, or sex, can develop virtually any identity that lies within the human ambit (Lewontin 1992, from author's précis on the book jacket).

By claiming nearly limitless plasticity for both psychic and physical development,

Lewontin suggested that ambitious parents can make their child not only into a doctor, lawyer, or, no doubt, a genius, at will, but also into a tennis champion or a basketball superstar, if that is what the child aspires to. Watson had only hubris and wishful thinking to back up his assertions. Lewontin's challenge was greater because he had 60 years' accumulation of data to contend with, most of it adverse to his startling hypothesis. That he chose to state it anyway is a triumph of ideology over reason and evidence. If it were true, Lewontin's claim would impose a heavy burden of guilt on the parents of children who fail to achieve whatever 'identity' they hoped for.

Nazi racism

The views and deeds of Adolf Hitler may have had more influence on the nature–nurture question than Marx or Mead or any other thinker. Nazi notions about racial differences and Aryan superiority, the cruel experiments on twins conducted by Dr Mengele and, above all, the barbaric 'final solution' for the millions alleged to be genetically inferior, made it difficult for an entire generation of civilized people to be dispassionate about the role of heritable differences in human affairs. Radical environmentalism was no longer just an arguable scientific hypothesis but it became an article of antifascist faith. The issue was no longer debatable in politically correct society, not even on University campuses.

The decline and fall of radical environmentalism

The long night of radical environmentalism seems to be coming to an end. Throughout the period, occasional studies appeared showing that, psychologically, adoptees resembled their biological parents more than they resembled the adoptive parents who reared them. Twin and family studies accumulated, showing that the degree of resemblance of pairs of related individuals tends to parallel their degree of genetic relatedness. In recent years there has been a crescendo of twin and adoption studies with mutually corroborative results, and the pendulum of informed public opinion seems to be swinging in the direction toward which these findings point.

It is once again possible for reasonable, educated people to acknowledge that we humans differ remarkably from one another in nearly every way imaginable. Moreover, life would be unbearable, perhaps impossible, if this were not so. 'Individual differences are what make horse races' as Mark Twain pointed out, and of course he meant 'horses races' as a metaphor for all of social living . If every other person had precisely my own innate gifts and limitations I know that life would be hell. Our species since the earliest times has been dependent for its survival upon a division of labour within social groupings; an organization of specialists being more efficient than a mere congeries of individuals, the extended-family bands formed by our ancestors were therefore greater than just the sum of their component members.

The human genome

The human genome, the book of instructions for the fabrication of an individual, consists of some 100 000 pairs of genes strung out rather like beads along the DNA molecules packed within each of our 23 pairs of chromosomes. This complete genetic blueprint is contained within the nucleus of nearly every cell of the body. Genes serve as patterns for making enzymes and other proteins. Each cell is like a chemical factory in which the enzymes are the chemists that synthesize the special molecules required for life. Most of the genes in the human genome are identical in all normal persons; they constitute the instructions that caused us to develop into *Homo sapiens* rather than into chimpanzees or butterflies or toadstools. Perhaps one-quarter of our genes are polymorphic; from one person to another in the human population there may be two to twenty or more slightly different genes, different alleles that can occupy the locus of a given polymorphic gene. For example, there is one pair of genes that primarily determines eye colour and there are two different alleles that can occur in that locus. If both of your eye-colour genes are of the blue type, then your eyes will be predominantly blue (although other genes will influence the particular shade of blue). If either or both of your eye-colour genes are of the brown type, then your eyes will be predominantly brown, since the brown-eye gene is dominant over the blue type.

Most traits that are of psychological interest are metrical traits rather than binary characteristics, and vary continuously from person to person. They are similar to stature in being polygenic traits, which means they are determined by the combined activity of many polymorphic genes. Your stature is the sum of the lengths of your head, your neck, your back and the long bones of your legs. Each of these components is designed by a different group of genes, some of them polymorphic, so that people differ from one another genetically in the lengths of each component part. Other polymorphic genes influence the length of all the parts so that the components are correlated in respect to size; people with long heads tend to have long femurs also. For these reasons, we say that stature is determined by the additive action of many different polymorphic genes. As we shall see, most metrical psychological traits also owe an important portion of their variation among people to polygenic variation within the breeding group.

The great genetic lottery

At conception, the mother's ovum contains in its nucleus one gene more-or-less randomly selected from each of the approximately 100 000 gene pairs in her genome. The fertilizing sperm similarly contains some 100 000 single genes, one from each of the father's complete set of gene pairs. At fertilization, these two random halves of the two parents' genomes combine to form the genome of the child. If only 1000 of the 100 000 gene pairs in the human genome were polymorphic, the number of different, genetically unique offspring from all possible matings would exceed 10 followed by more than 600 zeros ($2^{1000} \times 2^{1000}$). From this we can safely conclude that each child produced by the great lottery of conception possesses a genetic blueprint that differs in at least some respects from any heretofore seen on earth.

Twins

On the other hand, fortunately for science, there are twins. After conception, the fertilized ovum divides into two identical daughter cells each of which then divides again, and those four daughters again divide—beginning the embryological process that will lead to the creation of a human fetus. About four times in every 1000 conceptions, the embryo splits into two equal and separately viable parts. These two half-embryos will continue to develop into two separate children who, because they began as a single zygote or fertilized egg, are known as monozygotic or identical twins. Because of their origins, identical twins share the same genome and are genetically indistinguishable.

Dizygotic or fraternal twins occur when the mother produces more than one fertile ovum in the same ovulation period. When two ova are present, each can be fertilized by a different sperm and begin to develop into pairs of siblings who are genetically related just like ordinary siblings. Each of them possesses different random halves of each parent's genome so that, on the average, they will share about half of their polymorphic genes. Fraternal twins, like ordinary siblings, can share many more than half of their parent's polymorphic genes and thus be remarkably similar, or they may share many fewer than half, and thus be genetically quite different. I have a photograph of one pair of fraternal twins, young men who participated in one of our twin studies, who do not appear to be even from the same generation.

Because of their genetic identity, we know that differences within pairs of identical twins must be due to environmental causes. Environmental influences begin well before birth. Identical twin babies differ in size, often in handedness, and sufficiently in other little ways so that their parents and close friends can generally tell them apart— and these small differences all are due to idiosyncratic environmental differences during development. However, as they grow up, identical twins usually prove to be remarkably similar in temperament, in aptitudes, and interests, more so than pairs of fraternal twins. It was Charles Darwin's cousin, Sir Francis Galton, who first realized the possibilities of using twins to study the heritability of psychological characteristics.

Heritability

It is meaningless to ask whether Isaac Newton's genius was due more to his genes or his environment, as meaningless as asking whether the area of a rectangle is due more to its length or its width. But if a certain group of rectangles vary in width between 1 and 10 inches but vary in length from 1 to 100 inches, then we can say that the variation in their areas is more affected by the variation in their lengths than by the lesser variation in their widths. Similarly, for people in general, it is meaningful to ask whether their genetic differences are more or less important than their differences in experience in producing the variation we observe in the traits involved in genius. The proportion of the total variation in any trait that is associated with genetic variation is called the *heritability* of that trait.

It is important to understand that the heritability of most psychological traits tells us as much about the given culture as it does about human nature. It is likely (although we cannot be sure of this) that the amount of genetic variability among people within each human culture or breeding group is about the same. But environmental opportunities vary widely both within and between cultures. We would not expect to find a literary genius in a preliterate tribe in Papua New Guinea. In the Middle Ages, peasant children had much less opportunity to develop their intellectual capacities than the children of princes and the heritability of IQ then would have been decreased by this large amount of environmental variation. On the other hand, the fact that the heritability of IQ among the citizens of modern western democracies is on the order of 75 per cent suggests that these cultures have succeeded in providing environmental opportunity that is tolerably equal for all their children (at least for their white children).

Estimating heritability

As Galton anticipated, we can make use of both the social experiment of adoption and the biological experiment of twinning to estimate the heritability of traits. Children reared from infancy by adoptive parents will resemble their biological parents solely for genetic reasons. If the adoptive placements are random, then any similarity between the children and their adoptive parents will be due solely to environmental influences provided by the adoptive home. Twins reared together will resemble each other both for genetic reasons and because of their shared rearing experiences. If we assume that these environmental influences are the same for both identical and fraternal twins, then the greater similarity within identical pairs must be due to the fact that they share all their polymorphic genes while fraternal twins share, on average, only 50 per cent. A standard formula computes the heritability of a trait from twice the difference between the correlations of identical and fraternal twins on that trait.

Twins who are adopted away in infancy and reared apart represent a rare and valuable combination of Galton's two methods. The correlation on any trait within pairs of identical twins reared apart is therefore a direct estimate of the heritability of that trait. It turns out that, for most traits, identical twins reared apart resemble one another just about as much as do identical twins reared together. This fact has two important implications. First, it indicates that being reared together in the same home does not usually serve to make siblings more alike psychologically when they are assessed as adults. This implication is confirmed by studies of unrelated adoptive siblings reared together who, as adults, do not resemble one another psychologically more than do random pairs of people. The second implication is that, since correlations between identical twins reared apart directly estimate trait heritability, we can also use correlations between identical twins reared together for this purpose. Identical twins reared apart are rare and very expensive to study, while there are nearly a million pairs of identical twins reared together in just the United States alone. They tend to be wonderfully cooperative about participating in research.

Estimating heritability directly from identical twin correlations is not only convenient but also conservative. As we shall see later in this chapter, not all polygenic effects are additive but some are configural, in the sense that the effect on the trait of certain genes may depend on the presence or absence of certain other genes. Identical twins, who share all their genes, will also share all such configural or *emergenic* traits, while fraternal twins who share only half their polymorphic genes, may be unlikely to share the full set in the required configuration and are therefore unlikely to share the trait in question (Lykken *et al.* 1992).

Are psychological traits influenced by genetic differences?

Nearly all psychological traits or tendencies that can be reliably measured turn out to have heritabilities ranging from about 25 to 75 per cent (e.g. Bouchard *et al.* 1990). That is, among persons of European ancestry—for IQ, extroversion, neurotic tendency, musical talent, creativity, scientific and other interests, even for religiousness, authoritarianism, and for happiness—from one to three-quarters of the variation from person to person is associated with genetic differences between those persons.

How do we know this? In the case of IQ, countless studies have shown that the correlation between pairs of related individuals is proportional to their genetic correlation. Identical twins are twice as similar within pairs in IQ as are fraternal twins, whose genetic correlation is .50. The IQ correlation for fraternal twins, in turn, is about four times that of first cousins, whose genetic correlation is .125. Moreover, pairs of unrelated adoptive siblings reared together, once they are grown and out of the adoptive home, correlate in IQ about zero (Bouchard and McGue 1981). Perhaps the best evidence we have of the heritability of IQ among adults of European ancestry comes from five studies of identical twins reared apart, carried out in Britain, Denmark, Sweden, and in the United States and totalling 163 of these rare twin pairs. The IQ correlations in these studies (each one a direct estimate of heritability) ranged from .64 to .78 and the grand average correlation was .75 (see McGue *et al.* 1993).

Extroversion, considered to be one of the handful of basic traits of temperament, was correlated .54 for more than 500 pairs of adult identical twins from the Minnesota Twin Registry, indicating a heritability of at least 50 per cent. Neurotic tendency or neuroticism showed an identical twin correlation of .48 in the same sample. Similar results were found in the Minnesota Study of Twins Reared Apart (Bouchard *et al.* 1990). About half of the variance in measures of creativity has been shown by the Minnesota studies to derive from genetic variation (Bouchard and Lykken, in press). Self-rated musical talent correlated .69 among the 512 pairs of adult identical twins reared together, but the correlation was smaller (only .44) among the Minnesota identical twins reared apart. This suggests perhaps that musical ability is one trait for which shared family experience does make a difference, augmenting the genetic influence.

Strength of scientific interests, in contrast, correlated .45 among identical twins reared together and .57 among those reared apart. Interest in religious matters produced correlations above .50 in both groups as did a measure of commitment to traditional values (Lykken *et al.* 1993; Tellegen *et al.* 1988). Altemeyer's well-validated measure of right-wing authoritarianism produced correlations of about .60 in both types of identical twin pair. Finally, self-report measures of happiness or subjective well-being show a heritability approaching 50 per cent (Lykken and Tellegen 1996).

How do genetic differences produce psychological differences?

We cannot yet begin to trace the many steps that intervene between the protein-making activities in which the genes are directly engaged and their ultimate influence upon individual differences in complex psychological traits. We assume that behavioural differences are associated with nervous system differences. Some of the latter undoubtedly are 'hard-wired,' biological differences. We can imagine, for example, that some brains work faster or more consistently than others or that the inhibitory mechanisms that enable focused concentration are biologically stronger or more reliable in some brains than in others. But surely many of the brain differences that account for differences in personality, interests, and attitudes are differences in the 'software,' are the result of learning and experience. Yet, if nurture or experience is the proximal cause of individual differences in these traits, how can one explain the strong association between these differences and genetic variation (i.e. nature)?

A major insight of behaviour genetics is that one important way in which the genome exerts its influence upon the brain is indirect; the genes help to determine the effective environment of the developing child through the correlation or the interaction of genes with environment (Plomin *et al.* 1977; Scarr and McCartney 1983). There are several ways in which these interrelationships operate. *Passive gene-environment correlation* is exemplified by the example of John Stuart Mill; bright parents tend to give their children both 'bright genes' and intellectual stimulation. Children reared by athletic biological parents are likely to receive strong bodies as well as athletic encouragement and example. Partly for genetic reasons, some infants are fussy and irritable whereas others are happy and responsive; these differences elicit different responses from their adult caretakers. This process, which of course continues throughout life as our (primarily social) environment reacts differentially to our innate temperament, talents, and physical appearance, is called reactive or evoked gene-environment correlation. Partly for genetic reasons, different children attend to different aspects of their environment, and seek out or create environments attuned in some way to their genetic make-up. These are examples of active gene-environment correlation. The first day in school or a first roller-coaster ride will be a pleasurable excitement for some children, stimulating growth and self-confidence, but a terrifying and destructive experience for other children; that is, the same fire that melts the butter hardens the egg—this is gene-environment interaction.

An illustrative example[3]

A distinguished amateur ornithologist was relieved to learn, at the age of 11, that he was adopted. This discovery explained for him why he was so different from his parents and their relatives. His adoptive parents did not read or own books but the boy always had a library card and used it regularly. The parents had no talent for, nor interest in, sports but the youngster, in summer, always carried his baseball mitt with him in case of the chance for a game and won recognition for his prowess at basketball and tennis. This man's biography is a chronicle of active gene-environment correlation, and his quest for experiences compatible with his innate proclivities contrasts with his failure to respond to influences that were readily available but to which he did not resonate. One interest that the other members of his adoptive family shared was in religion but our acquaintance never joined with them in this.

In his late middle-age, this man set about discovering his biological parentage. He found that his parents had married after he had been given up for adoption and they had produced several other children. He discovered that his full-siblings were well educated, active, and successful people like himself. One uncle had been Dean of my university's graduate school. This man's adoptive parents, like most parents, were 'permissive' in the sense that they did not determinedly or effectively shape his behaviour nor influence him by their provocative or charismatic example. Had they been readers themselves with quick minds and lively intellectual interests, they might have given different or additional directions to his reading and thought. Had their religious practices been either emotionally or intellectually stimulating, he might well have been more interested in them. On the other hand, had this man found that he had an identical twin reared by a different set of 'permissive' adoptive parents in some other American town, I believe they would have discovered that they shared not only similar aptitudes and interests, but similar developmental histories as well.

Emergenesis: genetic traits that do not run in families

Secretariat

Old-fashioned hereditarians used to make much of the notion of breeding, a concept that has been pushed to the extreme by exponents of the sport of horse racing. Through careful breeding in the early part of the nineteenth century, the Thoroughbred race horse got steadily stronger and faster and the record times recorded at old English race courses steadily fell. Around about 1900, however, this curve levelled off as the initial additive variance was bred out of the line. The modest improvements in performance during the following seventy years or so have been largely attributed to better training, nutrition, and veterinary techniques.

---

[3] This man, an acquaintance of my colleague T. J. Bouchard, Jr, was kind enough to provide our research group with an outline of his autobiography.

And then along came Secretariat, a great red American stallion who lay down and took a nap on the day of his Kentucky Derby[4] and then got up and broke the course record, not by just a whisker but by seconds. He did the same thing at Pimlico and then won the Belmont—and the Triple Crown—by more than 30 lengths. Put out at once to stud, where only the most promising mares could afford his fees, Secretariat sired more than 400 foals—most of them disappointments, none of them remotely in their sire's class. Secretariat had a distinguished lineage, of course, although none of his forebears could have run with him, but whatever he received at the great lottery of his conception could not be easily passed on in random halves. It seems a reasonable conjecture that Secretariat's qualities were configural, emergenic.

At last, in 1988, one of Secretariat's sons, Risen Star, finished third in the Kentucky Derby, won the Preakness, and then won the Belmont by some 14 lengths, albeit a full two seconds behind his sire's record pace. After more than 400 attempts, Secretariat managed to produce a winner. Although emergenic traits do not 'run in families', they are more likely to reappear in a carrier family than in a random lineage. No doubt Risen Star's dam contributed key elements of the emergenic configuration.

Although running speed is a metrical variable, Secretariat so far exceeded the limits of the normal distribution as to suggest a qualitative difference, a new natural class or taxon. The arena of human achievement appears to offer many similar examples, singular individuals whose accomplishments so far exceed the norm that we classify them separately from the common herd. An important example of such an emergenic class includes those people we call 'geniuses'.

Genius

How did it come about that a man born poor, losing his mother at birth and soon deserted by his father, afflicted with a painful and humiliating disease, left to wander for twelve years among alien cities and conflicting faiths, . . . suspected of crime and insanity, and seeing, in his last months, the apotheosis of his greatest enemy—how did it come about that this man, after his death, triumphed over Voltaire, revived religion, transformed education, elevated the morals of France, inspired the Romantic movement and the French Revolution, influenced the philosophy of Kant and Schopenhauer, the plays of Schiller, the novels of Goethe, the poems of Wordsworth, Byron, and Shelley, the socialism of Marx, the ethics of Tolstoy, and, altogether, had more effect upon posterity than any other writer or thinker of that eighteenth century in which writers were more influential than they had ever been before? Here, if anywhere, the problem faces us: what is the role of genius in history . . .?

In this celebrated first sentence of their *Rousseau and revolution*, Will and Ariel Durant (1967) pose as well the psychological problem of genius itself, its mysterious irrepressibility and its ability to arise from the most unpromising of lineages and to flourish even in the meanest of circumstances.

---

[4] The Kentucky Derby, the Pimlico, and the Belmont Stakes comprise the three great annual events—the 'crowning' events—of American Thoroughbred flat-racing.

Human genius has always been a problem for both environmentalists and hereditarians to understand. There have been families of genius, of course, the Bernoullis and the Bachs, the Darwins and the Huxleys, the musical Marsalis family. But it is the solitary genius, rising like a great oak in a forest of scrub and bramble, who challenges our understanding. Carl Friedrich Gauss, ranked with Archimedes and Newton as one of the 'Princes of Mathematics,' had uneducated parents, his mother was illiterate, yet the boy had taught himself to read and to do simple arithmetic by the time he was three years old (Buhler 1981). When Gauss was 10, the village schoolmaster thought to keep his large class occupied by computing the sum of the integers from one to 100. Moments later he was startled to see little Carl at his desk with just a single number on his slate; 'there 'tis,' said the boy and then sat with his hands folded while the rest of the class toiled on. In the end, only Carl had the correct answer (Dunnington 1955). The boy had at once perceived that the problem reduced to $(1+100) + (2+99) + \ldots + (50+51) = 50(101) = 5050$. To believe that some extraordinary accident of experience created this Prince out of ordinary clay is to believe in magic.

Another example is the great Hindu mathematician, Srinivasa Ramanujan, discussed by Robert Albert in Chapter 6. Described as a 'magical genius' (Kolata 1987), Ramanujan was reared in a one-room adobe hut in southern India and his mathematical education consisted primarily of two books, both in a foreign language (Borwein and Borwein 1988). In 1913, with the help of a better-educated friend, Ramanujan wrote from Madras to the great G. H. Hardy at Cambridge, asking his opinion of some 120 theorems which were enclosed. Hardy reports that some of these were classical though obscure; others were in Hardy's own area and he managed to prove them himself:

though with a good deal more trouble than I had expected . . . The formulae 110–113 are on a different level and obviously both difficult and deep . . . I had never seen anything the least like them before. A single look at them is enough to show that they could only be written down by a mathematician of the highest class. They must be true because, if they were not true, no one would have had the imagination to invent them. (G. H. Hardy 1940)

Suppose that Gauss or Ramanujan had been born with a healthy identical twin who was spirited away to be reared by some country parson in Oxfordshire. Barring cholera or other accident, is it not likely that the parson's surname too would now be immortal? Ramanujan died young without offspring; his parents and one brother apparently were unexceptional. Although Gauss provided rich stimulation and opportunity for his six offspring (by two different and highly cultivated wives), none of them distinguished themselves.[5] But if the genius of these men was prefigured in their genes, why was it never manifested elsewhere in their lineage? The answer is, I think, that genius consists of unique configurations of attributes that cannot be transmitted in half-helpings.

---

[5] Gauss's second son, Eugene, emigrated to the United States in 1830, enlisted in the army, and later went into business in Missouri. Eugene is said to have had some of his father's gift for languages and the ability to perform prodigious arithmetic calculations, which he did for recreation after his sight failed him in old age.

Michael Faraday, the premier experimental scientist of his generation, was the self-taught son of a humble blacksmith (see Chapter 5). Knight refers to Faraday's 'curious mixture, or perhaps we should say compound, of humility and pride' (Knight 1985). Biographers of people of genius often allude in this way to interactions or configurations of their subjects' attributes. We know that Shakespeare also came from undistinguished stock, that this foremost wordsmith in our history had numerous siblings and several children, none of whom left any trace—or any word—behind them (Parrott 1938). An American genius, Benjamin Franklin, was one of a large family and sired two children of his own, all of them members of the common generality of humankind (Garfield 1982). The configurality of genius is dramatically illustrated in the life' work of another extraordinary American, Gutzon Borglum, the sculptor, engineer, inventor, entrepreneur who carved Mount Rushmore (Shaff 1985). However one evaluates the aesthetic or the ecological impact of transforming a mountain into a frieze of presidential heads, this prodigious monument will survive the millennia because of the configuration of prodigious talents, each of them essential to the project, that were combined in this singular individual. One of the luminaries of twentieth century science, John von Neumann, was capable of such extraordinary intellectual feats that some of his colleagues were led to suggest that von Neumann's brain 'might be an emergent organ, of a different order of complexity than those of ordinary mortals' (Campbell 1988, p. 103). Genius of this calibre seems to be not just an abundance of one or several components such as IQ, but rather a harmony of attributes, a compound rather than merely a mixture.

Exceptional endowment or exceptional endeavour?

On reading *Hereditary genius*, by his cousin, Francis Galton, Charles Darwin wrote, 'You have made a convert of an opponent in one sense, for I have always maintained that, excepting fools, men did not differ much in intellect, only in zeal and hard work; and I still think [this] is an eminently important difference'. Thomas Edison, too, believed that genius was ninety-nine per cent perspiration and one per cent inspiration and he 'often work[ed] as many as 112 hours a week' (McAuliffe 1995). Isaac Newton, asked how he made his remarkable discoveries, replied: 'I keep the subject constantly before me and wait until the first dawnings open little by little into the full light' (Andrade 1956).

Hardy told of a visit he made to Ramanujan 'when he was lying ill at Putney. I had ridden in taxi-cab No. 1729, and remarked that the number seemed to me rather a dull one, and that I hoped it was not a bad omen. "No," he replied, "it is a very interesting number; it is the smallest number expressible as a sum of two cubes in two different ways" ' (Newman 1956). It was said of Ramanujan that every number was his friend and he had plainly thought about and stored away many interesting facts about most of the lower integers. At the age of 10 or 12 he could recite the values of *pi* and the square root of two to any number of decimal places. Because mathematics was his only interest as a boy, he had failed his scholarship examinations in India. Could it be that Ramanujan's exceptional achievements resulted, not from exceptional endowments but, rather, from the fact that, like Newton, he had kept the one subject of his interest constantly before him since his childhood?

In 1960, at the Center for Advanced Study in the Behavioral Sciences in Palo Alto, Dutch psychologist Adrian de Groot, an expert on the psychology of chess and a chess master himself, simultaneously played and defeated 20 chess duffers like myself. He was not allowed even to see one chess board presided over by two of the Center Fellows who thought themselves to be relatively accomplished players. Well into the game, after they announced the next move they had decided on, de Groot pointed out that their proposed move was impossible; although they had the chess pieces arrayed before them while he had only his mental image to rely on, they got it wrong while he got it right. De Groot himself had played—and been easily beaten—by the future grand master, Bobby Fischer, when Fischer was a boy of twelve. De Groot was careful to point out, however, that even by that early age Fischer had played many thousands of chess games and had derived from this experience a vast armamentarium of chess positions and strategy.

The late Richard Feynman frequently disconcerted physicist colleagues by inter-rupting their explanations of new findings, to which they had devoted weeks or months of work, and quickly scrawling on a blackboard a more general result of which theirs was just a special case. Was this lightning-like calculation or was Feynman able to draw upon a 'storehouse of previously worked-out—and unpublished—know-ledge'? Feynman's biographer, James Gleick, describes a research seminar at which astrophysicist Willy Fowler proposed that the recently discovered quasars were super-massive stars.

Feynman immediately rose, astonishingly, to say that such objects would be gravitationally unstable. Furthermore, he said that the instability followed from general relativity. The claim required a calculation of the subtle countervailing effects of stellar forces and relativistic gravity. Fowler thought he was talking through his hat. A colleague later discovered that Feynman had done a hundred pages of work on the problem years before. The Chicago astrophysicist Sub-rahmanyan Chandrasekhar independently produced Feynman's result—it was part of the work for which he won a Nobel Prize twenty years later. Feynman himself never bothered to publish. Someone with a new idea always risked finding, as one colleague said, 'that Feynman had signed the guest book and already left,' (Gleick 1992).

K. A. Ericsson (1990; Ericsson and Charness 1994; see also the chapter by Lehmann and Ericsson in this volume) has shown that remarkable feats of memory can be achieved by apparently unremarkable people after extensive practice. He has also shown that most examples of exceptional performance, including those by people known as geniuses, are preceded by years of intense and single-minded application and practice.

Ericsson and his colleagues have amassed a truly impressive body of evidence in sup-port of their view that it is deliberate and intensive practice, rather than differences in native ability, that separates elite performers from the rest of us. With hundreds of hours of guided practice spaced over weeks or months, ordinary college students can learn to increase their digit span—the number of digits correctly repeated after hearing them read only once at a rate of one per second—by 10 times. There are techniques of calculation with which, after extensive practice, one can accomplish feats of mental arithmetic impossible for the untrained mind. The conditioning and practice of elite athletes changes their muscle strength, aerobic capacity, the speed of their reflexes, the size of their hearts, and even the relative proportions of fast and slow-twitch muscle fibres, and it is these practice-produced effects rather than just native ability that is responsible for extraordinary athletic performance. The celebrated violinist at last night's concert almost certainly practises more intensely and consistently than the members of the orchestra's violin section. Elite performers tend to do less well as they get older but many of them also tend to practise less intensely as they age.

Ericsson believes not only that genius and exceptional performance depends upon intensive years of practice but that most of us, given the same teachers and similar preparation, could do as well as these elite performers do. Ericsson and Charness (1994, p. 744) are willing to acknowledge that genetic differences in temperament and 'preferred activity level' may determine which of us go for the gold but, curiously, they cling to the assumption that individual genetic differences in both physical and mental capacities are not important, perhaps non-existent. This would require us to believe that most children could acquire perfect pitch and the ability to reproduce compositions after a single hearing if only we listened to music as long and as intently as Blind Tom and Leslie Lemke did, or drawn from memory a construction site after a brief glance, as Sack's savant Steven did. We should have to suppose, as Lewontin seems to imply, that almost any of our children could become world-class athletes, given the right training and the appropriate temperament. We must also accept the proposition that the young Gauss's ability to correct his father's arithmetic at three and confound his school master at ten resulted, not from extraordinary mental hardware, but from mental software acquired through self-directed practice in an intellectually unstimulating environment.

Those of us who have studied identical twins reared apart from one another find these assumptions incredible. We cannot believe that these twins correlate 0.75 in IQ merely because, in their separate environments, their similarities in temperament led them to indulge in very similar amounts of practice on very similar topics. One set of Bouchard's identical triplets reared apart were each on their high school's wrestling team before they ever knew of each other's existence. I think this was because they shared a configuration of genetic traits, physical and mental, that made them interested in, and good at, this particular sport. More generally, I think that one reason, although not the only reason, that most elite performers engage in the dedicated pursuit of excellence in their specialty is that they are naturally good at it from the start so that their early efforts are rewarded by early success.

I think we must agree with Ericsson, however, that works of genius tend to be the product of minds enriched by years of concentrated effort. Isaac Newton often became so caught up in cerebration that he would forget to eat or sleep. Edwin Land, inventor of the instant Polaroid camera and of a sophisticated computational theory of colour vision, sometimes worked at his desk for 36 hours or more, unaware of the passage of time until he felt faint on standing up. Similar stories were told of Edison. It does not follow, however, that these were ordinary minds to begin with.

Edison, Feynman, Land, and Newton all from their boyhood had intense curiosity, an enthusiasm or zeal for discovery and understanding. Each of them was able to take seriously hypotheses that others thought to be implausible (or had not thought about at all). All four possessed a kind of intellectual arrogance that permitted them to essay prodigious tasks, to undertake to solve problems that most of their contemporaries believed to be impossible. And each of them had quite extraordinary powers of concentration. Even Darwin, plagued as he was by physical miseries that would have invalided most men, somehow mustered mental energy enough to pursue the painstaking researches that yielded the thousands of facts with which he built his theory and defended it against so many critics.

Mental energy

What is this 'mental energy' that powers minds of genius, from Newton to Mozart to Ramanujan? Surely it is partly a function of motivation. I can think longer and harder about ideas that interest me or, to phrase it differently, about problems I see to be steps toward some goal that I covet. But I cannot think long and hard about Fermat's Last Theorem because I haven't a clue about how to solve that problem, no matter how much I should enjoy being the one to achieve that objective. If, as a boy, I had been able to run faster or kick a football further than my fellows could, I might have worked long and hard on improving those talents. But I could not and I did not. Who can doubt that one reason Bobby Fischer played so many games of chess so young was that he found from the start that he had a gift for the game? Yet, mental energy is not entirely a function of motivation and a sense of making progress. I have an eminent colleague, the psychologist Paul Meehl, who has always been able to read at least six books to my one. He does not read faster than I do nor with greater initial interest. I do not believe that he is more strongly motivated than I am to learn what the books have to teach (although, with his superior memory, he does have the advantage of knowing that more of what he reads will stay with him!). The fact is that, although I am probably his equal in physical energy, while reading technical material my eyelids begin to droop long before his do. During my life I have spent untold hours happily reading, writing, analysing data, writing computer programs, full of the sense of enjoyable accomplishment, but never for more than four or five hours at a stretch, 10 or 12 hours in a day. It is inconceivable that I could work productively at any intellectual task for 36 consecutive hours, not if my life depended on it.

Most recognized geniuses, in contrast, seem to possess remarkable powers of concentration. Archimedes's 'awesome mathematical talent was augmented by an ability to devote himself single-mindedly to any problem at hand in extraordinary periods of intense, focused concentration. At such times, the more mundane concerns of life were simply ignored. We learn from Plutarch that Archimedes would, 'forget his food and neglect his person, to that degree that when he was occasionally carried by absolute violence to bathe or have his body anointed, he used to trace geometrical figures in the ashes of the fire, and diagrams in the oil on his body, being in a state of entire preoccupation, and, in the truest sense, divine possession with his love and delight in science' (Dunham 1990).

Referring to Newton, John Maynard Keynes has said:

His peculiar gift was the power of holding continuously in his mind a purely mental problem until he had seen straight through it. I fancy his preeminence is due to his muscles of intuition being the strongest and most enduring with which a man has ever been gifted. Anyone who has ever attempted pure scientific or philosophical thought knows how one can hold a problem momentarily in one's mind and apply all one's powers of concentration to piercing through it, and how it will dissolve and escape and you find that what you are surveying is a blank. I believe that Newton could hold a problem in his mind for hours and days and weeks until it surrendered to him its secret. Then being a supreme mathematical technician he could dress it up, how you will, for purposes of exposition, but it was his intuition which was pre-eminently extraordinary . . . 'so happy in his conjectures', said de Morgan, 'as to seem to know more than he could possibly have any means of proving' (J. M. Keynes 1956).

Psychologists are not yet able to measure individual differences in mental energy, independent of motivational factors, but there can be no doubt at all that some people have more of this resource than others and I am confident that these are differences in native endowment. If I seem to be claiming here to know, like Newton, more than I possibly have any means of proving, let me explain how I do know it. There is no doubt that now, at age 69, my own stores of mental energy—my poor 'muscles of intuition'—are considerably weaker now than they were at 29. In his *A mathematician's apology* (1969), G. H. Hardy remarks that 'mathematics, more than any other art or science, is a young man's game . . . I do not know an instance of a major mathematical advance initiated by a man past fifty' (p. 78). It seems a reasonable postulate that powers which vary within an individual at different times must also vary between individuals at any time. Quoting Hardy again, Newton's 'greatest ideas of all, fluxions and the law of gravitation, came to him about 1666, when he was twenty-four' (p. 78). Surely Newton's mind, at fifty, was even more enriched by years of concentrated effort than it was at twenty-four. Yet he had given up mathematics by age fifty, presumably because some power of mind, already in full flood at twenty-four, had ebbed.

If Edison, Feynman, Gauss, and Newton had all been intensely tutored from the age of three by brilliant parents, as J. S. Mill was, then I might at least consider the possibility that my own mental muscles might have been stronger if my own parents had been more demanding. But they were not and I will not. 'When you see [Edison's] mind at play in his notebooks, the sheer multitude and richness of his ideas makes you recognize that there is something that can't be understood easily—that we may never be able to understand.' (historian Paul Israel, quoted in McAuliffe 1995). I think what lies at the heart of these mysteries is genetic, probably emergenic. The configuration of traits of intellect, mental energy, and temperament with which, during the plague years of 1665–6, Isaac Newton revolutionized the world of science were, I believe, the consequence of a genetic lottery that occurred about nine months prior to his birth, on Christmas Day, in 1642.

References

Andrade, E. N. Da C. (1956). Isaac Newton. In *The world of mathematics*, Vol. I, (ed. J. Newman), p. 275. Simon and Schuster, New York.

Borwein, J. M., and Borwein, P. B. (1988). Ramanujan and pi. *Scientific American*, **258**, 112–17.

Bouchard, T. J. Jr, and Lykken, D. T. (in press). Genetic and environmental influence on correlates of creativity. In *1995 Henry B. and Joselyn Wallace National Symposium on Talent Development* (ed. N. C. Colangelo and S. G. Assouline). Iowa City, Iowa.

——, and McGue, M. (1981). Familial studies of intelligence: A review. *Science*, **212**, 1055–9.

——, Lykken, D. T., McGue, M., Segal, N. L., and Tellegen, A. (1990). Sources of human psychological differences: the Minnesota study of twins reared apart. *Science*, **250**, 223–8.

Buhler, W. K. (1981). *Gauss: a biographical study*. Springer-Verlag, Berlin.

Campbell, J. (1988). *Grammatical man*. Simon and Schuster, New York.

Degler, C. N. (1991). *In search of human nature*. Oxford University Press, Oxford.

Dunham, W. (1990). *Journey through genius*. John Wiley and Sons, New York.

Dunnington, G. W. (1955). *Carl Friedrich Gauss: titan of science*. Hafner, New York.

Durant, W., and Durant, A. (1935). *The story of civilization*. Simon and Schuster, New York.

Ericsson, K. A. (1990). Theoretical issues in the study of exceptional performance. In *Lines of thinking*, Vol. 2, (ed. K. Gilhooly, M. Keane, R. Logie, and G. Erdospp), pp. 5–28. John Wiley and Sons Ltd, London.

——, and Charness, N. (1994). Expert performance: its structure and acquisition. *American Psychologist*, **49**, 725–47.

Freeman, D. (1992). Paradigms in collision. *Academic Questions*, **5**, 23–33.

Garfield, E. (1982). Benjamin Franklin: philadelphia's scientist extraordinaire. *Current Contents*, **40**, 5–12.

Gleick, J. (1992). *Genius: the life and science of Richard Feynman*. Pantheon Books, New York.

Hardy, G. H. (1940). *Ramanujan: twelve lectures suggested by his life and work.* Cited by Newman, J. R. (1956). Srinivasa Ramanujan. In *The world of mathematics*, Vol. I, (ed. J. Newman), pp. 368–80. Simon and Schuster, New York.

——, (1969). *A mathematician's apology*. Cambridge University Press, Cambridge.

Keynes, J. M. (1956). Newton the man. In *The world of mathematics*, Vol. I, (ed. J. R. Newman), pp. 277–85. Simon and Schuster, New York.

Knight, D. M. (1985). In *Faraday rediscovered*. (ed. D. Gooding and F. James), pp. 149–63. Stockton, New York.

Kolata, G. (1987). Remembering a 'magical genius.' *Science*, **236**, 1519–21.

Lewontin, R. C. (1992). *Human diversity*. Scientific American Books, New York.

——, Rose, S., and Kamin, L. J. (1984). *Not in our genes*. Pantheon, New York.

Lykken, D. T. (1995). *The antisocial personalities*. Lawrence Erlbaum Associates, Mahwah, NJ.

——, and Tellegen, A. (1996). Happiness is a stochastic phenomenon. *Psychological Science* **7**, 186–9.

——, Bouchard, T. J., McGue, M., and Tellegen, A. (1992). Emergenesis: genetic traits that do not run in families. *American Psychologist,* **47**, 1565–77.

——, Bouchard, T. J., McGue, M., and Tellegen, A. (1993). Heritability of interests: a twin study. *Journal of Applied Psychology,* **78**, 649–61.

McAuliffe, K. (1995). The undiscovered world of Thomas Edison. *The Atlantic Monthly,* December, 80–93.

McGue, M., Bouchard, T. J. Jr, Iacono, W. G., and Lykken, D. T. (1993). Behavior genetics of congnitive ability: a life-span perspective. In *Nature, nurture and psychology* (ed. R. Plomin and G. E. McClearn), pp. 59–76. American Psychological Association, Washington, DC.

Mead, M. (1949). *Male and female.* William Morrow, New York.

Newman, J. R. (1956). Srinivasa Ramanujan. In *The world of mathematics*, Vol. 1 (ed. J. Newman), pp. 368–76. Simon and Schuster, New York.

Parrott, T. M. (1938). *Shakespeare.* Scribner's Sons, New York.

Plomin, R., DeFries, J. C., and Loehlin, J. C. (1977). Genotype-environment interaction and correlation in the analysis of human behavior. *Psychological Bulletin,* **84**, 309–22.

Sacks, O. (1995). *An anthropologist on Mars.* Knopf, New York.

Scarr, S., and McCartney, K. (1983). How people make their own environments: a theory of genotype-environment effects. *Child Development,* **54**, 424–35.

Shaff, H. (1985). *Six wars at a time: The life and times of Gutzon Borglum.* Permelia, Darien, CN.

Solomon, A. (1996). Questions of genius. *The New Yorker*, (3 Aug.), 113–23.

Tellegen, A., Lykken, D. T., Bouchard, T., Wilcox, K., Segal, N., and Rich, S. (1988). Personality similarity in twins reared apart and together. *Journal of Personality and Social Psychology,* **54**, 1031–9.

Watson, J. B. (1924). *Behaviorism.* University of Chicago Press, Chicago.

Wilson, E. O. (1978). *On human nature.* Harvard University Press, Cambridge, MA.

ALBERT EINSTEIN

CHAPTER 3

Creativity and genius: a systems perspective

Mihaly Csikszentmihalyi

Introduction

THE title of this volume, *Genius and the mind*, suggests that one should look for the explanation to the mysteries of genius inside the human cranium. My goal in this chapter will be to argue that while the mind has quite a lot to do with genius and creativity, it is not the place where these phenomena can be found. The location of genius is not in any particular individual's mind, but in a virtual space, or system, where an individual interacts with a cultural domain and with a social field. It is only in the relation of these three separate entities that creativity, or the work of genius, manifests itself. In popular usage, 'genius' is sometimes used as a noun that stands by itself, yet in reality it appears always with a modifier: musical genius, mathematical genius, scientific genius, and so forth. Genius cannot show itself except when garbed in a concrete symbolic form.

The attribution of genius is not based on any precise criterion; it depends on a consensus of peers. Generally genius is attributed to a person who can perform with ease feats that even the experts in a given field can achieve only with great difficulty. In science, some of the central criteria for which genius is attributed include exceptional memory, fast calculation, original insights, and perhaps more than anything else, the ability to see problems from unusual perspectives. A leading astronomer gives a good summary of the traits that lead to the attribution of genius in describing her teacher, George Gamow:

Gamow was a fascinating person to work with . . . not just because he was so brilliant . . . he truly belongs in the genius class . . . No amount of my attempting to follow him would have made it possible for me to think the way he thought. He just could raise questions that had not been raised before . . . Some people have some kind of intuition about how the universe works . . . Maybe that is what you mean when you say 'genius'. People that take these enormous leaps. (see end note 1)

This ability to 'take enormous leaps' is probably grounded in some peculiarity of the nervous system. Perhaps it is a function of that superabundance of glial cells in the left inferior parietal lobe found in the autopsy of Einstein's brain (Gardner *et al.* 1996, p. 135). But to tell the truth, at present there is no firm evidence on which to base a structural, or even a functional explanation of genius. In other words, there is no anatomical evidence about differences in brain structure, and there are no measures of thought processes that differentiate geniuses from ordinary mortals, except anecdotal accounts and the direct evidence of superior accomplishments.

At this point in the state of knowledge, it seems more useful to examine genius not as an intra-psychic phenomenon, but as a historical process which takes place in a social and cultural context. And instead of genius, I shall focus on the creative process, which is a much more broadly researched area. Although not all geniuses produce creative works, and not all creative achievements involve genius, the overlap between these two concepts is large enough to treat them as closely related.

Creativity research in recent years has been increasingly informed by a systems perspective. Starting with the observations of Morris Stein (1953, 1963), and the extensive data presented by Dean Simonton showing the influence of economic, political, and social events on the rates of creative production (Simonton 1988, 1990), it has become more and more clear that variables external to the individual must be taken into account if one wishes to explain why, when, and where new ideas or products arise and become established in a culture (Gruber 1988; Harrington 1990). A good example of this trend can be seen in the recent special issue of the *Creativity Research Journal* and the debate surrounding its lead article (Kasof 1995), which claims that 'creativity' and 'genius' are purely social attributions without any objective basis. We need to believe in the existence of special gifts, of exceptionally gifted individuals, and so we select successful individuals who possess certain likely characteristics (such as good luck, or the ability to overcome obstacles), and attribute to them the disposition of 'genius'.

The particular systems approach developed here is not that extreme. It has been described before, and applied to historical and anecdotal examples, as well as to data collected to answer a variety of different questions (Csikszentmihalyi 1988*b*, 1990; Csikszentmihalyi *et al.* 1993; Csikszentmihalyi and Sawyer 1995; Feldman *et al.* 1994). In the present context, I will expand the model more rigorously, and develop its implication for a better understanding of how the work of genius can be studied.

Why do we need a systems approach?

Like most psychologists, when I started studying creativity over thirty years ago, I was convinced that it was a purely intra-psychic process. I simply assumed that one could understand creativity with reference to the thought processes, emotions, and motivations of individuals who produced novelty. But each year the task became more frustrating. In our longitudinal study of artists, for instance, it became increasingly clear that some of the potentially most creative persons stopped doing art and pursued ordinary occupations, while others who seemed to lack creative personal attributes persevered and eventually produced works of art that were hailed as important creative achievements (Csikszentmihalyi 1990; Csikszentmihalyi and Getzels 1988; Getzels and Csikszentmihalyi 1976). To use just a single example, young women in art school showed as much, or more creative potential than their male colleagues. Yet twenty years later, not one of the cohort of women had achieved recognition, whereas several in the cohort of men were successful.

The same situation holds in science. As Sir Francis Darwin said long ago, '. . . in science the credit goes to the man who convinces the world, not to the man to whom the idea first occurs' (Darwin 1914). New ideas in any discipline—from technology to religion—are very common; the question is, will they make a difference? And to make a difference, one must be able to 'convince the world', and have the idea become part of the cultural heritage of humankind.

Confronted with this situation, one can adopt one of two strategies. The first one was articulated by Abraham Maslow and involves denying the importance of public recognition (Maslow 1963). It is not the outcome of the process that counts in his opinion, but the process itself. According to this perspective a person who re-invents Einstein's formula is as creative as Einstein was. A child who sees the world with fresh eyes is creative; it is the quality of the subjective experience that determines whether a person is creative, not the judgement of the world. Although I believe that the quality of subjective experience is the most important dimension of personal life, I do not believe that creativity can be assessed with reference to it. It is a question, in the words of the Bible, 'to render unto Caesar the things which are Caesar's' (Matthew 22: 21). If creativity is to retain a useful meaning, it must refer to a process that results in an idea or product that is recognized and adopted by others. Originality, freshness of perceptions, divergent thinking ability are all well and good in their own right, as desirable personal traits. But without some form of public recognition they do not constitute creativity, and certainly not genius. In fact, one might argue that such traits are not even necessary for a creative accomplishment.

In practice, creativity research has always recognized this fact. Every creativity test, whether it involves responding to divergent thinking tasks or whether it asks children to produce designs with coloured tiles, is assessed by judges or raters who weigh the originality of the responses. The tacit assumption is that an objective quality called 'creativity' is revealed in the products, and that judges and raters can recognize it. But we know that expert judges do not possess an external, objective standard by which to evaluate 'creative' responses. Their judgements rely on past experience, training, cultural biases, personal values, idiosyncratic preferences. Thus whether an idea or product is creative or not does not depend on its own qualities, but on the effect it is able to produce in others who are exposed to it. Therefore it follows that what we call creativity is a phenomenon that is constructed through an interaction between producer and audience. Creativity is not the product of single individuals, but of social systems making judgements about individuals' products.

A second strategy that has been used to accommodate the fact that social judgements are so central to creativity is not to deny their importance, but to separate the process of creativity from that of persuasion, and then claim that both are necessary for a creative idea or product to be accepted (Simonton 1988, 1991, 1994). However, this stratagem does not resolve the epistemological problem. For if you cannot persuade the world that you had a creative idea, how do we know that you actually had it? And if you do persuade others, then of course you will be recognized as creative. Therefore it is impossible to separate creativity from persuasion; the two stand or fall together. The impossibility is not only methodological, but epistemological as well, and probably ontological. In other words, if by creativity we mean the ability to add something new to the culture, then it is impossible to even think of it as separate from persuasion.

Of course, one might disagree with this definition of creativity. Some will prefer to define it as an intra-psychic process, as an ineffable experience, as a subjective event that need not leave any objective trace. This is especially so in our days, when creativity is seen by many as the last admirable quality for which human beings can legitimately take credit and therefore something that must be preserved at all costs in its own aura of mystification. But any definition of creativity that aspires to objectivity will have to recognize the fact that the audience is as important to its constitution as the individual to whom it is credited.

An outline of the systems approach

Thus, starting from a strictly individual perspective on creativity, I was forced by facts to adopt a view that encompasses the environment in which the individual operates. This environment has two salient aspects: A cultural, or symbolic aspect which here is called the domain; and a social aspect called the field. Creativity is a process that can be observed only at the intersection where individuals, domains, and fields interact.

The domain is a necessary component of creativity because it is impossible to be a genius, at least by the definition used here, in the absence of a symbolic system. Original thought does not exist in a vacuum. It must operate on a set of rules, of representations, of notations. One can be a creative carpenter, cook, composer, chemist, or clergyman because the domains of woodworking, gastronomy, music, chemistry, and religion exist and one can evaluate performance by reference to their traditions. Without rules there cannot be exceptions, and without tradition there cannot be novelty.

Creativity occurs when a person makes a change in a domain, a change that will be transmitted through time. Some individuals are more likely to make such changes, either because of personal qualities, or because they have the good fortune to be well-positioned with respect to the domain—they have better access to it, or because of social conditions that allow them free time to experiment. For example, until quite recently the majority of scientific advances were made by men who had the means and the leisure—clergymen like Copernicus, tax collectors like Lavoisier, or physicians like Galvani—men who could afford to build their own laboratories and concentrate on their thoughts. All of these individuals lived in cultures with a tradition of systematic observation of nature, and a tradition of record-keeping and of mathematical symbolization which made it possible for their insights to be shared and evaluated by others who had equivalent training.

But most novel ideas will be quickly forgotten. Changes are not adopted unless they are sanctioned by some group entitled to make decisions as to what should or should not be included in the domain. These gatekeepers are what we call here the field. The term 'field' is often used to designate an entire discipline or kind of endeavour. In the present context, however, I want to define the term in a more narrow sense, and use it to refer only to the social organization of the domain—to the teachers, critics, journal editors, museum curators, agency directors, and foundation officers who decide what belongs to a domain and what does not. In physics, the opinion of a very small number of leading university professors was enough to certify that Einstein's ideas were creative. Hundreds of millions of people accepted the judgement of this tiny field, and marvelled at Einstein's creativity, without understanding what it was all about. It has been said that in the United States ten thousand people in Manhattan constitute the field in modern art. They decide which new paintings or sculptures deserve to be seen, bought, included in collections and therefore added to the domain.

In creativity research the field usually consists of teachers or graduate students who judge the products of children or other students. It is they who decide which test responses, mosaics, or portfolios, are to be considered creative. In this sense it is true that creativity tests can measure creativity—as long as it is recognized that what is meant by 'creativity' here is acceptance by the field of judges. Such creativity, while part of the domain of creativity research, may have nothing to do with creativity in any other domain. At every level, from Nobel Prize nominations to the scribbles of 4-year olds, judges are busy assessing new products and deciding whether or not they are creative—in other words, whether they are enough of an improvement to be included in a domain.

The systems model is analogous to the model that scholars have used to describe the process of evolution. Evolution occurs when an individual organism produces a variation which is selected by the environment and transmitted to the next generation (see for example Campbell 1976; Csikszentmihalyi 1993; Mayr 1982). The variation which occurs at the individual level corresponds to the contribution that a person makes to creativity; the selection is the contribution of the field, and the transmission is the contribution of the domain to the creative process. Thus creativity can be seen as a special case of evolution; it is to cultural evolution as mutation, selection, and transmission of genetic variation are to biological evolution.

In biological evolution it makes no sense to say that a beneficial step was the result of a particular genetic mutation alone, without taking into account environmental conditions. For instance, a genetic change that improved vision may contribute little to the evolution of a nocturnal species, whereas a change that enhanced hearing would be beneficial to it. Moreover a genetic mutation that cannot be transmitted to the next generation is also useless from the point of view of evolution. The same considerations apply to creativity when the latter is seen as the form evolution takes at the cultural level.

The cultural context

What we call creativity always involves a change in a symbolic system that has a counterpart in a mental structure. A change that does not affect the way we think, feel, or act will not be creative. Thus genius presupposes a community of people who share ways of thinking and acting, who learn from each other and imitate each other's actions. It helps to think about creativity as involving a change in memes, or the units of imitation that Dawkins (1976) suggested were the building-blocks of culture. Memes are similar to genes in that they carry instructions for action. The notes of a song tell us what to sing; the recipes for a cake tells us what ingredients to mix and how long to bake. But whereas genetic instructions are transmitted in the chemical codes we inherit on our chromosomes, the instructions contained in memes are transmitted through learning. By and large we learn memes and reproduce them without change; when a new song or a new recipe is invented, then we have creativity.

Memes seems to have changed very slowly in human history for a very long time. One of the earliest memes was the shape that our ancestors gave to the stone tools they used for chopping, carving, scraping, and pounding. The shape of these flint blades remained almost unchanged during the Palaeolithic, or Old Stone Age, for close to a million years—99.5% of human history. It is not until about 50 000 years ago, in the Upper Palaeolithic, that humans began to use new tools: blades specialized for performing specific functions, and even tools for making other tools. The first change in the meme of the tool took almost a million years; once this first step was taken, however, new shapes followed each other in increasingly rapid succession. For thousands of generations, men looked at the stone blades they held in their hands, and then reproduced one exactly alike, which they passed on to their children. The meme of the tool contained the instructions for its own replication. But then someone discovered a more efficient way of chipping stone blades, and a new meme appeared, which started reproducing itself in the minds of men, and generating offspring, that is new tools that had not existed before, which were increasingly different from their parent.

The meme of a flint scraper or a flint axe is part of the domain of technology, which includes all the artefacts humans use to achieve control over their material environment. Other early domains were those of language, art, music, religion, each including a set of memes related to each other by rules. Since the recession of the last Ice Age about 15 000 years ago, memes and corresponding domains have of course proliferated to an extent that would have been impossible to foresee only a few seconds earlier in evolutionary time. Nowadays the single domain of technology is subdivided into so many subdomains that no single individual can master even a minute fraction of it.

Cultures as symbolic domains

It is useful in this context to think about cultures as systems of interrelated domains. This is not to claim that culture is nothing but a system of interrelated domains; after all, there are over a hundred different definitions of culture being used by anthropologists, and no single definition can be exhaustive. The claim is simply that in order to understand creativity, it is useful to think of culture in this way.

It then follows that cultures differ in the number of domains they recognize, and in the hierarchical relationship among domains. For example in Western cultures, philosophy tended to develop out of religion, and then the other scholarly disciplines separated out of philosophy. For a long time religion was the queen of disciplines, and it dictated what memes could be included in different domains. Now scholarly domains are much more autonomous, although it could be claimed that mathematics has become the benchmark by which other domains are judged.

The multiplication and gradual emancipation of domains has been one of the features of human history across the planet. For a long time almost every aspect of cultural thought and expression was unified in what we would call a religious domain. Art, music, dance, narrative, proto-philosophy, and proto-science were part of an amalgam of supernatural beliefs and rituals. Now every domain strives to achieve independence from the rest, and to establish its own rules and legitimate sphere of authority.

It is usually the case that a domain with time develops its own memes and system of notation. Natural languages and mathematics underlie most domains. In addition there are formal notation systems for music, dance, logic; and other less formal ones for instructing and assessing performance in a great variety of different domains. For instance Jean Piaget (1965) gave a very detailed description of how rules are transmitted in a very informal domain: that of the game of marbles played by Swiss children. This domain is relatively enduring over several generations of children, and it consists in specific names for marbles of different sizes, colour, and composition. Furthermore, it consists in a variety of arcane rules that children learn from each other in the course of play. So even without a notation system, domains can be transmitted from one generation to the next through imitation and instruction.

Creativity as change in domains

Typically, the memes and rules that define a domain tend to remain stable over time. It takes psychic energy to learn new terms and new concepts, and in so far as psychic energy is a very scarce and necessary resource (Csikszentmihalyi 1988b), and provided that the old terms and rules are adequate to the task, it makes sense for domains to remain stable. Thus the Egyptian civilization, for example, seems to have suffered no ill effects for intentionally keeping its religion, art, technology, and political system unchanged for several thousands of years.

The common belief is that if creativity is rare, it is because of supply-side limitations; in other words, because there are few geniuses. The truth seems to be that the limits to creativity lie on the demand-side. If there is too little creativity, it is because both individually and collectively we cannot change our cognitive structures rapidly enough to recognize and adopt new ideas. For example, each year about 100 000 new books are published in the United States alone. Assuming they all contain new ideas, how many of them will be read by enough people to change the culture? At the last census, about 500 000 individuals claimed to be artists. Even if they all produced exceptionally creative works, how many of them could we pay attention to, and remember? Surveys suggest that the average American can name fewer than two living artists.

A good example of how difficult it is to overcome the inertia that protects traditional memes is the history of the metric system. Before the metric system was adopted, weights and measures were not translatable into one another, and differed from culture to culture. The metric system was a perfect expression of rationalism, and it was introduced in France in the late eighteenth century as a way to make measurement simpler and more comparable. In this sense, the 'metre' was a very creative new meme that saved much time and needless mental effort. By 1875 this new system had been adopted by almost every European nation, and then by the rest of the world. Even Great Britain capitulated in the second half of the twentieth century. But in the United States the system is still resisted, partly because there is too much money invested in the older, more awkward system, and partly because it would take too much mental effort to learn the new system.

Domains tend to change when one culture is exposed to the memes of another, usually equally advanced but different culture. Thus ancient Greece, being at the crossroads of trade between the North and the South, and between the East and the West, was influenced by ideas and practices converging from the Asiatic steppes and from Egypt, and from Europe as well as Persia and the Middle East. In Europe, similar melting pots for ideas arose later in Venice, Florence, Burgundy, the Hanseatic ports and the great sea-faring nations such as Portugal, Spain, England, and the Netherlands. Another source of change comes from conflicts between or within cultures; as Simonton has documented, social unrest is typically linked with the adoption of new memes (Simonton 1990).

Creativity is the engine that drives cultural evolution. The notion of 'evolution' does not imply that cultural changes necessarily follow some single direction, or that cultures are getting any better as a result of the changes brought about by creativity. Following its use in biology, evolution in this context means increasing complexity over time. In turn complexity is defined in terms of two complementary processes (Csikszentmihalyi 1993, 1996). First, complexity means that cultures tend to become differentiated over time—they develop increasingly independent and autonomous domains. Second, the domains within a culture become increasingly integrated; that is, related to each other and mutually supportive of each other's goals by analogy to the differentiated organs of the physical body that help each others' functioning.

In this sense, creativity does not always support cultural evolution. It generally contributes to differentiation, but it can easily work against integration. New ideas, technologies, or forms of expression often break down the existing harmony between different domains, and thus might, at least temporarily, jeopardize the complexity of a culture. The separation of physics from the tutelage of religion accomplished by Galileo's discoveries ushered in an era of tremendous differentiation in science, but at the expense of a corresponding loss of integration in Western culture. Presumably, if the evolution of culture is to continue, creative insights will in the future restore the interrelation between the currently divergent domains, thus temporarily restoring the complexity of the culture, at least until new steps in differentiation again sunder it apart.

What characteristics of domains enhance creativity?

According to this perspective, at any given point in time domains differ from one another (or from the same domain at earlier and later times) in terms of how easy it is to make a creative contribution to them. We shall review some of these characteristics below.

One obvious factor is the stage of development that the domain has attained. There are times when the symbolic system of a domain is so diffuse and loosely integrated that it is almost impossible to determine whether a novelty is or is not an improvement on the *status quo*. Chemistry was in such a state before the adoption of the periodic table, which integrated and rationalized knowledge about the elements. Earlier centuries may have had many potentially creative chemical scientists, but their work was too idiosyncratic to be evaluated against a common standard. Or conversely the symbolic system may be so tightly organized that no new development seems possible; this resembles the situation in physics at the end of the last century, before the revolution in thinking brought about by quantum theory. Both of these examples suggest that before a paradigmatic revolution, creativity is likely to be more difficult. On the other hand, the need for a new paradigm makes it more likely that if a new viable contribution does occur despite the difficulty, it will be hailed as a major creative accomplishment.

At a given historical period, certain domains will attract more gifted young people than at other times, thus increasing the likelihood of creativity. The attraction of a domain depends on several variables: its centrality in the culture, the promise of new discoveries and opportunities they present, and the intrinsic rewards that working in the domain gives. For instance, the Renaissance in early fifteenth century Florence would have not happened without the discovery of Roman ruins which yielded a great amount of new knowledge about construction techniques and sculptural models, and motivated many young people who otherwise would have gone into the professions, to become architects and artists. The quantum revolution in physics at the beginning of this century was so intellectually exciting that some of the best minds for several generations flocked to physics, or applied its principles to neighbouring disciplines such as chemistry, biology, medicine, and astronomy. Nowadays similar excitement surrounds the domains of molecular biology and computer sciences. As Thomas Kuhn (1962) remarked, potentially creative young people will not be drawn to domains where all the basic questions have been solved and therefore appear to be boring, offering few opportunities to experience the intrinsic and extrinsic rewards of solving important problems. A domain with clear rules, where novelty can be evaluated objectively, with a rich and complex symbolic system, and a central position in the culture, will be more attractive than one lacking such characteristics.

Domains also vary in terms of their accessibility. Sometimes rules and knowledge become the monopoly of a protective class or caste, and no-one else is admitted to it. Creative thought in Christianity was renewed by the Reformation, which placed the Bible and its commentaries in reach of a much larger population that had previously been excluded by an entrenched priestly caste. The enormously increased accessibility of information available on the Internet might also bring about a new peak in creativity across many different domains, just as the printing press did over four centuries ago.

Finally some domains are easier to change than others. This depends in part on how autonomous the domain is from the rest of the culture, or from the social system that supports it. Until the seventeenth century, it was difficult to be creative in Europe in many branches of science, since the Church had a vested interest in preserving the *status quo*. In Soviet Russia, the Marxist–Leninist dogma took precedence over scientific domains, and many new ideas that conflicted with it were not accepted. The most notorious case, of course, was Lysenko's application of the Lamarkian theory of evolution to the development of new strains of grain. This theory was considered to be more 'Marxist' than the Darwinian–Mendelian paradigm. Even in our time, some topics in the social (and even in the physical and biological) sciences are considered less politically correct than others, and are given scant research support as a consequence.

The social context

Even the most individually-oriented psychologists agree that in order to be called creative, a new meme must be socially valued. Without some form of social valuation it would be impossible to distinguish ideas that are simply bizarre from those that are genuinely creative. But this social validation is usually seen as something that follows the individual's creative act, and can be, at least conceptually, separated from it. The stronger claim made here is that there is no way, even in principle, to separate the reaction of society from the person's contribution: the two are inseparable. As long as the idea or product has not been validated we might have originality, but not creativity.

Nowadays everyone agrees that van Gogh's paintings show that he was a very creative artist. It is also fashionable to sneer at the ignorant bourgeoisie of his period, for failing to recognize van Gogh's genius and letting him die alone and penniless. The implication, of course, is that we are much smarter, and if we had been in their place we would have loved van Gogh's paintings. But we should remember that a hundred years ago those canvases were just the hallucinatingly original works of a sociopathic recluse. They became creative only after a number of other artists, critics, and collectors interpreted them in terms of new aesthetic criteria, and transformed them from substandard efforts into masterpieces.

Without this change in the climate of evaluation, van Gogh would not be considered creative even now. But would he have been creative anyway, even if we didn't know it? In my opinion, such a question is too metaphysical to be considered part of a scientific theory. If the question is unanswerable in principle, why ask it? The better strategy is to recognize that in the sciences as well as in the arts, creativity is as much the result of changing standards and new criteria of assessment, as it is of novel individual achievements. Having adopted such a convention, it becomes easier to understand how new memes are accepted in the domain, and in the culture (see note 2).

Who decides what is creative?

The recognition that culture and society are as involved in the constitution of creativity as the individual may set the course of investigation on the right footing, but it certainly does not answer all the questions. In fact, it brings a host of new questions to light. The major new question this perspective reveals is; 'Who is entitled to decide what is creative?' According to the individual-centred approach, this issue is not problematic. Since it is assumed that creativity is located in the person and expressed in his or her works, all it takes is for some 'expert' to recognize its existence. So if some kindergarten teachers agree that a child's drawing is creative, or a group of Nobel Prize physicists judge a young scientist's theory creative, then the issue is closed, and all we need to find out is how the individual was able to produce the drawing or the theory.

But if it is true, as the systems model holds, that attribution is an integral part of the creative process, then we must ask', 'What does it take for a new meme to be accepted into the domain? Who has the right to decide whether a new meme is actually an improvement, or simply a mistake to be discarded? How can creativity be influenced through the attributional process?'

In the systems model, the gatekeepers who have the right to add memes to a domain are collectively designed as the field. Some domains, such as Assyrian languages and literature, may have a very small field consisting of a dozen or so scholars across the world. Others, such as electronic engineering, may include many thousands of specialists whose opinion would count in recognizing a viable novelty. For mass market products such as soft drinks or motion pictures, the field might include not only the small coterie of product developers and critics, but the public at large.

In some domains it is almost impossible to do novel work without access to capital. To build a cathedral or to make a movie requires the collaboration of people and materials, and these must be made available to the would-be creative artist. Not surprisingly, creativity in the arts and sciences has flourished historically in societies that had enough surplus capital to finance experimental work. For example, the masterpieces of Florence were built with the interest that accumulated on the ledgers of the city's bankers throughout Europe; the masterpieces of Venice were the fruit of that city's sea-going trade. The Dutch painters and scientists took off after Dutch merchants began to dominate the sea lanes. As resources accumulate in one place, they lay down the conditions for innovation.

Occasionally fields become extensions of political power, responsible to society at large. For instance, the works of Renaissance artists were not evaluated by a separate aesthetic field, but had to pass muster from ecclesiastical authorities. When Caravaggio painted his vigorously original portrait of St Matthew in a relaxed pose, it was not accepted by the Prior of the church that had commissioned it because it looked too unsaintly. In the Soviet Union, specially trained party officials had the responsibility of deciding which new paintings, books, music, movies, and even scientific theories were acceptable, according to how well they supported political ideology.

Some of the most influential new ideas or processes seem to occur even though there is no existing domain or field to receive them. For instance, Freud's ideas had a tremendous diffusion even before there was a domain of psychoanalysis, or a field of analysts to evaluate them. Personal computers were widely adopted before there was a tradition and a group of experts to judge which were good, which were not. But the lack of a social context in such cases is more apparent than real. Freud was immersed in the domain of psychiatry, and simply expanded its limits until his conceptual contributions could stand on their own as a separate domain. The first field of psychoanalysis was composed of medical men who met with Freud to discuss his ideas, and were convinced by them to the point of identifying themselves as practitioners of the new domain. Without peers and without disciples, Freud's ideas might have been original, but they would not have had an impact on the culture, and thus would have failed to be creative. Similarly, personal computers would not have been accepted had there not been a domain, in this case computer languages, that allowed the writing of software and therefore various applications; and an embryonic field, that is people who had experience with mainframe computers, with video games, and so on, who could constitute themselves as a field of 'experts' in this emerging technology.

In any case, the point is that how much creativity there is at any given time is not determined just by how many original individuals are trying to change domains, but also by how receptive the fields are to innovation. It follows that if one wishes to increase the frequency of creativity, it may be more advantageous to work at the level of fields than at the level of individuals. For example, some large organizations such as Motorola, where new technological inventions are essential, spend a large quantity of resources in trying to make engineers think more creatively. This could be a good strategy, but it will not result in any increase in creativity unless the field, in this case management, is able to recognize which of the new ideas are good, and has ways for implementing them, that is including them in the domain. Whereas engineers and managers are the field who judge the creativity of new ideas within an organization such as Motorola, the entire market for electronics becomes the field that ultimately evaluates the organization's products. Thus at one level of analysis the organization is the entire system, with innovators, managers, and production engineers as its parts; whereas at a higher level of analysis the organization becomes just one element of a broader system including the entire industry.

Characteristics of fields that enhance creativity

Fields vary on a variety of dimensions, such as the extent to which they are autonomous. Some fields can make judgements about creativity irrespective of the society in which they are embedded, whereas others do little more than mediate public opinion. The autonomy of a field is to a certain extent a function of the codification of the domain it serves. When the domain is arcane and highly codified, like Assiriology or molecular biology, then the decision as to which new meme is worth accepting will be made by a relatively small field. On the other hand in the domains of movies or popular music, which are much more accessible to the general public, the specialized field is notoriously unable to decide which works will be creative. For the same reasons, creativity is much more ephemeral in the arts compared to the sciences. Works of art that seemed to shine with originality to audiences at the beginning of this century may seem trite and pointless to us. It is instructive to compare the list of Nobel Prize winners in literature against that of the winners of the science prizes; fewer of the writers from years past are now recognized as creative compared with the scientists.

Another important dimension along which fields vary is the extent to which they are open or closed to new memes. The openness of a field depends in part on its internal organization, in part on its relation to the wider society. Highly hierarchical institutions, where knowledge of the past is greatly valued, generally see novelty as a threat. For this reason churches, academies, and certain businesses based on tradition seek to promote older individuals to leadership positions, as a way of warding off excessive change. Creativity is not welcome in fields whose self-interest depends on keeping a small cadre of initiates performing the same routines, regardless of efficiency; some of the trades unions come to mind in this context.

In addition to autonomy and openness, there are many other features of a field that will make it either more or less likely to stimulate the acceptance of new memes. One of the most important ones is access to resources. A field is likely to attract original minds to the extent that it can offer scope for experimentation, and promises rewards in case of success. Even though, as we shall see, individuals who try to develop domains are in general intrinsically motivated—that is, they enjoy working in the domain for its own sake—the attraction of extrinsic rewards such as money and fame are not to be discounted.

Leonardo da Vinci was one of the most creative people on record in terms of his contributions to the arts and the sciences, and constantly moved during his lifetime from one city to another, in response to changing market conditions. The leaders of Florence, the Dukes of Milan, the Popes in Rome, and the King of France waxed and waned in terms of how much money they had to devote to new paintings, sculptures, or cutting-edge scholarship. As their fortunes changed, Leonardo moved to wherever he could pursue his work with the least hindrance.

The great flowering of impressionism in Paris was in part due to the willingness of the new middle classes to decorate their homes with canvasses. This in turn attracted ambitious young painters from every corner of the world to the banks of the Seine. The first beneficiaries of the new affluence were academic painters, but as their craft became so perfect it became boring. Subsequently, new photographic techniques made life-like pictures no longer unique, benefiting those painters who broke with tradition and introduced new memes.

How central a field is in terms of societal values will also determine how likely it is to attract new persons with an innovative bent. In the present historical period, bright young men and women are attracted to a range of often contrasting domains, all of which, however, have widespread ideological and/or material support. Some might be attracted to computer sciences because they provide the most exciting new intellectual challenges; some to oceanography because it might help to save the planetary ecosystem; some to currency trading, because it provides access to financial power, and some to family medicine, because it is the new medical speciality in demand. Any field that is able to attract a disproportionate number of bright young persons is more likely to witness creative breakthroughs.

Societal conditions relevant to creativity

We have already considered some of the societal conditions that make a field more responsive to novel ideas. It is useful, however, to focus more explicitly on the traits of societies that facilitate the entire creative process, including all three elements: the domain, the field, and the person.

As mentioned earlier, other things being equal a society that enjoys a material surplus is in a better position to help the creative process for several reasons. It makes information more readily available, it allows for a greater rate of societal differentiation and experimentation, and it is better equipped to reward and implement new ideas. A subsistence society has fewer opportunities to encourage and reward novelty, especially if it is expensive to produce. Only societies with ample material reserves can afford to build great cathedrals, great universities, great scientific laboratories. Even the composition of music, the writing of poetry, or the painting of pictures seems to require a market where subsistence needs are not primary. But it seems that there is often a lag between social affluence and creativity, and the impact of wealth may take several generations to manifest itself. So the material surplus of nineteenth century America was first absorbed by the need to build a material infrastructure for society (canals, railways, factories), before it was invested in supporting novel ideas, such as the telephone or the mass production of cars and planes.

A further and more controversial requirement might be that an egalitarian society is less likely to support the creative process than one where relatively few people control a disproportionate amount of the resources, especially in relation to the arts. Aristocracies or oligarchies may be better able to support creativity than democracies or socialist regimes, simply because when wealth and power are concentrated in a few hands, it is easier to use part of it for risky and 'unnecessary' experiments. The development of a leisure class often results in a refinement of connoisseurship that in turn provides more demanding criteria by which a field evaluates new contributions.

Societies located at the confluence of diverse cultural streams can benefit more easily from that synergy of different ideas which is so important for the creative process. It is for this reason that some of the greatest art, and the earliest science, developed in cities that were centres of trade. The Italian Renaissance was in part stimulated by the Arab and Middle Eastern influences that businessmen and their retinues brought into Florence and the seaports of Venice, Genoa, and Naples. The fact that periods of social unrest often coincide with creativity is probably due to the synergy that results when the interests and perspectives of usually segregated classes are brought to bear on each other. The Tuscan cities supported creativity best during the fourteenth and fifteenth centuries, a period in which noblemen, merchants, and craftsmen fought each other bitterly, and when every few years a good portion of the citizenry was banished.

But it is not enough to be exposed to new ideas, it is also important to be interested in them. There have been societies with great resources at the confluence of trade routes where new ideas have been shunned. In Egypt, for example, a unique burst of creativity resulted in astonishing accomplishments in architecture, engineering, art, technology, religion, and civic administration. Following this, the leaders of society apparently agreed that the best policy was to leave well enough alone. Thus most of Egyptian art for several thousand years was produced in a few central workshops supervised by priests or bureaucrats, relying on universally binding rules, common models, and uniform methods. '. . . originality of subject-matter,' writes the sociologist of art Arnold Hauser 'was never very much appreciated in Egypt, in fact was generally tabooed, the whole ambition of the artist was concentrated on thoroughness and precision of execution . . .' (Hauser 1951, p. 36).

Whether a society is open to novelty or not depends in part also on its social organization. For instance, a farming society with a stable feudal structure would be one where tradition counts more than novelty, whereas societies based on commerce, with a strong bourgeois class trying to be accepted by the aristocracy, have usually favoured novelty. Whenever the central authority tends towards absolutism, it is less likely that experimentation will be encouraged. Chinese society is another good example of a central authority supported by a powerful bureaucracy that resisted the spread of new ideas for centuries. Despite enormous early cultural advances, and a great frequency of creative individuals, Chinese authorities believed that the uses of gunpowder for weapons, or of movable type for the printing of books, were bad ideas. Of course, they might have been right. Nevertheless, currently China is trying to catch up as fast as possible with the new ideas that in the past they had elected politely to ignore.

The creative person

When we get to the level of the person in creativity research, we are immediately on more familiar ground. After all, the great majority of psychological research assumes that creativity is an individual trait, to be understood by studying individuals. A recent analysis of doctoral dissertations on the topic found that six out of ten theses written by psychology PhDs in 1986 were focused on individual traits (Wehner *et al.* 1991) and none dealt with the effects of culture and social groups. Cognitive processes, temperament, early experiences, and personality were the most frequently studied topics.

The systems model makes it possible to see the contributions of the person to the creative process in a theoretically coherent way. In the first place, it brings to attention the fact that before a person can introduce a creative variation, he or she must have access to a domain, and must want to learn to perform according to its rules. This implies that motivation is important—a topic already well understood by scholars in the field of creativity. But it also suggests a number of additional factors that are usually ignored; for instance that cognitive and motivational factors interact with the state of the domain and the field.

Second, the system model reaffirms the importance of individual factors that contribute to the creative process. People who are likely to innovate tend to have personality traits that favour breaking rules, and early experiences that make them want to do so. Divergent thinking, problem finding and all the other factors that psychologists have studied are relevant in this context.

Finally, the ability to convince the field about the virtue of the novelty one has produced is an important aspect of personal creativity. The opportunities one has to get access to the field, the network of contacts, the personality traits that make it possible for one to be taken seriously, the ability to express oneself in such a way as to be understood, are all part of the individual traits that make it easier for someone to make a creative contribution.

But none of these personal characteristics is sufficient, and probably they are not even necessary; conservative and unimaginative scientists have made important creative contributions to science by stumbling on important new phenomena. Primitive painters like le Douanier Rousseau or Grandma Moses, who were trying to be traditional but could not quite paint realistically enough, have been seen as having contributed creatively to the history of art. At the same time, it is probably true that those who can master a domain, and then want to change it, will have a higher proportion of their efforts recognized as creative. So we now review briefly the characteristics of such persons.

Accessing the domain

In order to bring about a novel change, a person has to have access to the information contained in a given domain. How much access a person has depends on two sets of factors: one external and structural, the other subjective and internal. The external factors include the amount of cultural capital a person can dispose of, and the domain-related roles available in the social environment. Cultural capital consists of the educational aspirations of one's parents, the non-academic knowledge one absorbs in the home, and the informal learning that one picks up from home and community. Moreover, it involves learning opportunities which include schooling, mentoring, exposure to books, computers, museums, musical instruments, and so forth. Domain-related roles are those opportunities for expressing one's creative potential that vary from culture to culture, from social class to social class, and from historical epoch to epoch. For example, whether a person will be able to study physics or music long enough to be able to innovate in it depends in part on whether there are laboratories or conservatories in which one can practice and learn state-of-the-art knowledge in the particular domain.

Whether people will avail themselves of existing knowledge does not depend only on these external, structural factors. It depends also, perhaps more, on subjective traits such as curiosity, interest, and intrinsic motivation. At this point we do not know to what extent such dispositions are inherited and form part of a person's temperament, and to what extent they are learned and cultivated in the early family environment. In either case, the fact is that traits such as curiosity and motivation vary considerably between people. For instance one of the subjects of our study, Manfred Eigen, was drafted into the German air defence out of high school, at age 15. He was taken to Russia to man an anti-aircraft battery on the Eastern front, and at the end of World War II he was taken prisoner by the Soviet troops. He escaped from the prisoner of war camp and walked for over 500 miles without money or food, evading Russian soldiers, until he reached the doors of the University of Göttingen. Here he was resolved to study science, having heard that Göttingen had the highest reputation in the field. The University had not reopened yet after the war, but when it did the young Eigen was admitted even without his High School diploma. He went to work with a vengeance, received his doctorate at age 23, and by 1967—at age 40—his discoveries in chemistry had earned him a Nobel prize.

This example shows the extent to which internal factors like curiosity and determination can compensate for the lack of structural opportunities. There are similarities to the ways in which Michael Faraday (described in Chapter 5 by Michael Howe) overcame obstacles in his determination to become a scientist. It would have been easy for Eigen to resign himself to the lack of educational opportunities in the prison camp, or in post-war Germany—in which case it would have been impossible for him to contribute creatively to science. However, it should be added that his curiosity and determination seem, at least in part, to be the result of the cultural capital he had accumulated in his early years. Eigen's father was a musician, and he grew up in a family where culture was held in high esteem, where children were expected to be proficient in a variety of subjects, and where training in music and science was provided as a matter of course. By the age of 15, when he was drafted into the Army, Eigen's desire to access the domain of science was so firmly established that the enormous obstacles in his way scarcely slowed down his progress. Nevertheless, if for example he had been taken to a Siberian gulag, or if Germany had been prevented from rebuilding its scientific infrastructure, it is probable that Eigen would not have been able to overcome this lack of opportunity.

Producing novelty

Being able to access a domain is indispensable but certainly not sufficient, for a person to make a creative contribution. He or she must also have the ability and inclination to introduce novelty in the domain. It is convenient to divide the personal qualities that help the production of novelty into four kinds: innate ability, cognitive style, personality, and motivation.

Innate ability refers to the fact that it is easier to be creative if one is born with a physical endowment that helps to master the skills required by the domain. Great musicians like Mozart seem to be unusually sensitive to sounds from the earliest years, and artists seem to be sensitive to colour, light, and visual shapes even before they start practising their craft. If we extend the definition of creativity to domains such as basketball—and in principle there is no reason for not doing so—then it is clear that a creative player like Michael Jordan benefits from unusual physical co-ordination. At this point, we know very little about the relationship between brain organization and the ability to perform in specific domains. It would not be surprising, however, to discover that interest or skill in certain domains can be inherited, as suggested by David Lykken in Chapter 2. Howard Gardner's postulate of seven or more separate forms of intelligence (Gardner 1983, 1993) also seems to support the notion that each of us might be born with a propensity to respond to a different slice of reality, and hence to operate more effectively in one domain rather than another. Many of the subjects in our study displayed unusual early abilities that were almost at the level of the child prodigies described by Feldman (1986). On the other hand, a roughly equal number of individuals who achieved comparable creative contributions appeared to have rather undistinguished childhoods, and were not recognized as exceptional until early adulthood.

Clearly very little is known as yet about the relationship of central nervous system structures and creativity, although many claims are being made these days with limited support. For instance, cerebral lateralization research has led many people to claim that left-handers or ambidextrous individuals, who are presumed to be using the right side of their brains more, are more likely to be creative. Left-handers are apparently over-represented in such fields as art, architecture, and music. Many exceptional individuals from Alexander the Great to Leonardo da Vinci, Michelangelo, Raphael, Picasso, Einstein were all left-handers (Coren 1992; Paul 1993). Suggestive as such trends might be, there is also evidence that left-handers are much more likely to be prone to a variety of unusual pathologies (Coren 1992, p. 197–220). Thus whatever neurological difference handedness makes might not be directly linked to creativity, but rather to deviancy from the norm that can take either a positive or a negative value.

The most salient attributes of the cognitive style of potentially creative individuals appear to be divergent thinking (Guilford 1967) and discovery orientation (Getzels and Csikszentmihalyi 1976). These are, of course, some of the most thoroughly researched dimensions of creativity to be found in the psychological literature. Divergent thinking, usually indexed by fluency, flexibility, and originality of mental operations, is routinely measured by psychological tests given to children, and shows modest correlations with childish measures of creativity, such as the originality of stories told or pictures drawn (Runco 1991). Whether these tests also relate to creativity in 'real' adult settings is not clear, although some claims to that effect have been made (Milgram 1990; Torrance 1988). Discovery orientation, or the tendency to find and formulate problems where others have not seen them, has also been measured in selected situations, with some encouraging results (Baer 1993; Runco 1995). As Einstein and many others have observed, the solution of problems is a much simpler affair than their formulation. Anyone who is technically proficient can solve a problem that is already formulated, but it takes true originality to formulate a problem in the first place (Einstein and Infeld 1938).

Some scholars dispute the notion that problem finding and problem solving involve different thought processes. For example, the Nobel-prize winning economist and psychologist Herbert Simon has claimed that all creative achievements are the result of normal problem-solving (Simon 1985, 1988). However, the evidence he presents is based on computer simulation of scientific breakthroughs. This is not relevant to the claim, since the computers are fed pre-selected data, logical algorithms, and a routine for recognizing the correct solution—all of which are absent in real historical discoveries (Csikszentmihalyi 1988*a*, *c*).

The personality of creative persons has also been exhaustively investigated (Barron 1969, 1988). Psychoanalytic theory has stressed the ability to regress into the unconscious while still maintaining conscious ego controls as one of the hallmarks of creativity (Kris 1952). The widespread use of multi-factor personality inventories suggest that creative individuals tend to be strong on certain traits such as introversion and self-reliance, and low on others such as conformity and moral certainty (Csikszentmihalyi and Getzels 1973; Getzels and Csikszentmihalyi 1976; Russ 1993). Some examples of this approach are provided by Robert Albert in his evaluation of the mathematicians Srinivasa Ramanujan and G. H. Hardy (Chapter 6).

There is a long tradition of associating creativity with mental illness, or genius with insanity (Jacobson 1912; Lombroso 1891). Recent surveys have added new credence to this tradition by demonstrating rather convincingly that the rate of various pathologies such as suicide, alcoholism, drug addiction, and institutionalization for nervous diseases is much higher than expected in certain 'creative' professions, such as drama, poetry, music, and so forth (Jablow and Lieb 1988; Jamison 1989; Martindale 1989; Richards 1990). These results, however, only demonstrate that some fields, which in our culture get little support, are associated with pathology either because they attract persons who are exceptionally sensitive (Mitchell 1972; Piechowski 1991), or because they can offer only depressing careers. They may have little or nothing to say about genius itself. Another perspective on these issues is provided by Gordon Claridge in Chapter 10.

One view this author has developed on the basis of his studies is that creative persons are characterized not so much by single traits, but rather by their ability to operate through the entire spectrum of personality dimensions. So they are not just introverted, but can be both extroverted and introverted depending on the phase of the process. When gathering ideas a creative scientist is gregarious and sociable; when he starts working, he might become a secluded hermit for weeks on end. Creative individuals are sensitive and aloof, dominant and humble, masculine and feminine, as the occasion demands (Csikszentmihalyi 1996). What dictates their behaviour is not a rigid inner structure, but the demands of the interaction between them and the domain in which they are working.

The importance of motivation for creativity has long been recognized. If one had to bet on who is more likely to achieve a creative breakthrough—a highly intelligent but not very motivated person, or one less intelligent but more motivated—one should always bet on the second (Cox 1926). Because introducing novelty in a system is always a risky and usually unrewarded affair, it takes a great deal of motivation to persevere.

One recent formulation of the creative person's willingness to take risks is the 'economic' model of Sternberg and Lubart (1995).

In order to want to introduce novelty into a domain, a person should first of all be dissatisfied with the *status quo*. It has been said that Einstein explained why he spent so much time on developing a new physics by saying that he could not understand the old physics. Greater sensitivity, naiveté, arrogance, impatience, and higher intellectual standards have all been adduced as reasons why some people are unable to accept the conventional wisdom in a domain, and feel the need to break out of it.

Values also play a role in developing a creative career. There are indications that if a person holds financial and social goals in high esteem, it is less likely that he or she will continue long enough braving the insecurities involved in the production of novelty, and will tend to settle for a more conventional career (Csikszentmihalyi *et al.* 1984; Getzels and Csikszentmihalyi 1976). A person who is attracted to the solution of abstract problems (theoretical value) and to order and beauty (aesthetic value) is more likely to persevere.

Perhaps the most salient characteristic of creative individuals is a constant curiosity, an ever renewed interest in whatever happens around them. This enthusiasm for experience is often seen as part of the 'childishness' attributed to creative individuals (Csikszentmihalyi 1996; Gardner 1993). Another way of describing this trait is that creative people are intrinsically motivated. A recurrent refrain among them goes something like this, 'You could say that I worked every day of my life, or with equal justice you could say that I never did a lick of work in my life.' In other words, work and enjoyment are so deeply intertwined that they cannot be disentangled.

How these patterns of cognition, personality, and motivation develop is still not clear. Some may be under heavy genetic control, while others develop under the conscious direction of the self-organizing person. In any case, the presence of these traits is likely to make a person more creative if the conjunction with the other elements of the system—the field and the domain—happen to be propitious.

Convincing the field

To make a creative contribution, a person must not only be able to produce a novelty in the domain, but must also be able to present the novelty in such a way that the field will accept it as an improvement over the *status quo,* and thus worth including in the canon of the domain. If this does not happen, the novelty is likely to disappear from the record without affecting human consciousness any further. There are exceptions, as when a painting or a theory that had been ignored in the author's lifetime is rediscovered posthumously. In such cases what changes is not the creative contribution, but the field or the domain that receives it. As the totality of the system changes with time, a painting or theory that was simply different may become 'creative', or vice-versa. In most cases, however, the author's own actions will help determine whether the novelty is accepted or not.

Every model of the creative process recognizes that after the phases of preparation, incubation, and insight there must follow a phase of elaboration during which the novel idea or product is polished and prepared for public scrutiny. For a scholar this might involve many months of hard work readying an article for publication; for an inventor it involves building a prototype that will pass the scrutiny of the patent office; for an artist it might involve convincing a gallery or a collector that a canvas is worth exhibiting. This phase of the creative process is often the least appealing, and it involves skills and behaviours that are often at variance with the preceding phases. For instance if the beginning of the creative process involves a great deal of flexibility, idiosyncrasy, and divergent thinking, its end requires convergent thinking, social skills, and sheer endurance. It is partly for this reason that the creative personality includes opposite dimensions; the creative process requires opposite personality traits.

In our longitudinal study of artists, it became apparent that the kind of young people who in art school were considered to be the most promising embodiments of the 'artist', had a great deal of trouble once they left college. Art teachers rewarded students who were highly original, reclusive, abrasive, unconcerned about material rewards and success. But after graduation, such students had a very hard time getting public support for their work. They antagonized the 'field' of critics, gallery owners, and collectors, and pretty soon found themselves without contacts or commissions. At that point most of them lost heart and took up some other occupation, refurbishing old houses, customizing cars, starting a plumbing company, thereby forfeiting any claims to changing the domain. The young artists who left their mark on the world of art tended to be those who in addition to originality also had the ability to communicate their vision to the public, often resorting to public relations tactics that would have been abhorrent in the pure atmosphere of the art school. It is interesting that in the analysis presented by Andrew Steptoe in Chapter 11, the more successful artists of the Italian Renaissance also appear to have coupled creativity with social and diplomatic skills.

This is how George Stigler, a winner of the Nobel prize in economics, expressed this requirement in his interview for our study:

I've always looked upon the task of a scientist as bearing the responsibility for persuading his contemporaries of the cogency and validity of his thinking. He isn't entitled to a warm reception. He has to earn it, whether by the skill of his exposition, the novelty of his views . . . Everybody has to sooner or later say, unless he's insane, 'I have to accept the judgement of the people around me. I can't say I'm great if everybody else says I'm not.' Or if I do say it and don't bring it to fruition, I am clearly a romancer or a utopian, not an active participant in my society.

In order to persuade one's contemporaries, it is important for a person to be able to internalize the rules of the domain and the opinions of the field, so that one can anticipate its judgements and avoid having to beat one's head against a wall. Practically all creative individuals say that one advantage they have over their peers is that they can tell when their own ideas are bad, and that they can immediately forget the bad ideas without investing too much energy in them. Linus Pauling, the winner of two Nobel prizes, was asked at his sixtieth birthday party how he had been able to come up with so many epochal discoveries. 'It's easy', he is said to have answered, 'You think of a lot of ideas, and throw away the bad ones'. To be able to do so, however, implies that one has a very strong internal representation of which ideas are 'good' and which are 'bad', a representation that matches closely the one accepted by the field.

An extremely lucid example of how a person internalizes the system is given by the inventor Jacob Rabinow, who has 250 patents on a variety of very different inventions. In addition to being a prolific inventor himself, he is also prominent in the field, because he works for the patent office, and hence decides which inventions by other individuals deserve recognition. In describing what it takes to be an original thinker, Rabinow mentions first the importance of what I have called the *domain*:

So you need three things to be an original thinker. First, you have to have a tremendous amount of information—a big database if you like to be fancy. If you're a musician, you should know a lot about music, that is, you've heard music, you remember music, you could repeat a song if you have to. In other words, if you were born on a desert island and never heard music, you're not likely to be a Beethoven. You might, but it's not likely. You may imitate birds but you're not going to write the Fifth Symphony. So you're brought up in an atmosphere where you store a lot of information.

So you have to have the kind of memory that you need for the kind of things you want to do. And you do those things which are easy and you don't do those things which are hard, so you get better and better by doing the things you do well, and eventually you become either a great tennis player or a good inventor or whatever, because you tend to do those things which you do well and the more you do, the easier it gets, and the easier it gets, the better you do it, and eventually you become very one-sided but you're very good at it and you're lousy at everything else because you don't do it well. This is what engineers call positive feedback. The small differences at the beginning of life become enormous differences by the time you've done it for 40, 50, 80 years as I've done it. So anyway, first you have to have the big database.

Next, Rabinow brings up what the person must contribute, which is mainly a question of motivation, or the enjoyment one feels when playing (or working?) with the contents of the domain:

Then you have to be willing to pull the ideas, because you're interested. Now, some people could do it, but they don't bother. They're interested in doing something else. So if you ask them, they'll, as a favor to you, say: 'Yeah, I can think of something.' But there are people like myself who *like* to do it. It's fun to come up with an idea, and if nobody wants it, I don't give a damn. it's just fun to come up with something strange and different.

Finally he focuses on how important it is to reproduce in one's mind the criteria of judgement that the field uses:

And then you must have the ability to get rid of the trash which you think of. You cannot think only of good ideas, or write only beautiful music. You must think of a lot of music, a lot of ideas, a lot of poetry, a lot of whatever. And if you're good, you must be able to throw out the junk immediately without even saying it. In other words, you get many ideas appearing and you discard them because you're well trained and you say, 'that's junk.' And then you see the good one, you say, 'Oops, this sounds interesting. Let me pursue that a little further.' And you start developing it. . . . And by the way, if you're not well trained, but you've got ideas, and you don't know if they're good or bad, then you send them to the Bureau of Standards, National Institute of Standards, where I work, and *we* evaluate them. And *we* throw them out.

Conclusion

It is certain that those who are interested in the phenomenon of genius will continue to focus on the individual and his or her thought processes. After all, the unique qualities of those whose mind takes 'enormous leaps' are so attractive that we can't curb our curiosity about them. What the present chapter seeks to accomplish, however, is to point out that genius cannot be recognized except as it operates within a system of cultural rules, and it cannot bring forth anything new unless it can enlist the support of peers. If these conclusions are accepted, then it follows that the occurrence of genius is not simply a function of how many gifted individuals there are, but also of how accessible the various symbolic systems are, and how responsive the social system is to novel ideas. Instead of focusing exclusively on individual geniuses, it will make more sense to focus on communities that may or may not nurture genius. In the last analysis, it is the community and not the individual who makes genius manifest.

Acknowledgement

The research reported herein was supported by a grant from the Spencer Foundation.

Notes

1. This quote and the subsequent ones are taken from interviews conducted by the author with 100 creative individuals in the context of a study supported by the Spencer Foundation.
2. The parameters of the systems model are very simple, but difficult to understand. Its implications are so counter-intuitive that most people exposed to the model dismiss it out of hand, even before they have a chance to reflect on it. A typical objection is the following caveat from one of the reviewers of this volume: 'My only criticism concerns the author's consistent confusion of creativity with the recognition and acceptance of creativity. Is the universe still there if no humans are around to recognize its existence? . . . Was Herman Melville not a genius until a critical mass of individuals began to really like *Moby Dick?* If so, how many people did it take to recognize him as a genius before he became one . . .' I would love to be able not to confuse creativity with its recognition and its acceptance. But how would I go about it? Unfortunately, as a scientist, I must resign myself to observe creativity only after it has been recognized. There is no other way to do it. For creativity, unlike the universe, is not a physical entity that would exist even if humans were not around to recognize its existence. The first obstacle in the way of understanding the systems model is to think that creativity is a 'natural kind'—something on the order of atoms or molecules. My

contention is that if no humans had ever existed, and all of Shakespeare's works were to miraculously materialize on a distant planet, no entity in the universe would know whether they were 'creative'—for they would lack the essential element of human response. This argument is not the same conundrum that George Berkeley proposed almost three centuries ago, when he asked whether there would be a sound in the forest if a tree fell, and no one was there to hear it. If by 'sound' we mean the vibrations of molecules in the air, then certainly there is sound regardless of human presence. But the same argument does not hold for creativity, which is a judgement people make of certain ideas or products, and which therefore cannot exist without people.

The reviewer proceeds with the rhetorical question: 'Was Melville not a genius . . .?' The answer is 'No'. If a critical mass of individuals had not begun 'to really like *Moby Dick*' then the reviewer would not have used Melville as an example, and the readers could not have understood the reviewer's reference. In other words, whether Melville is or is not a genius as long as he is unrecognized is a metaphysical question which cannot be answered in empirical terms. The reason the question can be asked in the first place is that a critical mass has already identified Melville as a genius. 'How many people does it take . . . to recognize him as a genius' is an empirical question, and one of the purposes of the systems model is to begin answering it.

References

Baer, J. (1993). *Creativity and divergent thinking.* Lawrence Erlbaum, Hillsdale, NJ.

Barron, F. (1969). *Creative person and creative process.* Holt, Rinehart and Winston, New York.

——(1988). Putting creativity to work. In *The nature of creativity* (ed. R. J. Sternberg), pp. 76–98. Cambridge University Press, Cambridge.

Campbell, D. T. (1976). Evolutionary epistemology. In *The library of living philosophers: Karl Popper* (ed. D. A. Schlipp), pp. 413–63. Open Court, La Salle, Ill.

Coren, S. (1992). *The left-handed syndrome: the causes and consequences of left-handedness.* The Free Press, New York.

Cox, C. (1926). *The early mental traits of three hundred geniuses.* Stanford University Press, Stanford, CA.

Csikszentmihalyi, M. (1988*a*). Motivation and creativity: toward a synthesis of structural and energistic approaches to cognition. *New Ideas in Psychology*, **6**, 159–76.

——(1988*b*). Society, culture, person: a systems view of creativity. In (ed. R. J. Sternberg), pp. 325–39. *The nature of creativity* Cambridge University Press, Cambridge.

——(1988*c*). Solving a problem is not finding a new one: a reply to Simon. *New Ideas in Psychology*, **6**, 183–6.

——(1990). The domain of creativity. In *Theories of creativity* (ed. M. A. Runco and R. S. Albert, pp. 190–212. Sage Publications, Newbury Park, CA.

——(1993). *The evolving self: a psychology for the third millennium.* HarperCollins, New York.

——(1996). *Creativity: flow and the psychology of discovery and invention.* HarperCollins, New York.

——, and Getzels, J. W. (1973). The personality of young artists: an empirical and theoretical exploration. *British Journal of Psychology*, **64**, 91–104.

——, —— (1988). Creativity and problem finding. In *The foundations of aesthetics, art, and art education* (ed. F. G. Farley and R. W. Neperole), pp. 91–106. Praeger, New York.

——, and Sawyer, K. (1995). Shifting the focus from individual to organizational creativity. In *Creative action in organizations* (ed. C. M. Ford and D. A. Gioia), pp. 167–72. Sage Publications, Thousand Oaks, CA.

——, Getzels, J. W., and Kahn, S. P. (1984). *Talent and achievement: a longitudinal study of artists.* [A report to the Spencer Foundation] The University of Chicago, Chicago.

——, Rathunde, K., and Whalen, S. (1993). *Talented teenagers: the roots of success and failure.* Cambridge University Press, New York.

Darwin, F. (1914). *The Galton lecture.* The Eugenic Society, London.

Dawkins, R. (1976). *The selfish gene.* Oxford University Press, Oxford.

Einstein, A., and Infeld, L. (1938). *The evolution of physics.* Simon and Schuster, New York.

Feldman, D. (1986). *Nature's gambit: child prodigies and the development of human potential.* Basic Books, New York.

——, Csikszentmihalyi, M., and Gardner, H. (1994). *Changing the world: a framework for the study of creativity.* Praeger, Westport, CT.

Gardner, H. (1983). *Frames of mind: the theory of multiple intelligences.* Basic Books, New York.

—— (1993). *Creating minds.* Basic Books, New York.

——, Kornhaber, M. L., and Wake, W. K. (1996). *Intelligence: multiple perspectives.* Harcourt Brace, Fort Worth, TX.

Getzels, J. W., and Csikszentmihalyi, M. (1976). *The creative vision: a longitudinal study of problem finding in art.* John Wiley and Sons, New York.

Gruber, H. (1988). The evolving systems approach to creative work. *Creativity Research Journal*, **1**, 27–51.

Guilford, J. P. (1967). *The nature of human intelligence.* McGraw-Hill, New York.

Harrington, D. M. (1990). The ecology of human creativity: a psychological perspective. In *Theories of creativity* (ed. M. A. Runco and R. S. Albert), pp. 143–69. Sage Publications, Newbury Park, CA.

Hauser, A. (1951). *The social history of art.* Vintage Books, New York.

Jablow, H. D., and Lieb, J. (1988). *The key to genius: manic-depression and the creative life.* Prometheus Books, Buffalo, NY.

Jacobson, A. C. (1912). Literary genius and manic depressive insanity. *Medical Record*, **82**, 937–39.

Jamison, K. R. (1989). Mood disorders and patterns of creativity in British writers and artists. *Psychiatry*, **52**, 125–134.

Kasof, J. (1995). Explaining creativity: The attributional perspective. *Creativity Research Journal*, **8**, 311–66.

Kris, E. (1952). *Psychoanalytic explorations in art.* International Universities Press, New York.

Kuhn, T. S. (1962). *The structure of scientific revolutions.* The University of Chicago Press, Chicago.

Lombroso, C. (1891). *The man of genius.* Walter Scott, London.

Martindale, C. (1989). Personality, situation, and creativity. In *Handbook of creativity* (ed. R. R. J. Glover and C. R. Reynolds), pp. 211–32. Plenum, New York.

Maslow, A. H. (1963). The creative attitude. *The Structuralist*, **3**, 4–10.

Mayr, E. (1982). *The growth of biological thought.* Belknap Press, Cambridge, MA.

Milgram, R. M. (1990). Creativity: an idea whose time has come and gone? In *Theories of creativity* (ed. M. A. Runco and R. S. Albert), pp. 215–33. Sage Publications, Newbury Park, CA.

Mitchell, A. R. (1972). *Schizophrenia: the meaning of madness.* Taplinger, New York.

Paul, D. (1993). *Left-handed helpline.* Dextral Books, Manchester, UK.

Piaget, J. (1965). *The moral judgment of the child.* The Free Press, New York.

Piechowski, M. J. (1991). Emotional development and emotional giftedness. In *Handbook of gifted education* (ed. N. Colangelo and G. A. Davis), pp. 285–306. Allyn and Bacon, Boston.

Richards, R. (1990). Everyday creativity, eminent creativity, and health. *Creativity Research Journal*, **3**, 300–26.

Runco, M. A. (1991). *Divergent thinking*. Ablex, Norwood, NJ.

—— (ed.) (1995). *Problem finding*. Ablex, Norwood, NJ.

Russ, S. W. (1993). *Affect and creativity*. Lawrence Erlbaum, Hillsdale, NJ.

Simon, H. A. (1985). Psychology of scientific discovery. Keynote presentation at the *93rd Annual Meeting of the American Psychological Association*, Los Angeles, CA.

—— (1988). Creativity and motivation: a response to Csikszentmihalyi. *New Ideas in Psychology*, **6**, 177–81.

Simonton, D. K. (1988). *Scientific genius*. Cambridge University Press, Cambridge.

—— (1990). Political pathology and societal creativity. *Creativity Research Journal*, **3**, 85–99.

—— (1991). Personality correlates of exceptional personal influence. *Creativity Research Journal*, **4**, 67–8.

—— (1994). *Greatness: who makes history and why*. Guilford, New York.

Stein, M. I. (1953). Creativity and culture. *Journal of Psychology*, **36**, 311–22.

—— (1963). A transactional approach to creativity. In *Scientific creativity* (ed. C. W. Taylor and F. Barron), pp. 217–27. John Wiley, New York.

Sternberg, R. J., and Lubart, T. I. (1995). *Defying the crowd: cultivating creativity in a culture of conformity*. The Free Press, New York.

Torrance, E. P. (1988). The nature of creativity as manifest in its testing. In *The nature of creativity* (ed. R. J. Sternberg), pp. 43–75. Cambridge University Press, Cambridge.

Wehner, L., Csikszentmihalyi, M., and Magyari-Beck, I. (1991). Current approaches used in studying creativity: an exploratory investigation. *Creativity Research Journal*, **4**, 261–71.

LUDWIG VAN BEETHOVEN

CHAPTER 4

Historical developments of expert performance: public performance of music

Andreas C. Lehmann and K. Anders Ericsson

Introduction

THROUGHOUT history, some creative achievements have gone beyond what contemporaries considered possible. These achievements have changed our cultural heritage forever, often in a revolutionary fashion. Many have seemed inexplicable to people at the time, so their creators were assumed to have been endowed with special capacities such as innate talent and genius. One of the domains in which the notion of innate talent remains powerful even today is music, and anecdotal accounts abound of the almost magical technical wizardry of exceptional musicians. Adult soloists, composers, and especially child prodigies, have all been described as having exceptional talent or genius.

In this chapter, we want to address the issue of whether it is really necessary to attribute unique capacities to particular individuals. We will examine the possibility that their creative achievements can be explained by factors based on cultural conditions, environmental factors, and acquired skills. In other areas of revolutionary discovery, such as the geographical explorations of Columbus and others, the individuals involved are usually described today in terms of their exceptional motivation, bravery, dedication, or persistence (Wilcox 1977). Their travels and subsequent discoveries are explained without recourse to unique and unknown capacities, but rather to developments in science, technology, and accumulation of knowledge. Can we likewise suggest that for the domain of music performance, the current standards of training of professional musicians allow a large number of individuals to attain the very high levels of skill that only a century ago appeared virtually unobtainable? Such an explanation necessarily reduces the mystique surrounding some famous individuals, but it also provides us with a more objective account of their achievements.

Following a number of authors such as Boden (1994), we understand creativity to be achievement that goes beyond existing knowledge or practice in a domain of activity such as science or music. In addition, the achievement has to be recognized by the field and incorporated into the canon, as noted by Mihaly Csikszentmihalyi in Chapter 3, and discussed by others (Schaffer 1994). This view positions creativity outside the individual as a process that relies on societal factors. Indeed, performers themselves may not always be aware of their creative contribution until it is recognized by others. What constitutes a creative act? In this chapter we are less interested in the cognitive processes that underlie creativity than in the creative contributions themselves and the conditions that made them possible. Creative achievements in the sciences may consist of discoveries of natural laws or novel theories. In music, creativity is manifest in the development of new musical styles and pieces, new playing techniques, innovative training techniques, and other displays of exceptional skills.

Creative achievements have often been perceived as emerging at one particular point in time. Anecdotes are told about the exact moments when discoveries were allegedly made, for example when Newton discovered gravity, or Archimedes his 'principle'. More recent research, however, has shown that discoveries—at least in the sciences— are processes that develop over long periods of time (cf. Gruber 1989). In addition, while creative achievements often appear to be isolated successful efforts to solve certain problems, Simonton (1997) has shown that the more important contributions of a creative individual tend to be associated with phases of high productivity in general. It follows that creative achievements are related to an individual's knowledge and skills and professional involvement in a domain.

In addition to the skills they acquire, musicians and other performers need incentives to make creative contributions. For example, the desire to overcome previous performance limitations or to compete successfully with other musicians will motivate individuals to search for new solutions to technical problems. In the quest for these solutions, they may take advantage of changing circumstances that offer possibilities which were hitherto unknown. We assume that a field such as music tends to stimulate ever higher and more complex levels of performance—as long as there are incentives for performers to be drawn into the business. Incentives to choose a domain such as music are, as Csikszentmihalyi (1996) points out, strongly related to the possibility of earning a living.

In this century, many philosophers and scientists have discussed the issue of progress in Western civilization (e.g. Nisbet 1980). Although everyone agrees that scientific and technological advances have led to higher productivity and affluence, there is considerable controversy about whether quality of life has improved as a result of these changes. Likewise, evaluative judgements about what type of performance or what type of music is more enjoyable to listeners in a given historical period cannot be made, as the aesthetic criteria are likely to differ across periods. Indeed, enjoyment is not based only on the difficulty of the music or on instrumental virtuosity. This chapter will focus on the activity of performing music in public, and leave aside aspects of musicianship such as composing, teaching, or directing.

Outline of the chapter

This chapter proposes that the skills of performing musicians have gradually improved over the last three centuries at least. We argue that this is a result of competition and of the efforts of individual musicians to surpass their contemporaries. We first assess changes in public music performance across historical periods. Aspects of performance are then identified that allow us to study music performance objectively, irrespective of style or period. The third section reviews the development of music performance along with the constraints imposed on it by general changes within society. The site of performance, including the ambient noise level and acoustical features of the location, is one factor which favours some musical instruments over others. Another factor concerns the emergence of instrumental music for individual performers or soloists; this has allowed audiences to compare the performances of different artists. We also document historical trends toward increased competition among musicians for fame and fortune. The next section discusses the increases in preparation and specialization over time that have led to the achievement of higher levels of performance. We then examine the strong evidence for our claim that the skills required of musicians have increased. In addition, we describe other mechanisms that allow musicians to excel, such as innovative playing techniques and improvements made to musical instruments. We go on to discuss the assimilation of these changes into a body of shared knowledge which has allowed later generations of performers to acquire superior techniques and thus surpass their predecessors. Increases over recorded history in the amount of deliberate practice carried out by developing musicians are described, as are improvements in the effectiveness of their education. The final section summarizes and integrates our findings into a model of competition and increase of performance skills.

This chapter has been written for the general reader, and does not assume prior experience in playing an instrument or knowledge of music history. Some sections, however, will provide more detail than is strictly necessary to understand our general claims, because we felt it important to include sufficient historical facts to allow the scientific evaluation of our argument.

Assessing performance skills of the past

Since we lack sound recordings of musicians from previous centuries, the level of skilled performance of earlier musicians has to be inferred from other sources. In particular, we can use the music itself. Some pieces of music are evidently much easier than others, and the levels of skill required for performance vary correspondingly. Since most music was performed in public, we think it safe to assume that contemporary musicians were able at least to play what was written down more or less accurately. Unfortunately, this type of inference is only appropriate for certain periods and musical cultures. In other periods, performers added extra-notational features such as ornaments, and the complexity and skill demands of pieces are clearly underestimated by the notes that appear on the manuscript or printed page.

Objective data about the expressive playing skills and artistic interpretations of past musicians are virtually impossible to obtain. However, the capacity of instruments at any given historical time can be studied. By analyzing changes in musical instruments over time, it is possible to draw conclusions about the skills required for effective performance. We have focused on the piano and the time period over which it was developed. One can try to infer the realm of possibilities for performance and composition from the performance traditions and playing techniques of different time periods. These may in turn be compared with other periods.

Improvements in expert music performance over time: the general framework

Despite numerous historical changes in performance conditions, the musician's job of performing music for the entertainment of a public has remained the same well-defined task. This task is constrained by various factors. Although most of our examples relate to traditional Western art music, it is plausible to assume that our model could also be modified to apply to jazz, popular music, or music of non-Western cultures. Let us take a look at some of the constraints on playing music in public.

The organization of society during a particular historical period will dictate in a rather unpredictable fashion how, where, and when music is made. The performance conditions for instrumental music have undergone significant changes throughout history (see Grout 1980; Seaton 1991, for overviews). The most relevant change has been the increasing independence or autonomy of instrumental music, which was previously subservient to singing. Secondly, musicians have come more and more to play notated music which is not necessarily their own, and in the process to rely less on their improvisational skills. In general, expert musicians have to accept the performance conditions they encounter as part of what they are expected to do (task demands). They adapt and strive to improve their performance within the limits imposed by these demands.

Today, the situations that stimulate public performances of the greatest technical sophistication and involve the highest personal motivation are probably international competitions for pianists and violinists. Winning a prestigious competition is necessary for a career as an international soloist (Sosniak 1985), so these competitions are probably the best available objective measure of outstanding music performance today. A comparison between performances by contemporary participants in international competitions and the performance conditions of past eras throws up several differences that are listed in Table 4.1. Later in the chapter, these aspects will be discussed in more detail.

The first three aspects listed in Table 4.1 concern elements of the performance task, namely what music is played, the amount of preparation prior to performance, and the musical instruments used. The first difference between contemporary and past performers concerns the selection of music. Modern performers select their music from a host of pieces that have been composed for their instrument. They will typically select pieces that have stood the test of time and are somewhat popular, but contain sufficient technical challenge to allow the performers to display their technical facility. As will be shown below, recent piano music tends to be more complex and technically challenging than music that was available to earlier pianists. This does not of course mean that the modern performer cannot also choose less complex music for aesthetic reasons. Before the middle of the nineteenth century, elite solo performers largely relied on their own compositions, whereas later soloists could choose their repertoire from a large existing body of music written by established composers.

Table 4.1   Common elements of public music performance and main characteristics of elite keyboard performers today versus centuries ago.

	Performers of past centuries	Modern performers
Music to be played	Mostly own compositions	Selected music by others
Preparation for a specific performance	Relatively short due to improvisation or sight-reading	Preparation extended for months and years to perfect rehearsed and memorized performance
Instruments	Original instruments	Extensively modified instruments to increase flexibility, control of tonal production, and range
Specialization	Many professional responsibilities (perform on several instruments, lead ensembles, compose, teach)	High degree of specialization as solo performers of a particular instrument
Training	Often informal with later start of instrumental training	Training designed by professional teacher with early ages for start of practice

The biographies of famous performers attest to the fact that today's elite musicians spend months and years preparing and perfecting their performance of a single programme before it is presented at a competition or concert. In contrast, the preparation for a public performance was generally shorter in earlier times. Contemporary records indicate that many pieces were more or less sight-read due to lack of rehearsal time (Carse 1940). Keyboard and other performers often relied on their improvisational skills when working from short-hand notation, most obviously in the seventeenth and eighteenth centuries when the system of thorough-bass (harmonies being indicated by figures) was commonplace (Bailey 1992).

Because sight-reading or *ad hoc* improvisations are carried out spontaneously or under severe time constraints, performers may not be able fully to take advantage of all their technical and artistic prowess. By allowing more time for preparing an improvisation or rehearsing and memorizing notated music, a performance of higher quality with fewer mistakes, faster speeds, and greater technical difficulty becomes possible. The notion that public music making can be improved through prior preparation is important, because the audience does not know how prepared a performance is. Another goal of preparation today is to reduce the variability of performances. Present day audiences expect musicians to entertain them with performances of reliable and reproducible quality, despite the immense technical complexity of many pieces of music. Of course, we do not know what expectations audiences had in former times. However, reports dating from earlier this century about famous musicians such as Anton Rubinstein, Alfred Cortot, and Fritz Kreisler, suggest that day-to-day variability in performance was more acceptable than it is now (Dubal 1990; Elder 1993).

Today's performers seek out the best musical instruments that they can afford. Although to an untrained eye some instruments, such as the violin, look very similar to instruments used centuries ago, they have actually changed considerably. Virtually all of the changes have involved increases in the instruments' capacity for changes in loudness (dynamics), and have tended to give the musician more flexibility and control when playing technically difficult passages. Over the last three centuries, the violin has been fitted with a chin and shoulder rest, a slightly longer neck, metal strings, and fine-tuners (Dilworth 1992). The extended possibilities of instruments, which will be documented later in this chapter for the piano, have led to more difficult playing techniques being possible, and also to longer periods of learning.

Concurrent with the changes in public music performance, there are at least two other significant differences between contemporary players and musicians of the past (see Table 4.1). During the last three centuries, the role of musicians has changed to allow them more time to develop their instrumental skills, at the expense of other music-related skills they used to possess. Virtually all of today's elite performers specialize on a single instrument and perform a small number of rehearsed music pieces (repertoire) for that instrument. In contrast, musicians in earlier historical periods usually played several different instruments, composed, led ensembles, and taught. Furthermore, today's élite performers start their music training at an early age, often between the ages of 4 and 5. Highly experienced teachers design training programmes to allow these students to make maximal progress from the start (Sosniak 1985; Ericsson *et al.* 1993). It might be tempting to think that musicians in other eras simply worked harder or had fewer distractions. However, the amount of concentrated practice that can be sustained over extended periods of time appears to be limited to four or five hours a day (Ericsson *et al.* 1993 for examples of different domains). Attempts to maintain practice beyond this optimal limit may lead to overuse injuries and burnout. Even so, by the age of 20 the better musicians of the present day have engaged in over 10 000 hours of deliberate practice. In contrast, many musicians of earlier times acquired their initial music skills as apprentices at considerably older ages. Antonio Salieri, Mozart's contemporary, started in his teens, while Bach's students in Leipzig gained access to instrumental music instruction only after age 12 (Wolff *et al.* 1983). Musicians in the seventeenth and eighteenth centuries were expected to become competent in a number of different musical activities, and explicit instruction and formal practice activities may have been scarce. In those cases where appropriate instructional materials were available, scholars have noted an associated surprisingly rapid increase in level of performance (e.g. Woodfield 1984, for the viol; Baldauf-Berdes 1993, for singing; and Blume 1955, vol. 4, p. 338, for recorder playing).

In sum, elite musicians of the present day are highly focused on public performance, and make every effort to exhibit their best abilities in front of the audience. Instrumentalists of previous eras did not concentrate with the same degree on performance, because it was only one aspect of their professional responsibilities.

The task of performing music in public

The music that audiences have wished to hear and the physical location of performances have varied throughout history in response to changing philosophical ideas and social conditions (see Hildebrand 1988; Loesser 1954/1990, for examples regarding piano music; Seaton 1991, for a general description). One of the foremost functions of music is the entertainment of an audience, and professional musicians have fulfilled this function differently in different times. In this section, we discuss the suitability of instruments for different performance conditions, the emerging importance of individual players or soloists, and the opportunities the audience has to evaluate the quality of the players.

How performance conditions favour different musical instruments

Public music performance requires external support and organization. In the Middle Ages and Renaissance, there were three major employers for musicians, namely the church, the courts, and the cities. From the eighteenth century onwards, an increasingly affluent middle class became the main supporter of music performance. Depending on the employer and the occasion, public music performances were given in small or medium-sized rooms, large or noisy halls, or even out of doors.

The indoor production of music in the Renaissance favoured soft sounds, particularly the voice accompanied by lutes, and ensembles of viols or recorders (Polk 1991). During this period, music was also performed on the harpsichord or lute in a virtuosic improvisatory fashion. Later, in the Baroque, the harpsichord, clavichord, and smaller string ensembles were used to entertain in quiet environments. The music of the *salons* of the nineteenth century included voice (accompanied for example by the piano), solo piano music, and smaller string ensembles.

More spacious environments such as large dining halls or outdoor settings require louder instruments and larger ensembles. In the Renaissance, these would have been consorts of shawms, trombones, and trumpets. The Baroque witnessed the birth of the opera, which has remained one of the major genres up to the present day. Partly because audiences were much more noisy than they are today, bigger locations required larger accompanying ensembles and more powerful singers to provide adequate volume. A similar trend was seen at courts throughout Europe during the Classical period, where instrumental ensembles grew in size and diversity. This trend culminated in the large concert halls of the nineteenth and early twentieth century which were designed to accommodate a romantic orchestra and large choir (Salmen 1988).

Philosophical and aesthetic changes have also influenced the preferred styles of music. In the Baroque period, music conveyed static emotional states (*Affekte*) using idiomatic ornamentations, figures, and phrases. Since the early Classical period, there has been an increase in the dramatic expressiveness of music that is paralleled by developments both in other arts and in philosophy. Improvements in instrument design have supported these trends. For example, the development of Christofori's piano allowed for variability in loudness in contrast with the harpsichord which did not, permitting increased expressivity (Komlos 1995). Thus, public music performance has changed as a function of preferred styles and playing conditions, and successful musicians have adapted to the demands of their times.

The role of the individual performer

The opportunity for individual instrumentalists to stand out as soloists has depended on the performance practices of the period. Initially, instrumental music primarily served as an accompaniment to singing. Later, instruments began to imitate the vocal lines, and performance practices allowed alternation between voice and instruments. Finally, a genuine instrumental music evolved that allowed players to come to the forefront and display their skills. Generally, the opportunities for virtuosic performance are reserved for outstanding musicians, and accompanying instruments are left with simpler parts. But the highest degree of exposure is gained when an individual plays an entire concert. In the eighteenth and nineteenth century, several artists took part in the same concert or recital, until Liszt started to play entire concerts by himself. Breaking with custom, he also included works by other composers rather than just playing his own works.

Soloists sometimes show off their skills, and on many occasions virtuosi have been accused of devaluing their performances for the purpose of self-enhancement (Baillot 1835/1991; Rowland-Jones 1992). While this may be permissible in secular settings, the situation is theoretically different for church music. Given the importance of the words in religious settings, church music can only be used to spotlight the individual musician to a limited extent. At various times, the church has tried to increase the participation of the congregation or increase the intelligibility of the words, both at the expense of musical artistry and virtuosity. Virtuosic church music does exist against all the odds, partly because some compositions were primarily written for state occasions rather than for everyday services, and partly because some church music is not set to words.

Our assumption that evaluation and competition influence the level of creative achievement in performance leads to testable predictions. For those instruments that are used for solo performance, compared with those that usually have accompanying functions, more opportunities for the evaluation of individual performances exist, and we would consequently expect more rapid increases in the level of playing skills.

The evaluation of musical performances and competition between musicians

Whenever employers or audiences are provided with choices among performing musicians, they will select the one who is viewed as better or has the better reputation. Therefore, in order to make a living, musicians have to compete with each other to attract audiences, fame, and patronage.

As a result, local musicians may not always be the first choice, and musicians from distant cultural centres may be favoured. The opportunities for such comparisons arrived when musicians began to travel with nobility, or when musicians migrated in search of work. Such was the case in the fifteenth century, when German musicians were sought after in Italy because of their superior skills (Polk 1994). Once they had taught their new skills to local musicians, their stranglehold on employment decreased and 'importation' of musicians was no longer the norm (Polk 1991). Outstanding musicians disseminated their creative achievements through travelling and teaching, and aspiring musicians including the young Mozart, travelled to places with advanced musical cultures such as Italy, so as to work with eminent musicians and learn new styles.

Musicians of different periods in history are known to have tried to outperform each other in veritable 'playoffs'. The evidence is anecdotal and therefore not always reliable, but its mere existence is certainly telling. Liszt and Thalberg met for a personal piano competition (Walker 1990), as did Mozart and Clementi (Komlos 1995), and Handel and Scarlatti (Blume 1956). Even today, jazz players continue to engage in friendly 'cutting contests' (Berliner 1994). Thus despite the fact that there are aspects of musical performance that are difficult to evaluate objectively, playing in public is partly an exhibition of skills in which musicians compete for their audiences and for the respect of their peers.

Over time, the expectations of audiences have increased and they have been able to make more informed comparisons between different performers. Widespread music training has allowed many concert-goers to attain a considerable level of skill themselves, especially on solo instruments such as the piano and the violin. Along with their appreciation for the highest levels of music performance, audiences have gained a greater ability to detect imperfections. With the emergence of the radio and recordings, many members of concert audiences will already have heard the music being performed. Listening to recordings by the world's foremost musicians on high-fidelity stereo systems creates high expectations for the concert soloist—a problem that earlier musicians encountered to a lesser degree.

In summary, over the last couple of centuries, conditions for the public performance of music have become more uniform. The music being played is mostly selected from a restricted repertoire of known pieces. Many members of modern-day concert audiences have received formal music training or have at least heard the same or similar music recorded by the world's best musicians. These developments have led to better opportunities for evaluating public performances, a rise in expectations and, we believe, higher levels of performance skill. In the next section we will examine in more detail the trade-offs and adaptations that musicians have made over time to accommodate these demands.

Improvements in musical performance through preparation and specialization

As in all other areas of human performance, longer preparation for a given concert or musical event will naturally lead to higher levels of performance accuracy and reproducibility. The audience typically has no way of knowing how much preparation was involved in a given performance. The following anecdote illustrates these central points (see Gerig 1974). In 1834, the pianist Kalkbrenner improvised a fifteen minute piece for the music theorist A. B. Marx, who was very impressed. The next day Marx received some newly published music from Paris. He was outraged when, among the new pieces, he found the very same piece Kalkbrenner had allegedly 'improvised' for him. In this section, we elaborate the importance of preparation by returning to two issues that were introduced earlier, namely improvisation and playing from notated music.

The simplest form of improvisation is to add embellishments to a melody, and experienced singers and instrumentalists can rely under these circumstances on their intuitions. However, real-time demands make it difficult to plan out larger structures and complex ornamentations due to cognitive factors such as limitations in working memory. Alternatively, the singer can draw on a well-rehearsed set of ornaments and use these patterns to create more complex and fluent embellishments. In the Middle Ages and Renaissance, manuals were written that taught musicians how to use standard ornaments for voice and instruments (Brown 1976). If a song was performed several times, the singer could work on the improvised ornamentation iteratively in a trial-and-error fashion, retaining pleasing parts and altering less suitable ones on each occasion. Likewise, the nineteenth-century virtuosi who performed variations on operatic tunes had the opportunity to play them repeatedly, thereby refining their performance through practice. This process, which can be called 'precomposition' (Berliner 1994) is akin to that of a university teacher who refines a specific lecture over time, and as a creative process is consistent with 'variation-selection' models of creativity (Simonton 1997).

An advantage of a patterned or 'precomposed' improvisation is that it increases the chances of a high quality performance, and safeguards the musician from interfering factors such as noise, health problems, or lack of motivation. The fact that extensive preparation results in a performance in which loudness and timing become stable and reproducible was originally demonstrated by Seashore (1967/1938), and has since been replicated in a number of laboratory studies (Gabrielsson in press; Kopiez 1996). Another more or less intentional by-product of extended preparation of a given piece of music is performance from memory. This is commonplace today but was rare before the nineteenth century, when it initially stunned audiences.

At first, playing from memory was looked upon with similar wonder to that which had been elicited by the exhibition of enormous technical prowess, and it is practised for its drawing powers to this day, as exemplified in the public performance, from memory, of the complete works of Beethoven, Bach, Chopin and other masters . . . From the adoption of memory-playing as a presumptive of public concerts, resulted its introduction as a requirement for nearly every music student. (Wier 1940, p. 301)

Since the end of the eighteenth century, the music of past and contemporary composers has been increasingly disseminated, and performers have come to play notated music

that is not their own. Walker (1990) reports anecdotal evidence that piano solo performers in the eighteenth and early nineteenth century performed in public with little
or no preparation, and some examples from Mozart's life are described by Andrew Steptoe in Chapter 7. Sight-reading was also common for orchestral music. Beethoven's
orchestral works, which were extremely difficult for the time, were premiered after only
a few rehearsals by orchestras that included amateurs (Cook 1993; McVeigh 1993). In
1816, the composer Anton Reicha advised others to write orchestral parts that could be
sight-read (Brown 1993). Virtuosi guarded their music against plagiarism by handing
out the orchestral parts only for a few rehearsals prior to the concert, thus forcing members of orchestras to sight-read the music. The exceptional occasions that involved
highly rehearsed performances were sufficiently rare to be specially noted by contemporaries (see Carse 1948, for the orchestra of the Paris conservatory in the 1830s, and
Baldauf-Berdes 1993, for the orchestra of the Venetian orphanages under Vivaldi).

Reading of unfamiliar music at first sight is only possible at skill levels below a musician's technical best, because much music involves intricate fingerings in complex passages and the need to anticipate future sections, and these have to be worked out in
advance. Even experienced musicians may not interpret the emotional atmosphere of
a piece of music correctly without studying it carefully. In past centuries, hand-written
or poorly engraved manuscripts further hindered the actual reading process (Komlos
1995). Studies have shown that when pianists are given repeated trials to perform an
unfamiliar piece of music, they tend to optimize their fingerings (Lehmann and Ericsson 1995). For similar reasons, playing fast may only be possible when sight-reading
simple material, while the mastery of highly complex music at rapid speeds requires
extended preparation. In the course of the nineteenth century there was a move to
rehearsed performance of published works. This change was brought about partly
because composers insisted that their works be played as written, but one can specu-
late that it was also because of the pressures of competition and the expectations of
audiences.

Although sight-reading and improvisation can be learned and improved with training
and experience, there are limits to how complex, fast, and reliable an unrehearsed performance can be. This is not to say that sight-reading or improvisation skills are not
beneficial, but longer preparation will ultimately yield a performance of higher quality.
In the next section we extend the preparation argument to show that not only does the
performance of individual pieces improve, but that extending and intensifying the
acquisition of musical skills will lead to higher levels of mastery in general.

The historical trend toward increased specialization of musicians

Musicians in the Western European tradition have always undergone a rigorous training,
although training conditions have varied across historical eras. In general, training is
limited by the starting age for a particular period, and by the age at which the individual enters the profession. Higher levels of performance in several domains have
been related to larger amounts of lifetime practice (Ericsson *et al.* 1993; Sloboda *et al.*

1996, for music; Starkes *et al.* 1996, for wrestling; Charness *et al.* 1996, for chess). When future performers devote all their training exclusively to those aspects of the task that are most desired, they should attain a higher final level of skill, often at the expense of other skills. Thus if musicians wish to become solo performers, a specialized training will lead to higher levels of skill than will a more general educational program. Using keyboard players as an example, we will illustrate this process of professional specialization, which can incidentally also be observed for other domains of expertise such as science and sport (Ericsson 1996).

Beginning in the Middle Ages and continuing during the Baroque period, most musicians were relatively diversified. J. S. Bach, for example, was a composer, performer, music director, improviser, music teacher, and Latin teacher. Mozart's multiple roles are also well known (see Chapter 7). As a rule, instrumentalists of the past were able to perform on more than one instrument in public, and keyboard players customarily played all possible instruments including the organ, harpsichord, and clavichord (Woodfill 1953; Bowers 1992). Initially, music for keyboards was interchangeable, but during the seventeenth century composers started taking advantage of the specific characteristics of each individual instrument (Komlos 1995). During the Classical period, musicians such as the pianist Muzio Clementi started to specialize in public performances on a single instrument.

As musicians specialized on one instrument, their careers also became more focused. Prior to the nineteenth century, most performers were still composing to some degree, or at least arranging and modifying existing compositions. By the beginning of the twentieth century, most had completely specialized in the performance of the standard repertoire. Others such as Carl Czerny, specialized exclusively in teaching. Teachers like Theodor Leschetizky, Josef Hofmann, and Artur Schnabel trained their students to play unique and creative interpretations note-perfect from memory. Unfortunately, sight-reading in public declined, and opportunities for playing less rehearsed music are now restricted to pianists who specialize in accompanying (coaching, chamber music, ballet). Some performers of our century even specialize in one particular era or a limited number of composers, or become known for their interpretation of individual works (Glenn Gould for Bach's *Goldberg Variations*, or Vladimir Horowitz for Rachmaninoff's Third Piano Concerto). Similar trends toward specialization can be observed for performers of orchestral instruments such as the flute and violin (Bowers 1992; McVeigh 1993).

Changes in performance expertise

When music educators assign music to their students, they are faced with the problem of assessing the difficulty of particular pieces. The music chosen needs to be appropriately challenging without exceeding the student's current abilities. To assist teachers in their decision, there exist educational plans which are designed by experienced educators (e.g. the Piano Syllabus of the Toronto Conservatory 1986; the 'P-F' system devised by Pierce and Fuszek 1987; and the Associated Board and Guildhall School of Music Examinations in the UK). In these plans, individual techniques and pieces are listed in terms of their grades of difficulty.

Grades in educational plans are usually organized such that the average student can master about one grade per year of instruction. Depending on the intended starting age and duration of instruction, the different educational plans contain between 10 and 15 grades. The criteria applied by music experts for grading music are not explicitly stated, and are most likely based on their experience as performers and teachers. Technical problems such as speed seem to be important criteria. For example, the demands on playing speed for scales increase from less than 150 notes per minute at level 1 to over 500 notes per minute at level 12 (Piano Syllabus 1986). Interpretational complexity may also play a role, but there is less indication as to how this type of complexity is assessed. In a recent diary study with an advanced pianist who was preparing for a public performance, we found that complexity ratings for a given set of pieces correlated 0.71 ($p < 0.05$) with the accumulated practice time for these same pieces (Lehmann and Ericsson 1996).

There is also some consensus about the level of difficulty of pieces in the repertoire. We found, for example, that intercorrelations between gradings of the same pieces in the Piano Syllabus and Pierce and Fuszek were high ($r = .84, p < 0.001$, Lehmann and Ericsson 1996). Thus, modern experts' perceptions of the difficulty of a piece, as indexed by the number of years of training that educational plans recommend prior to attempting it, appear to be valid measures of complexity.

If it is difficult to compare performances in the present day, one can imagine that comparing past performances is even harder. By choosing our modern perception of performance complexity as the standard for cross-historical comparisons, we will not capture additional technical difficulties that stemmed from performance practices in the past. However, we can analyse the difficulty that pieces from different times would pose for today's performers, and determine when in history the more difficult techniques (by today's standards) were invented and introduced.

The increase in the skill requirements of piano music over time

Our first analysis focused on the piano sonata. Baillot (1835/1991) describes the sonata as 'a sort of concerto stripped of its accompaniment, [which] gives [the performer] the occasion to let his power shine and to develop a part of his resources'. Collections of such sonatas—well known to most amateur piano players—by Clementi, Haydn, Mozart, Beethoven, and Schubert, span roughly one hundred years starting from 1750. The correlation between complexity ratings, given in Pierce and Fuszek (1987), and compositional dates is significant ($r = 0.68, p < 0.001$), indicating that piano sonatas became more technically difficult over this time period. Confirmation for our statistical results comes from the comments of the composers themselves. For example, Joseph Haydn realized that his piano sonatas were becoming increasingly difficult as he grew older (Rosenblum 1988). Interestingly, analysing only Haydn's sonatas also reveals a significant correlation between difficulty and year of composition ($r = 0.58$, $p < 0.01$) which is shown in Fig. 4.1. Another such analysis could be made for the piano étude, a somewhat later genre that performers have used to display their skills. For example, Liszt rewrote his études several times, usually with an increase in technical difficulty (Ganz 1960). Of course, not all earlier pieces are less complex than later ones. A great number of Baroque keyboard pieces were originally composed for the harpsichord but are played on the piano today, thus adding a layer of complexity in allowing changes in dynamic. Our results allow us to infer that the pianistic skills necessary to perform sonatas and other pieces must also have increased.

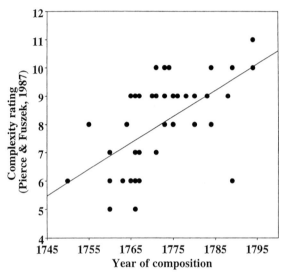

Fig. 4.1 Increase of technical complexity in the piano sonatas by Joseph Haydn.

Based on the abovementioned educational plans, it is also possible to infer the difficulty of particular playing techniques by the grade level at which they are introduced. For a number of these techniques there is an approximate historical date at which they were invented and appeared in compositions (see Fig. 4.2). Some techniques are of course linked to the development of the instrument, while others emerged after the instrument had reached its modern form. Not surprisingly, dynamic change, which was impossible on the harpsichord, is taught to piano students from the very beginning of instruction. The increased complexity of the left hand of Mozart's works compared to those of Haydn (Wier 1940) requires at least level 5. Czerny's studies for the left hand and a whole range of specialized left hand repertoire were written throughout the Romantic period and into the twentieth century. The standard fingering for double octave scales, codified by Johann Cramer, appears at level 7. Scales in double thirds and sixths, which appear at level 12 or higher, became necessary for the works of the nineteenth century virtuosi. The use of the damper pedal in a modern way was introduced by John Field around 1800, and complex pedalling is necessary to perform the music of our century. Unfortunately, Pierce and Fuszek (1987) do not give a level at which the use of the pedal is introduced in the learning sequence.

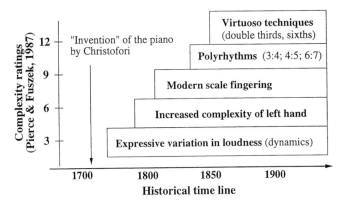

Fig. 4.2 Introduction of new pianistic techniques since the early development of the piano.

Finally, an important technical device is the polyrhythm, which consists of a simultaneous bimanual performance of complex rhythmic patterns with proportions such as 2:3 or 3:4 (starting at level 6 with simple 2:3 cross-rhythms). The mathematically precise execution of triplets is a prerequisite for creating polyrhythms. It only became necessary in the last quarter of the eighteenth century, and was considered difficult at that time (Türk 1789/1982). The frequency of simple polyrhythms increased in later compositions, and more complex polyrhythms exist in works by Frédéric Chopin and in teaching materials such as Johannes Brahms' études.

In summary, the playing techniques that require more training for modern music students were introduced later in history. This finding is one of the strongest pieces of evidence for our claim that the technical mastery of musicians has increased over time. The next section explores some of the reasons for this increase in complexity.

Development of musical instruments and associated skills

Increases in skill occur when individual élite performers go beyond the existing, and invent new techniques that make the most efficient use of instrumental capabilities. These capabilities will continue to change as long as instrument makers are innovative in response to design problems. The success of makers in turn depends on their ability to produce superior musical instruments, and to win the endorsement of their instruments by famous performers. Admittedly, changes in instrument design involve trade-offs, as certain sound effects, nuances, and playing techniques are replaced by new ones (Baines 1992).

The emergence of the piano was partly a result of efforts to produce a keyboard instrument that allowed changes in volume, by combining the clavichord's ability to produce dynamic shadings with the harpsichord's sonic power. Instrument makers strove to produce increasingly louder instruments with full-sounding high (treble) and low (bass) ranges by adding more strings per note and increasing the strings' diameter (Marcuse 1964). The structural properties of the piano body were also modified to withstand heavier stringing, and larger hammers were built.

It seems clear that the first pianos, especially the English ones, gained their dynamic range at the expense of speed. They could not be played as rapidly as harpsichords, whereas the earlier Viennese pianos still preserved some of the harpsichord's facility (Komlos 1995). Clementi, a performer-composer who was also a piano builder, improved the hammer action to allow for faster repetition of notes, and Sébastien Erard perfected this mechanism with the development of the so-called double-escapement mechanism in 1821 (Parrish 1953; Sadie 1980, vol. 14, p. 702). While the initial slower action clearly represented a decrease in task demands—as slow movements are easier to control than fast ones—today's pianists can achieve the same fast tempi on modern concert grands that can be played on the softer earlier Viennese pianos (Rosenblum 1988).

The extension of range (number of notes) of the piano can be viewed as the continuation of a process that began in the Middle Ages. The modern piano has a range of almost eight octaves. In the eighteenth century alone, the tonal range of the piano grew from four to six octaves. A similar extension is documented for other instruments such as the recorder (Ganassi 1535/1956) and violin (Blume 1966, vol 13, p. 1722). Initially, the sounds produced at the extremes of the range were not very pleasing musically, forcing composers of the eighteenth century such as Lodovico Giustini to write for a more restricted range than the instrument nominally had to offer (Sheveloff 1987). However, instrument makers soon remedied this problem. The expansion of the tonal range in compositions can be observed through the lives of composers such as Domenico Scarlatti, Haydn, and Beethoven. In a number of instances, performer-composers collaborated with instrument makers on extending the range of their instruments. For example, both Jan Dussek and Beethoven requested larger tonal ranges from their instrument makers (Komlos 1995; Rosenblum 1988). Successful mastery of the new range required the playing of larger horizontal leaps, and the dexterity to cover a broad span with scales and patterns (arpeggios), despite sometimes awkward hand positions or even hand crossings.

Innovations in playing techniques at the highest levels of performance

During many periods of musical history, virtuoso players have made creative contributions by incorporating their personal playing experience and styles into their written compositions. Mozart was known for his agile left hand, and is said to have increased the complexity of the left hand in his compositions. Chopin's style took into account ergonomic factors related to the location of the black and white keys, and his music is consequently full of 'black keys' or accidentals (Letnanova 1991). One specific technique, sometimes referred to as 'third hand' impression, was developed by the pianist

Sigismund Thalberg in the 1830s (Hitchcock 1971; Walker 1990). It involves distrib-uting the melody notes between the hands in the middle of the keyboard (see Fig. 4.3), while the accompaniment is played in scales and patterns to the left and right of the melody. This technique not only requires a large span, it also destroys the classical map-ping of hands onto the keyboard, with the right hand playing the melody while the left provides the accompaniment. Maintaining a dynamic difference between the melody (louder) and the accompaniment (softer) on one keyboard, often within one hand, imposes heavy skill requirements on the performer.

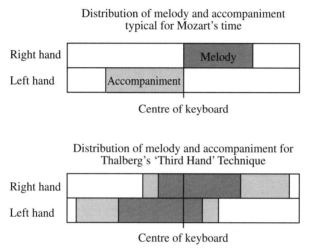

Fig. 4.3 Mapping of hands and dynamics to the keyboard layout for Mozart's time (top) and for Thalberg's 'third hand' technique (bottom).

Note. Horizontal range of the keyboard is shown schematically in top view. Centre of keyboard suggests 'Middle C'.

The interaction between performers and composers is also a source of new playing techniques. Composers from the Middle Ages to the twentieth century have incorpor-ated the most advanced contemporary skills into their works, and have consulted with expert performers to identify the full range of possibilities of particular instruments. The following examples derive from several centuries; Giovanni Gabrieli incorporated into his music ornaments published by his virtuoso cornettists Girolamo Dalla Casa and Giovanni Bassano in the late sixteenth century (unpublished master's thesis, Pringle 1996); Vivaldi is known to have tailored his compositions to the particular strengths of his soloists in eighteenth century Venice (Baldauf-Berdes 1993); Bach con-sulted with some of the finest flute players of his time (Powell and Lasocki, 1995); Mozart worked with the oboe virtuosi Ramm and the clarinetist Anton Stadler (Haynes 1992); Beethoven consulted the double bass virtuoso Dragonetti (Blume 1954, vol. 3, p. 739), and from the piano virtuoso Steibelt he probably borrowed the special pianis-tic effect of rapid alteration between two notes (Stillings 1972). Compositions that introduced these techniques presented ordinary musicians of the time with difficulties during rehearsal and performance. But today, these parts are standard fare for instrumentalists.

There are numerous anecdotes about works that were regarded as unplayable at the time of their composition. Virtuoso performers impressed their audiences by playing exactly those works, as when Liszt played Beethoven's *Hammerklavier* sonata. Anecdotes about 'impossible' pieces exist for virtually all instruments, as an informal survey we conducted among the performing faculty at Florida State University's School of Music confirmed. Some composers of the late nineteenth and early twentieth century wrote without considering the performer's limitations, relying on a perfectly trained and willing professional to overcome any problems that might arise. Loesch (1992) gives telling examples of this in relation to the cello.

Other innovative playing techniques were based on methods that had been previously developed for a different instrument or the voice. For example, seventeenth century texts suggest that expert singers and instrumentalists imitated each others' techniques and ornamentation (Brown 1976). In the fifteenth century, the organist Conrad Paumann transferred the playing of several simultaneous voices (polyphonic playing) from the keyboard to the lute (Polk 1994). Thalberg's 'third hand' technique was inspired by the English harpist Parish-Alvars (Walker 1990), while Niccolò Paganini is known to have transferred his extensive knowledge of the guitar to the violin. Liszt in turn attempted to transfer Paganini's virtuosic violin technique to the piano. In all cases, the creative contribution of the expert performer has consisted in recognizing the potential for transfer and then developing a corresponding technique. A more recent example is of some modern wind instrumentalists, who perform the technique of 'circular breathing' which allows for concurrent continuous tone production while breathing. This technique has long been used with certain non-Western instruments such as the Australian didgeridoo (Schellberg 1993). Transferred techniques are likely to disregard some of the standard constraints of the instrument, thus adding to the level of difficulty. New techniques are usually added to the pool of existing techniques rather than replacing the old (Read 1993; Mather 1980).

Optimizing training and practice for instrumental performance

Regardless of when they were developed, new and improved techniques have often extended the range of music that could be composed and performed on an instrument. By their appearance in compositions, innovations are assimilated into the standard set of skills for anyone who wants to succeed as a professional musician. This section will show that the increased complexity of music performance at the highest levels has implications for training, because it forces music teachers to find ways to facilitate the acquisition of new techniques. We will also show that the acquisition of instrumental skills among children has accelerated over the last 250 years.

Evidence for the accelerated acquisition of performance skills

Detailed historical records of the relationship between instruction or practice and levels of performance are virtually non-existent. However, in the case of child prodigies, we believe one can make the assumption that they have at all historical times been maximally immersed in learning and performing music. We can therefore compare the change in rate at which piano playing prodigies have attained certain levels of music performance skill, and test our hypothesis that the acquisition of skills has accelerated over time. For this analysis, we have identified solo pieces played by child prodigies, and the ages at which they performed these pieces in public. The musician had to be under 13 years of age at the time of performance to qualify as a child prodigy. Our sample is not random, but consists of some of the best known keyboard prodigies from Johann Sebastian Bach (born 1671) onwards. Their names are listed in the legend to Fig. 4.4. After finding the earliest public performance known for each individual, we assessed the difficulty level of the piece that was performed, by looking it or a comparable piece up in the standard lists of graded repertoire. We then computed an index by dividing the number of years of study that would on average be required for the piece (extracted from modern curricula) by the actual number of years of study the prodigy had undertaken prior to playing the piece in public. This fraction was then multiplied by 100. For example, if a modern-day student played Schubert's *Moments musicaux* (rated level 7 by Pierce and Fuszek 1987), after seven years of instruction, this student would receive a score of 100 ($[7/7] \times 100$). If another student performed the same pieces after only 3.5 years of instruction, a score of 200 would be assigned ($[7/3.5] \times 100$). Thus, the precocity of performers of the past relative to today's standards would be indicated by numbers higher than 100.

As can be seen in Fig. 4.4 (filled squares), there is a significant tendency for prodigies of later generations to play more difficult pieces after shorter periods of training than did earlier prodigies ($r = 0.67$, $p < 0.05$). This index reflects an acceleration of skill acquisition once training is initiated. A second index was then computed to look at the age when certain pieces were performed. This was done by dividing the projected age of performance from modern curricula by the age at which a given prodigy actually performed the piece. Figure 4.4 (open circles) shows another significant correlation ($r = 0.85$, $p < 0.01$). This indicates that by today's standards, more recent prodigies have been more advanced in their performance skills than prodigies from earlier times. But given that the difficulty of music in the repertoire has also increased over time, it is possible that the relationship we observed is merely due to more recent prodigies playing music that was unavailable to earlier generations. However, even after statistically controlling for the difficulty level of the performed piece, we found that precociousness has increased reliably over time.

The empirical evidence presented here is endorsed by a host of anecdotes that point to an increase in performance skills over time (among others, see Bischoff 1876, p. vii, p. 147; Auer 1921/1980, p. 72; Wier 1940, p. 266; Carse 1940, p. 162; Ganz 1960, p. 134; Young 1967, p. 147; Phillips 1978, p. 195; Mather 1980, p. 1; Matuschka 1987;

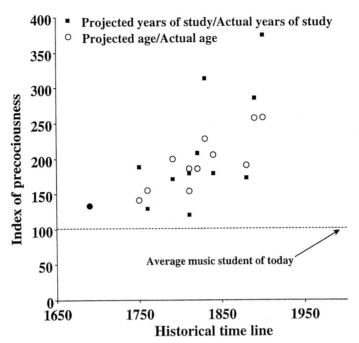

Fig. 4.4 Evidence for accelerated skill acquisition of 12 piano prodigies (J. S. Bach, W. A. Mozart, M. A. Mozart (Nannerl), C. Czerny, Fe. Mendelssohn, F. Liszt, C. Schumann, Ar. Rubinstein, An. Rubinstein, C. Saint-Saëns, E. Nyiregyhazi, J. Hofmann).

Zaslaw 1989, p. 9; McVeigh 1993, p. 221). A problem with anecdotes is of course that they cannot be sampled systematically, so contradictory sources may be overlooked. We have searched carefully, and have been able to locate anecdotal evidence of a decline in florid singing skills (Henderson 1921) and in improvisation skills (Donington 1963). But we have not found any examples contradicting the increase in technical proficiency of the performance of rehearsed music.

Factors that contribute to successful instruction and practice

Systematic formal training becomes necessary when the demands of music making go beyond the skills that can be acquired through mere participation. The intensity and structure of specialized training will also reflect the level of skill demanded of successful performers. For example, the evolution of more sophisticated church music from the seventh century onwards made the *Schola Cantorum* and other ensembles necessary (Mahling 1972). The systematic training of singers has a long tradition compared to that of instrumentalists, and method books survive from many periods (see Harris 1989; Crutchfield 1989a, b; Butt 1994). This may in part account for the fact that in the era under investigation here (the eighteenth to twentieth centuries), we do not see the same dramatic increase in singing skills as in instrumental skills. The success of systematic instruction depends partly on the availability of suitable instructional material. Important examples are Johann Quantz's flute method from 1752, Leopold Mozart's violin primer published in 1756, C. P. E. Bach's piano methods from 1753 and 1762, and Baillot's violin method of 1835. These manuals were written by the foremost music educators of their time, but once they had been published, they could be used even by mediocre teachers to train large numbers of music students.

Several investigators have looked at the number and quality of the teachers of expert musicians (Howe and Sloboda 1991; Manturzewska 1990; Sosniak 1985). It is clear that better performers received lessons with fewer and more qualified teachers than did less good performers. As a matter of fact, master teachers of earlier centuries also advised beginners to seek instruction with the best available mentors (e.g. Türk 1789/1982). Studies of the orphanages in Venice, which became famous in the eighteenth century for their musical achievements, support the role of highly qualified teachers. Baldauf-Berdes (1993) describes how instruction for new members of the choirs and orchestras progressed gradually from simple peer tutoring in the sixteenth and seventeenth century, to instruction by local outside teachers, culminating with instruction by internationally renowned musicians such as Nicola Porpora and Antonio Vivaldi in the eighteenth century.

Practice is known to be the most important factor for increasing skills, but there are certain conditions that need to be met in order for practice to be effective (Ericsson *et al.* 1993; also Ericsson and Charness 1994). Deliberate practice is effortful, and it involves the setting of specific goals and the monitoring of results. We can see from contemporary reports how famous musicians used specific practice to build their exceptional techniques (Gerig 1974). For example, the violinist Paganini developed a technique of playing on one string by practising pieces in different positions and on selected strings, while Liszt and Thalberg perfected their novel techniques through specific exercises of scales and leaps. It appears that for young performers, external monitoring in the form of supervised practice is necessary (see Lehmann 1997, for historical prodigies; Frederickson 1995, for a contemporary example).

A limiting factor on daily practice is the amount of time that it can be sustained with optimal intensity. This is about four to five hours for adults. Various master teachers have suggested a similar length for practice; three hours according to Chopin and Hummel, four hours according to some others. The amount of practice that young beginners can manage increases over time (Sloboda *et al.* 1996). Similar increases of deliberate practice times have been documented in domains where individuals start training at older ages (see Starkes *et al.* 1996, for wrestling). Interestingly, scientific and anecdotal evidence from different domains indicates that experts prefer to do their most mentally demanding activities in the morning hours (Ericsson *et al.* 1993; Lehmann and Ericsson 1996; Hofmann 1920/1976). Finally, because it takes roughly a decade to acquire the levels of skill required for competing internationally (Simon and Chase 1973; Ericsson *et al.* 1993), performers need to balance the amount of daily practice they do with recuperative rest so as to avoid burnout and physiological fatigue.

Ericsson *et al.* (1993) have suggested that an earlier start in training leads to higher performance at younger ages. Winning a competition at a young age is likely to result in extra resources and access to the foremost teachers. The skills that are encouraged have varied through history. Stevens (1982) found a predominance of child vocal prodigies in the Renaissance period, organ prodigies in the Baroque period, piano prodigies in the nineteenth century, and violin prodigies in the twentieth century. We have also found that expert pianists had started earlier than amateur pianists and that world-class pianists had started earlier than less accomplished professional pianists of the same age cohort (Ericsson *et al.* 1993). The average starting age for the best pianists in our sample was 5.8 years of age. Some older books on piano teaching advocate later ages for the average student (Hofmann 1920/1976: 6–7 years of age; Türk 1789/1982: 7–8 years of age). Some modern-day teachers encourage earlier starting ages, but these may be partly limited by the instruments themselves. Edler-Busch (1993) suggests that improvements in flute construction in the nineteenth century allowed for a younger starting age than was previously customary, while Rainey (1985) claims that adding a curved headjoint may reduce it even further by overcoming the lack of muscle strength in children. These ergonomic adaptations also enable longer practice and playing times. For the violin and other stringed instruments, specially designed smaller versions of the original instruments have existed for a long time. W. A. Mozart is known to have used a small instrument as a child. In summary, the early start of training and continued deliberate practice allow children an earlier mastery of performance skills than their peers. This performance advantage will benefit the prodigious child by increasing access to master teachers and societal resources.

Summary and discussion

Many aspects of playing music in public have changed dramatically over the past several centuries. The repertoire has increased substantially through the steady accumulation of compositions, and—at least for the piano—more recent compositions tend to be more complex and technically challenging than older ones. We have attributed the increases in complexity to improvements in instrumental design and to innovations and advances in performance technique. Concurrently, the increased time spent preparing for performances, coupled with growing professional specialization, have given the performer the opportunity to master more complex pieces of music. Finally, the optimization of training has allowed young pianists to attain the high level of skills necessary for modern virtuosi.

We have developed a model that describes how the level of performance within a well-defined domain increases, without having to assume exceptional innate capacities. When individuals gain recognition in a field by surpassing existing performance standards, these achievements set new standards of excellence. These standards go on to determine the limits of adult performance, until they too are surpassed. New standards and achievements are assimilated into education and training, allowing future musicians to match and to surpass the previous level of final, high quality performance.

At any given time in history, a certain number of performers achieve the highest levels of adult skills for that era. These individuals receive rewards and recognition, and may gain employment at a court or church, fill concert halls, or make commercial recordings. Although it is always the contemporary audience that judges the quality of a performance, their criteria may vary with the performance practices of the time. Improvisation, for example, may be judged on the basis of its expressiveness, novelty, and complexity, while performance of known (notated) music will be based on accuracy, authenticity, or reproducibility. The eminent performers of their time will distinguish themselves by fully exploring the instrument's capacities, or by surpassing existing skills in creative ways. Eventually, these creative achievements are taught to others by the performers themselves, or by specialized pedagogues. Teachers are eager to transmit new techniques, because their reputations rest on the students who reach the highest levels of performance. Similarly, students will strive to display the greatest possible skills compared with their peers, so as to gain access to the best available teachers and resources. Ultimately, the implementation of new techniques through instruction leads the entire community of élite music performers to a higher level of music performance skill.

Supporting evidence for our claims was based primarily on data regarding solo piano performance. However, similar evidence could be assembled for a number of other instruments such as violin, some wind instruments, percussion, and in particular the harpsichord. As was pointed out earlier, instruments without strong solo functions are unlikely to show the same degree and rate of increase in skill. Of course, for different instruments the development may fall in different periods of Western music history. A slightly different pattern exists for the solo voice. Because of the high levels of performance and refined teaching systems attained already even before the Middle Ages, it appears that solistic singing may not have seen the same dramatic increase in performance skills over the last 300 years as has the piano. In general, the different rates of progress in technical skill of instrumentalists and singers underline the importance that changes in the instrument design have on the development of playing skills. Naturally, our analysis is also limited to those periods of Western music for which written sources exist, and when music was approximately performed as written.

Our analysis is not meant to make any evaluative statements about the aesthetic achievements and importance of specific musical compositions. Regarding the expressive aspects of music performance, we follow Gerig (1974) and Ferrucio Busoni (1968) who have argued that complete mastery of technical problems is a prerequisite for the production of expressive interpretations. A number of expressive aspects of performance, such as tempo changes and beat length, are mostly transmitted orally and are therefore subject to the tastes of the time. This process has resulted in many equally valid alternative interpretations of the same piece of music. In fact, when one looks at the different performance speeds on commercial recordings (e.g. Palmer 1968, for J. S. Bach's *Inventions*; Repp 1992, for Schumann's *Traumerei*), it is clear that those expressive aspects are played in an extremely variable fashion. However, compositions in the twentieth century often prescribe musical expression quite explicitly, and it is reasonable to assume that performers will try to follow these instructions. Given the availability of recordings, it is now possible to assess whether performers have become more skilled at adhering to complex expressive markings. One could also use recordings to trace skill developments for primarily orally transmitted performance practices in jazz, non-Western music, or popular music, thereby broadening the scope of our claims regarding increases in expert performance.

For many performance traditions, instruments, and repertoires of written music, historical developments have for now come to a halt. However, the accumulation of music and the knowledge of how to play it enables modern-day performers to play works that in former times were considered the peak of artistic achievement, or almost unplayable. Sometimes, as in the case of Renaissance music, we may not know at first how to perform the music. But as scholarly materials become available, musicians and singers learn how to recreate historically informed performances (e.g. Kite-Powell 1994).

We would like to return to our opening question about the need to attribute special innate capacities to innovators and exceptional music performers. Based on an earlier review of expert performance in many different domains (Ericsson and Lehmann 1996), we find that experts adapt maximally to the typical demands of their domain through training and practice. Following the historical approach to expert performance taken in this chapter, we extend this claim to the *community* of instrumental performers. The community of performers adapts to changes in demands by designing better training methods, and by allocating more time for skill acquisition through specialization. The creative contributions of eminent experts change the nature of the task itself, sometimes by simply altering existing skills, at other times by creating unusual and hitherto unknown methods. The fact that the outstanding performance skills of one generation are later matched and surpassed by large numbers of later musicians clearly suggests that performers are not endowed with any inexplicable capacities or extraordinary innate talents. Rather, they seem to have acquired their exceptional skills in much the same way that later and modern-day performers have acquired theirs.

Given the sophisticated instruments of today, established training methods, early starting ages for practice, and high levels of daily deliberate practice among young musicians, it is tempting to believe that the present generation of élite solo performers may already have reached the ultimate level of mastery of their instruments—a level that cannot be surpassed but only matched by future generations. However, such claims have been made before in the history of music, including for example Beethoven's claims about his *Hammerklavier* sonata, and Schönberg's assertions about his violin concerto. As we now know, these claims were premature. Considering the unpredictable and creative nature of past achievements in music performance, it is reasonable to assume that as long as society offers appropriate incentives and élite performers keep striving to surpass the achievements of current and past masters, creative innovations will never cease to be made.

Acknowledgments

This paper would have not been possible without Jeffery Kite-Powell, director of the Early Music program at FSU, who has been a constant source of support and advice since we started exploring expert performance from a historical perspective three years ago. We would also like to thank Neil Charness, Peter Delaney, Reinhard Kopiez, Benjamin Pringle, and John Sloboda for comments on earlier versions of this paper, and Andrew Steptoe for his help in finalizing the chapter.

References

Auer, L. (1980). *Violin playing as I teach it* (original published in 1921). Dover, New York.

Bailey, D. (1992). *Improvisation: its nature and practice in music.* Dacapo, New York.

Baillot, P. (1991). *The art of the violin* (ed. and trans. L. Goldberg; original published in 1835). Northwestern Illinois Press, Evanston, IL.

Baines, F. (1992). Musical instruments and performers of the past. In *Companion to contemporary musical thought*, Vol. 2 (ed. J. Paynter, T. Howell, R. Orton, and P. Seymour), pp. 961–76. Routledge, London.

Baldauf-Berdes, J. L. (1993). *Women musicians of Venice: musical foundations 1525–1855.* Clarendon, Oxford, UK.

Berliner, P. F. (1994). *Thinking in jazz: the infinite art of improvisation.* University of Chicago Press, Chicago.

Bischoff, H. (ed.) (1876). *Die Aesthetik des Klavierspiels von Adolph Kullak* (2nd revised edn) Guttentag, Berlin.

Blume, F. (ed.) (1949–1986). *Musik in Geschichte und Gegenwart*, Vols 1–17. Bärenreiter, Kassel, Germany.

Boden, M. A. (1994). What is creativity? In *Dimensions of creativity* (ed. M. A. Boden), pp. 75–118. Bradford, Cambridge, MA.

Bowers, J. (1992). Mozart and the flute. *Early Music*, **20**, 31–8.

Brown, C. (1993). String playing practices in the classical orchestra. *Basler Jahrbuch für historische Musikpraxis*, **17**, 41–64.

Brown, H. M. (1976). *Embellishing 16th-century music.* Oxford University Press, Oxford.

Busoni, F. (1968). *Exercises and studies for the piano: Part I* (ed. F. Goebels). Breitkopf and Härtel, Wiesbaden, Germany.

Butt, J. (1994). *Music education and the art of performance in the german baroque.* Cambridge University Press, Cambridge.

Carse, A. (1940). *The orchestra in the 18th century.* Heffer, Cambridge, UK.

——(1948). *The orchestra from Beethoven to Berlioz.* Heffer, Cambridge, UK.

Charness, N., Krampe, R., and Mayr, U. (1996). The role of practice and coaching in entrepreneurial skill domain: an international comparison of life-span chess skill acquisition. In *The road to excellence: the acquisition of expert performance in the arts, sciences, sports, and games* (ed. K. A. Ericsson), pp. 51–80. Erlbaum, Mahwah, NJ.

Cook, N. (1993). *Beethoven symphony no. 9.* Cambridge University Press, Cambridge.

Crutchfield, W. (1989a). The classical era: voices. In *Performance practice: music after 1600* (ed. H. M. Brown and S. Sadie), pp. 292–322. Norton, New York.

Crutchfield, W. (1989*b*). The 19th century: voices. In *Performance practice: music after 1600* (ed. H. M. Brown and S. Sadie), pp. 424–60. Norton, New York.

Csikszentimihalyi, M. (1996). *Creativity, flow, and the psychology of discovery and invention.* Harper Collins, New York.

Dilworth, J. (1992). The violin and bow—origins and development. In *The Cambridge companion to the violin* (ed. R. Stowell), pp. 1–29. Cambridge University Press, Cambridge.

Donington, R. (1963). *The interpretation of early music.* Faber, London.

Dubal, D. (1990). *The art of the piano.* Tauris, London.

Edler-Busch, E. (1993). Trompeten waren auch mal gerade: zum Anfangsalter für das Querflötenspiel. *Üben and Musizieren*, **10**, 26–9.

Elder, D. (1993). Edward Kilenyi remembers Dohnanyi. *Clavier*, **32**, 11–18.

Ericsson, K. A. (1996). The acquisition of expert performance: an introduction to some of the issues. In *The road to excellence: the acquisition of expert performance in the arts, sciences, sports, and games* (ed. K. A. Ericsson), pp. 1–48. Erlbaum, Mahwah, NJ.

——and Charness, N. (1994). Expert performance. Its structure and acquisition. *American Psychologist*, **49**, 725–47.

——and Lehmann, A. C. (1996). Expert and exceptional performance: evidence for maximal adaptations to task constraints. *Annual Review of Psychology*, **47**, 273–305.

——Krampe, R. T., and Tesch-Römer, C. (1993). The role of deliberate practise in the acquisition of expert performance. *Psychological Review*, **100**, 363–406.

Frederickson, D. (1995). Van Cliburn remembers his remarkable mother. *Clavier*, **35**, 6–9.

Gabrielsson, A. (in press). Music performance. In *The psychology of music*, (2nd edn) (ed. D. Deutsch).

Ganassi, S. (1956). *Opera intitulata fontegara* (original published 1535). Lienau, Berlin.

Ganz, P. F. (1960). The development of the etude for pianoforte. *Dissertation Abstracts International (UMI 60–6546).*

Gerig, R. R. (1974). *Famous pianists and their technique.* Luce, Washington.

Grout, D. J. (1980). *A history of Western music* (3rd edn, with C. V. Palisca). Norton, New York.

Gruber, H. (1989). The evolving systems approach to creative work. In *Creative people at work* (ed. D. B. Wallace and H. E. Gruber), pp. 3–24. Oxford University Press, Oxford.

Harris, E. T. (1989). The Baroque era: voices. In *Performance practice: music after 1600* (ed. H. M. Brown and S. Sadie), pp. 97–116. Norton, New York.

Haynes, B. (1992). Mozart and the oboe. *Early Music*, **20**, 43–62.

Henderson, W. J. (1921). *Early history of singing.* Longmans Green, New York.

Hildebrand, D. (1988). *Pianoforte: a social history of the piano.* G. Braziller, New York.

Hitchcock, D. (1971). Sigismund Thalberg: an evaluation of the famous composer-pianist, and the 100th anniversary of his death. *Piano Quarterly*, **20**, (77), 12–16.

Hofmann, J. (1976). *Piano playing with piano questions answered* (original published in 1920). Dover, New York.

Howe, M. A. and Sloboda, J. A. (1991). Young musicians' accounts of significant influences in their early lives. 1. The family and the musical background. *British Journal of Music Education*, **8**, 39–52.

Kite-Powell, J. (ed.) (1994). *A performer's guide to Renaissance music.* Schirmer, New York.

Komlos, K. (1995). *Fortepianos and their music: Germany, Austria, England, 1760–1800.* Clarendon Press, Oxford, UK.

Kopiez, R. (1996). Aspekte der Performanceforschung. In *Handbuch der Musikpsychologie* (2nd edn), (ed. H. Motte-Haber), pp. 505–587. Laaber, Laaber, Germany.

Lehmann, A. C. (1997). Acquisition of expertise in music: efficiency of deliberate practice as a moderating variable in accounting for sub-expert performance. In *Perception and cognition of music* (ed. J. Sloboda and I. Deliege), pp. 165–91. Taylor and Francis, London.

—— and Ericsson, K. A. (1995). *Fingerings in piano performance as evidence for the mental representation of music: a preliminary study.* Paper presented at the Conference of the Society for Music Perception and Cognition, Berkeley, CA, June 22–25.

—— and Ericsson, K. A. (1996). *Preparation of a public piano performance: the relation between practice and performance.* Paper presented at the 10th Annual Florida Conference on Cognition, Perception, Sensation, and Action. Tallahassee, FL, March 22–23, 1996.

Letnanova, E. (1991). *Piano interpretation in the 17th, 18th, and 19th century.* McFarland, Jefferson, NC.

Loesch, H. V. (1992). *Das Cellokonzert von Beethoven bis Ligeti.* Lang, Frankfurt, Germany.

Loesser, A. (1990). *Men, women and pianos: a social history* (original published in 1954). Dover, New York.

McVeigh, S. (1993). *Concert life in London from Mozart to Haydn.* Cambridge University Press, Cambridge, UK.

Mahling, C.-H. (1972). Die Ausführenden der Kirchenmusik im Mittelalter. In *Geschichte der katholischen Kirchenmusik*, Vol. 1 (ed. K. G. Fellerer), pp. 409–15. Bärenreiter, Kassel, Germany.

Manturzewska, M. (1990). A biographical study of the life-span development of performing musicians. *Psychology of Music*, **18**, 112–39.

Marcuse, S. (1964). *Musical instruments; a comprehensive dictionary.* Doubleday, Garden City, NY.

Mather, R. (1980). *The art of playing the flute: a series of workbooks,* Vol. 1. Romney Press, Iowa City, IO.

Matuschka, M. (1987). *Die Erneuerung der Klaviertechnik nach Liszt.* Katzbichler, Munich.

Nisbet, R. (1980). *History of the idea of progress.* Basic Books, New York.

Palmer, W. A. (ed.) (1968). *J. S. Bach: inventions and sinfonias.* Alfred Music.

Parrish, C. G. (1953). *The early piano and its influence on keyboard technique and composition in the eighteenth century.* Research Microfilms Publishers, Superior, WI.

Phillips, P. (1978). Performance practice in 16th-century English choral music. *Early Music,* **6**, 195–9.

Piano Syllabus (1986). *Royal Conservatory of Music Toronta: Piano Syllabus.* Royal Conservatory, Toronto, Canada.

Pierce, R., and Fuszek, R. (1987). *The P-F guide: a conceptual approach to piano instruction.* R. Pierce Music, West Covina, CA.

Polk, K. (1991). Patronage and innovation in instrumental music in the 15th century. *Historical Brass Society Journal,* **3**, 151–78.

—— (1994). Innovation in instrumental music 1450–1510: the role of German performers within European culture. In *Music in the German Renaissance* (ed. J. Kmetz), pp. 202–14. Cambridge University Press, Cambridge.

Powell, A., and Lasocki, D. (1995). Bach and the flute: the players, the instruments, the music. *Early Music,* **23**, 9–30.

Pringle, B. (1996). Vocal and instrumental ornamentation from 1535–1624: its emergence as a virtuosic art and its effects on written compositions in the Italian manner. Unpublished Master's thesis. Florida State University, Tallahassee, Florida.

Rainey, T. E. (1985). *The flute manual.* University Press of America, Lanham, MD.

Read, G. (1993). *Compendium of modern instrumental techniques.* Greenwood Press, Westport, CN.

Repp, B. (1992). Diversity and commonality in music performance: an analysis of timing microstructure in Schumann's 'Träumerei'. *Journal of the Acoustical Society of America*, **92**, 2546–68.

Rosenblum, S. (1988). *Performance practices in classic piano music*. Indiana University Press, Bloomington, IN.

Rowland-Jones, A. (1992). *Playing recorder sonatas: interpretation and technique*. Clarendon Press, Oxford, UK.

Sadie, S. (ed.) (1980). *The New Grove dictionary of music and musicians* (6th edn), Vols 1–20. Macmillan, London.

Salmen, W. (1988). *Das Konzert: eine Kulturgeschichte*. Beck, Munich.

Schaffer, S. (1994). Making up discovery. In *Dimensions of creativity* (ed. M. A. Boden), pp. 13–52. Bradford, Cambridge, MA.

Schellberg, D. (1993). *Didgeridoo. Ritual origins and playing techniques*. Binkey Kok, Diever, Holland.

Seashore, C. E. (1967). *Psychology of music* (original published in 1938). Dover, New York.

Seaton, D. (1991). *Ideas and styles in the Western musical tradition*. Mayfield, Mountain View, CA.

Sheveloff, J. (1987). Domenico Scarlatti: tercentenary frustrations (Part II). *Musical Quarterly*, **72**, 90–118.

Simon, H. A., and Chase, W. G. (1973). Skill in chess. *American Scientist*, **61**, 394–403.

Simonton, D. K. (1997). Creative productivity: a predictive and explanatory model of career trajectories and landmarks. *Psychological Review*, **104**, 66–89.

Sloboda, J. A., Davidson, J. W., Howe, M. J. A., and Moore, D. (1996). The role of practise in the development of expert musical performance. *British Journal of Psychology*, **87**, 287–309.

Sosniak, L. A. (1985). Learning to be a concert pianist. In *Developing talent in young people* (ed. B. S. Bloom), pp. 19–67. Ballantine, New York.

Starkes, J., Deakin, J., Allard, F., Hodges, N., and Hayes, A. (1996). Deliberate practice in sports: what is it anyway? In *The road to excellence: the acquisition of expert performance in the arts, sciences, sports, and games* (ed. K. A. Ericsson), pp. 81–106. Erlbaum, Mahwah, NJ.

Stevens, G. H. (1982). *Das Wunderkind in der Musikgeschichte*. Unpubl. Dissertation, University of Münster, Germany.

Stillings, F. S. (1972). *The sonatas of Beethoven as he played and taught them*. Music Teachers National Association, Cincinnati.

Türk, D. G. (1982). *School of clavier playing* (trans. R. H. Haggh, original published in 1789). University of Nebraska Press, Lincoln, NE.

Walker, A. (1990). *Franz Liszt*, Vol. 1. Knopf, New York.

Wier, A. E. (1940). *The piano: its history, makers, players, and music*. Longmans and Green, London.

Wilcox, D. (1977). *Ten who dared* (preface by Anthony Quinn). Little, Boston.

Wolff, C., Emery, W., Jones, R., Helm, E., Warburton, E., and Derr, E. (1983). *The New Grove: Bach family*. Norton, New York.

Woodfield, I. (1984). *The early history of the viol*. Cambridge University Press, Cambridge, UK.

Woodfill, W. L. (1953). *Musicians in English society from Elizabeth to Charles I*. Princeton University Press, Princeton, NJ.

Young, P. M. (1967). The foundation of modern keyboard techniques. Abelard-Schumann, London.

Zaslaw, N. (ed.) (1989). *The classical era: From the 1740s to the end of the 18th century*. Macmillan, London.

CHARLES DARWIN

CHAPTER 5

Early lives: prodigies and non-prodigies

Michael J. A. Howe

SOME geniuses have been widely acknowledged to be exceptionally able well before reaching adulthood. But there have also been geniuses such as Charles Darwin, who were never considered to be exceptional during their childhood. There are no inevitable connections between prodigy and genius, and the vast majority of child prodigies do not develop into exceptionally creative adults. One is tempted therefore to wonder whether there is any relationship at all between mature genius and prodigious early talent. In fact, there are a number of links, and examining them can yield insights into the ways in which the experiences of childhood and early life make it possible for some individuals to prepare themselves for major creative achievements in their maturity. I would argue that in some cases, the outstanding early progress that leads children to be called prodigies was necessary to equip those individuals for their adult achievements. There have been instances in which the recognition of early talents by influential adults has opened up vital new learning experiences and educational opportunities that would not otherwise have been available. In other cases, the factors that contributed to a young person becoming a child prodigy have had less desirable effects, diminishing rather than increasing the chances of that individual becoming capable of mature creative accomplishment. These patterns are discussed in this chapter through an examination of the early experience of four intellectual giants of the nineteenth century: John Stuart Mill, Charles Darwin, Michael Faraday, and George Stephenson.

Ostensibly, it would be helpful to assess the links between prodigy and genius quantitatively. One might ask what proportion of child prodigies turn into adult geniuses, and how many geniuses were identified as being prodigies in childhood. However, that kind of exercise would only be valid if there existed objective ways of defining child prodigies and adult genius. No such methods exist. When people decide that someone is a genius, they do not base this judgement on the individual's abilities or other qualities, but by recognizing the person's achievements (Howe 1994). As noted by Mihaly Csikszentmihalyi in Chapter 3, whether or not someone becomes known as a genius does not depend on any direct measurement of inherent qualities, but the acknowledgement of their feats by other people (such as professional groups or aficionados). Consequently, genius can only be defined in the limited way in which terms like 'a successful person' or 'a prize winner' can be defined. This may depend as much upon luck and good fortune as upon the individual's special capabilities. Not surprisingly, therefore, there is no universal agreement about who belongs in the 'genius' category.

As soon as one moves beyond a very small number of individuals—Newton, Einstein, and a few dozen others—there is considerable dispute concerning whether or not particular people belong in that exclusive club.

Similarly, there is no agreed method of deciding who is a child prodigy, and there is much room for subjectivity and arbitrary influences. There are no recognized criteria for specifying just how superior a child's performance has to be with respect to peers of his or her age, in order to count as evidence of prodigiousness. Even if that could be decided, it would be extremely difficult to ensure equivalence between children showing promise in different fields of ability or areas of expertise. For example, it is not really possible to guarantee comparable standards for young tennis players and budding scientists.

An additional and separate complication stems from the fact that there are differences in the extent to which the abilities of exceptional children are placed on display and can be apparent to adults. When a child is exceptionally competent at a performing skill such as playing a musical instrument or a particular sport, the chances are that knowledgeable people will notice this ability. The likelihood of the child being regarded as a prodigy will then be enhanced, as in the case of Mozart (see Chapter 7). But some young people have abilities that take a form which is not easily exhibited, so their superiority may not be obvious to observers. The young Albert Einstein was not regarded as a prodigy, because as a child he did not exhibit the kinds of exceptional feats that might have drawn attention to his abilities. Yet it is clear from the accounts of those who knew him well, that by early adolescence his intellectual skills were remarkable, and were on a par with those of children who were considered prodigies (Clarke 1979). Srinivasa Ramanujan, whose extraordinary life is described by Robert Albert in Chapter 6, was regarded as exceptional from his earliest years, despite the rather abstruse nature of his mathematical abilities. However, this appears to be because his family regarded him as a 'special' child favoured by the gods, rather than because his mathematical creativity was understood.

The problems of defining and identifying genius and prodigy appear to rule out quantitative investigation of their relationships. Nevertheless, there is much to be learned from a more qualitative approach. The emphasis here is less on making generalizations about prodigies and geniuses than on eliciting insights from a relatively detailed knowledge of the progress of the early lives of particular individuals. By examining and comparing a small number of prodigies and non-prodigies, and by charting the different routes by which they progressed through their early lives, it may be possible to discern chains of events that are not apparent with the coarser-grain methods of quantitative analysis. A young person's progress through early life is analogous in some respects to a journey. Each individual follows a route that is partly unique, and tracing that route makes it possible to begin to understand how and why that person became capable of their particular accomplishments.

Studying the course of a person's early life needs to be a largely descriptive undertaking. Otherwise, the blinkering preconceptions that are liable to follow from holding a particular theoretical position strongly may colour the investigation. Studies that are primarily descriptive in nature are sometimes considered inferior to those that have a more theoretical basis. None the less, a detailed description of a person's development in which their early progress is carefully charted may go some way towards explaining why and how the person's life took the course it did. I have argued elsewhere that in order to trace early lives effectively, it is necessary to combine the resources of the science of psychology with the art of biography (Howe 1982, 1996, 1997). Scientific psychology has advantages that accrue from insisting on rigour, and from paying careful attention to the quality of the evidence on which conclusions are based. However, when applied on its own, the scientific approach to psychology is restricted by the fact that its techniques are better suited to examining general phenomena than to discovering what happens to particular individuals. That limitation is especially crucial when the objects of study are unusual and far removed from the fictitious 'average person' evident in the combined data typically presented in empirical developmental psychology research (Belmont 1978). By comparison, the output of biographical scholarship has enormous advantages in focusing on the unique qualities of particular individuals. Unfortunately, biographers are sometimes not sufficiently aware of the factors that limit the reliability of their evidence. In other instances, scholars may fail to appreciate how readily evidence from biographical sources can be misinterpreted or misused as a basis for drawing inferences (Garraty 1958; Sturrock 1993).

Mixtures of psychology and biography are not uncommon. Psychologists interested in the development of particular individuals have often drawn upon biographical information, just as biographers have looked to psychology. In the latter case, however, the work has usually taken the form of a 'psychobiography' in which the psychological content is psychodynamic or psychoanalytic. From the perspective of many scientific psychologists, this approach is regarded as outmoded, lacking a firm foundation of hard facts based upon empirical evidence, and involving sometimes implausible theorizing. At its worst, authors using the psychobiographical approach may be content to assume that explanations of psychological phenomena are correct simply because they are consistent with a certain psychological theory. There may be a failure to realize that some theoretical accounts of human development are highly speculative and lack empirical support. Indeed, many theories initially devised earlier in the century have been called in question, if not entirely discredited, by factual evidence obtained from research about what actually happens to young people in the course of their development. Many writers of psychobiographies draw on the work of Sigmund Freud and other psychodynamic psychologists. Undoubtedly, Freud and his contemporaries did much to promote awareness of irrational and unconscious forces in peoples' mental lives, thus providing valuable insights into human nature. Nevertheless, it is likely that the factual evidence made available with modern scientific psychology can make an even larger contribution, because it is founded on observations of the ways in which individual children really develop.

Empirical findings that have emerged from modern research in psychology have contributed in a number of ways to our understanding of human development. Firstly, they make it possible to understand biographical phenomena that might at first sight appear inexplicable. For example, some of the phenomenal early feats of the young Mozart (described by Andrew Steptoe in Chapter 7) have appeared in the past to defy explanation, leading to suggestions about divine intervention. However, research findings relating to the emergence of high abilities suggest that exceptional skills can be acquired by ordinary people, and can be explained without resource to any special powers (Sloboda *et al.* 1994). Knowing this does not make Mozart's early progress any less admirable. But it does suggest that when we try to discover the causes of exceptional abilities, it may be fruitful to look for general mechanisms, rather than causes that are totally different from those present in the rest of humanity. Secondly, psychological research draws attention to the importance of avoiding certain kinds of faulty inference. A common problem is attributing too much importance to particular striking events that take place early in a person's life. The results of many research studies have shown that, contrary to popular belief, it is unusual for single childhood incidents to have long-lasting effects. The routine every day incidents and events that make up a person's life are generally much more influential than the more dramatic occurrences to which biographers are prone to attach importance. Thirdly, scientific psychology demonstrates the need to ensure that evidence is accurate. Studies have shown that memories are often less accurate than they are believed to be, and that people's autobiographical recollections of incidents in the earliest years of their lives are likely to be unreliable (Usher and Neisser 1993).

Sketching the early lives of four geniuses

My argument in this chapter is that the combination of knowledge obtained from undertaking psychological research, with information gained from close inspection of biographical narratives, can help to clarify the nature of links between child prodigy and genius. In the remainder of this chapter, I shall consider some aspects of the early lives of four individuals, all of whom can be regarded as geniuses. They differ enormously in their early experiences. None the less, in each case an examination of the biographical evidence shows that a route can be traced through which the young child (starting in some cases from unpromising beginnings) had experiences and opportunities that enabled him to acquire the qualities, knowledge and skills on which later creative achievements were founded. When early lives are traced in detail, some aspects of creative people and their accomplishments that at first appear to be entirely mysterious often become more explicable. The life course of these unusual individuals may have taken unexpected turns, but there are no sudden leaps or inexplicable gaps. If close inspection of the events of early life leaves some mysteries still unexplained, findings from psychological research may cast light on the causes of the person's exceptional attainments. The significance for adult accomplishment of being a child prodigy (or being regarded as a child prodigy) differs considerably from case to case. In most instances, the effects have been beneficial, although not always for the same reasons (Howe 1990).

John Stuart Mill

John Stuart Mill, who was born in 1806, is a prototypical example of a person who is widely and quite appropriately regarded as having been a child prodigy. His adult life was filled with major scholarly achievements, mostly related to political theory, philosophy, education, and the fields of enquiry that could now be seen as forming the social sciences. However, unusually in a prodigy, Mill was never encouraged until he was well into adolescence to perceive his abilities as being unusual. This was a consequence of his education and moulding at the hands of his father, James Mill. James Mill (1773–1836) was an austere scholar, closely associated with Jeremy Bentham and the economist David Ricardo, and was a pioneer of the Utilitarian tradition. He devised an educational programme that was intended to equip his son to continue his own work, and regarded his son's early achievements as the inevitable consequence of this regime. He therefore saw nothing at all extraordinary about the fact that his son's intellectual progress was outstanding.

John Stuart Mill wrote an account of his early education in his celebrated *Autobiography* (1971, first published in 1873). This is as candid, detailed, and accurate an account as any autobiography can be expected to be. Mill makes it clear that his father took great pains with his education, and that most of his waking hours from early childhood were devoted to learning. As a distinguished and diligent scholar, James Mill ensured that the intellectual grounding his son received was excellent, although the child's self-esteem and emotional development were greatly neglected in this rigorous regime. He paid little attention to motivating or encouraging the boy, but constantly told him how disappointing he was, and how slowly and lazily he worked. In consequence, John Stuart Mill may have been regarded by others as a prodigy, but was more of a dullard in his own eyes.

To modern readers with an understanding of the importance of a growing child's emotional needs, the consequences of John Stuart Mill's early life and education are to some extent predictable. By early adulthood, the intellectual equipment of his mind was superb. He was exceptionally knowledgeable and highly literate, and possessed enviable analytic skills and a capacity both to examine and dissect the detailed arguments of others and to develop abstract ideas of his own. In other respects, he was disastrously ill-prepared for a productive and fulfilling life. His social skills were poor, since his dominating father did little to enable him to become an independent or self-directed adult. John Stuart Mill himself did not have a sense that he had chosen the direction of his life, and lacked the personal ambitions that motivate people and their activities. Not surprisingly, John Stuart Mill found it very difficult to make the transition from being a clever young prodigy to becoming an autonomous adult with self-confidence and the maturity to utilize his mental powers. He did eventually surmount most of these difficulties, but not before experiencing a lengthy crisis in his early twenties. This was characterized by a severe breakdown that lasted for a number of years, in which he suffered depression and felt his life to be largely pointless. Interestingly, he recovered from this episode partly through interest in the poetry of William

Wordsworth, and acquired a passion for romantic lyricism that was completely antithetical to his own intellectual concerns.

John Stuart Mill recognized himself to be a kind of manufactured genius, formed by a father who had deliberately set out to produce a son with superior intellectual powers. His *Autobiography* provides an insightful account both of the benefits and dangers of such an exercise. While I would not wish to dismiss the negative consequences of his upbringing, there is no denying that Mill's unusual early life experiences helped him to become a child prodigy, and provided him with the intellectual resources that made possible the numerous scholarly achievements of his adult life (Howe 1990). There are strong grounds for believing that the remarkable early training provided by his father was a necessary if not sufficient condition for his emergence as a child prodigy. Had there been a delay until a later stage of his life in the process of equipping him intellectually, the likelihood that he would have become such a knowledgeable and powerful analytic thinker would have been much diminished.

Exceptional childhood progress appears to have been a necessity for John Stuart Mill. There are a number of areas of expertise in which similar circumstances apply. For example, it is rare for a person to become a supremely skilful musician unless he or she has made a good start in childhood. This point is elaborated in detail by Andreas Lehmann and Anders Ericsson in Chapter 4. The reason is partly because it is hard for an adult beginner to spend the substantial amount of time needed not only to acquire basic skills but to catch up with people who start training in childhood. Accomplished musicians may have already devoted as much as ten thousand hours to practice and training by the time they reach adulthood (Ericsson, *et al.* 1993; Sloboda *et al.* 1996). For a classical musician, there is little chance of having a successful career unless one has already carried out a substantial amount of training and practice in early life. Young musicians consequently devote many hours to mastering their instruments, and standards are so high that admiring adults are sometimes happy to describe them as prodigies.

Substantial amounts of early specialized training may be less essential for other fields of expertise than is the case for music. Nevertheless, in virtually any domain in which it is necessary to undertake deliberate practice in order to build up skills, someone who reaches adulthood without having undergone special training will be at a considerable disadvantage. Catching up may be extremely difficult, if not impossible. Consequently, amongst mathematicians, scientists, and performers at various sports, it is usually found that successful individuals have been at least highly competent before reaching the end of childhood. Even if in principle it is possible for an adult beginner to devote the time to the training tasks necessary to achieve high levels of expertise, it would be very unusual for them to have the sheer single-mindedness to make the commitment.

However, granted that considerable training in childhood is often essential, it does not follow that those children who make the most progress become the most successful adults. Lauren Sosniak (1985) interviewed a sample of extremely successful American classical pianists in their early thirties. She found that all had trained hard throughout their childhood and had become highly competent players at relatively early ages. However, few of them were seen by adults as being any more successful than the hundreds of other young people who were aspiring to careers as concert pianists.

These considerations suggest that whereas a particular child being regarded as a prodigy may increase the likelihood of substantial achievement later in life, the reason for the connection is not that being a prodigy *per se* is essential. Rather, labelling a child as a prodigy is an indication that he or she has had a valuable early start, and has already gained at a young age some of the skills conducive to mature achievement in the relevant field of expertise. If this account is correct, we would expect to find some people who are eventually regarded as being geniuses who were not seen as at all prodigious or exceptional in their early lives.

Charles Darwin

Charles Darwin (1809–1882) was one such person. As a child, he was considered reasonably intelligent but by no means unusual, and at school he never came close to winning prizes or distinguishing himself in any way. Darwin was a keen collector from his earliest years, and much of his collecting activity was related to natural history. However, this was unremarkable in itself, and although he was enthusiastic he displayed no particular expertise. No science was taught at his school, and his growing devotion to natural history was frowned upon by his headmaster, who saw it as a waste of time. Nevertheless, perhaps because of rather than despite his headmaster's disapproval, his hobby gradually developed into a serious interest. Darwin was fortunate to enjoy the advantages of growing up in a wealthy family which took a lively interest in scientific matters. His older brother allowed him to assist and then to collaborate in practical experiments in chemistry. Through this, he acquired the beginnings of the scientific education his school failed to provide. His family's wealth made it possible to travel, so he was able to go on walking holidays that brought him into contact with new environments and unfamiliar varieties of fauna and flora. It is possible that had science been taught at school, it would have become associated in Darwin's mind with the compulsory and competitive elements of school work that he disliked. His interest in natural history might then have been extinguished at an early stage.

Darwin's transition from naive child collector to enthusiastic teenage naturalist and competent young scientist was a steady progress, in which his knowledge and skills gradually increased as his horizons broadened. From the time he became a student at Edinburgh University at the age of 16, he came into contact with professional biologists and other scientists who were prepared to help him. This good fortune continued when he moved to Cambridge University, and was due to several factors. He came from a distinguished family and was known to be the grandson of the respected scientific thinker Erasmus Darwin. The biologists who helped him were also attracted by his enthusiasm and the seriousness of his interest. Perhaps most importantly, Darwin was notably successful at getting on with other people and developing friendships. In this respect he differed strikingly from John Stuart Mill. In fact, Darwin's ability to co-operate with others and to gain their respect was crucial to his scientific achievements. In later years, he was obliged to gather large amounts of evidence from a wide range of sources in order to provide the empirical support for the theory of evolution by natural selection. He was assisted by being able to draw upon information provided by numerous collaborators from many different walks of life. He used his charm to extract scientific data from others that he could not have collected himself. Similarly, the social and personal skills and capacity for friendship that he developed during his childhood (unimpeded by the restriction placed on the somewhat friendless John Stuart Mill) equipped him well for gaining co-operation from some difficult individuals. These included his father, who was initially strongly opposed to his decision to leave England to circumnavigate the world on the voyage of *HMS Beagle*. Another was the *Beagle's* Captain, Robert Fitzroy, who was a temperamental and often hot-tempered individual. Darwin managed to remain on friendly terms with him, despite close confinement on a tiny ship for almost six years (Sulloway 1985).

It can therefore be argued that Darwin's achievements depended almost as much on his personal qualities as on his intellectual capacity. Had he been a child prodigy, any advantage this might have given him would very possibly have been out-weighed by a childhood in which his intellect was fostered at the expense of personal qualities and social skills. These skills, and his reputation for dependability, were greatly needed in later years as he relied on the support of others to carry out his greatest work.

Michael Faraday

The life of Charles Darwin provides a clear demonstration of the fact that it is possible for someone to become a genius despite never having been regarded as any kind of prodigy in childhood. However, it might be argued that Darwin's case merely proves that an early start is unnecessary for those fortunate individuals who have the support of wealthy and stimulating families and a good general education. Perhaps a 'prodigious' early start is still necessary for those children whose early years are not so favoured by material resources. However, this suggestion is contradicted by the early years of another great scientist, Michael Faraday. Faraday was born in 1791, the son of a blacksmith. He left school at the age of thirteen to work for a small firm in London where he was employed as an apprentice bookbinder (Jones 1870: Cantor 1991; Gooding and Jones 1985). That hardly seems to have been a promising start for a man who was to become one of the dominant scientists of the nineteenth century. However, Faraday had some important advantages. Firstly, he was intellectually curious and eager to learn. Although bookbinding does not seem to be an especially good preparation for science, he had plenty of access to books and came into frequent contact with literary and intellectual people. Secondly, he was fortunate in that his employer was a kindly man who gave his apprentices plenty of help and encouragement. In fact, Faraday was not the only apprentice of the firm to have a distinguished adult career. Thirdly, his family were members of a religious sect that placed considerable emphasis on the virtue of self-help, and on the importance of what would be called 'family values'. His family was close and supportive, as is evident from the fact that most members maintained close contact with each other and supported one another throughout their lives.

The combination of intellectual stimulation which the young Michael Faraday received at work, and a supportive family life in which people helped and depended on one another, has been shown by modern research to be particularly effective in enabling young people to achieve. For example, Mihaly Csikszentmihalyi and his co-workers have investigated the study practices and time-management of adolescents (Csikszentmihalyi and Csikszentmihalyi 1993: Csikszentmihalyi *et al*. 1993). A majority of adolescents find it difficult to engage in studying and practising the activities that are necessary for progress towards higher levels of competence. But a minority of young people report that they do not dislike studying, and make very effective use of their study time. In most cases, these well placed young people are those whose home backgrounds are not only educationally stimulating, but also relatively structured and supportive. These adolescents tend to come from homes in which everyone helps each other and everyone has their own responsibilities, so that children learn to get on with their lives and the jobs they have to do. In doing so, they acquire good working habits, and do not spend their days in time-wasting activities such as squabbling with siblings, complaining their life is unfair, or arguing about whose turn it is to do jobs around the home.

With this supportive background and level of intellectual stimulation, Faraday's limited schooling was not such an obstacle to becoming a scientist as it would be today. It should be remembered that advanced schooling in that era was founded on a classical education, so that Faraday would probably have learned virtually nothing about science at school. Instead, he went to enormous pains to educate himself, supplementing his learning from books with attendance at lectures and discussion groups. As a learner, he was strikingly energetic and well-organized, as well as being extremely thorough and conscientious. For someone who studied as hard as he did, his progress was not outstandingly fast. What was extraordinary about Faraday was his sheer determination and persistence. He maintained a rigorous study schedule despite working at a full-time job. He was fortunate to encounter an excellent 'how to study' guide in Isaac Watts' *The improvement of the mind* (1801). This was an ideal source of inspiration and advice for any young learner, especially one who was largely self-taught. *The improvement of the mind* is one of the best in a long tradition of self-help books addressed to general readers. It has twenty chapters on a wide range of topics such as reading, lectures, acquiring new languages, 'fixing the attention', memory, reasoning, observation, and learning from conversations. Isaac Watts emphasized the necessity for students to take positive steps to ensure that the process of learning was active and meaningful. His book would have helped Faraday to select effective day-to-day study activities, and would have given him a good appreciation of the ways in which students can extend their own knowledge and skills.

Faraday not only read Watts's book, but diligently and conscientiously followed the advice contained in it. So, for example, after he had attended a lecture and taken notes on it, he would re-write and expand his work, referring to books where necessary in order to provide the additional information that was needed to fill gaps in his knowledge. Like many conscientious young learners, Faraday was careful to prepare himself for any good fortune that might come his way. When the time came that an assistant was required in the laboratory of the Royal Institution, Faraday had already made sure that the fashionable and celebrated chemist Humphry Davy knew of his existence, and that he was the best man for the job.

George Stephenson

Charles Darwin's early life demonstrates that it is possible to become a genius without exhibiting the early signs of excellence that lead some highly promising children to being labelled as prodigies. Faraday's experience shows that even without the benefits of good schooling and an educated family background, a young person who is enormously determined and has the good fortune to be provided with help and encouragement may also aspire to greatness. But what are the chances for a child brought up in real poverty, without any of the benefits of schooling? Is it ever possible for such a child to overcome these obstacles, and become capable of creative achievements that might later be acknowledged on the world stage?

The handicaps facing a child brought up in these circumstances are severe, and individuals who have managed to surmount them are rare. There are a handful of such people, one of whom was George Stephenson (1781–1848). Stephenson was a railway engineer, and is justly regarded as a genius for his immense achievements in developing steam locomotion to the point at which passenger travel became possible. The engines he designed as an adult travelled at speeds unimaginable at the time of his birth. In addition to this pioneering work, Stephenson also made important contributions to the design of railway lines and to the construction of routes. His railways crossed terrains that had been thought impassable by previous engineers, and he was consulted about railways in many parts of the world. Yet the man who achieved these feats started life as the son of a colliery fireman in a mining village near Newcastle in the north of England. His father was so poor that he could never afford to send any of his six children to school. George Stephenson himself received no formal education as a child, but was employed as a cowherd from an early age, and began work at the mine assisting his father to stoke one of the colliery engines when he was 14 years old. It was not until the age of 18 years that he learned to write his name after he had started attending classes in reading and basic arithmetic. He walked to the house of a local teacher in the evenings three times a week for his lessons, after finishing his twelve-hour shift in the mine where he was then working (Smiles 1881; Rolt 1960; Davies 1975).

The early life of George Stephenson was one continuous hard struggle. Like Michael Faraday he was unusually ambitious, energetic, and determined, but his disadvantages were considerably more severe. The period of time over which it was necessary for him to work at acquiring engineering skills and knowledge was much longer than in Faraday's case. Faraday had established himself as a promising young scientist by his early twenties. It was not until Stephenson was over 30 years old that he had become sufficiently qualified and experienced to be placed in a position in which he was given the opportunity to display his capabilities.

How is it possible for a child with no schooling to become a great engineer? Engineering in the early nineteenth century depended less on science and mathematics than does modern engineering. George Stephenson was able to gain the relatively small amount of theoretical knowledge that was essential for his work only much later, and in this he was helped by his own son Robert. Stephenson's lack of early education would have been crippling for any would-be engineer starting a couple of decades later.

One of the positive influences on his development was the intense interest he had in engines from his earliest days. His work in the mines as an adolescent often involved primitive engines, so he had plenty of opportunities to study their operation. He watched them and built models of them when he was still a child, and in later years observed how they worked, repaired them when they went wrong, took them to pieces and rebuilt them. In doing this, he gained an intimate practical knowledge of the capabilities and weaknesses of the early steam engine, and this was vital to his later career.

For instance, Stephenson's first biographer Samuel Smiles (1881) notes that at the age of 17 years, he was employed as a 'plugman', responsible for a pumping engine. This was a relatively skilled job since his interest in engines had already been recognized. When an engine suffered a serious breakdown, the usual response would be to send for the chief engineer. But Stephenson:

applied himself so assiduously and successfully to the study of the engine and its gearing—taking the machine to pieces in his leisure hours for the purpose of cleaning it and understanding its various parts—that he soon acquired a thorough practical knowledge of its construction and mode of working, and very rarely needed to call the engineer of the colliery to his aid. His engine became a sort of pet with him, and he was never wearied of watching it and inspecting it with admiration. (Smiles 1881, p. 9)

At about this point in his life, it seemed possible that despite his disadvantages, the young Stephenson might eventually become an unusually competent and innovative engineer. As well as closely observing the engines for which he was responsible, he capitalized on his childhood pastime of building model steam engines. He even began to conduct small experiments to test ideas that came to him when he was told about scientific findings that had been reported in the newspapers, despite the fact that he could not yet read. This acute interest in the detailed working of machines, the delight in giving close attention to their operation, and never tiring interest in how the parts act together, are almost the defining marks of mechanical inventors even today (Colangelo 1993). As Samuel Smiles noted:

The daily contemplation of the steam engine, and the sight of its steady action, is an education of itself to an ingenious and thoughtful man. And it is a remarkable fact, that nearly all of that has been done for the improvement of this machine has been accomplished, not by philosophers and scientific men, but by labourers, mechanics, and enginemen. Indeed, it would appear as if this were one of the departments of practical science in which the higher powers of the human mind must bend to mechanical insight. (Smiles 1881, p. 10)

For an engineer at the beginning of the nineteenth century, practical activities of this kind were crucial. Just as musicians, chess players, and experts in other fields gradually master skills over the course of thousands of hours of training and practice, Stephenson's mind was engaged with engines. He gradually built up a deep and extensive knowledge, and in this way acquired practical skills that could not be matched even by engineers with greatly superior scientific and theoretical knowledge. Although in his early life George Stephenson had none of the educational opportunities that appear important today for creative achievement, he did not lack experiences that made it possible to acquire engineering skills. These were of great value to this pioneer and inventor in the field of steam locomotion.

Conclusion

In some circumstances, the events that lead a young person to be regarded as a child prodigy closely parallel the experiences that prepare an individual for truly creative achievement. If only for this reason, prodigy and genius are related states. But for a number of reasons outlined in this chapter, it is by no means inevitable that a prodigy will ever become capable of substantial accomplishments. As I have shown in the case of John Stuart Mill, the early experiences that encourage a child to prodigious feats can also have outcomes that constrain the individual. They may indeed make it harder rather than easier for the child to gain the qualities such as a sense of purpose and direction that are needed in order to sustain the immense and prolonged efforts required for the most substantial of human achievements. The fact that a child is regarded as a prodigy may provide an indication that he or she has had a good early start in acquiring skills and knowledge that may be beyond the reach of someone who delays training until adulthood. But as the accomplishments of people such as Charles Darwin and George Stephenson demonstrate, there is nothing to stop a person whose early progress has not been remarkable from becoming capable of major creative acts.

References

Belmont, J. M. (1978). Individual differences in memory: the case of normal and retarded development. In *Aspects of memory* (ed. M. M. Gruneberg and P. E. Morris), pp. 153–85. Methuen, London.

Clark, R. W. (1979). *Einstein: the life and times.* Hodder and Stoughton, London.

Cantor, G. (1991). *Michael Faraday: sandemanian and scientist.* Macmillan, Basingstoke.

Colangelo, N., Assouline, S. G., Kerr, B., Huesman, R., and Johnson, D. (1993). Mechanical inventiveness: a three-phase study. In *CIBA Foundation Symposium No 178: the origins and development of high ability* (ed. G. R. Bock and K. Ackrill), pp. 160–70. Wiley, Chichester.

Csikszentmihalyi, M., and Csikszentmihalyi, I. S. (1993). Family influences on the development of giftedness. In *CIBA Foundation Symposium No 178: the origins and development of high ability* (ed. G. R. Bock and K. Ackrill), pp. 187–200. Wiley, Chichester.

——, Rathunde, K., and Whalen, S. (1993). *Talented teenagers: the roots of success and failure.* Cambridge University Press, Cambridge.

Davies, H. (1975). *George Stephenson.* Weidenfeld and Nicolson, London.

Ericsson, K. A., Tesch-Romer, C., and Krampe, R. T. (1993). The role of deliberate practice in the acquisition of expert performance. *Psychological Review*, **100**, 363–406.

Garraty, J. A. (1958). *The nature of biography.* Jonathan Cape, London.

Gooding, D., and James, A. J. L. (1985). Introduction: Faraday rediscovered. In *Faraday rediscovered: essays on the life and work of Michael Faraday, 1791–1867* (ed. D. Gooding and F. A. J. L. James), pp. 1–13. Macmillan/Stockton Press, Basingstoke.

Howe, M. J. A. (1982). Biographical evidence and the development of outstanding individuals. *American Psychologist*, **37**, 1071–81.

—— (1990). *The origins of exceptional abilities.* Blackwell, Oxford.

—— (1994). Genius. In *Encyclopedia of Intelligence, Vol 1* (ed. R. J. Sternberg), pp. 483–8. Macmillan, New York.

—— (1996). The childhoods and early lives of geniuses: combining psychological and biographical evidence. In *The road to excellence: the acquisition of expert performance in the arts and science, sports and games* (ed. K. A. Ericsson), pp. 255–70. Erlbaum, New York.

—— (1997). Beyond psychobiography: towards more effective syntheses of psychology and biography. *British Journal of Psychology*, **88**, 235–48.

Jones, B. H. (1870). *The life and letters of Faraday.* Longmans, Green and Co, London.

Mill, J. S. (1971). *Autobiography.* Oxford University Press, London. First published in 1873.

Pearce Williams, L. (1965). *Michael Faraday: a biography.* Chapman & Hall, London.

Rolt, L. T. C. (1960). *George and Robert Stephenson.* Longman, London.

Sloboda, J. A., Davidson, J. W., and Howe, M. J. A. (1994). Is everyone musical? *The Psychologist*, **7**, 349–54.

——, ——, ——, Davidson, J. W., Howe, M. J. A., and Moore, D. G. (1996). The role of practice in the development of performing musicians. *British Journal of Psychology*, **87**, 287–309.

Sosniak, L. A. (1985). Learning to be a concert pianist. In *Developing talent in young people* (ed. B. S. Bloom), pp. 19–67. Ballantine, New York.

Smiles, S. (1881). *Life of George Stephenson* (Centenery Edition), originally published in 1857. Murray, London.

Sturrock, J. (1993). *The language of autobiography.* Cambridge University Press, New York.

Sulloway, F. J. (1985). Darwin's early intellectual development: an overview of the *Beagle* voyage. In *The Darwinian heritage* (ed. D. Kohn), pp. 121–54. Pinceton University Press, Princeton.

Usher, J. A., and Neissser, U. (1993). Childhood amnesia and the beginnings of memory for four early life events. *Journal of Experimental Psychology: General*, **122**, 155–65.

Watts, I. (1801). *The improvement of the mind.* J. Abraham, London.

SRINIVASA RAMANUJAN

Mathematical giftedness and mathematical genius: a comparison of G. H. Hardy and Srinivasa Ramanujan

Robert S. Albert

Introduction

THE major issues explored in this chapter appear distinct, but at the same time they blend into each other. The heart of the chapter is about two mathematicians—G. H. Hardy (1877–1947) and Srinivasa Ramanujan (1887–1929)—who alone and in collaboration did important work during the first quarter of this century. The comparison between them makes it possible to look for differences between people who are gifted, talented and make great professional achievements, and those rare self-launched people who defy our definitions and well-worked out assumptions, people who from their earliest years appear so tailor-made for their lives that we need to find other explanations for them. Throughout the chapter, I ask if the comparison between these two men might help us to identify gifted children and assist them in maximizing their potential. My confidence in doing this grows out of a prediction I made years ago, when I described how early accurate parental identification and encouragement of young talent could have advantages. My example was an All-Star basketball player who, after learning that his two-year old son would grow up to be 6 feet 6 inches tall, practised basketball with him for the next ten years (Albert 1980). Twenty years later, the son is a star basketball player at his father's old university.

Over the years, creativeness has been compared with eminence, implying that where you find one, you will find the other. In my own work, however, I have found that creativeness and eminence do not necessarily appear together at all. In this chapter, I try to show why creativity is a special and relatively rare type of behaviour. It is a way of thinking about problems, and in the broadest sense about oneself. Throughout the development of creativity, there is much exploration of deeply-held values, ideals, and what one can expect of oneself in life.

Why Hardy and Ramanujan?

I should like to explain why I have chosen to focus primarily on Hardy and Ramanujan, and somewhat less on Hardy's lifelong collaborator and colleague at

Trinity College Cambridge, J. E. Littlewood (1885–1957). What we learn from them may teach us important lessons about giftedness and genius. Because they lived in the same era and worked in the same discipline, their similarities and differences can give us insights into the higher levels of eminence, where talent parts company from genius.

The first question to ask is how eminent were Hardy, Littlewood, and Ramanujan. This not a rhetorical question. We want to learn from these men to discover what distinguishes them from less eminent individuals. Hopefully, this will help us identify early giftedness, and facilitate its transformation into creativity.

There are standard methods of answering the question of eminence, including assessment of their output, the number of citations to the work they produced, how often they are listed in standard biographical dictionaries and encyclopaedias, and their prominence in the basic texts in a field. Obviously, the methods are not independent of one another, but the most objective measure in mathematics and the sciences is citation count. Once an article is sent to a journal or a book is published, its use and evaluation are out of the author's hands. Articles and books are susceptible to the judgement of hundred of peers throughout the world (see Garfield 1987 for a discussion of the use and misuse of citations). The frequency with which scientists and mathematicians cite another's work is indirectly related to that individual's creativity, productivity, and ability to generate ideas. I believe that the length of time the work continues to be cited tells us even more about its significance. Obviously, as the number of references made to an individual's work increases, that person's reputation grows. Therefore, eminence that is built on the quantity and judged quality of work in public domain argues against the notion that there are unknown hidden geniuses (see the discussion by Mihaly Csikszentmihalyi in Chapter 3).

Since the *Science Index* first appeared in 1961, it has been possible to calculate the reputations of scientists with hard numbers. It has been found that citation counts correlate with other indices of reputation such as honours. They can tell us who is likely to be publicly recognized in the future by prestigious honours such as Fellowship of the Royal Society. Hardy, Littlewood, and Ramanujan were all elected Fellows of the Royal Society, but Ramanujan received his Fellowship at a much earlier age. All three men were prolific writers in mathematics. Hardy accumulated 305 publications, mostly in collaboration with Littlewood. Ramanujan published 37 (or 96, depending on one source), but his life was much shorter. These figures are impressive, and for good reason. Cole and Cole (1967) have calculated that of the 250 000 scientists whose work was mentioned in the 1961 *Science Index*, just over 1% had 58 citations. This is the average level of Nobel laureates between 1955 and 1965. Their honours and the quality and quantity of their publications attest to the fact that Hardy, Littlewood, and Ramanujan were eminent mathematicians.

How accurate are citations as a measure of influential productivity and as a predictor of eminence? The sheer amount of production in most scientific fields has increased continuously over the last 300 years. Yet at any one time, only a few men and women are responsible for the majority of publications, and these individuals can be identified by their citations. Garfield (1970) demonstrated that it was possible to predict likely candidates for the Nobel science prizes in this way, and did in fact identify the next two Nobel laureates on the basis of citations. But mere productivity is never the basis of eminence. It is a combination of quantity and quality of work that matters (e.g. Rushton and Endler 1979). Correlations between quantity and quality range from 0.49 for Nobel laureates in the sciences, to 0.50–0.59 among creative architects, to nearly 0.70 for psychologists and physicists (Albert 1975; MacKinnon 1965).

Another way of assessing eminence is to study dictionaries of biography or encyclopaedias, since these give an indication of the extent to which people are recognized outside their own field of expertise. The *Dictionary of National Biography* is the best model, although its selections are posthumous and supposedly limited to British subjects. The biographies of eminent people who died in the twentieth century appear in supplements to *Dictionary of National Biography*, each of which covers 10 years. Hardy's biography appeared in the 1941–1950 edition, and Littlewood's in the next edition. The two pages of Hardy's biography emphasize his collaborations with Littlewood and Ramanujan, which were judged to be his 'best work'. His career is summarized as having a 'profound influence on modern mathematics'. Littlewood's entry is shorter, and contains as much information about Hardy as it does about Littlewood himself. Ramanujan was not included in the *Dictionary of National Biography*, possibly because of his Indian origin. However, this is made up for in the *Encyclopaedia Britannica* (1965 edition), in which Hardy and Ramanujan are discussed in short biographies, while Littlewood is not mentioned.

The selections in the *Dictionary of National Biography* and the *Encyclopaedia Britannica* might be a matter of their editor's interest in mathematics. I have therefore examined standard histories of mathematics (Barton 1985; Cajoni 1980; Campbell and Higgins 1984). Hardy and Ramanujan are acknowledged in two of them. Barton (1985 p. 246) describes Ramanujan as a 'Hindu genius' with uncanny manipulative ability, whose 'disorganized character' was related to his intuitive reasoning. Cajoni (1980) places Hardy and Ramanujan high in the history of mathematics. He developed a chronology of major contributions to mathematics starting at 500 BC with evidence of counting. The collaboration between Hardy and Ramanujan on the theory of numbers is listed for 1917.

Hardy and Ramanujan were apparently more eminent than Littlewood. Perhaps the best reason for this is given by Hardy himself (1940, p. 20): 'the reputation of a mathematician cannot be made by failures or by rediscoveries, it must rest primarily and mightily on actual and original achievement.'

Hardy

Readers may find it helpful to consult the chronologies of Hardy and Ramanujan's lives given in Appendix A as they move through the short biographies. Godfrey Harold Hardy (always known as G. H. Hardy) was born in 1877, the only son and oldest child of a modest professional family. As a young man his father had been a successful teacher in geography and drawing in Lincolnshire. He moved to work at Cranleigh School in

Surrey, and was promoted and given a salary rise after three years of teaching. He married Sophia Hall, who was also trained as a teacher, and from all accounts both parents were bright and had higher than average mathematical ability. Hardy's only sister Gertrude was born two years after him.

G. H. Hardy's father Isaac is described by biographers as gentle, indulgent, and somewhat ineffectual. But along with his kindly disposition, he was bright and ambitious both for himself and his family. The family's talent for mathematics and music indicate the 'genetic possibilities' for Hardy and his sister (discussed by David Lykken in more detail in Chapter 2). Hardy's sister Gertrude was also mathematically talented, and a family history of similar talents is relatively common among eminent people (Albert 1994*b*). It is not unusual therefore that young children who are gifted mathematically will have parents, perhaps a sibling, and even one or more grandparents who are also mathematically talented (Albert 1980). Hardy's mother had a similar background to his father. She came from a working-class family, and was ambitious and talented in music (mathematics' first cousin). It is in her temperament where she differed most from Isaac Hardy. Isaac was religious in the conventional sense, but Hardy's mother (like Ramanujan's formidable parent) was definitely religious, quite determined to do right, and somewhat obsessively involved with her children's welfare and education.

It appears then that Hardy's parents were devoted, ambitious, and well-educated for their time and social origins. Each was aware and proud of their only son's obvious gifts and mathematical talent. The family in which G. H. Hardy was brought up fits well with what we know about gifted children in general.

Littlewood

I put John Littlewood's biography here to indicate how similar he was to Hardy, and how different they both were from Ramanujan. These similarities give us a good sense of the family constellation of talent, birth-order, ambition, socio-economic status, and resources that are often found among high achieving gifted children. In various psychological studies such as Cox's work on geniuses, Roe's eminent scientists and Zuckerman's (1977) American Nobel laureates, more than 80% came from professional or semi-professional homes (Ochse 1990). The same is true in my two samples of exceptionally gifted boys, while Gibson's (1970) sample of university scientists shows more than 70% come from backgrounds of this type.

Littlewood was the oldest child of a family that traced its roots as far back as the Battle of Agincourt. Like Hardy, he was middle-class, but with more of a professional background. Both his father and paternal grandfather were educated in mathematics at Pembroke College, Cambridge. People who knew both Littlewood and Hardy described the former as the more balanced, steady and unexceptional (Snow 1967). Not that he was a dull fellow. He had a number of outside interests, and appears to have been more at ease socially than was Hardy. In the case of Littlewood, becoming a mathematician seemed like growing into a career. Academic mathematics had already been in his family over several generations, so such a career would seem in the natural order of things. In fact, his father was so certain of his 15-year-old son's talent that he sent him from South Africa, where he believed the education could not match his son's gifts, to St Paul's School in London. Here he was able to study for three years under a prominent teacher, and in 1902 at the age of 17 he entered Trinity College, Cambridge.

Ramanujan

Readers will notice that I have written more about Ramanujan than Hardy and Little-wood combined, and for good reason. All three men were first children and the oldest sons of mathematically-gifted parents. But beyond this, the differences between Ramanujan and his contemporaries far outweigh whatever he might have had in common with them. This is not because Hardy and Littlewood were Westerners and Ramanujan was Indian. It is ironic that despite his obscure origins, we nevertheless know more about Ramanujan than the two Englishmen. From all we know, we find that Ramanujan was an 'original' who seemed to come out of nowhere, much like Isaac Newton and Albert Einstein.

Ramanujan's personality meshed with his mathematical power and originality. He has been characterized by Western and Indian writers alike as singular, serious yet also ebullient, impulsive, and always possessed by mathematics. He was simultaneously pleasant and detached, perhaps even indifferent, in most social relationships. Above all, Ramanujan was intense, obsessed, and self-centred, to some extent addicted to doing mathematics. Both Hardy and Littlewood were deeply involved in their work, but not to the near total exclusion of other people and interests. Nandy (1980) describes Ramanujan as 'self-born', and Kanigel (1991) adds 'self-willed, self-directed, self-made . . . conceivably . . . selfish'. My own view is that to the degree that Ramanujan was absorbed in mathematics, he was also self-absorbed. C. P. Snow's characterization of another original also applies to Ramanujan: 'Those who spent much time with Einstein . . . found him grow stranger, less like themselves, the longer they knew him' (Snow 1967). Ramanujan was also similar to Einstein in his self-confidence. 'It was like him (Einstein) to begin his work . . . with the aid of nothing but his own pure unaided thought. No one else would have started from that suspension of mathematical techniques . . . He had absolute confidence . . . absolute faith in his own insight.' Hardy and others tell us that this was true of Ramanujan as well. Ramanujan was absolutely certain about the correctness of his concept of mathematics, and he left his professional colleagues in no doubt of this certainty.

He was born on 22 December 1887 in his maternal grandmother's house, following South Indian custom. His birthplace was the first evidence of what would be a lifelong bond between Ramanujan and his mother and indirectly with his maternal grand-mother. His place of birth bestowed upon him his 'special' place within the family, and was a source of his early serenity. He was born into a devout Brahmin family that although very poor, nevertheless maintained its high social status. Both his mother and grandmother were intensely religious and believed their family gods often intervened on their behalf. The best proof of this was Ramanujan's own birth. There were no children in the early years of his parent's marriage, and his grandfather, grandmother and mother prayed continuously to their family goddess Managini. After years of unanswered prayer, the family was 'blessed' (the mother's word) with his birth. Ramanujan was always treated as a special child, almost as sacred by his mother and grandmother. He was tended carefully, thereby surviving at a time when four out of every ten infants died. The 'blessing' was confirmed by the early deaths of three siblings born over the next few years. Indeed, Ramanujan was an only child for the first ten years of his life. By then, his own extraordinary talent in mathematics was evident and this drew Ramanujan and his mother closer together. She too was mathematically able, and had predicted long before her son's birth that he would share these gifts. Ramanujan spent most of his early years intimately bonded with his mother, isolated from his father and other males.

I emphasize his early years for good reason. The families in which Hardy and Littlewood grew up are similar to those of many gifted children in Western society. By contrast, the degree of imbalance between Ramanujan's mother and father is rarely found in the families of Western scientists. In Western research, it is often the father–son relationship which guides the early development of a young scientist. Ramanujan's father existed almost totally outside the family, removed from most of the important decisions regarding his son in a way that was standard for many Indian families at the time. If Ramanujan never talked with his father about mathematics or about the influence of his personal gods in his life (and by age ten they had become one and the same), the mother and son rarely spoke of anything else (Nandy 1980; Ram 1972; Ranganathan 1967). Many biographies dwell on his mother's mathematical ability and profound religious belief, with scarcely any mention of his father's lesser abilities. Curiously enough, however, it was Ramanujan's father who asserted himself when his son's precocity became apparent. Against his wife's wishes, he insisted that his five year old son was sent to school. Yet in general, Ramanujan's isolation was so complete that it cannot be understood primarily in terms of culture or personal ineffectiveness. Instead, we must appreciate the sources of power and deep involvement in the mother. Even by the standards of her time, Ramanujan's mother was an exceptional and strong woman.

The education of Hardy and Ramanujan

Hardy and Ramanujan were alike in gender and formal birth-order, and to a lesser degree in their parents' talents and ambitions. Despite these similarities, the two men and their families were worlds apart, and these differences raise several questions about their education and the originality of their work. It is in the dynamics and relationships within families that the greatest environmental differences exist. Ramanujan's family was the antithesis of Hardy's, and that of any other eminent scientist with whom I am familiar. Did these differences influence the developing gifts and careers of the two boys?

No one ever doubted that both were bright boys, and their talents were recognized by parents and neighbours within their first few years. Hardy spoke early and intelligently, and by the age of two he was reading and writing numbers into the millions. During boring church services, he occupied himself by working out the factors of the hymn numbers (for example hymn 84 must be $2 \times 2 \times 3 \times 7$). He was enrolled in his first formal school when he was three years old, since his parents had by then seen the reliable markers of giftedness—very early adult-like speech, independent reading, and an interest and facility with numbers. When he was eight years old, Hardy wrote his own newspaper filled with editorials, advertisements, and a detailed account of a local cricket match. At the age of ten, he was deeply impressed by the Bayeux Tapestry depicting the Norman conquest of England, and immediately began writing his own detailed history of the events.

The story is very different for Ramanujan. He began school at the age of five only because his father overcame his mother's resistance. At the age of seven he passed his primary school examination with little effort, but he resented the lack of mathematics (not arithmetic) in the curriculum. At age nine, he came first in a competition for academic scholarships and was awarded a half-fee scholarship. But from the next year onwards, he was primarily self-taught because even with a scholarship, his family could not afford schools. This was not taken as a setback, because by now Ramanujan and his mother were supremely confident of 'his mathematics'. Behind this confidence was Ramanujan's absolute religious belief in the worth and legitimacy of his work and its destiny.

It is at the age of ten, therefore, when Hardy and Ramanujan part ways in their development and education (see Appendix A). Hardy continued to progress smoothly. When he was twelve, he received the first public acknowledgement of his mathematical talent by being awarded a scholarship to Winchester, a school renowned for its strength in this subject. Recognition of Ramanujan's exceptional talent also came when he was twelve years old, and teachers, students and friends were by then referring to him as a genius. But the most solid proof came between the ages of twelve and thirteen, when he independently repeated the discoveries of the great mathematician Euler. He was upset to learn that his work was rediscovery and not new. It is interesting that Ramanujan was close to the age at which Pascal and Einstein also made independent discoveries (Albert 1975). This phenomenon is quite rare, and demonstrates one indisputable sign of exceptional giftedness, which is a burst of immediate knowledge described by Morelock (1995) as 'spontaneous knowing' in her studies of children with IQs of more than 200.

In contrast, Hardy's giftedness was in no way exceptional. If we look at his career choice, it was made at an age close to that of many young men and women entering college. His apparent lack of passion for mathematics is in stark contrast to Ramanujan. Hardy took up a scholarship at Trinity College, Cambridge after leaving Winchester. No doubt this scholarship was instrumental in helping to consolidate his interest in mathematics. But its greater significance was that it enabled him to go to Trinity, his clear ambition from the age of 15 when he read a popular book called *A Fellow of*

Trinity. From that time on, Hardy later wrote 'mathematics meant to me primarily a Fellowship at Trinity'. Looking back, Hardy recalled that from then on he only wanted to be a mathematician, but the evidence is weak. In fact, he was nearly twenty years old when he made the decision to become a mathematician, after being stimulated by reading Jordan's *Cours d'analyse de l'Ecole Polytechnique*.

What contributes to eminence?

The early identification and selective influences on giftedness

There are three good reasons for paying close attention to the identification of giftedness. Left on its own, giftedness remains at best a potential until it acquires direction and definition. Like all children, the gifted require specific stimulation and encouragement. There is little evidence of a genetic influence on creativity independent of intelligence or IQ (Plomin 1986). Creativity is nurtured. The importance of accurate early identification is supported by the growing evidence that after age 12 or so, childhood malleability decreases sharply. This is apparent in changes in children's abilities to learn a new language or complex musical skills. What makes identification of giftedness difficult is that high IQ often brings a versatility in ability (Anderson 1992; Ludwig 1995; White 1931). Hardy certainly showed this versatility. Nevertheless, most parents can and often do make reasonable assessments of their children's giftedness (e.g. Laband and Lentz 1985; Monsaas and Englehard 1990). Robinson (1981) showed that the parents of a sample of exceptionally gifted youngsters could give precise straight-forward descriptions of their children's capabilities at age two in reading, adding etc, which were accurate predictors of the children's IQ four or five years later.

However, there are two questions to settle. If parents can identify giftedness, what calls their attention to the child in the first place? And what gives direction to their encouragement? My answer to these questions is the degree of parent–child similarity. We know that similar gifts and talents run in families, so it should be relatively easy for parents to spot early signs. Two other characteristics determine the interests and attention of parents: gender and birth-order. First-born or only sons often receive a disproportionate amount of their parents' attention, encouragement and resources, especially in families of middle and high socio-economic status (e.g. Albert 1994a, b; Cox 1926; Ochse 1990). Together, these factors give added direction to the family's interest, and the lines of family–child attraction are established. So much so that it is fair to conclude that the development of a child's talents reflects its family rather than changes it, imparting continuity between family and personal development:

For the young child, intellectual achievement is largely determined by others (e.g. parents and teachers), and because the child who inherits genes conducive to high intellectual achievement, is also likely to develop within a family that provides effective intellectual stimulation, genetic and experiential effects are passively correlated during the early stages of development. (McGue *et al.* 1993, p. 73)

Figure 6.1 illustrates the changing 'sources' and families' influence in a child's develop-ment. What is fascinating is how the contributions of family environment and heredity go in contrary directions from what many of us have been taught to believe. For all of its early influence, the formative power of family environment declines rapidly from adolescence, while the influence of the individuals' heredity increases from ages 12 to 16. It is interest-ing that the chronologies of the lives of Hardy and Ramanujan diverge at this age.

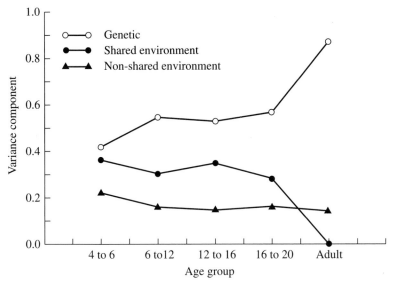

Fig. 6.1 IQ variance component estimates derived from published twin IQ correlations. Estimates are based on the standard assumptions used with the Falconer heritability formula (McGue *et al.* 1993).

Differences between creative and non-creative scientists

In this section, I will diverge briefly from discussing Hardy and Ramanujan to consider the question of why so many aspiring scientists meet the personality and cognitive requirements of their chosen fields, yet only a few establish genuinely creative careers. Professional scientists and mathematicians make up a homogeneous groups of adults, who have not only chosen their careers but have also been 'recruited' into it by parents, teachers, and mentors on the basis of their apparent aptitudes. The fact noted earlier that eminent scientists typically come from professional, semi-professional, or man-agerial backgrounds underscores the importance of family resources and values. None the less, important differences regularly appear between creative and non-creative sci-entists. As a rule, creative scientists and mathematicians make their career decisions earlier than the less creative (Busse and Mansfield 1984). They receive their PhDs an average of three years earlier than the less creative, begin to publish an average of three to six years sooner, and are more prolific for longer periods into their careers (Helson 1971; Helson and Crutchfield 1970).

How can we account for these career differences? It is not simply a question of temperamental fit, although this is certainly relevant to early interests and an orientation towards science. Nor is it a matter of differences in curricular or educational programmes. What matters most is the family and students' on-going intellectual and educational emphases. Table 6.1 summarizes differences that are typically seen between what have been called 'Schoolhouse gifted' in contrast to the 'Creative-productive gifted', and illustrates the characteristics that have been described in the previous paragraphs.

Table 6.2 is an overview of the traits that have been observed by researchers as being

Table 6.1 Dimensions of differences between schoolhouse-gifted and creative-productive gifted people.

Dimension	Schoolhouse gifted	Creative-productive giftedness
Typical age at which studied	Children	Adults
Nature of contributions	Learning what is known	Discovery
Level of achievement	Very good	Profound
Time frame to achieve goal	Minutes to months	Months to years
Role of creativity	Often unnecessary	Necessary
Level of task commitment required	Variable	High
Level of self-concept required	Variable	High

Siegler and Kotovsky 1992

Table 6.2 Traits most often observed by researchers for creative writers,[1] mathematicians,[2] and architects[3].

1. Has high aspiration level for self; is certain 'of the worth and validity of one's creative efforts'.
2. Values own independence and autonomy; is resolute.
3. Is productive; gets things done.
4. Appears to have a high degree of intellectual capacity.
5. Genuinely values intellectual and cognitive matters.
6. Tends to be rebellious and non-conforming; is critical, sceptical, not easily impressed.
7. Thinks and associates to ideas in unusual ways; has unconventional thought processes; is intuitive.
8. Has a wide range of interests.
9. Is an interesting, outstanding person, with 'a measure of egotism'.
10. Does not judge self and others in conventional terms like 'popularity', 'the correct thing to do'.
11. Often 'has a sense of destiny about (themself) as a human being'.
12. Enjoys sensuous experiences (including touch, taste, smell, physical contact).

[1] Barron (1969);   [2] Helson (1971);   [3] MacKinnon (1978)

typical of creative writers, mathematicians, and architects. It indicates that adults who are creative in the real world trust their own interests, judgement, impulses, and intuitions. Along with being intellectually and aesthetically engaged in their ideas, they are less defensive and less self-controlled than others. Taken together, these findings show us important differences. The first is that the fundamental differences between creative and non-creative adolescents or adults are not in their intelligence, but in the deeper and more personal levels of their self-image, and the way in which their experience determines how their aptitudes and interests function. Nevertheless, the relationship between intelligence, educational attainment, and creativity deserves further discussion.

Intelligence, education, and creativity

The intelligence quotient (or IQ) is just one number that represents performance on a variety of sub-tests, yet surprisingly enough this one number predicts a child's educational potential quite well (Brody 1992). However, IQ has much less to tell us about creative potential, particularly when we consider groups of people with high intelligence (Feldman 1984; Hedges and Nowell 1995; Hollingworth 1942; Terman 1947). The fact is that individuals with exceptionally high childhood IQs of 170 or more generally do not differ in their adult academic and social achievement from those whose childhood IQs were around 130. However, high IQ often goes along with talent; according to O'Connor and Hermelin (1981, 1983), better than average talent in art and music is often accompanied by moderately high to very high IQ. This relationship is so pervasive among talented people that Anderson (1992) has concluded that as a general rule 'specific talents are most obvious at high IQs'.

Where is creativity in this mix? At best, it is only indirectly associated with intelligence and education. Creativity has its own defining characteristics and development, and we can see this by considering the three most cited characteristics of creative performance. These are the responses to environmental change, to gaps in one's knowledge and expectations, and to novelty. Creative responses must have relevance (and not be bizarre, off-the-wall, or random efforts), and they must show noticeable novelty, originality, and individuality (Amabile *et al.* 1994; Snow 1994). Certainly Srinivasa Ramanujan's work met these criteria. But the question remains of why so few people produce genuinely creative work.

No one to my mind has improved on the research of Getzels and Jackson (1962) or MacKinnon (1992) on the differences between the homes of highly gifted but not creative people, and their peers who were also highly gifted and considerably more creative. The differences are mainly the result of the parent–child relationship experience. Effective but not especially creative adults have conventional roles and expectations, while creative adults experience conflicting and often distant relationships, sometimes even involving harsh treatment. The gifted but not creative adults in these studies came from what they themselves described as happy homes with affectionate, approving parents and successful fathers. The home lives of the creative individuals were far from happy, with significant emotional overlay, and they were often socially ill-at-ease. Another aspect of the two configurations relates to health. Gifted but uncreative adults and their parents are reported nearly always to have enjoyed good physical and psychological health, with few illnesses or accidents in childhood. On the other hand, creative people have often experienced a series of illnesses in their childhood, sometimes with accompanying periods of loneliness (Albert 1994*b*).

Education and eminence

What are the implications of these arguments for IQ and the achievement of eminence? This question cannot be ignored, if for no other reason than that the relationship between IQ, formal education, and social and career success is perhaps the best empirically established association in social science. Thus American high school graduates have a mean IQ of 111, while those who go on to college average 118. Students who graduate with BA or BSc degree have a mean IQ of 123, while those people who earn a PhD average 132 (Roe 1952; Simonton 1994). Table 6.3 summarizes data on IQ from a number of samples ranging from acknowledged geniuses (Cox 1926) to qualified university scientists. It can be seen that the mean IQ of all professional groups, whether creative or not, is much higher than that of the general population (a mean of 100). Most interestingly however, the average IQ of the 'creative' groups and comparison subjects are almost identical. We do not unfortunately know what level of eminence was achieved by most of the creative individuals included in Table 6.3. Nevertheless, when we look at the IQ of people of known exceptional eminence (as studied by Cox and Roe), we find that they are consistent with their achievements. The mean is 154 for Roe's scientists, and 159 for Cox's sample. Cox derived her IQ estimates from biographical material. The agreement between the measures of IQ she derived and the actual test scores from the samples studied by Roe should increase our confidence in Cox's method. Taken together, these data should convince us that exceptionally high IQ is not superfluous, when it is accompanied by the qualities listed in Table 6.2. G. H. Hardy's observation is pertinent here: 'For any serious purpose, intelligence is a very minor gift'.

How adolescents' experiences influence their careers

A successful and satisfying career depends on an individual's personality, aptitudes and interests working together. An important step in continued career success is making sense of one's experience. When the *Achievement of eminence* project began in 1975, I assumed that exceptionally gifted middle-class boys of well educated parents would have little trouble finding their ways into careers that matched their gifts. The boys' success might not be of the highest level, but rarely would there be failures. At the time, this was the main message both from biographies and systematic research, because one rarely heard about people who fell by the wayside. The truth, as I have since learned, is that if one is to achieve a 'good fitting' career, that career will almost always be the result of personal search, experimentation, and thought. No child, however bright and

Table 6.3 Eminence: IQ × creativeness.

Groups	*n*	Average	Range
Highly creative, clearly eminent			
Total sample[a]	301	159	120–200
Philosophers[a]	22	173	
Scientists[a]	39	164	
Scientists[b]	59	152	121–177
verbal		163	123–164
spatial		137	123–164
mathematical		160	128–194
Some clearly creative, but of unknown levels of eminence			
Architects (most creative)[c]	26	132	120–141
Architects (least creative)[c]	30	128	107–143
Research scientists (most creative)[c]	19	133	121–142
Research scientists (least creative)[c]	18	132	117–143
Male mathematicians (most creative)[c]	18	135	119–151
Male mathematicians (least creative)[c]	15	135	124–142
Female mathematicians (most creative)[c]	7	128	116–140
Female mathematicians (least creative)[c]	20	133	114–144
All creative male and female subjects, combined[c]	70	133	116–151
All comparison male and female subjects, combined[c]	115	131	107–144
Only IQs reported			
University mathematicians[d]	16	130	124–136
University physical scientists[d]	62	129	113–136
University social scientists[d]	10	122	112–132

[a] Cox's geniuses (1926)
[b] Roe's eminent scientists according to type of test (1952, 1970)
[c] MacKinnon and Hall's samples of creative and uncreative gifteds (1973)
[d] Gibson and Light's university scientists (1967)

talented, understands the possibilities that lie ahead, unless he is a Ramanujan or a Mozart, Chatterton, Babe Ruth, or Duke Ellington (Albert 1994*b*).

Early in our research, we noticed configurations of family traits, emphases and patterns of creativity scores that were specific for each of two different samples of gifted 12-year-old boys and their parents (Albert and Runco 1987; Runco and Albert 1987). One sample was labelled math/science with an average SAT-mathematics score of 635 at age 12, a score which is at the 98th percentile in the USA, and far higher than that of many college students. The second sample was labelled exceptionally high IQ, with an average IQ of 158 at age 12. At age 12, the boys had far above average scores on two standard creativity tests as well (Albert 1980). Their personality scores on the California Personality Inventory were nearly identical to those of the 12-year-old budding scientists studied by Parloff and Datta (1965) and Parloff *et al.* (1968). That is where matters stood until the boys were 22 years old. At that point, there appeared a sizeable group (between one quarter and one third) of the boys who had changed so dramatically from their early personality dispositions and education, that they now fitted better with the other sample than with their original one. Accordingly, these young men were labelled 'crossovers', to contrast them with the remaining non-crossovers (Albert and Spangler 1992).

Obviously, even exceptionally high aptitude at age 12 was not a good predictor of an educational career in science or mathematics. Apart from concluding that the early test results were simply wrong, we searched for an explanation by looking at personality scores at age 22 on the *Adjective check list*. The personality differences between math/science crossovers and non-crossovers made psychological sense (Albert and Spangler 1992). The personality profile of the math/science non-crossovers was what we expected of most professional scientists and mathematicians. These young men were not expressive emotionally or socially dominant, nor were they inclined to need or to solicit attention from others. They were quite self-controlled and not of a playful disposition. None of these characteristics were prominent in the crossovers.

We also found important differences in cognitive aptitude, as distinct from IQ and specific scores on mathematical and verbal tests. In another longitudinal study, the *Study of mathematically precocious youth*, eight ability tests were given to 12-year-old boys (Stanley *et al.* 1974). Each boy's scores were converted into standardized scores, which allowed one individual's performance to be compared with others (I am grateful to Dr Stanley for making these data available). We found that the scores of our math/science crossovers on cognitive aptitude tests were generally substantially below the mean levels recorded in the *Study of mathematically precocious youth*. Their average scores were also significantly lower than those of non-crossovers. Taken together, these results imply that cognitive aptitudes and personality were associated with career choice.

We are continuing to study these young men as they grow up. The majority of the math/science non-crossovers have careers related to these disciplines, including basic research, research project management, and computer science. The careers of the crossovers are much more diverse, including the church, medicine, and social work.

Comparison with Hardy and Ramanujan

In the final section of this chapter, I will summarize an analysis in which I attempted to quantify the personality traits of Hardy, Littlewood, and Ramanujan, and compare them with a mathematically gifted group and a sample of world-class social scientists. The purpose of this analysis is twofold. The first goal is to determine if our three great mathematicians (Hardy, Littlewood, and Ramanujan) shared personality traits with each other, even though they were from different cultures. The second aim is to determine if the personalities of young men who at age 12 tested as exceptionally gifted in mathematics and science (the non-crossovers), resembled the three great mathematicians. A contrast was provided by a group of eminent social scientists who I also assessed.

Both the social scientists and the exceptionally gifted math/science non-crossovers were interviewed individually by me. Each interview lasted between one and three hours, and immediately afterwards I completed an *Adjective check list* for that individual. For Hardy. Littlewood, and Ramanujan, I completed the *Adjective check list* on the basis of information provided by biographies and autobiographical writings. This is not a novel procedure, since others have used the *Adjective check list* on people with whom they had no personal contact (Gough and Heilbrun 1983; Historical Figures Assessment Collaborative 1977; MacKinnon 1978; Simonton 1991). The *Adjective check list* itself has been widely used over many decades; it consists of 300 adjectives, all or none of which may be selected to describe an individual. These adjectives are combined into sets which make up 33 personality scales (Gough and Heilbrun 1983).

The results are shown in Table 6.4. These indicate that the 22-year-old mathematically gifted men have very similar personality profiles to Hardy and to Littlewood. All these respondents were low in their need for affection and emotional support (scale 13), a trait supposedly rooted in the 'scientific temperament'. However, the young mathematicians do not match either Hardy nor Littlewood in their sense of personal worth (scale 20). This makes sense, in that the older men were successful and their careers had validated them as eminent scientists. What makes scale 20 especially interesting is that it incorporates three of the items seen in Table 6.2, namely 'Has a wide range of interests', 'Is productive, gets things done', and 'Has a high aspiration level for self'. Two other interesting differences are seen in scales 29 and 32. The 22-year-old mathematicians' scores on scale 29 were average. It is Hardy, Littlewood, and the social scientists who, like so many creative men and women, are low in self-discipline, and in a need to conform. These are the scores of autonomous adults who strive for power, success and tangible accomplishments. The three adult professional mathematicians also had relatively low scores on scale 32. This picks up characteristics such as preference for complexity, asymmetry, and thinking in analogies and metaphors.

Hardy and Littlewood: gifted careers

For the most part, the *Adjective check list* personality profiles for Hardy and Littlewood are alike. One particular rating that may appear curious to readers with knowledge of Hardy's homosexual inclinations and romantic attachments to young men is his average score on scale 8 (heterosexuality). I do not have an explanation for this finding, but it may be a reflection of a lack of sensitivity in this particular scale. The scales (3, 20, 23, 27, 31, and 33) on which there are noticeable differences between the two men make psychological sense. It was Littlewood who was described by others as being the better adjusted, more conventional man. He had a more rounded if less complex personality than Hardy, who was reflective, sensitive, and extremely self-conscious. He appeared to C. P. Snow (1967) to have been 'born with three skins too few'. In contrast, Littlewood was physically adventurous, interested in skiing, hiking, and mountain climbing. A cognitive difference between them is indicated by scale 31,

Table 6.4 Adjective check list[1, 2] comparing Hardy, Littlewood, and Ramanujan with other gifted mathematicians and social scientists (50 is the norm for all scales).

	Math-ematically gifted	Mathematicians Hardy		Littlewood		Ramanujan		Social scientists
Need scales								
1. Achievement: To strive to be outstanding in pursuits of socially recognized significance	48	59		58		58		64
2. Dominance: To seek and maintain a role as leader in groups, or to be influential and controlling in individual relationships	46	54		49		53		53
3. Endurance: To persist in any task undertaken	48	50		62	>	47	<	57
4. Order: To place special emphasis on neatness, organization, and planning in one's activities	49	50		59	>	43	<	57
5. Intraception: To engage in attempts to understand one's own/behaviour or the behaviour of others	53	57		53	>	38	<	54
6. Nurturance: To engage in behaviours that provide material or emotional benefits to others	48	49		48	>	32	<	44
7. Affiliation: To seek and maintain numerous personal friendships	47	47		49	L>	40		45
8. Heterosexuality: To seek the company of and derive emotional satisfaction from interactions with opposite-sex peers	48	49		51		48		48
9. Exhibition: To behave in such a way as to elicit the im-mediate attention of others	49	46		44	<	60	>	52
10. Autonomy: To act independ-ently of others or of social values and expectations	52	51		47	<	72	>	55

11. Aggression: To engage in behaviours that attack or hurt others	49	47	45	<	71	>	54
12. Change: To seek novelty of experience and to avoid routine	50	52	45	<	63	>	51
13. Succorance: To solicit sympathy, affection, or emotional support from others	48	38	35	<	58	>	42
14. Abasement: To express feelings of inferiority through self-criticism, guilt or social impotence	48	44	46	>	37	<	44
15. Deference: To seek and maintain subordinate roles in relationships with others	50	43	48	>	28	<	43

Topical scales
Nine scales assessing attributes, potentialities, and role characteristics

16. Counselling readiness scale: Readiness to accept counselling or professional advice in regard to personal problems, psychological difficulties, and the like	52	49	42	H>	33	<	48
17. Self-control: The extent to which self-control is imposed and valued	49	41	47		39		44
18. Self-confidence: Self-confidence, poise, and self-assurance	47	58	59		57		60
19. Personal adjustment: Good adjustment in the sense of the ability to cope with situational and interpersonal demands, and a feeling of efficacy	49	46	54	L>	43	<	52
20. Ideal self-scale: Strong sense of personal worth, or harmony between what one is and what one wants to be	48	80	56	H>	50	<	67

	Math-ematically gifted	Hardy	Mathematicians Littlewood	Ramanujan	Social scientists
21. Creative personality scale: The desire to do and think differently from the norm, and a talent for originality	54	61	60	66	64
22. Military leadership: Steadiness, self-discipline, and good judgement of the kind required in positions of military (or related) leadership	48	47	56 >	34 <	50
23. Masculine attributes scale: Role-qualities such as ambition, assertiveness, and initiative associated with everyday notions of masculinity	48	48	55	50	55
24. Feminine attributes scale: Role-qualities such as helpfulness, sympathy, and affection associated with everyday notions of femininity	49	39	47 <H	49	46

Transactional analysis scales

25. Critical parent scale: Attitudes of evaluation, severity, and scepticism associated with the concept of a 'critical parent'	50	46	45 <	57	57
26. Nurturing parent scale: Attitudes of support, stability, and acceptance associated with the concept of a 'nurturing parent'	49	54	59 >	33 <	49
27. Adult scale: Attitudes of independence, objectivity, and industriousness associated with the concept of a 'mature adult'	50	51	62 >	40 <	56
28. Free child scale: Attitudes of and playfulness, impulsiveness, self-centredness associated with the concept					

of a 'free or very expressive child'	48	50	55	<	67	>	54
29. Adapted child scale: Attitudes of deference, conformity, and self-discipline associated with the concept of an 'adapted' or very dutiful child	51	42	38	>	55	>	42

Origence–intellectence scales

30. High origence, low intellectence: Feelings and emotion (high origence) valued more highly than detachment and rationality (low intellectence). High scores suggest informality, vitality, and playfulness	49	51	46		50		44
31. High origence, high intellectence: High value placed on both affect (origence) and rationality (intelligence). High scores suggest versatility, unconventionality, and individuality	52	53	38	<	72	>	53
32. Low origence, low intellectence: No particular value placed on either origence or intellectence. High scores suggest contentment, conventionality, and optimism	48	28	43		35		43
33. Low origence, high intellectence: Rationality and analysis (intellectence) valued more highly than feelings and emotion (origence). High scores suggest logicality, industriousness, and cognitive clarity	52	55	72	L>	54		59

[1] Definitions (Gough and Heilbrun (1980)
[2] Only scales being presented
> Hardy and Littlewood scores are significantly higher than Ramanujan's
L> Only Littlewood's or H> only Hardy's score significantly higher than Ramanujan's
< Ramanujan's score significantly higher than Hardy, Littlewood and/or social scientists'
< Social scientists' scores significantly higher than Ramanujan's

32, and 33. Littlewood's interest in mathematics was not restricted to abstract issues, nor were his results achieved through intuition or presented with Hardy's clarity and style. Hardy was strongly motivated by the aesthetic aspects of his work, whereas Littlewood's approach was one of 'power'. Interestingly, it was Littlewood who usually worked out the details of a problem, and Hardy who wrote the final elegant draft. Hardy in fact believed that Littlewood had more mathematical talent than him. Littlewood's approach to life and mathematics was rational, characterized by more clarity and logic than by what Hardy called 'spin'—obvious individuality and subtlety.

We can see the differences between Hardy and Littlewood in their diametrically opposed responses to two situations. The first was the very difficult annual Tripos examination taken by mathematics students at Cambridge University. Success at this examination placed a mathematician in high esteem for the rest of his life, particularly if he was a high scoring 'Wrangler', or even 'Senior Wrangler'. James Maxwell, J. J. Thompson (the discoverer of the electron), and Lord Kelvin had all been senior wranglers, while Bertrand Russell had ranked seventh wrangler in 1897. Hardy detested the examination system and fought throughout his career to have it eliminated, even though he had come fourth after only two years at Trinity. Littlewood agreed that the examinations were useless, but took them without complaint. Their other shared experience was in growing old. It is impossible to imagine Littlewood contemplating, much less attempting, suicide as his health and mathematical powers waned. Hardy on the other hand, did attempt suicide. His masterpiece, *A mathematicians apology* (1969), was both an early warning of his suicide attempt and an explanation for it. Ageing was the gravest insult to him, while Littlewood was less bothered, continuing to publish into his eighties (Bollobás 1986; Kanigel 1991).

Ramanujan: genius

Many of the *Adjective check list* scores for Ramanujan are opposite to those of my other subjects. These differences are mostly in the 'need' scales and in the 'transactional' scales. The easiest way to understand his profile is to see it as that of a creative artist rather than scientist. His most extreme scores show little concern for others, low self-control, low self-criticism, and low conventional thinking, with high needs for autonomy, novelty and attention, and emotional assistance from others. These scores, when combined with his impulsiveness, aggression, and individuality, tell us that Ramanujan was definitely his mother's son. If he resembled anyone besides his mother, it is a Mozart or a Beethoven, a Dylan Thomas, a Chatterton, any number of artists, and a few military men (Napoleon and Patten come to mind). But he is not like Handel, or T. S. Eliot, or Eisenhower. There are other differences between Ramanujan and the two English mathematicians that we should note. They include the magnitude of his achievements, the manner by which he reached them, and their striking individuality. These place him among great artists and near to Einstein as far as mathematics is concerned (Snow 1967).

Conclusions

Building a career is never easy, even for the most gifted, talented, or ambitious person. Smoothing out individual differences, I believe there are three periods in life during which significant age and career transitions occur together. Whether they are the result of (or markers for) genetically timed sensitive periods in maturation and development is not clear. Nevertheless, these transitions and their sequence appear more prominent in the early years of creative than non-creative people. It should not be surprising that these transitions follow an age-based sequence. Much of Western education and social organization is age-graded (Aries 1962), and tracks fundamental changes in cognitive and social competence between ages five and seven, and around puberty (Rogoff *et al.* 1975; White 1970).

The three ages are: The Age of Discovery, the Age of Ascent, and lastly the Age of Consolidation. The Age of Discovery (age 0–14 years) involves, more than anything else, the early signs of giftedness and talent, and their identification. The experiences of Hardy, Littlewood, and Ramanujan were all on schedule. Changes in competencies, career choices and self-image at around age 12–15 regularly appear in the developmental histories of many gifted children and eminent adults. This is a period when intense 'focal' relationships with knowledgeable and undemanding non-family individuals are often formed (Albert 1991). These involved tutors for Hardy and Littlewood, and class-mates and neighbours for Ramanujan. Another equally significant event may take place during a 'crystallizing' experience (Walters and Gardner 1986). This is a powerful, unpredictable moment of self-discovery of individual talent and identity. The essence of a crystallizing experience was caught by the French novelist Stendhal, when he used 'crystallizing' to describe the effect of falling in love. Both Hardy and Ramanujan had crystallizing experiences. Ramanujan's experience was earlier than for Hardy, and it seems to have involved the far rarer experience of 'spontaneous knowing'. Interestingly, it took place around the same age as the experiences reported by Pascal, Gauss, Einstein, and Bertrand Russell.

The Age of Ascent (age 15–20) is the period during which the domain of a child's giftedness or talent clearly appears, along with evidence of its power and final dimensions. The mathematical talents of Hardy and Littlewood became evident during this period, although Ramanujan's genius appeared several years earlier. It is during this period that we see Hardy and Littlewood being deliberately shaped and orientated towards appropriate careers by their parents and schools. The difference between Hardy and Ramanujan in development during this period marked the first unquestionable difference between giftedness and genius. Incontrovertible evidence for Ramanujan's special status emerged when he was twelve with his spontaneous rediscovery of Euler's theories. There is no evidence that any similar event occurred in the lives of Hardy or Littlewood.

The Age of Consolidation (age 20–30) is the period during which budding eminence takes a clear form (perhaps with early publications) and becomes public (Albert 1975;

Raskin 1936; Simonton 1991). Viewed in sequence, the three periods tell us that maturation continues well after childhood, furnishing some of the resources for careers as well as their developmental limits. The age at which dramatic increases in competencies occur is an important marker of maturation and talent. Changes at ages 12–14 years are very specific and important for genius, but less so for giftedness. By the age of 12, Ramanujan appeared to have been an astounding mathematician, while Hardy remained a very gifted child with a variety of interests.

The identification of giftedness and genius

These differences raise the question of whether giftedness and genius have defining moments in their development. For all its individuality, genius is not easy to identify at an early stage, and it seems easy to mistake the early signs of giftedness in mathematics and music for genius.

There is no way of our knowing the IQ of Hardy or Ramanujan. No matter, we will never discover the Ramanujans, Mozarts, Newtons, or Picassos of this world through IQ tests or other psychometrics. The comparison of Ramanujan, Hardy, and Littlewood shows us that giftedness, talent, and creativeness are three separate developmental issues. Because giftedness can be measured, it is more susceptible than genius to the influence and encouragement of others. This means that accurate identification and appropriate education are relevant to its development. What we can or should do for the Ramanujans of this world is far from clear to me. In common with other self-launched geniuses, Ramanujan had an uncanny ability to teach himself from an early age in near isolation from textbooks and teachers.

Gifted people have a wider scope of careers than geniuses. Although there may be one or two careers that are best suited to a gifted person they are rarely the only accessible ones. For a genius, there is only one route, suggesting a wide difference between the malleability of genius and giftedness. Gifted people can be educated for more than one career, whereas there are far fewer careers in which genius can be accommodated. 'Reality' is more limiting for genius, and this poses an educational dilemma. Again, we turn to Hardy for the last word. After years of reflection, Hardy wished to make clear what he knew of Ramanujan's 'profound and invincible originality'. Interestingly, he recognized the risk that formal education held for such an individual:

He would probably have been a greater mathematician if he had been caught and tamed a little in his youth; he would have discovered more that was new, and that, no doubt, of greater importance. On the other hand, he would have been less a Ramanujan, and more of a European professor, and the loss might have been greater than the gain. (Hardy 1979)

Acknowledgement

I wish to express my appreciation to Professor Steptoe for his invitation and the John D. and Catherine T. MacArthur Foundation for support in the preparation of this chapter.

Appendix A: Chronologies

Hardy	Their ages	Ramanujan
1877, born into a very stable, mathematically gifted, 'typical' Victorian semi-professional family		1887, born into a desperately poor, matriarchal, Indian family. His mother was notably gifted mathematically and extremely religious.
The oldest child and only son. Had a younger sister who was to tend to him all his life.		After years of parents' infertility Ramanujan's birth is followed by the deaths of two newborns, making him very 'special' to family. He is oldest child and son, and is family's only child for 10 years before brothers are born.
At age 2, speaking in full sentences, writing numbers. Amuses self in church by factoring numbers. Age 3 in formal school.	2–4	Does not speak until age 4.
	5	Takes examination and is first in whole district. Father overrules mother and enrolls him in local school.
	7	Passes primary school examination.
Writes and publishes his own newspaper in which cricket has a large share of space; cricket remains a lifelong passion.	8–9	Already recognized as mathematically exceptional. Constantly doing 'his' mathematics. Scores first on school exams and wins a half-fee scholarship.
Mesmerized by the Bayeux Tapestry. He begins writing his own history of Norman Conquest.	10–11	
Awarded scholarship to Winchester School: a school noted for its strength in mathematics. He never forgives the school for not placing him on the cricket team.	12–13	Is given *Loney's Trigonometry*. It is his first formal instruction at College level mathematics. His mathematical 'genius' is specifically acknowledged by many of his teachers. At the same age as Pascal and a few other mathematical greats, Ramanujan also demonstrates 'spontaneous knowing' by independently discovering some of Euler's formal theorems derived 150 years earlier. When told of this, Ramanujan was greatly upset.

Hardy	Their ages	Ramanujan
Does well with facility, but little passion.	14	
Inspired to go to Trinity College, and earn a fellowship, after reading a popular novel about it; studying mathematics was secondary, except as his ticket to Trinity.	15	Read Carr's *Synopsis of elementary results in pure and applied mathematics*. This is a 'crystallizing experience'; it electrifies him.
Awarded the Duncan Prize in mathematics by Winchester.	16	Passes entrance examination at University of Madras with first class ranking.
	18	Fails in first year of college, but scores 100 in mathematics. Discontinues study at university.
Enters Trinity College, but it is the study of history that still tempts him; professor raises doubts about it. Hardy stays with mathematics.	19	Resumes studies, falls ill, does not take examinations.
His tutor suggests that Hardy read a relatively obscure book, Jordan's *Cours d'analysis*; now commits self to mathematics.	20	Moves about home region looking for employ ment, fails examination for FA (Highschool diploma) because he refused to devote time to any course not connected to 'his' mathematics.
Placed very high, but not highest marks on Tripos exam; publishes first mathematical paper.	21	
Hardy graduates in 1898.	22	Marries, falls ill again, operated on for kidney troubles.
Passes Part 2 Tripos, highest score. Awarded a fellowship to Trinity.	23	Meets founder of Indian Mathematical Society to whom he shows his notebooks. This mathematician is amazed by them.
Wins prestigious Smith prize. From now to age 34 publishes ten or more. papers yearly.	24	Is given small financial assistance; first publication, Hardy which later calls 'his first substantial paper.'
	25	Given clerkship to get by on.
	26	Writes the first of two letters to Hardy. The letter is dated 16 January 1913, which would make Ramanujan 26 years old, but in the letter he says he is '23 years of age'. Hardy sends a friend to 'learn more' about Ramanujan.

	27	Hardy learns he is exceptional, just as Ramanujan had described himself. Ramanujan receives scholarship from University of Madras. Hardy arranges invitations to Trinity.
	28	Now at Trinity, begins working with Hardy.
	29	Receives Honorary BA degree from University of Cambridge.
Publishes *A course in pure mathematics*; for next 75 years and 10 editions this is the greatest influence on teaching college level mathematics.	30	Becomes seriously ill with tuberculosis. Elected Fellow of Royal Society.
Put up for Royal Society.	31	
	32	Leaves for home, still seriously ill, no signs of recovery. Arrives home, writes last letter to Hardy
	32 1/2	Dies, after which Hardy says 'there is not much to say about the rest of Ramanujan's life'.
Elected Fellow of Royal Society.	33	
Begins lifelong collaboration with Littlewood.	34	
Hardy discovers Ramanujan. Intensive collaborative work with Littlewood and Ramanujan, separately. Hardy publishes his 'first key paper'.	36	
From this time on, Hardy was prime British mathematician. For all his honours and work he never claimed to be a genius, but believed Ramanujan was, and championed wide acceptance of Ramanujan's original mathematics the rest of his (Hardy's) life.	40	

References

Albert, R. S. (1975). Toward a behavioral definition of genius. *American Psychologist*, **30**, 140–51.

—— (1980). Exceptionally gifted boys and their parents, *Gifted Child Quarterly*, **24**, 174–9.

—— (1991). People, processes and developmental paths to eminence. In *Counseling gifted and talented children*, (ed. R. M. Milgram), pp. 75–93. Ablex Publishing Corp., Norwood, NJ.

Albert, R. S. (1994*a*). The achievement of eminence: a longitudinal study of exceptionally gifted boys and their families. In *Beyond Terman: contemporary longitudinal studies of giftedness and talent* (ed. R. F. Substrik and K. D. Arnold), pp. 282–315. Ablex Publishing Corp., Norwood, NJ.

—— (1994*b*). The contribution of early family history to the achievement of eminence. In *Talent development II: Proceedings from the 1993 Henry B. and Jocelyn Wallace National Research Symposium on Talent Development* (ed. N. Colangelo, S. G. Assouline, and D. L. Ambroson), pp. 311–60. Gifted Psychology Press, Scottsdale, AZ.

—— and Runco, M. A. (1987). Possible different personality dispositions of scientists and non-scientists. In *Scientific excellence: origins and assessment* (ed. D. Jackson and J. P. Rushton), pp. 67–97. Sage Publications, Beverly Hills, CA.

—— and Spangler, D. (1992). Giftedness, creative efforts and identity: Their relationships to one another. In *Advances in cognition and educational practice,* Vol. 1 (ed. J. Carlson), pp. 181–205. JAI Press, Inc, Greenwich.

Amabile, T., Phillips, E., and Collins, M. A. (1994). Person and environment in talent development: the case of creativity. In *Talent Development II: Proceedings from the 1993 Henry B. and Jocelyn Wallace National Research Symposium on Talent Development* (ed. N. Colangelo, S. G. Assouline, and D. L. Ambroson), pp. 265–79. Gifted Psychology Press, Scottsdale, AZ.

Anderson, M. (1992). *Intelligence and development: a cognitive theory*. Blackwell, Oxford.

Aries, P. (1962). *Centuries of childhood*. Knopf, New York.

Barron, F. X. (1969). *Creative person and creative process*. Bolt, Rinehart and Winston, New York.

Barton, D. M. (1985). *The history of mathematics: an introduction*. Allyn and Bacon, Inc., Boston.

Bollobás, B. (ed.) (1986). *Littlewood's miscellany*. Cambridge University Press, Cambridge.

Brody, N. (1992). *Intelligence* (2nd edn). Academic Press, New York.

Busse, T. V. and Mansfield, R. S. (1984). Selected personality traits and achievements in male scientists. *Journal of Psychology*, **116**, 117–31.

Cajoni, F. (1980). *A history of mathematics* (3rd edn.). Chelsea Publishing, New York.

Campbell, D. M. and Higgins, S. C. (1984). *Mathematics, people, problems, results*, Vol. 1. Wadsworth, Belmont, CA.

Cole, S., and Cole, J. R. (1967). Scientific output and recognition: a study in the operation of the reward system in science. *American Sociological Review*, **32**, 377–90.

Cox, C. M. (1926). *Genetic studies of genius*, Vol. 2: *the early mental traits of three hundred geniuses* Stanford University Press, Stanford.

Feldman, D. H. (1984). A follow-up study of subjects who scored above 180 IQ in Terman's 'Genetic studies of genius.' *Exceptional Children*, **50** , 518–23.

Garfield, E. (1970). Citation indexing for studying science. *Nature*, **222**, 669–70.

—— (1987). Mapping the world of science: Is citation analysis a legitimate evaluation tool? In *Scientific excellence: origins and assessment* (ed. D. N. Jackson and J. P. Rushton), pp. 18–37. Sage Publications, Newbury Park, CA.

Getzels, J. W., and Jackson, P. W. (1962). *Creativity and intelligence: explorations with gifted students*. Wiley, New York.

Gibson, J. B. (1970). Biological aspects of a high socio-economic group: IQ, education, and social mobility. *Journal of Biosocial Science*, **2**, 1–16.

Gibson, J., and Light, P. (1967). Intelligence among university scientists. *Nature*, Feb. 4, pp. 441–3.

Gough, H. G., and Heilbrun, A. B. (1983). *The adjective check list manual*. Consulting Psychologists Press, Palo Alto, CA.

Hardy, G. H. (1969). *A mathematician's apology*. Cambridge University Press, Cambridge.

—— (1979). *Collected papers of G. H. Hardy, Volume 7*. Clarendon Press, Oxford.

Hedges, L. V., and Nowell, A. (1995). Sex differences in mental test scores, variability and numbers of high-scoring individuals. *Science*, **269**, 41–5.

Helson, R. (1971). Women mathematicians and the creative personality. *Journal of Consulting and Clinical Psychology*, **36**, 210–20.

——and Crutchfield, R. S. (1970). Mathematicians: The creative researcher and the average Ph.D. *Journal of Consulting and Clinical Psychology*, **34**, 250–7.

Historical Figures Assessment Collaborative (1977). Assessing historical figures: The use of observe-based personality descriptions, *Historical Methods Newsletter*, **10**, 66–76.

Hollingworth, L. S. (1942). *Children above 180 IQ*. World Books, Yonkers, NY.

Kanigel, R. (1991). *The man who knew infinity*. Washington Square Press, New York.

Laband, D., and Lentz, B. (1985). *The roots of success*. Praeger Publishers, New York.

Ludwig, A. M. (1995). *The price of greatness: resolving the creativity and madness controversy*. The Guilford Press, New York.

MacKinnon, D. W. (1965). Personality and the realization of reactive potential. *American Psychologist*, **20**, 273–81.

——(1978). *In search of human effectiveness: identifying and developing creativity*. Creative Education Association, Inc, Buffalo, NY.

——(1992). The highly effective individual. In *Genius and eminence* (2nd edn), (ed. R. S. Albert), pp. 179–93. Pergamon Press, Oxford.

——, and Hall, W. B. (1973). Intelligence and creativity. In *Science as a career choice: theoretical and empirical studies* (ed. B. T. Eiduson and L. Beckman), pp. 148–65. Russell Sage Foundation, New York.

McGue, M., Bouchard, T. J., Iacono, W. G., and Lykken, D. T. (1993). Behavioral genetics of cognitive ability: A lifespan perspective. In *Nature, nurture and psychology* (ed. R. Plomin and G. E. McClearn), pp. 59–76. American Psychological Association, Washington DC.

Monsaas, J. A., and Engelhard, G. J. (1990). Home environment and the competitiveness of highly accomplished individuals in four talent fields. *Developmental Psychology*, **26**, 264–8.

Morelock, M. J. (1995). The profoundly gifted child in family context. Unpublished Dissertation: Tufts University.

Nandy, A. (1980). *Alternative sciences: creativity and authenticity in two Indian scientists*. Allied Publishers, New Delhi.

Ochse, R. (1990). *Before the gates of excellence: the determinants of creative genius*. Cambridge University Press, New York.

O'Connor, N. and Hermelin, B. (1981). Intelligence and learning: specific and general handicaps. In *Intelligence and learning*. (ed. M. Friedman, J. P. Das, and N. O'Connor), pp. 51–65. Plenum Press, New York.

——, ——(1983). The role of general and specific talents in information processing. *British Journal of Developmental Psychology*, **4**, 389–403.

Parloff, M. B., and Datta, L. (1965). Personality characteristics of the potentially creative scientist. In *Communications and Community: Science and Psychoanalysis*, Vol. 8 (ed. J. H. Masserman), pp. 91–106.

——, ——, Kleman, M., and Handlon, J. H. (1968). Personality characteristics which differentiate creative male adolescents and adults. *Journal of Personality*, **36**, 528–52.

Plomin, R. (1986). *Development, genetics and psychology*, Erlbaum, Hillsdale, NJ.

Ram, S. (1972). *Srinivasa Ramanujan*. National Book Trust, New Delhi.

Ranganathan, S. R. (1967). *Ramanujan ~ the man and the mathematician*. Asia Publishing House, Bombay.

Raskin, E. A. (1936). Comparison of scientific and literary ability: a biological study of eminent scientists and men of letters of the nineteenth century. *Journal of Abnormal and Social Psychology*, **31**, 20–35.

Robinson, H. B. (1981). The uncommonly bright child. In *The uncommon child* (ed. M. Lewis and L. Rosenblum), pp. 57–81. Plenum Press, New York.

Roe, A. (1952). *The making of a scientist*. Dodd, Mead, New York.

——(1970). A psychologist examines sixty-four eminent scientists. In *Creativity* (ed. P. E. Vernon), pp. 43–51. Penguin Books, Baltimore, MD.

Rogoff, B., Sellers, M. J., Pirrotta, S., Fox, N., and White, S. H. (1975). Age of assignment of roles and responsibilities to children: a cross-childhood study. *Human Development*, **18**, 353–69.

Runco, M. A., and Albert, R. S. (1987). Exceptionally gifted chldren's personality dispositions and their relationship to parental personality and the family environment. Presented at the meeting of *The Society for Research in Child Development*, Baltimore, M.D.

Rushton, J. P., and Endler, N. S. (1979). Assessing impact and quality in psychology: the use of citation counts. *Personality and Social Psychology Bulletin*, **5**, 17–18.

Siegler, R. S., and Kotovsky, K. (1992). Two levels of giftedness: shall ever the twain meet? In *Genius and Eminence*, (2nd edn) (ed. R. S. Albert), pp. 95–108. Pergamon Press, Oxford.

Simonton, D. K. (1991). Career landmarks in science: individual differences and interdisciplinary contrasts. *Developmental Psychology*, **27**, 119–30.

——(1994). *Greatness: who makes history and why*. The Guilford Press, New York.

Snow, C. P. (1967). *Variety of men*. Macmillan, London.

Snow, R. E. (1994). Aptitude development and talent achievement. In *Talent development II. Proceedings from the 1993 Henry B. and Jocelyn Wallace National Research Symposium on Talent Development* (ed. N. Colangelo, S. G. Assouline, and D. L. Ambroson), pp. 101–20. Gifted Psychology Press, Scottsdale, AZ.

Stanley, J. C., Keating, D. P., and Fox, L. H. (ed.) (1974). *Mathematical talent: discovery, description and development*. The Johns Hopkins University Press, Baltimore.

Terman, L. M. (1947). Subjects of IQ 170 or above. *Genetic studies of genius,* Vol. 4, Chap. 21. Stanford University Press, Stanford, CA.

Walters, J., and Gardner, H. (1986). The crystallizing experience: discovering an intellectual gift. In *Conceptions of Giftedness* (ed. R. J. Sternberg and J. E. Davidson), pp. 306–31. Cambridge University Press, Cambridge.

White, R. K. (1931). The versatility of genius. *Journal of Social Psychology*, **2**, 460–89.

White, S. H. (1970). Some general outlines of the matrix of developmental changes between five and seven years. *Bulletin of the Orton Society*, **20**, 41–57.

Zuckerman, H. (1977). *Scientific elite: Nobel Laureates in the United States*. The Free Press, New York.

WOLFGANG AMADEUS MOZART

CHAPTER 7

Mozart: resilience under stress

Andrew Steptoe

MOZART'S character and creativity hold great fascination both for admirers of his music, and for students of the creative process. His extraordinary life as a child prodigy, coupled with the apparently effortless musical outpouring of his adult life, have led to a perception that Mozart possessed a natural or God-given talent. This view emerged soon after his death in 1791, but since then opinions about his life and personality have varied greatly (Stafford 1991). Commentators of the Romantic era portrayed him as a gentle genius unrecognized in his time but composing for posterity, while later writers have regarded him as feckless and immature. Musical historians of the present day tend to emphasize his connections with the rationalism of the Enlightenment epoch, and his disciplined and business-like approach to the task of composition (Robbins Landon 1988; Zaslaw 1989; Steptoe 1990).

My purpose in this chapter is to outline the ways in which an understanding of psychological and social research can illuminate and deepen appreciation of Mozart's life and achievements. I begin by discussing the composer's early life, and the manner in which he epitomizes many of the problems of the nature–nurture debate. His transition from child prodigy to mature adult artist illustrates the pressures that typically confront juvenile successes in other fields. As an adult, Mozart enjoyed periods of great popularity, but at the same time experienced many difficulties, frustrations, and sorrows. His capacity to transcend these problems is a tribute to exceptional resilience. I hope to show how systematic methods of investigation help to identify the key personal and social resources that enabled Mozart to flourish despite the adverse experiences of his adult life. Finally, I will argue that far from being a timeless genius, Mozart seems to have been particularly responsive to the social and cultural fashions of the era, and to have had a creativity closely attuned to the demands of a professional artistic life.[1]

A prodigy of nature

The phrase 'prodigy of nature' was used repeatedly in the public press to describe Mozart when he was seven and eight years old, and with good reason. Wolfgang

[1] I have outlined some of these arguments in a preliminary form in *Mozart's personality and creativity* (Steptoe 1996*a*).

Amadeus Mozart was born in 1756 in Salzburg, then a small independent ecclesiastical principality governed by the Prince-Archbishop, and part of the loose confederation of German States known as the Holy Roman Empire (see Steptoe 1996b, for further details of the composer's life). His father Leopold was a violinist in the employ of the Prince-Archbishop and the Cathedral, while his mother Maria Anna was the daughter of a civil administrator. Mozart had an older sister, known in the family as Nannerl, who was being taught to play the harpsichord and clavichord by Leopold. Just before Wolfgang's fifth birthday, Leopold began to make notes in the margins of Nannerl's work book stating, for example 'This piece was learned by Wolfgangerl on 24th January 1761, three days before his fifth birthday, between 9.00 and 9.30 in the evening' (Deutsch 1966, p. 12). These were the first signs of prodigious development, and within a year the family had travelled to Vienna so that Wolfgang and his sister could perform before the Empress Maria Theresa and the high nobility of Austria and Hungary.

The family embarked on an extensive European tour in June 1763 when Mozart was seven years old. Over the first six months they made a leisurely progression through Germany to Brussels, stopping at courts or large cities such as Frankfurt and Munich so that the children could perform. From Brussels they moved to Paris, where Wolfgang and his sister played for King Louis XV and delighted the court with their childish charm. The young boy had the singular honour of waiting on the Queen at table, talking to her and eating from her plate at dinner. It was in Paris that he completed his first published compositions, a set of six sonatas for piano with violin which were dedicated to one of the Royal Princesses. They left Paris in April 1764 and travelled to London, where within three days they were asked to perform before King George III and Queen Charlotte.

During their time in London, Wolfgang was put through a series of rigorous musical tests by Daines Barrington, an aristocratic lawyer who published an account in the transactions of the Royal Society. His ability to play at sight, to fill in harmonies, and to improvise in styles appropriate to different emotions, was astonishing. Mozart's father Leopold was convinced of the divine origins of his son's talent, stating 'Every day God performs fresh miracles through this child'.[2]

Was Mozart's early talent the result of the educational input provided by his father Leopold? Leopold was a formidable musical pedagogue, and the author of a standard text on violin playing. He devoted his life to nurturing his children's musical skills, and gave them intensive instruction. They led a disciplined life in which music was the central focus, and were required to practise relentlessly. This dedication is neatly illustrated by Leopold's concern about the disruption to their lives that might be produced by moving house in Salzburg:

Every moment I lose is lost forever. And if I ever guessed how precious for youth is time, I realise it now. You know that my children are accustomed to work, but if with the excuse that one thing prevents another they were to accustom themselves to hours of idleness, my whole plan would crumble to pieces. Habit is an iron shirt. (Letter 10/11/1766)

The general issue of the origins of musicality has been vigorously debated over recent

---

[2] Quotations from the letters of Mozart and his family are taken from Anderson (1985).

years. Sloboda and colleagues (1994), for example, have argued that 'although it appears to be the case that musical ability runs in families, inheritance of innate talent is not necessarily a satisfactory explanation'.

However, Leopold Mozart not only nurtured his son's abilities through teaching and support, he also provided his genes. It might equally well be supposed that Wolfgang's prodigious ability arose from an exceptional combination of genes, perhaps through the process of emergenesis described by David Lykken in Chapter 2. Modern behavioural genetics suggests that genes may influence general abilities and specific talents, while at the same time affecting background characteristics such as persistence and capacity for hard work. Genetic factors may even promote exposure to particular sets of environmental stimuli (Plomin 1994). It can be argued that Wolfgang Mozart's willingness to comply with his father's instruction, and his enthusiasm for hard practice, were themselves genetically determined.

There would appear, therefore, to be an inextricable confound between genetic make-up and early environmental stimulation, allowing the champions of both causes to use Mozart as an exemplar. The problem in studying individual cases is that there are seldom good comparisons available; either genetically similar people separated at birth, or individuals exposed to the same environmental stimuli (in this case encouragement, intensive instruction and an atmosphere saturated with music) as the creative person. Such examples could help determine whether the early exposure factors are sufficient.

Nannerl Mozart

Fortunately, in the case of Wolfgang Mozart, there is someone with whom he can be directly compared. Mozart's sister Nannerl was taught in a virtually identical way to her brother. Indeed she had the advantage over him, since she was four and a half years older and so was trained without any competition until she was more than nine years old. Up until this age, Leopold's efforts and ambitions were focused on her. As Albert (1995) and Sulloway (1996) have shown, first born or lone children have inestimable advantages in terms of parental investment. If the environmental stimulation provided by living and training within this musical family was enough, then Nannerl Mozart would also have become a great musician and composer.

The evidence is that Nannerl developed into an impressive performer, but nothing more. The English musicologist Charles Burney knew the Mozarts in London when Nannerl was 14 years old, and described her as a 'neat player'. Friedrich Melchior Grimm, the author of the celebrated *Correspondence Litteraire*, said that she had 'most beautiful and most brilliant execution on the harpsichord' (Deutsch 1966, p. 36). Andreas Lehmann and Anders Ericsson (Chapter 4) have included her among the select group of keyboard prodigies in their analysis of early talent and practice effects.

Yet it appears that good performer as she was, she was not creative musically in the manner of her brother. Was this because Leopold Mozart held her back because it was not considered seemly for a woman to have a musical career? Probably not, because

Leopold was extremely ambitious, and music was one of the few fields in which young women in the eighteenth century were permitted to excel. There are several contemporary examples, such as Maria Theresia von Paradis, a blind Austrian piano virtuoso who played professionally from her teenage years, and toured through Germany, France, and England. Mozart wrote the piano concerto in B flat major (K456) for her, and she also composed concertos and operas that played successfully on the stage (see Steptoe 1986). Regina Strinasacchi was a violin virtuoso who played throughout Italy from her sixteenth year, and had toured the major cities and courts of Europe before she was twenty years old. Nancy Storace, the Anglo-Italian soprano who created the role of Susanna in *The Marriage of Figaro*, was singing leading roles in Italian opera houses by the age of sixteen, while the first Barbarina in *Figaro* (Anna Gottlieb) was only thirteen years old when the opera was produced in 1786.

I suggest the explanation for Nannerl Mozart's lack of progression beyond performance is that she lacked the capacity for creating original music. Leopold was an excellent teacher of playing and drilled her well, just as he did other talented children such as the future concert pianist Heinrich Marchand. Wolfgang Mozart's ability was of a different order altogether, and this was recognized at an early stage. In Paris, Baron Grimm considered the seven-year-old Mozart's technical abilities to be only part of his precocity:

What is really incredible is to see him improvise for an hour on end and in doing so give reign to the inspiration of his genius and to a mass of enchanting ideas, which moreover he knows how to connect with taste and without confusion. (Deutsch 1966, p. 26)

Although Leopold was a composer himself, his works were in the *Kapellmeister*-tradition of small German courts. He produced attractive but generally unremarkable music on demand for the regular cycle of church celebrations and civic events. He composed almost nothing after his son began to write music, even though he lived for over twenty more years.

It is extremely unlikely that Wolfgang Mozart's genius was a simple product of his training. Seldom has there been such a clear case of a creative individual and a close relative living in the same family and undergoing similar dedicated training in a particular domain of activity. There is a strong case for supposing that the differences between the capacities of the two people who emerged were the product of their personal biological endowments. On the other hand, it is indisputable that without the intense nurturance provided by Leopold, Wolfgang's creativity would not have blossomed (for a more critical appraisal of Leopold's role, see Solomon 1995). He not only acquired his musical education from his father, but his entire early life was moulded by Leopold's beliefs and attitudes.

Adolescence and the development of self-esteem

Mozart returned from his spectacular journey across Europe at the end of 1766, shortly before his eleventh birthday. Although the next few years contained notable successes, he also began to experience disappointments in the hitherto effortless development of his career. The first lengthy period of frustration and difficulty arose in Vienna during 1768. The family had travelled from Salzburg so that the talents of the children could be displayed once again in the capital city. After a few months in Vienna, the suggestion was made that Wolfgang should write an Italian comic opera (*opera buffa*) for the Court Theatre, and the result was the three act opera *La Finta Semplice*. Leopold Mozart saw the plan as a way of making his son's transition from youthful performer to member of the adult world of composition and commissioned music. However, Leopold misjudged the situation, assuming that fellow professionals would be only too delighted with competition from a 13-year-old boy. The impresario responsible for the opera was reluctant to commit himself to the project, and production and payment became enmeshed in intrigue. The family lost money and reputation, culminating in a petition of complaint from Leopold to the Emperor that probably did further damage. For the young Mozart to have been encouraged to write an opera, only to have it denigrated and suppressed, must have been an unhappy experience.

More disappointments occurred over the next few years. Both Leopold and his son were convinced that Salzburg was too small and insignificant for their talents, so looked for employment elsewhere. Italy was the focus for European musicians, so father and son made journeys there in 1769, 1771, and 1772. Their hopes were initially centred on Milan, then the capital of the Habsburg province of Lombardy. Wolfgang scored a notable success there with his first Italian *opera seria, Mitridate,* in 1770. In the autumn of the following year, they returned to Milan so that he could compose *Ascanio in Alba* for the wedding celebrations of one of the Habsburg Archdukes. The work was ostensibly commissioned by Empress Maria Theresa, so the Mozarts hoped that it might lead to an Imperial appointment. Indeed, the Archduke Ferdinand suggested that he employ Wolfgang, but unknown to the Mozarts the Empress responded negatively: 'You ask me to take the young Salzburger into your service . . . I do not know why, not believing that you have need of a composer or of useless people' (Deutsch 1966, p. 138). Their final visit to Italy took place a year later, and this time they set their sights on Florence, and the possibility of employment by the ruler of Tuscany, Duke Leopold (the brother of the Emperor). Leopold Mozart even feigned a rheumatic illness so as to lengthen their stay in Italy, but to no avail.

Mozart returned to Salzburg where he spent the next four and a half years in the service of the Prince-Archbishop. Here he became increasingly frustrated by the narrow social circle, the boorishness of the musicians, the parochial musical tastes and the tedium of the demands of the Court and Cathedral. Just as importantly, he was now treated like a subordinate servant-musician, not like in his childhood as an exceptional and talented individual.

These setbacks might have led to a loss of confidence in his destiny, to doubt in his ability, and even to questioning of his father Leopold's plans and strategies. But there is little evidence of any such feelings, for it was during these years that Mozart developed the high level of self-esteem and confidence in his own ability that was to stand him in such good stead in later life. Self-esteem is not the same as conceit, but describes a confidence in abilities, self-acceptance, and perceptions of competence in different areas of life. High levels of self-esteem are valuable when a person experiences emotional losses and other traumas, since they help to prevent the development of feelings of worthlessness and guilt (Brown *et al.* 1990). People with high self-esteem are less likely than others to respond to disappointments with despair and despondency. Wolfgang Mozart's self-esteem was nurtured by the encouragement and praise of his father. Indeed, his father was probably excessively doting, as the distinguished opera composer Johann Hasse noted when he met them in 1771:

Young Mozart is certainly marvellous for his age, and I do love him infinitely. The father, as far as I can see, is equally discontented everywhere . . . He idolises his son a little too much, and thus does all he can to spoil him: But I have such a high opinion of the boy's natural good sense that I hope he will not be spoiled in spite of his father's adulation, but will grow into an honest fellow. (Deutsch 1966, p. 134)

Allied to Mozart's self-esteem was a particular outlook on life that prevented him from becoming discouraged when things did not go his way. Both Mozart and his father tended not to blame themselves for set-backs, but blamed them on other people or external circumstances. This is strikingly illustrated by Leopold's account of the fiasco surrounding the composition of *La Finta Semplice* in 1768. His petition to the Emperor places the responsibility firmly on other people. He recounts in detail the perfidy of the opera management and the impresario, their obstructiveness and lack of good faith; not once does he suggest that he may have been over-ambitious in believing his young son could write an opera, or that professional musicians might be uneasy about a work written by a child with no experience of *opera buffa*, and probably very little command of Italian.

This 'attributional style' became marked in Mozart's adult life, and will be described in more detail later in this chapter. It is an orientation that seems to be so contrary to depression and other dysphoric mood states that efforts have been made to train vulnerable school-children to think this way. The results of these studies suggest that it may indeed help to prevent later depressive problems (Gillham *et al.* 1995).

Transition to adulthood: Mozart's two opportunities

The difficulties that many child prodigies encounter as they grow up have been described by several authors (Horowitz and O'Brien 1985; Radford 1990), and are discussed by Michael Howe in Chapter 5 of this volume. The transition from a childhood dominated by a parent (usually the father) or mentor to independent adult life is fraught with problems. Many child prodigies have combined early creativity and intellectual development with late emotional maturity. The people who have been most successful in maintaining and developing their creative output in adult life have typically been those who realigned their emotional attachments in early adult life, breaking away from the dominant parent, often against fierce opposition. Mozart is an interesting example of this process because we know a good deal about these years of his life, and also because he had two attempts at independence. The first ended in disappointment and disarray, and was followed by several more years of subservience before a successful rite of passage was achieved.

Mannheim and Paris 1777–1778

The first opportunity occurred in 1777 when Mozart was 21 years old. The growing frustration with Salzburg reached a climax early in the year, when Leopold petitioned the Archbishop for leave to travel with his son. The unsympathetic Archbishop Colloredo refused, so a few months later a second request was submitted in Wolfgang Mozart's own name. This piece of sanctimonious self-justification infuriated the Archbishop, who promptly dismissed both father and son. Leopold was distraught and fell ill, and it was eventually agreed that he would be reinstated while his son set out on his travels in the company of his mother.

Their 15-month journey through Germany to Paris was eventful but ultimately unsuccessful. Mozart failed in the main purpose of the tour, which was to secure a permanent post as director of music (*Kapellmeister*) at a Court outside Salzburg. He composed relatively few major works, even though he spent several months in Paris and Mannheim, two of the great musical centres of the era. Instead of making money through performing and composing, the family ended up in debt, and the saddest event of all was the death of Mozart's mother, lonely and far from home. Although the composer could not be held responsible, his father implicitly blamed him for lack of care and attention to his mother. A month after she died, Leopold wrote to Wolfgang saying that 'She was fated to sacrifice herself for her son' (letter 3/8/1778). Two years later he repeated 'If I had been with your mother during her illness, she might still be alive' (letter 30/11/1780).

Mozart's failure on this tour was the result of several factors. He was travelling first and foremost as a keyboard virtuoso (though his skill on the violin was not insignificant), playing his own works and improvising. The hope was that he would impress patrons by his skills, and that they would offer him commissions for new music or a position within their musical establishments. What he failed to realize was that a career of this type required considerable entrepreneurial skills. In an era in which communication was limited, it could not be anticipated that aristocrats and other patrons would even have heard of him in advance, let alone know of his reputation. His passage as a child had been smoothed by Leopold, who collected letters of introduction and established contacts, flattered local musicians and waited on those in authority so as to secure entrées into the highest circles. Mozart knew little of this business and found it difficult. He was not active in seeking work, but waited for it to come to him. Baron Grimm, his early admirer who re-established contact in Paris, identified the problem succinctly:

He is too trusting, too inactive, too easy to catch, too little intent on the means that may lead to fortune. To make an impression here one has to be artful, enterprising, daring. To make his fortune I wish he had but half his talent and twice as much shrewdness, and then I should not worry about him . . . In a country where so many mediocre and even detestable musicians have made immense fortunes, I very much fear that your son will not so much as make ends meet. (Deutsch 1966, p. 177)

A second impediment was that Mozart was not sure of his position socially. As a child he had been admired in the highest social circles, and had access to kings, emperors, and cardinals. His years in Salzburg had been spent as a servant-musician, where he was considered to be lower in the hierarchy than the Archbishops's valet (Steptoe 1990). Now travelling as a young independent artist, he did not know where he stood. This is illustrated most vividly by his experiences in Augsburg, Leopold Mozart's home town in which he still had relatives. When Mozart was in Italy, he had been awarded a knighthood by the Pope, and had been elected into the select company of the Golden Order, receiving a golden cross on a red sash. Leopold suggested that he wore this decoration in Augsburg so as to win honour and respect. But it had the reverse effect. The son of the Governor of the city and other youths mocked him mercilessly, asking how he had got the cross, where they could get one, whether it was really made of gold, and so on. Mozart was mortified and was unable to counter these bullies; as far as we know, he never wore the cross again, and did not use the title *Chevalier*.

Perhaps most importantly of all, Mozart was emotionally inexperienced. This lack of maturity may appear surprising in one who had already composed the 'little' G minor (K183) and A major (K201) symphonies, the five violin concertos and several religious works of great expressive profundity. In Mannheim, he became infatuated with Aloisia Weber, a soprano then aged about 18 and the daughter of a poor music copyist. All his ambitions and Leopold Mozart's carefully laid plans were instantly forgotten. Instead of moving on to Paris, he wanted to take Aloisia to Italy, to write operas for her in Venice, and to make her famous as a prima donna. Although he was already borrowing money, he paid her expenses when they travelled to the country residence of a noble family outside Mannheim.

Perhaps his naïvety is shown most of all by the fact that he conveyed all his enthusiasm to Leopold by letter, assuming that his father would be equally delighted. Not surprisingly, Leopold was horrified:

I have read your letter of the 4th with amazement and horror. I am beginning to answer it today, the 11th, for the whole night long I was unable to sleep and am so exhausted that I can only write quite slowly . . . It depends solely on your good sense and your way of life whether you die as an ordinary musician, utterly forgotten by the world, or as a famous Kapellmeister, of whom posterity will read—whether, captured by some woman, you die bedded on straw in an attic full of starving children, or whether, after a Christian life spent in contentment, honour and renown, you leave this world with your family well provided for and your name respected by all. (letter 12/2/1778)

In the event, Mozart did continue on to Paris, where he spent six months with comparatively little success. On his way back to Salzburg later in the year, he stopped at Munich where Aloisia was employed at the opera. Here he found that his feelings were not reciprocated; Aloisia may have been initially flattered by the enthusiasm of the talented young composer, but felt little more.

Vienna 1781

Fortunately for Mozart and for posterity, a second opportunity to break free presented itself in 1781. He had been commanded to travel to Vienna where Archbishop Colloredo was staying for Lent, so that he could provide entertainment as part of the household. However, he soon found that the Viennese nobility were enthusiastic about his talents as a performer, and he was patronized by leading figures in Enlightenment society circles. He therefore prevaricated when instructed to return to Salzburg at the end of April. In a series of letters to his father, he poured out his dislike of his home town and his employer, painting a rosy picture of the future in Vienna:

I shall say nothing whatever about all the injustice with which the Archbishop has treated me from the very beginning of his reign until now, of the incessant abuse, all the impertinencies . . . which he has uttered to my face, of my undeniable right to leave him . . . I have here the finest and most useful acquaintances in the world. I am liked and respected by the greatest families. All possible honour is shown me and I am paid into the bargain. So why should I pine away in Salzburg . . .? (letter 12/5/1781)

Leopold's replies unfortunately have not survived, but Wolfgang was deeply upset by the lack of support from his father:

I too do not know how to begin this letter, my dearest father, for I have not yet recovered from my astonishment and shall never be able to do so, if you continue to think and to write as you do. I must confess that there is not a single touch in your letter by which I recognise my father! (letter 19/5/1781)

Clearly, Leopold put pressure on his son to return home and maintain his subservient position for the sake of economic security. It is possible that Wolfgang would have succumbed, since despite the praise, he was earning little money. However, his resolution was bolstered by a new development, for in the summer he fell in love with his future wife Constanze. Leopold was predictably infuriated, particularly since Constanze was the younger sister of Aloisia Weber, and thus came from a family that he considered to be feckless and exploitative. Wolfgang tried to present Constanze in a way his father would like, as a thrifty housewife without any physical attractions, but it was no good. Leopold accused Constanze's mother of being a procurer, and thought that she should be put in chains, made to sweep streets, and have the words 'seducer of youth' hung round her neck. But Wolfgang Mozart was firm, asserting his continued affection for his father but resisting his pressure.

Leopold responded by refusing to give his consent to the marriage, and even went so far as to feign lack of interest in his son's activities. In the summer of 1782, the German opera *Die Entführung aus dem Serail* (The Abduction from the Seraglio) was produced in Vienna with considerable success. Mozart proudly sent the score for his father's opinion. He was devastated by the response:

I received today your letter of the 26th, but a cold, indifferent letter, such as I could never have expected in reply to my news of the good reception of my opera. I thought . . . that you would hardly be able to open the parcel for excitement and eagerness to see your son's work, which . . . is making such a sensation in Vienna . . . But you—have not had the time. (letter 31/7/1782)

He married on 4 August 1782 without his father's approval, and in the Webers found a supportive second family who helped him establish and maintain an independent adult existence.

Mozart's last ten years

Mozart spent the last ten years of his life living and working in Vienna. The facts about his experiences over this period are well known (see Steptoe 1996*b*). He was one of the first musicians to live outside the system of regular employment by a court, aristocratic household, or the church. He relied on performing, composition, and teaching for his income, and had none of the security enjoyed by contemporaries like Joseph Haydn, Karl Dittersdorf, and Antonio Salieri. Teaching was most important as a source of revenue over the first two years while he established himself in the city, but he soon became popular as a virtuoso pianist. The business of public concerts was not yet well established, so a great deal of music-making went on in the palaces of the nobility and in the households of civil servants and merchants (Morrow 1989). Mozart played regularly in chamber concerts, but perhaps used his virtuoso skills to greatest effect in his piano concertos. Between 1782 and 1786 he composed fifteen piano concertos, and these established the genre in the classical music repertoire. His first opera for Vienna was *Die Entführung aus dem Serail,* the Singspiel that became one of the mainstays of the German opera repertoire. His opera *Le Nozze de Figaro* (The Marriage of Figaro) of 1786 was one of the most eagerly anticipated works of the era. His material success can be gauged by the fact that in 1784, he and his family moved into a first floor apartment of the Camesina House in central Vienna at a rent of 480 gulden per year. This was more than the entire annual salary he had earned in Salzburg. His income was also bolstered by payments from publishers who actively competed for the opportunity to distribute his works.

However, this high level of popularity did not continue. The circle of potential patrons and audiences in Vienna (which then had a population of about 250 000) was relatively small, so it was difficult to sustain interest in a performer, however talented. Although his orchestral and chamber compositions continued to be played, Mozart's appearances as a virtuoso became more limited. There was some compensation from the high fees paid for works such as *Le Nozze de Figaro* (450 gulden) in 1786, and *Don Giovanni* (675 gulden) in 1787 and 1788. But there are signs that the market for his compositions also shrank, since his works became too complicated and subtle for amateur players and for the short rehearsal times typical at this time (see Lehmann and Ericsson's discussion of this issue in Chapter 4). In April 1787, the family moved from their costly apartment to cheap lodgings in one of the suburbs of Vienna, some distance from the palaces of the nobility on whose patronage Mozart depended. Over the remaining years of his life, he never entirely re-established financial security, and there were periods of acute want during which he had to turn to friends for small loans so as to keep afloat.

The struggles of an independent professional career were coupled with other sources of stress over the Vienna years. It is worth detailing the catalogue of difficulty and personal sorrow he endured, so as to understand why Mozart's mental strength is so striking.

Life events and long-term stressors

Research on life stress and health draws a convenient distinction between acute life events and long-term stressors. Acute events include such incidents as the death of a family member or close friend, the collapse of an important relationship, forced change of residence, or the loss of a job. These occurrences are acute in as much as they can be pinpointed in time, and the immediate trauma can be very severe. Of course, the impact of such events is not always brief, since there are usually long-term ramifications in terms of future relationships and life-style. Chronic stressors or long-term difficulties are ongoing problems of living that may be sustained for months or years. They include living in crowded conditions, looking after a disabled relative, or relentless work pressure. There is ample evidence from the research literature that acute events and long-term stressors increase risk of emotional disorders and various physical illness. Many studies have shown that major life events increase risk of depressive illness, and associations with anxiety disorders and other psychological problems have also been identified (Brown and Harris 1989). Chronic stressors such as looking after a dementing relative increase risk of depression, while also compromising physical health and resistance to infection (Kiecolt-Glaser *et al.* 1994). Jobs characterized as high in psychological demand and low in control appear to promote coronary heart disease in vulnerable individuals (Schnall *et al.* 1994). Unemployment and job insecurity has been liked with a variety of health consequences, including risk of suicide, premature death, and alcohol problems (e.g. Catalano *et al.* 1993). Studies of the types of event that appear to be particularly damaging indicate that 'losses' such as a death within the family or dissolution of key relationships are particularly salient.

To the eyes of a modern investigator of these issues, Mozart experienced an astonishingly high rate of acute events and long-term stressors over his ten years in Vienna. Between 1783 and 1789, four of his children died in infancy, living from between one day and six months. The view is sometimes expressed that in epochs of high infant mortality, people were accustomed to the death of children. However, this is not borne out by contemporary records, and is also belied by the experience of people in the developing world of today, where distress at the death of infants is palpable (Pollock 1983). Mozart also lost several friends and contemporaries through death, including the young cleric August Hatzfeld and the physician Sigmund Barisani. His father Leopold, who had been such a dominant influence, died in 1787, and Wolfgang became alienated from his sister Nannerl. There were acute setbacks in his professional life as well, such as his failure to be appointed piano teacher to the Princess Elizabeth of Würtenberg in 1782, his inability to obtain sufficient interest to publish his string quintets (K406, 515, and 516) by private subscription in 1788, and the conspicuous snub in 1790 when he was not included among the Viennese musicians involved in the wedding celebrations of the heir to the Habsburg crown.

Mozart also endured long-term stressors during this period. They included a series of illness in his wife Constanze. We do not know the precise nature of her problems, but they may have been associated with difficulties in pregnancy. These illnesses were costly, since they consulted the best physicians in Vienna who prescribed cures at the nearby spa of Baden. Her illnesses were also extremely distressing. In the summer of 1789, for example, Mozart wrote to a friend:

My wife was wretchedly ill again yesterday. Today leeches were applied and she is, thank God, somewhat better. I am indeed most unhappy, and am forever hovering between hope and fear! . . . I have been living in such *misery*, that for very grief not only have I not been able to go out, but I could not even write. At the moment she is easier, and if she had not contracted bedsores, which make her condition most wretched, she would be able to sleep. The only fear is that the bone may be affected. She is extraordinarily resigned and awaits recovery or death with true philosophic calm.

Mozart worked at a relentless pace, since his livelihood depended on being able to fulfil commissions and give performances when required. Over the Vienna years he composed more than 130 large scale works, including the piano concertos, six operas, six symphonies, ten string quartets, five quintets, other chamber works, and religious pieces such as the C minor Mass and the Requiem. By way of comparison, even the prolific Joseph Haydn wrote fewer than half this number of substantial pieces over the decade. At the same time, Mozart was giving piano lessons, mounting concerts, and organizing tours. For most of the decade, he lived with his wife and young children (two survived) in cramped conditions.

Yet despite all these burdens, Mozart persisted in his work and did not succumb to despondency. His creative output was also maintained, except for periods when he was ill or was on concert tours. This conclusion about productivity is endorsed by quantitative analyses of compositional output and 'biographical stress' reported by Simonton (1977). After controlling statistically for age, Simonton found no significant associations between stressful life experiences and productivity in a set of ten classical composers that included Mozart.

The apparent lack of impact of external circumstances on his output is illustrated strikingly by the events of 1788. This was a difficult period in Vienna. Emperor Joseph II had just declared war on the Ottoman Empire and a huge army was mobilized and sent to the front line in the Balkans. Many of the male aristocracy were in the army, so private entertainments were curtailed. One of the two main theatres was closed, and concert work was thin on the ground. Mozart and his family were obliged to move to cheap lodgings in the suburbs outside Vienna in the summer. His financial situation was so desperate that he wrote a series of letters to his friend Michael Puchberg begging for small loans. He pawned his goods, and even tried to sell the pawnbroker's tickets for further loans. The situation in Vienna deteriorated, and there were riots when bakers held back sales of cheap bread. In June, Mozart's six-month-old daughter Theresia died. His fortunes were at a very low ebb. Yet this was a period of extraordinarily creative fertility. Between June and September, he completed two piano trios, the delightful B major piano sonata (K545), and the violin sonata (K547). The symphony in E flat (K583) was completed in June, the famous G minor symphony (K550) in July, and the mighty C major 'Jupiter' symphony (K551) in August. Although these symphonies were not written in their entirety during the summer months, the very fact that Mozart was able to finish such complex and imaginative works during a period of intense strain is a mark of unusual resilience (see Wyn Jones 1991).

Mozart's social and personal resources

How can this resilience best be understood? Mozart illustrates most vividly how stress responses are not direct products of the traumas that are experienced. Rather, they are filtered by the social and personal resources that the individual can bring to bear on the situation. This 'transactional' model is well established in the clinical and research literature (Lazarus and Folkman 1984). It suggests that adverse consequences emerge only when resources are insufficient to cope with the experiences people have.

Mozart can almost be seen as a textbook example of the type of individual who had the social and personal resources to withstand the traumas of life. I described earlier how his childhood and stable family background helped promote a high level of self-esteem. His early years were successful not only financially, but in the sense that he was highly valued and nurtured by his family. It is features like family conflict, exclusion through favouritism, and failure of parental support that seem to increase vulnerability, and Mozart did not experience these (Brown *et al.* 1990). In addition, he possessed two characteristics that stood him in particularly good stead when it came to coping with the stresses and strains of his life: strong social ties, and an optimistic outlook.

Social ties and social support

There is considerable evidence that strong social networks and a supportive social circle are protective against emotional and physical health problems (see Cohen and

Syme 1985). This is not to say that all social contacts are good, and indeed difficulties at the interpersonal level can themselves constitute a major source of stress. Rather, research suggests that the help and emotional encouragement that people can mobilize in times of difficulty are very significant in predicting who will withstand traumatic experiences, and who will succumb. There are several facets of social support, ranging from the size and density of people's social networks to whether or not they have a particularly loving relationship with a partner.

One way to understand Mozart's experiences is to look at measures of social support used in present day research on stress and health. For example the Interpersonal Support Evaluation List is a questionnaire measure that clearly distinguishes four basic elements of the support system (Cohen *et al.* 1985). The first is tangible or practical support, assessed by questions about whether the respondent has people they can call on to help them with household chores when they are ill, with an emergency loan, or with looking after their home if they are away. Mozart had ample support of this kind, notably from Constanze's family; her mother came to help when their children were born, and her sister Sophie helped look after the composer himself during his terminal illness. His friend Michael Puchberg helped with small loans, so that even in the worst periods they were never destitute.

The second dimension is support through the provision of advice and information. Do we have people about us to whom we can really talk about difficulties, and who can give us advice about handling problems? All the evidence points to Mozart's wife Constanze as being his confidante in this respect. The longer they were married, the more reliant he became, as is touchingly evident in the letters he wrote to her. Indeed, they had been married for seven years before Mozart went on any journeys without her. But in the spring of 1789 he embarked on a concert tour through north Germany to Berlin. He wrote to her on the first day of the journey, saying 'Every other moment I look at your portrait—and weep partly for joy, partly for sorrow. Look after your health which is so precious to me and farewell, my darling! . . . I kiss you millions of times most tenderly and am ever yours, true till death' (letter 8/4/1789). In addition to his wife, Mozart could also call on an extensive social circle for advice. His membership of the Freemasons brought him into regular contract with distinguished people from many walks of life in an atmosphere of equality and brotherly support.

The third aspect of social support concerns the availability of people with whom to do things. An example from Cohen's questionnaire is 'When I feel lonely, there are several different people with whom I enjoy spending time'. Mozart was gregarious, and had a wide range of friends among the musicians, actors, and minor nobility of Vienna (see Steptoe 1990). Indeed, Feldman (1994) has remarked that Mozart's sociability was quite exceptional in comparison with most of the great creative talents of the modern era. Again, Constanze's extended family was valuable. In October 1791 the composer spent a few days alone in Vienna since Constanze was taking the cure at Baden. He described one day as follows:

This morning I worked so hard at my compositions that I went on until half past one. So I dashed off in great haste to Hofer simply in order not to lunch alone, where I found Mamma too. After lunch I went home at once and composed again until it was time to go to the opera. Leutgeb begged me to take him a second time and so I did. (letter 8/10/1791)

Franz Hofer was married to Constanze's sister Josepha, the soprano who created the role of the Queen of the Night in *The Magic Flute*; Mamma was Constanze's mother, and Joseph Leutgeb was the French horn-player for whom Mozart composed his four concertos. Clearly, this type of 'belonging' support was available to Mozart from many sources.

The last type of social support distinguished in the Interpersonal Support Evaluation List is 'self-esteem support', meaning the extent to which people express confidence in one's abilities and take an interest in one's activities. Despite reverses on the larger scale there is every indication that Mozart's close circle never doubted his ability. Distinguished contemporary composers such as Giovanni Paisiello and Joseph Haydn expressed admiration for Mozart, and recommended him to impresarios. Even his sometime rival Antonio Salieri was full of praise, as Mozart proudly told Constanze after a performance of *The Magic Flute*:

You can hardly imagine how charming they [Salieri and his companion] were and how much they liked not only my music but the libretto and everything. They both said it was an *operoni*, worthy to be performed for the grandest festival and before the greatest monarch, and that they would often go to see it, as they had never seen a more beautiful or delightful show. Salieri listened and watched most attentively and from the overture to the last chorus there was not a single number that did not call forth from him a bravo! or bello! (letter 14/10/1791)

Temperamental strengths

These features in Mozart's family background and his personal social circle might not have been sufficient in themselves, had they not been coupled with a temperament and outlook on life that provided additional strength. In speculating about Mozart's personality, I am conscious of the risks of drawing injudicious conclusions on the basis of selective and possibly biased assessments of the evidence. As for most historical figures, much of the 'evidence' about Mozart is second-hand, filtered by biographers or contemporaries who presented him in a particular light. Very substantial psychological studies have been based on biographical material rather than original evidence, including Cox's (1926) study of the intellect of 300 'geniuses', Cattell's (1963) application of a modern personality inventory to scientists of the past, and the analysis of psychopathology carried out by Post (1994). Although such procedures may be rigorous in themselves, they are constrained by the quality of their sources. There is no such thing as a completely objective biography, and accounts of historical figures can range from hagiography to the destructive. Biographers may not even be aware of the extent to which their own social, cultural, and psychological prejudices influence their treatment of the material (see Chapter 11 for further discussion of this issue). In Mozart's case, there have been many glosses on his personality, including Peter Davies's argument that he had depressive tendencies and a cyclothymic personality disorder (Davies 1987, 1989).

My own view is quite different, since my impression is that Mozart was rather robust temperamentally, and responded to the trials and tribulations of his life with remarkable equanimity. However, the question is whether one can get beyond trading viewpoints based on different interpretations of the same limited set of historical materials. It is my contention that progress is possible through the use of systematic analyses of Mozart's own writings. A method has been developed over recent years that holds considerable promise for investigations of this kind.

Mozart's reactions to events and 'explanatory style'

We all react to potentially distressing experiences in different ways, and some people are much more likely to become upset or even depressed by disappointments than others. One important factor influencing our reactions is how we account mentally for negative events. Over recent years, evidence has accumulated which suggests that a particular type of 'explanatory style' is characteristic of people who are prone to depression, while other explanatory styles are found in people with more optimistic outlooks (Peterson *et al.* 1993).

When something bad happens in our lives, most of us ask the question—why? We look for explanations of the causes of events in order to make the world more comprehensible. These causal explanations vary considerably, depending on the nature of the event and our personality predispositions (for example 'It is my fault that my children's teeth have cavities', 'It was just fate that I had that car crash'). There appear to be three important dimensions to these explanations. The first is whether the cause is construed as being internal, due to our own characteristics and behaviour, or external and due to other people and factors. How, for example, does one account for failure in an examination. An internal explanation would be 'I failed the exam because I did not study hard enough', while an external explanation is 'I failed the exam because I was not taught the right material'. The second dimension is whether one perceives the causes of bad events to be stable over time, or unstable. In the examination case, a stable explanation would be to attribute failure to an enduring characteristic such as one's stupidity or to prejudice against one's gender or race, while an unstable explanation would be a statement such as 'I failed because I felt ill during the exam'. The third dimension is whether the cause of the event is perceived as global, influencing a variety of situations, or specific to the particular incident in question. One individual might believe failure in an examination was a reflection on general intellectual ability, while another might conclude that he or she was simply not very good at the subject being tested. Whether or not these explanations are true is less important than how they account for our experiences.

There is now considerable evidence that depressed people tend to make attributions that are internal, stable, and global. That is, they regard bad events as being their own fault, and to be the result of enduring and general limitations or deficits. This type of explanation leads to a state of helplessness, and has been associated with other poor outcomes as well as depression, such as weak academic performance and lack of business productivity (Seligman and Schulman 1986; Petersen and Barratt 1987). The reason for this is that internal, stable, and global explanations attribute disappointments to enduring and unchangeable features of the individual, so do not lead to hope for the future. The opposite type of explanation is characteristic of optimists, who see the causes of bad events as being external, unstable, and specific.

This approach to understanding how people cope with bad events is relevant to Mozart, in that explanatory style can be assessed through content analysis of written material.

Analysing Mozart's explanatory style

Content analysis of written records has been used by many investigators for different purposes, and there are several examples in other chapters of this book. One problem about analyses of this kind for throwing light on temperament and personality is that much written material is intended for public consumption. It may therefore be a reflection of how the person wished to be seen rather than how they actually were. Mozart, for example, might have presented himself as cheerful when he was actually sad, so statements about his mood cannot be used as reliable indicators of mental state. In his surviving correspondence, there are occasions on which he clearly misled the recipient for particular purposes, as when he described his future wife Constanze to his father in mundane and muted terms:

She has no wit, but she has enough common sense to enable her to fulfil her duties as a wife and mother . . . She is accustomed to be shabbily dressed . . . She understands housekeeping and has the kindest heart in the world . . . Tell whether I could wish myself a better wife? (letter 15/12/1781)

This problem is overcome to some extent by the method known as Content Analysis of Verbatim Explanations, since the technique does not depend on overt expressions of mood. Rather, it analyses more automatic, sometimes unconscious processes that are less susceptible to biases arising from the desire to make a positive impression on the reader.

The technique involves extracting explanations of events from the written records, then rating these explanations on the three dimensions of internal/external, stable/unstable, and global/specific (Schulman *et al.* 1989). Each dimension is rated on a 7-point scale, ordered in such a way that low scores reflect greater optimism and high scores a depression-prone explanatory style. The three ratings are then summed, so that composite scores can range from 3 (highly optimistic) to 21 (highly pessimistic or depression-prone). To give an idea of scores that might be anticipated, composite scores averaging 10.3 (standard deviation 1.4) have been reported from American undergraduates (Schulman *et al.* 1989), while an average of 10.6 (standard deviation 1.3) was found in a sample of adults from the general population (Peterson *et al.* 1985).

An analysis of Mozart's explanatory style was carried out by the author in conjunction with Martin Seligman and Karen Reivich from University of Pennsylvania. The events and explanations were extracted from the 293 surviving letters and notes written by Mozart between September 1777 and his death in 1791. The standard English translation of the correspondence was used (Anderson 1985). Eighteen event-explanation units proved to be suitable for analysis. So as to reduce the possibility of bias, the identification of events and explanations was carried out in London, and all reference to Mozart was deleted. Ratings were then performed in Philadelphia by two independent raters who did not know that Mozart was the subject, and were not familiar with Mozart's life anyway. The scores of the independent raters showed good agreement ($r = 0.85$, $p < 0.001$), so averages were used.

The mean composite rating for Mozart's explanatory style was 9.67 with a standard deviation of 4.2. This is slightly more optimistic than results typically obtained from present day population samples. What is particularly interesting was the change in explanatory style score between Mozart's earlier years (1777–1781) and the last ten years in Vienna (1782–1791). The mean composite rating for events that took place in the earlier period was 11.1 (standard deviation 3.9), but this fell dramatically to an average of 7.88 (standard deviation 3.8) in the later years. In other words, Mozart's outlook on life as assessed with this method became substantially more optimistic in his later years.

The results of this content analysis suggests that in general, the composer had an optimistic way of thinking and that this may have helped to bolster his resistance to adverse events. His explanations for the causes of disappointments rarely display the characteristics of a person prone to depression. An example of this way of accounting for experiences comes from July 1782, when *Die Entführung aus dem Serail* was being performed in Vienna for the first time. The second performance of this opera was greeted with a great deal of displeasure from the audience and did not go down well. But instead of inferring that there was something wrong with the opera and that his composition needed revision, Mozart attributed the failure to organized opposition and to (temporary) errors on the part of the singers:

Can you really believe it, but yesterday there was an even stronger cabal against it than on the first evening! The whole first act was accompanied by hissing. But indeed they could not prevent the large shouts of 'Bravo' during the arias. I was relying on the closing trio, but, as ill-luck would have it, Fischer [Osmin in the opera] went wrong, which made Dauer [Pedrillo] go wrong too; and Adamberger [Belmonte] alone could not sustain the trio, with the result that the whole effect was lost and that this time it was not repeated. (letter 20/7/1782)

Another instance concerns the reception of the Paris symphony (K297/300*a*) at its première on 18 June 1778. Mozart had been particularly nervous about the reception of this symphony, and had written various features into it that he thought would appeal to the Parisian audience. However, after the first performance, he was asked by the impresario Joseph Legros to replace the central *andante*. For a young composer to be told that a movement of a recently composed major work was unsatisfactory and needed to be replaced might have seriously threatened his confidence. A person prone to depression might have believed that the criticism was correct, that his work was indeed inadequate, and that this only served to confirm what most people probably thought about his compositions in general. Mozart's response was quite different. He explained the impresario's opinion as being due to the fact 'The audience forgot to clap their hands and to shout as much as they did at the end of the first and last movements'. He therefore regarded the criticism as being due to an external, specific, and temporary state of affairs.

Of course, he was not always optimistic in his explanations of events, and there are some instances when he displayed the internal, stable, and global features characteristic of depression. However, they are outweighed by the dominant pattern of optimism and refusal to blame himself for failures. The increased optimism of Mozart's Vienna years might appear curious in the light of the problems he encountered in the last decade of his life. It was probably stimulated by two factors. The first is his involvement with Freemasonry. He enrolled in 1784, and remained an active participant for the rest of his life, regularly attending Lodge meetings and ceremonies, and writing several Masonic pieces. Freemasonry encouraged a tolerant, benign, and hopeful view of human life and progress, and Mozart's ability to cope was bolstered by this system of belief. A second factor underlying the optimism of these later years is that in his creative maturity, Mozart's confidence was strengthened through the confirmation of his own abilities. Indeed, it is difficult to imagine how anyone who managed to complete three great symphonies within the space of one difficult summer, or two operas of the calibre of *The Magic Flute* and *La Clemenza di Tito* within the space of five months, would not feel great exhilaration and self-confidence in his creative capacity.

Composition: motivation and creativity

The imaginative versatility of Mozart's music over his later years was extraordinary. Most of his original manuscripts have very few corrections, and have an uncluttered appearance that suggests he had worked out most of his ideas before consigning them to paper. There is more than one documented occasion on which he did not even write out the music fully before playing it, as with the piano part of the sonata for violin and piano (K379). The impression that writing the music was a late stage in the process was confirmed years later by Constanze. She recalled how her husband wandered around in a preoccupied fashion while thinking about his music. Then when he sat down to put pen to paper, he would ask her to keep him company and to chat to him about the latest news while he got on with his work. However, Mozart was not simply the mechanical instrument of some divine power, writing down music to order. Numerous sketches and manuscript fragments survive that attest to the difficulties he encountered in working out some pieces. Several fragments were abandoned after he had progressed some way with them. Others were set aside, only to be taken up months or years later to be reworked and completed (Tyson 1987).

His general approach was to write the main thematic line and possibly the bass first of all, then to fill in the inner voices, finishing off with supplementary parts or additional instrumentation. Sloboda (1985) has described the method as creating 'A structured and sectionalised representation which identified crucial parts within a superordinate plan. The first writing allowed Mozart to fix the crucial individuating elements of the composition on paper. These elements would allow the reconstruction of the rest even if the overall plan was lost from memory. For Mozart, writing out was not so much dictation as the negotiation, in a planned way, of a highly structured internal representation' (p. 114).

How was Mozart motivated to engage in this taxing and onerous work with such consistency over his adult life? Psychologists studying motivation for creative activities have highlighted the role of extrinsic versus intrinsic factors. Intrinsic motivation derives from a sense of inner satisfaction and enjoyment in the activity itself, while extrinsic factors include social and cultural rewards such as money, fame, and recognition. Experimental studies suggest that creativity is more strongly stimulated by intrinsic than extrinsic factors. Amabile (1983, 1985) has articulated this conclusion most clearly by stating that 'an intrinsically motivated state is conducive to creativity, whereas an extrinsically motivated state is detrimental'. It might be argued that many successful creators are stimulated both by intrinsic and extrinsic factors, but the experimental literature suggests that 'people who engage in an intrinsically interesting activity in the presence of salient extrinsic constraints will show less subsequent interest in that activity than people who do not work under such constraints' (Amabile 1985).

Authorities on this field of psychological research have cautioned against generalities from short-term studies with volunteers in laboratory settings to the exceptionally creative (Simonton 1994; Eysenck 1995; Eisenberger and Cameron 1996). This is certainly wise counsel as far as Mozart is concerned for his entire creative output was strongly influenced and driven by extrinsic factors. Mozart did not wait until inspiration struck, but worked to produce music as required by commissions or the needs of particular occasions. He was raised in the tradition of composers in the service of the Church or a court, writing music as and when it was required for solemn occasions or for recreation. Throughout his life, the type of music he wrote was determined by outside forces. While he was in Salzburg, he composed a great deal of ecclesiastical music, including numerous masses, litanies, and other pieces. Over his last ten years in Vienna he wrote very little religious music, since he was not employed by the church and elaborate church services were discouraged. When he was enjoying his greatest success in Vienna as a piano soloist (1782–1786), he composed 15 concertos, mainly for his own use. The genre then lost its popularity, and in the remaining five years of his life he composed only two more piano concertos. He composed different types of chamber music (piano trios, string quartets, sonatas) at different stages depending on the popularity of the form and the demands of publishers. For many people, Mozart's operas represent the pinnacle of his achievement, and he himself was devoted to writing for the stage. Yet he never embarked seriously on such work without a commission. Musicologists have concluded that there were virtually no occasions on which Mozart wrote any music that was not explicitly intended for a particular performance or to fulfil a commission (Zaslaw 1994).

It was not only in the type of music he wrote that Mozart was extrinsically motivated. The form of his works was also strongly influenced by the requirements of the occasion. For instance in 1789 he was commissioned by King Frederick William of Prussia to compose a set of string quartets. The King was an amateur cellist, and the quartets were written (with some difficulty) so as to give prominence to this instrument. The most extensive evidence for Mozart tailoring his music to the performer has come from studies of the operas (Steptoe 1988). Opera singers (then as now) were all powerful in the theatre, since the success of any company depended on the ability of its star singers to attract audiences. Singers expected music to be written for them that displayed their vocal prowess to best advantage. If they specialized in vocal leaps, these had to be included. If they were skilled at fast passage work, this was needed, and the overall range of the piece certainly had to suit them. Mozart was as compliant as any other composer of the era, and carefully studied each singer to make sure his music was appropriate. This flexibility was overtly articulated in 1778, when he wrote an aria for a distinguished tenor, Anton Raaff:

I asked him to tell me candidly if he did not like it or if it did not suit his voice, adding that I would alter it if he wished or even compose another . . . I made it a little long on purpose, for it is always easy to cut down, but not so easy to lengthen. (letter 28/2/1778)

The only time in his life when there are clear signs that he was adversely affected by extrinsic incentives was in 1790. He was commissioned to write music for a clockwork organ that would accompany a memorial tableau to a recently deceased military commander. This was displayed in a waxworks or museum of curiosities, and he accepted the work since he was in a poor financial state. He was clearly uninspired by the instrument and the situation:

As it is a kind of composition which I detest, I have unfortunately not been able to finish it. I compose a bit of it every day—but I have to break off now and then, as I get bored . . . If it were for a large instrument and the work would sound like an organ piece, then I might get some fun out of it. But, as it is, the works consist solely of little pipes, which sound too high-pitched and too childish for my taste. (letter 3/10/1790)

However, this was an unusual situation in that Mozart was being asked to write for a machine that he did not really regard as a musical instrument at all. The overwhelming impression is that Mozart was able to sustain a high level of creativity despite external demands and constraints; he could not afford the luxury of waiting for the right mood or peace and quiet before he composed. Contemporary psychological theory is beginning to reconcile the apparently deleterious effects of intrinsic motives with the evidence that industriousness is reinforced by rewards (Eisenberger 1992; Eisenberger and Selbst 1994).

Conclusions

This portrait of Mozart as a hard working, practical music maker might appear strange to readers familiar with the rude facetious genius of Shaffer's play *Amadeus*. What about his scatological letters, eccentric behaviour, and fecklessness? I would argue that although there is evidence for these features, they were not central to his character, but have subsequently been magnified by commentators struggling to comprehend Mozart's extraordinary achievements.

The view that Mozart led a bohemian existence, living for pleasure without thought for the future, is the creation of the late nineteenth and early twentieth centuries. It simply does not square with the information that is now available on his way of life and earnings (Steptoe 1996a, b). Earlier biographers underestimated the risks associated with working as an independent musician, and were poorly informed about the prevailing political and economic circumstances, so took the fluctuations in Mozart's fortunes to be signs of imprudence. His reputation for vulgarity comes in part from the set of letters that he wrote to his cousin Maria Anna Thekla Mozart, which are full of scatological word play and sexual innuendo. These letters date from his adolescence and mark a transitional phase. His family unashamedly used language of a strikingly vulgar type in their letters; even his mother signed off one letter to Leopold Mozart with 'I wish you good night, my dear, but first shit in your bed and make it burst'.

Mozart was also accused of vulgarity by a small number of acquaintances who later set down their reminiscences, notably the novelist and literary hostess Karoline Pichler:

Mozart and Haydn, whom I knew well, were men in whose personal intercourse there was absolutely no other sign of unusual power of intellect and almost no trace of intellectual culture, nor of any scholarly or other higher interests. A rather ordinary turn of mind, silly jokes and, in the case of the former, an irresponsible way of life, were all that distinguished them in society. (Deutsch 1966, p. 557)

Pichler was a member of the wealthy urban intelligentsia, and one senses a touch of social snobbery in her remarks, coupled with resentment that these low born individuals were endowed with exceptional abilities. Moreover, she wrote from the perspective of nineteenth century Romanticism, which liked its creative geniuses to be impressive and penetrating outside their field of expertise, and preferably of a turbulent disposition. The sanguine temperament and unexceptional approach to their creative task of composers like Mozart was difficult to accommodate, so a mythology was created. The combination of historical investigation coupled with the judicious use of systematic psychological studies can help to unearth a more probable profile.

References

Albert, R. S. (1995). The contribution of early family history to the achievement of eminence. In *Talent development* (ed. N. Colangelo and S. G. Assouline), pp. 311–60. Gifted Psychology Press, Scottsdale, AZ.

Amabile, T. M. (1983). *The social psychology of creativity*. Springer-Verlag, New York.

——(1985). Motivation and creativity: effects of motivation orientation on creative writers. *Journal of Personality and Social Psychology*, **52**, 1161–73.

Anderson, E. (1985). *The letters of Mozart and his family* (3rd edn). Prepared by S. Sadie and B. Smart. Macmillan, London.

Brown, G. W., and Harris, T. (1989). *Life events and illness*. Unwin, London.

——, Bifulco, A., Veiel, H. O. F., and Andrews, B. (1990). Self-esteem and depression. II. Social correlates of self-esteem. *Social Psychiatry and Psychiatric Epidemiology*, **25**, 225–34.

Catalano, R., Dooley, D., Wilson, G., and Hough, R. (1993). Job loss and alcohol abuse: a test using data from the Epidemiologic Catchment Area Project. *Journal of Health and Social Behavior*, **34**, 215–25.

Cattell, R. B. (1963). The personality and motivation of the researcher from measurements of contemporaries and from biography. In *Scientific creativity* (ed. by C. W. Taylor and F. Barron), pp. 119–31. John Wiley, New York.

Cohen, S., and Syme, S. L. (1985). *Social support and health*. Academic Press, New York.

——, Mermelstein, R., Kamarck, T., and Hoberman, H. M. (1985). Measuring the functional components of social support. In *Social support: theory, research and applications* (ed. I. G. Sarason and B. R. Sarason), pp. 73–94. Martinus Nijhoff, Dordrecht.

Cox, M. (1926). *The early mental traits of three hundred geniuses*. Stanford University Press, Palo Alto, CA.

Davies, P. (1987). Mozart's manic-depressive tendencies. *The Musical Times*, **128**, 123–6, 191–6.

——(1989). *Mozart in person: his character and health*. Greenwood, New York.

Deutsch, O. E. (1966). *Mozart: a documentary biography*, trans. E. Blom, P. Branscombe, and J. Noble. A & C Black, London.

Eisenberger, R. (1992). Learned industriousness. *Psychological Review*, **99**, 248–67.

——and Selbst, M. (1994). Does reward increase or decrease creativity? *Journal of Personality and Social Psychology*, **66**, 1116–27.

——and Cameron, J. (1996). Detrimental effects of reward—reality or myth. *American Psychologist*, **51**, 1153–66.

Eysenck , H. J. (1995). *Genius*. Cambridge University Press, Cambridge.

Feldman, D. H. (1994). Mozart and the transformational imperative. In *On Mozart* (ed. J. M. Morris), pp. 52–71. Cambridge University Press, Cambridge.

Gillham, J. E., Reivich, K. J., Jaycox, L. H., and Seligman, M. E. P. (1995). Prevention of depressive symptoms in schoolchildren: two-year follow-up. *Psychological Science*, **6**, 343–51.

Horowitz, F. D. and O'Brien, M. (1985). *The gifted and talented: a developmental perspective*. American Psychological Association, Washington, DC.

Kiecolt-Glaser, J. K., Malarkey, W. B., Cacioppo, J. T., and Glaser, R. (1994). Stressful personal relationships: immune and endocrine function. In *Handbook of human stress and immunity* (ed. R. Glaser and J. Kiecolt-Glaser), pp. 321–39. Academic Press, San Diego.

Lazarus, R. S., and Folkman, S. (1984). *Stress, appraisal and coping*. Springer-Verlag, New York.

Morrow, M. S. (1989). *Concert life in Haydn's Vienna*. Pendragon Press, Stuyvesant, NY.

Peterson, C., and Barratt, L. C. (1987). Explanatory style and academic performance among university freshmen. *Journal of Personality and Social Psychology*, **53**, 603–7.

——, Bettes, B. A., and Seligman, M. E. P. (1985). Depressive symptoms and unprompted causal attributions: content analysis. *Behaviour Research and Therapy*, **23**, 379–82.

——, Maier, S. F., and Seligman, M. E. P. (1993). *Learned helplessness: a theory for the age of personal control*. Oxford University Press, New York.

Plomin, R. (1994). *Genetics and experience*. Sage Publications, London.

Pollock, L. (1983). *Forgotten children: parent-child relations from 1500–1800*. Cambridge University Press, Cambridge.

Post, F. (1994). Creativity and psychopathology: a study of 291 world-famous men. *British Journal of Psychiatry*, **165**, 22–34.

Radford, J. (1990). *Child prodigies and exceptional early achievers*. Harvester-Wheatsheaf, New York.

Robbins Landon, H. C. (1988). *1791, Mozart's last year*. Thames and Hudson, London.

Schnall, P. L., Landsbergis, P. A., and Baker, D. (1994). Job strain and cardiovascular disease. *Annual Review of Public Health*, **15**, 381–411.

Schulman, P., Castellan, C., and Seligman, M. E. P. (1989). Assessing explanatory style: the content analysis of verbatim explanations and the Attributional Style Questionnaire. *Behaviour Research and Therapy*, **27**, 505–12.

Seligman, M. E. P., and Schulman, P. (1986). Explanatory style as a predictor of productivity and quitting among life insurance sales agents. *Journal of Personality and Social Psychology*, **50**, 832–8.

Simonton, D. (1977). Creative productivity, age and stress: a biographical time-series analysis of 10 classical composers. *Journal of Personality and Social Psychology*, **35**, 791–804.

Simonton, D. (1994). *Greatness: who makes history and why*. Guilford Press, New York.

Sloboda, J. (1985). *The musical mind: the cognitive psychology of music*. Oxford University Press, Oxford.

——, Davidson, J. W., and Howe, M. J. A. (1994). Is everyone musical? *The Psychologist*, **7**, 349–54.

Solomon, M. (1995). *Mozart*. Hutchinson, London.

Stafford, W. (1991). *Mozart's death*. Macmillan, London.

Steptoe, A. (1984). Mozart and poverty: a re-examination of the evidence. *The Musical Times*, **125**, 196–201.

—— (1986). Mozart, Mesmer and *Così fan tutte*. *Music and Letters*, **67**, 248–55.

—— (1988). *The Mozart-Da Ponte Operas*. Oxford University Press, Oxford.

—— (1990). Mozart as an individual. In *The Mozart compendium* (ed. H. C. Robbins Landon), pp. 102–31. Thames and Hudson, London.

—— (1996a). Mozart's personality and creativity. In *Wolfgang Amadè Mozart: essays on his life and music* (ed. S. Sadie), pp. 21–34. Oxford University Press, Oxford.

—— (1996b). *Mozart, Everyman-EMI music companion*. Everyman Library, London.

Sulloway, F. J. (1996). *Born to rebel: birth order, family dynamics, and creative lives*. Pantheon Books, New York.

Tyson, A. (1987). *Mozart: studies of the autograph scores*. Harvard University Press, Cambridge, Mass.

Wyn Jones, D. (1991). Why did Mozart compose his last three symphonies? Some new hypotheses. *The Music Review*, **52**, 280–9.

Zaslaw, N. (1989). *Mozart's symphonies: context, performance practice, reception*. Oxford University Press, Oxford.

—— (1994). Mozart as a working stiff. In *On Mozart* (ed. J. M. Morris), pp. 102–12. Cambridge University Press, Cambridge.

WILLIAM SHAKESPEARE

CHAPTER 8

The creative genius of William Shakespeare: historiometric analyses of his plays and sonnets

Dean Keith Simonton, Kathleen A. Taylor, and Vincent J. Cassandro

ANY home in the English-speaking world that features a library will almost certainly contain a volume entitled *The complete works of William Shakespeare*. Indeed, only the Bible is more likely to rank as the most widely distributed English-language book. Nor should this prominence surprise us. Shakespeare is often called the greatest creative writer in English literature, and sometimes enthusiasts will make the (decidedly ethnocentric) claim that he is the greatest literary genius who ever lived. Something of Shakespeare's exalted standing is reflected in Hart's (1987) popular book *The 100: a ranking of the most influential persons in history*. There we see Shakespeare ranked as 36, placing him almost in the top third of this elite group. Admittedly, this placement may seem a bit low to a genuine aficionado of the Bard, but we must recognize that he is *the* highest placed literary personality on Hart's list. Those above him are political leaders like Constantine the Great, military figures such as Genghis Khan, religious leaders like Buddha, scientists like Albert Einstein, or explorers such as Christopher Columbus. Indeed, only one other purely literary figure even made the list, namely Homer, who ranked 94. All other literary creators in the top 100 are more notable for their contributions to philosophy, such as Jean-Jacques Rousseau (number 71), Francis Bacon (number 78), and Voltaire (number 79). It is also impressive testimony to his celestial status to observe that Shakespeare ranks just behind Alexander the Great (33), Napoleon Bonaparte (34), and Adolf Hitler (35), and just ahead of Adam Smith (37) and Thomas Edison (38). He may not be up at the empyrean heights with Muhammad (1), Isaac Newton (2), or Jesus Christ (3), yet certainly Shakespeare is rubbing shoulders with some mighty distinguished company.

To be sure, many scholars would find such rankings pointless, if not outright silly. How can anyone compare the influence of a creative writer with those of a politician, general, religious leader, scientist, or inventor? Such an exercise may be even worse than adding apples and oranges. Yet the main point of this example is this: If there is any literary genius who has a claim to being considered among the important figures in history, Shakespeare certainly would have to be on the short list. After all, English is one of the most universally spoken languages, surpassed only by Chinese in the number of speakers. And it is exceeded by no other tongue in its global distribution, both as a second language and as the lingua franca of science, technology, and popular culture.

Furthermore, no single individual has done more to shape the nature of the English language than did Shakespeare. Much of the basic English vocabulary actually originated in words and expressions that Shakespeare coined in his poems and plays. This phenomenal impact is amply demonstrated in Macrone's (1990) book *Brush up your Shakespeare!*—a work that shows how easy it is for English-speakers to quote Shakespeare every day. Hundreds of words and expressions that permeate common speech were first placed on paper by Shakespeare's quill. Shakespeare's happy turns of phrase are often so commonplace, indeed, that many grammar checkers for word-processors will automatically tag many of these as clichés. It is a powerful sign of a writer's linguistic influence when novel expressions eventually become hackneyed phrases in mundane communication.

Nor is Shakespeare's literary genius confined to the English-speaking world. Translated into every major language of the world, his metaphors, images, characters, and plots have become the common stock of human civilization as well. His plays alone have inspired countless poets, dramatists, composers, and film makers throughout the world. For instance, a partial list of opera composers who have set his plays to music would have to include such notables as Adam, Barber, Bellini, Berlioz, Britten, Bruch, Goldmark, Gounod, Halévy, Holst, Nicolaï, Purcell, Rossini, Smetana, Vaughan Williams, Verdi, Wagner, and Wolf-Ferrari. Rightly, Shakespeare's contemporary Ben Jonson claimed that Shakespeare 'was not of an age, but for all time!' Indeed, centuries later the modern Chinese poet Liu Bo-duan could write an *Ode to Shakespeare* in which he could say,

> Three hundred years have passed 'twixt then and now,
> Yet all the world looks to that mountain's brow!

(quoted in Giles 1923/1965, p. 418)

Needless to say, Shakespeare has become the subject of an astronomical amount of literary scholarship. On occasion psychologists will even participate in these Shakespeare studies. A good example is the 1953 volume *The personality of Shakespeare: a venture in psychological method* by Harold McCurdy. For the most part, however, Shakespeare has not been the frequent subject of scientific study. This lack of attention we believe is most unfortunate. For reasons already expressed, Shakespeare can be seen as the prototypical literary genius. Therefore, if we wish to understand the nature of literary creativity and aesthetics, his own life and work may provide an excellent place to start our investigations. Granted this assertion, the only next issue is how to subject Shakespeare to rigorous study. Certainly the humanistic methods of the literary critic are ill-suited to the discovery of general principles. What we seek is a method that is quantitative and nomothetic in basic approach, in a fashion comparable to psychometric assessment and laboratory experiments. Just such a technique already exists. It is called *historiometry*.

Historiometry has been defined as 'a scientific discipline in which nomothetic hypotheses about human behaviour are tested by applying quantitative analyses to data concerning historical individuals' (Simonton 1990*b*, p. 3). This definition can be broken down into three components.

First, historiometry is dedicated to testing nomothetic hypotheses about human behaviour. In other words, it is a method that seeks out general laws or statistical regularities that transcend the names, dates, and places of history. Thus, when applied to the study of creative genius, historiometric research might evaluate conjectures or predictions about what personality traits, developmental experiences, or contextual factors might contribute to exceptional achievement. This orientation must be distinguished from the idiographic approach, which places special emphasis on the principles that guide the behaviour of singular persons, without worrying about whether these guidelines can be generalized (see for example Elms 1994; Runyan 1982, 1988).

Second, quantitative analyses are absolutely essential to the business of conducting historiometric research. To begin with, investigators must strive to assess the central variables on some quantitative scale, whether ordinal, interval, or ratio. For example, the researcher might evaluate intelligence, personality traits, or childhood trauma along some kind of dimension. Once these measures are obtained, the historiometrician subjects these data to often complex statistical analyses. Among the methods available are multiple regression, factor analysis, linear structural models, time series analysis, and cluster analysis. These techniques allow the hypotheses that inspire the study to be confirmed or rejected with the maximum possible scientific rigour.

Third, historiometric studies examine historic individuals—people who have made history in a particular human endeavour. Often this means that the subject pool consists of deceased luminaries, but this is not essential. It is certainly possible for contemporary individuals to have achieved sufficient greatness that their place in history is unquestionable. Someone like Albert Einstein, for instance, became a legend in his own lifetime. None the less, there are many advantages to narrowing the samples to historic personalities who are no longer living. In any case, we should stress the plural in the phrase 'historical individuals'. Historiometric inquiries are most often multiple-case studies. We must have a large sample size to apply the elaborate statistical techniques. And we must have a respectable sample size to make a convincing argument that our findings are truly nomothetic in nature. The only exceptions to this rule are those occasional historiometric inquiries that take a single notable, such as Beethoven or Napoleon, as prototypical exemplars of a particular kind of achievement domain (see for example Sears *et al.* 1978; Simonton 1979, 1987).

William Shakespeare would obviously fall in this highly distinguished group. Hence, he would seem to represent an appropriate subject for single-case historiometry. However, there appears to be one outstanding obstacle to applying historiometric methods to the Bard: the extreme dearth of reliable information about his life. Just how severe this limitation can be is evident in one of the classic historiometric inquiries *The early mental traits of three hundred geniuses* by Catherine Cox (1926). Cox had originally planned to calculate IQ scores for the most illustrious personalities in modern Western civilization. To accomplish this end, she had to compile accurate chronologies on the early childhood and adolescent accomplishments of the famous individuals who were part of her initial sample. This sample, of course, included Shakespeare. In fact, Cox obtained her collection of geniuses by taking the top names on a list of the 1000 most eminent figures in Western history, a list that placed Shakespeare *second*, just after Napoleon (Cattell 1903). Nevertheless, all of her efforts toward compiling an adequate database were in vain. She discovered that we know virtually nothing about Shakespeare's early years, and only a bit more about his adult career. So hidden in obscurity is his life that some scholars have argued that some other person besides Shakespeare actually wrote the works that now pass under his name. Anyhow, Cox reluctantly had to delete Shakespeare from her analysis.

Still, we must recognize that Cox's predicament was very special. She required some very special information in order to estimate IQ scores, and these data were not forthcoming in the historical record. In contrast, if the researcher has very different goals in mind, the information we possess about Shakespeare can become extremely rich. Above all else, he left a sizable body of plays and poems that we can subject to content analysis, one of the most useful of all historiometric techniques. In addition, we can combine this content analytical data with other information, such as the circumstances under which a piece was written or the ultimate artistic impact of a play or poem. We can thus construct a database that will help us understand how literary genius operates in an exemplary case like Shakespeare. Later research may then determine if these findings can be extended to creators of lesser renown.

We are not merely speculating here. In a series of historiometric inquiries conducted over the past dozen years, Shakespeare's life work has been the subject of quantitative and nomothetic scrutiny. Below we summarize those findings that contribute to our comprehension of literary creativity and aesthetics. The review falls naturally into two parts. First we examine studies that focused on Shakespeare's dramatic output, and then we look at the studies that concentrated on his poetic output.

The plays

Simple observation reveals that some of Shakespeare's plays are more successful than others. Indisputably, for instance, *Hamlet* is performed and read more frequently than any of the plays making up the *Henry VI* trilogy. But what is the basis for these contrasts in popularity? Are differences in aesthetic impact totally arbitrary, or are they determined by characteristics intrinsic to each play? Of course, literary critics and philosophers have been discussing issues like this ever since Aristotle's *Poetics*, and so we are hardly raising a new question. Where we depart from this humanistic tradition, however, is the quest for a quantitative and nomothetic answer. We want to find the content and form characteristics that predict differential aesthetic success across all of his plays. By 'content' we mean *what is said*, whereas by 'form' we mean *how it is said*.

Naturally, the predictive value of form and content is not the only question of interest in trying to fathom Shakespeare's dramatic genius. For example, we also must recognize that a play is created within a particular context, and hence the form and content of a dramatic creation may be a product of a particular set of biographical and historical variables. Again, literary critics have often explored how such distinct events affect the creative product, with much discussion analysing to what extent a particular dramatic work is autobiographical or reflects the times. We are most interested in learning whether there are general relationships between a play's attributes and various biographical and historical influences, particularly those historical and biographical factors that affect the very form and content characteristics that help differentiate the dramatic successes from the failures.

We may appear to have set ourselves an impossible task, but this same historiometric paradigm has already been useful in understanding the aesthetic success of works in classical music (Simonton 1994*a*). For example, popularity in the repertoire has been shown to be a curvilinear function of melodic originality (Simonton 1980*b*, 1987); melodic originality, in turn, was found to be function of biographical stress the composer experienced during the time of composition (Simonton 1980*a*, 1987). Furthermore, this same basic mode of attack has been applied with some success to dramatic literature, namely the extant plays of Aristophanes, Euripides, Aeschylus, and Sophocles as well as the very plays that define the traditional Shakespeare canon (Simonton 1983). Hence, we have good reason to suspect that we may apply this investigative strategy to just a single dramatic genius—that of William Shakespeare. Although there are only 37 plays to work with, this sample size is sufficient for addressing the key questions of the proposed research paradigm.

Popularity, aesthetic success, or greatness

Our empirical inquiries must begin with an operational definition of the differential popularity, aesthetic success, or greatness of Shakespeare's 37 plays. Simonton (1986*b*) accomplished this task by defining 19 different archival indicators that spanned more than a half century of literary taste. These measures gauged which plays are most read, produced, commended, heard, and discussed—as well as which plays are most ignored by the general public and scholars. These indicators included: the frequency of performance on-stage (e.g. at the Ashland Shakespeare Festival in Oregon, the New York Shakespeare Festival in Central Park, the Stratford Shakespeare Festival in Stratford, Connecticut, and the Stratford Festival in Stratford, Ontario); the number of complete audio recordings, single-play book editions, film versions, New York Times film reviews, and operatic renditions; the frequency of appearance in anthologies of general literature and drama, and in literary digests, general and literary histories, recommended literary guides, and scholarly criticism.

To assess whether the 19 indicators concurred on the relative status of the 37 plays, Simonton employed factor analysis, a mathematical technique for gauging whether alternative measures all converge on the same overall measurement. The results showed that all of the indicators are measuring the same underlying dimension. Accordingly, the 19 separate measures could be summed to produce a single set of highly reliable scores that quantify the relative 'popularity' of the 37 plays. The resulting quantitative scores are presented in Table 8.1 (along with the derived rank ordering). As is apparent, the popularity scores put *Hamlet* squarely on top, whereas the least-noticed play is *Henry VI*, Part 3. Other artistically unsuccessful plays include *Henry VI*, Parts 2 and 1, *Timon of Athens*, and *Pericles*.

To help validate these scores, it was determined whether the ratings found in Table 8.1 were consistent with a play's quotability (Simonton 1986*b*). The concordance between popularity and quotability was substantial. In particular, the popularity measure correlates positively with the number of distinct quotes in *Bartlett's familiar quotations* (Moreley 1953), *The Penguin dictionary of quotations* (Cohen and Cohen 1960), and *Quotations from Shakespeare* (Quennell 1971). This suggests that a successful drama may leave its mark on the audience by implanting memorable lines.

The scores provided in Table 8.1 may be criticized from both scientific and humanistic perspectives. From the former viewpoint, some scientists may worry about the wide gap between *Hamlet's* score and those of the other great tragedies, such as *Macbeth*. If this placement is considered a highly exaggerated 'outlier', we can always impose a logarithmic transformation that brings *Hamlet* much closer to his brethren below. However, empirical studies have indicated that it really does not make that much difference in subsequent analyses. The raw scores correlate so highly with the log-transformed measures that they each display almost equivalent associations with various other measures (Simonton 1986*b*).

Humanistic scholars, in contrast, may wonder whether the scores exhibited in Table 8.1 constitute anything more than mere popularity. Can we really go so far as to claim that these differences reflect contrasts in aesthetic success or dramatic greatness? To obtain an answer, Simonton (1986*b*) sought the independent judgements of two professors who taught the Shakespeare courses at a major university. These experts were specifically asked to rate each play in terms of greatness on a 15-point American grading system of A to F (with pluses and minuses), using whatever criteria they deemed appropriate. One professor gave the plays greatness grades along with a demarcation of the most personal plays, the landmark plays, the plays with the deepest characterization, and the plays with strongest mastery of social reality. The other professor, in contrast, gave a rating of 'amplitude' (how ambitious a play is in what it sets out to accomplish) and 'achievement' (how successful the play is in attaining its ambitions). Detailed statistical analysis of these subjective ratings revealed significant concordance with the objective archival measure. Factor analysis results revealed that when the seven subjective assessment items were combined with the 19 original measures, the original factor analysis results remained virtually unchanged. In fact, the reliability coefficient for the composite scores actually increased. Hence, the citation instrument may be claimed to assess such key attributes as social realism, characterization, personal expression, achievement, amplitude, and landmark achievement. Interestingly, the broader the scope of a particular subjective-attribute rating, the closer was its correspondence with the objective citation score.

Consequently, we conclude that these measures of popularity assess something more profound than mere fashion. It may even be appropriate to employ a word with

Table 8.1 Popularity ratings and estimated composition dates for 37 Shakespeare plays

Play	Popularity Score	Popularity Rank	Date Composite	Date Predicted
1. Henry VI, Part 1	16	36	1591	1592
2. Henry VI, Part 2	17	34	1591	1592
3. Henry VI, Part 3	15	37	1591	1592
4. Comedy of Errors	31	24	1592	1592
5. Richard III	44	18	1593	1593
6. Titus Andronicus	20	31	1593	1592
7. Love's Labours Lost	24	27.5	1593	1595
8. Taming of the Shrew	54	11	1594	1593
9. Two Gentlemen of Verona	20	31	1593	1593
10. Romeo and Juliet	84	4	1595	1596
11. Richard II	38	20	1595	1594
12. Midsummer Night's Dream	69	6.5	1595	1596
13. Merchant of Venice	68	8	1596	1598
14. King John	20	31	1596	1595
15. Henry IV, Part 1	45	17	1597	1596
16. Henry IV, Part 2	33	23	1598	1597
17. Much Ado About Nothing	46	15.5	1598	1599
18. Henry V	51	13	1599	1597
19. Julius Caesar	53	12	1599	1598
20. As You Like It	62	10	1599	1598
21. Merry Wives of Windsor	37	21	1600	1600
22. Twelfth Night	65	9	1601	1602
23. Hamlet	138	1	1601	1603
24. Troilus and Cressida	25	26	1602	1600
25. All's Well That Ends Well	26	25	1603	1604
26. Measure for Measure	47	14	1604	1603
27. Othello	77	5	1604	1602
28. Lear	85	3	1605	1604
29. Macbeth	94	2	1606	1606
30. Anthony and Cleopatra	46	15.5	1607	1609
31. Timon of Athens	16	35	1607	1605
32. Coriolanus	24	27.5	1608	1609
33. Pericles	18	33	1608	1608
34. Cymbeline	35	22	1610	1610
35. Winter's Tale	43	19	1610	1609
36. Tempest	69	6.5	1611	1609
37. Henry VIII	23	29	1613	1613

Note: Above table is adapted from Simonton (1986*b*), with the ranks inserted here. The composite dates are those based on the factor analysis of alternative datings, whereas the predicted dates are those indicated by stylistic evidence alone (i.e. 'verse tests').

stronger connotations than those engendered by the word 'popularity'—such as outright 'greatness'. However, this term is so value-laden and ambiguous that we may be better off sticking with the more modest variable name. Perhaps the term 'aesthetic success' provides a reasonable compromise between these two extremes.

Thematic content

The next task is to assess the content of the 37 plays. This can be achieved by taking advantage of the *Syntopicon* (Adler 1952) that comprises volumes 2 and 3 of the 54-volume *Great books of the Western world* (Hutchins 1952). In this ambitious reference published by *Encyclopaedia Britannica*, a team of 60 scholars compiled a detailed topical index to the nearly 500 works that make up the Western literary and intellectual tradition. The index consists of almost 3000 topics, and provides specific page citations to all books, novels, plays, poems, and essays contained in the *Great books* anthology. Because the complete works of Shakespeare are included in volumes 26 and 27, the *Syntopicon* thus provides an extensive content analysis of Shakespeare's entire literary output. The prevalence of any given theme in the plays was measured by counting the number of pages devoted to the issue and calculating in what percentage of the play the issue is evident. The study then focused on those issues to which Shakespeare dedicated at least one entire play. Only 46 themes in the entire *Syntopicon* satisfied this requirement (see Table 2 in Simonton 1986*b*).

A few general observations about these themes are in order. First, it is clear that Shakespeare had some favorite topics. In particular, he found three subjects especially attractive: family, love, and monarchy. Reflecting on Shakespeare's time, we can see that these three subjects were highly interrelated. Monarchies were family affairs swayed by love, as is well illustrated in the lives and deaths of the mothers of both Queen Elizabeth and King James, under whose reigns Shakespeare wrote his dramas. Plays such as *Lear*, *Macbeth*, and *Hamlet* are excellent examples of Shakespeare's fascination with love, monarchy, and family. Second, significant correlations exist among some of the 46 issues, revealing obvious links as well as more subtle instances of affinity between issues. An example of a less obvious linkage is the strong, positive association between 'the courage required of citizens and statesmen' and 'the definition of treason and sedition'. This relationship may represent Shakespeare's frequent discussion of the strength of will needed to initiate, join, or resist conspiracies that can be found in almost all of his plays about the monarchy, as well as in *Julius Caesar*.

After determining the major thematic content of Shakespeare's canon, we can analyse what relationships exist between content issues and the popularity index shown in Table 8.1. The following three themes correlated with both the raw and the log-transformed index of dramatic impact:

1. Popularity is negatively correlated with the theme 'the history of monarchy: its origin and developments'. Plays with a heavy historical emphasis, such as the *Henry VI* series, are not as likely to be read; analysed; made into films, recordings, or operas; staged or be studied as other types of work. Modern audiences prefer tragedies, comedies, and romances more than plays based on the English monarchy, the War

of the Roses and attendant events. Overall, the tragedies are significantly preferred over any other type of drama.

2. On the other hand, dramatic popularity is positively related to discussion of 'the care and government of children: the rights and duties of the child; parental despotism and tyranny'. These are issues as relevant today as they were in the days of the Globe Theatre, and the popularity of *Lear* and *Romeo and Juliet* are evidence that successful plays may be built around these eternal themes.

3. Evidently, appreciators seek out plays that feature 'madness or frenzy due to emotional excess'. Of all the themes considered, this demonstrates the greatest correlation with the objective measure of aesthetic success (Simonton 1986*b*). The three great tragedies *Hamlet*, *Othello*, and *Lear* all excite and stimulate audiences by offering an abundance of surprising and even shocking events. The emotional impulsiveness and irrationality displayed by the characters in these plays may provide a potent injection of arousal that contributes to aesthetic impact (Peckham 1967).

Formal attributes

In analyses discussed so far in this chapter, popularity is linked with specific content in the plays, but specific stylistic attributes have not yet been linked to aesthetic success. Proportions of lines written in prose or blank verse, run-on lines, double endings, speech endings, and light or weak endings simply did not predict differential popularity (for definitions, see Campbell 1966, pp. 931–3, Craig and Bevington 1973, pp. 39–41). Therefore, if Shakespeare's dramatic verse construction changed over the course of his writing career, this form variance did not significantly alter the likelihood of any given play becoming popular. Both good and bad dramas can be written in any verse form. Other form variables, including the absolute length of the play and the number of speaking roles, also were not relevant to a play's aesthetic success. Obviously, these form variables are a very limited sample of the multitude of ways in which to express poetic drama, so the lack of significant form correlations is not proof that popularity is determined more by content than by stylistic characteristics.

In fact, a study by Derks (1989) provides evidence that form and content may interact and influence play popularity. The particular focus of this inquiry was the way Shakespeare mixed tragic content with certain comic devices. Modern research on emotion suggests that enhancing one emotion by manipulating another may actually intensify aesthetic appreciation (Berlyne 1971; Solomon 1980). The phenomenon of 'comic relief' is a classic case. Derks (1989) specifically compared each play's popularity (as defined in Table 8.1) with frequency counts of both sexual and intellectual puns. Overall, pun frequency did not predict which plays in the canon would be popular. Sexual punning frequency also was not predictive of success; however, increased frequency of intellectual punning decreased comedy popularity and contributed to tragedy popularity. Although the implication here is that reducing intellectual punning might improve the success of a comedy, Derks suggests that adding intellectual puns to a tragedy would make a greater relative contribution as it enriches its theme.

Context

Before we can determine the historical and biographical context in which Shakespeare conceived his plays, we first must know when each play was written. Alas, assigning a date to each of Shakespeare's plays is not a straightforward task. Scholars have laboured for years to establish a chronology of the dramas, using both internal evidence (stylistic changes) and external evidence (supposed references to external events). Because there continues to be a lack of agreement on the correct composition dates, Simonton (1986b) chose to create his own dating system. Starting with the independent datings of seven experts (six of whom provided earliest and latest dates of composition for each work), Simonton generated a set of 13 individual dates for each play. He then carried out factor analysis on the relationships within each set to determine the degree of agreement between the separate estimates. Strangely enough, this data analysis revealed a nearly perfect consensus, as judged by the single-factor solution and the almost perfect reliability coefficient for a composite estimate made up of all 13 alternative dates. In other words, the disagreements about the composition date for any one play are extremely small relative to the total variation in the dates across all 37 plays. Hence, the new 'composite' dates presented in Table 8.1 may represent the best datings currently available.

Simonton further validated these dates by assessing the fit of internal evidence to the chronology (cf. Brainerd 1980). In particular, the proportion of double endings (extra syllables at the end of a line of blank verse), speech endings (dividing a line between two or more speakers), and light or weak endings (lines ending in propositions, conjunctions, a pronoun or an auxiliary verb) accounted for much of the variance found in chronology. Considering chronology from the earliest to the latest plays, frequency of light or weak endings increased, speech endings increased then decreased in frequency (inverted backward-J curve), and frequencies of double endings first decreased and then increased (U curve). The 'predicted' dates given in Table 8.1 are based on these stylistic measures alone. The two sets of dates are highly correlated. Although Shakespeare experts have asserted that relationships between stylistic changes and time should have been linear rather than curvilinear, and that blank verse and prose patterns should have been significant, these data reveal the scholars' qualitative impressions to be wrong.

In any case, with reliable datings in hand, we can now define the biographical and historical context in which Shakespeare's creativity operated.

Biographical background

So little is known about Shakespeare's life that we lack the biographical data such as the effects of life stress, that have proved useful in studying other prolific creators (cf. Simonton 1977, 1980*a*, 1987). However, given the dates of the plays, we can examine how dramatic content shifts as a function of the playwright's age (Simonton 1983). After introducing necessary statistical controls for the type of play, trend analyses of the 46 issue measures discovered four prominent thematic fluctuations across the course Shakespeare's writing career (Simonton 1986*b*):

1. The treatment of romantic, chivalrous, and courtly love first increased and then decreased dramatically (exhibiting an inverted-J curve). Evidently, Shakespeare was most preoccupied with love during his youth, whereas in maturity he chose broader issues for his dramas.

2. The issue 'man as object of laughter or ridicule' displayed a similar age function to that above (1). Discussion peaked early in the chronology of the Bard's repertoire: satirical or comical plays, such as the *Taming of the Shrew*, made way for more serious questions and plots.

3. As Shakespeare aged, a significant linear decline occurred in the treatment of commerce and rivalry in politics. Perhaps with the rebellion of the Earl of Sussex at the close of Queen Elizabeth's reign and the Gunpowder Plot at the beginning of King James' reign, this theme may have become increasingly dangerous to dramatize.

4. Discussion of conflict in human life first increased and then decreased as time passed (yielding an inverted-U curve). As Shakespeare's youthful interest in love, comedy and satire declined, his more mature fascination with human conflict intensified, peaking with the tragedies. For example contrast the intense and bloody conflicts that occur on-stage in *Macbeth*, *Lear*, and *Hamlet*, with those in *The tempest*. In *Tempest*, all substantial human conflict either occurs offstage or is mediated by a sprite. It appears that age mellowed the Bard.

Besides these agewise trends for content, the aesthetic effectiveness of Shakespeare's output also changed with age. Consistent with previous research on age and achievement (Simonton 1994*b*), the relationship between the popularity index and Shakespeare's age is described by a curvilinear inverted-U function shown in Fig. 8.1. Popularity or greatness first increases to a peak and then decreases, his most successful works appearing during his late 30s and early 40s. This popularity trend followed his evolution from apprentice status—when he wrote *Titus Andronicus*, inspired by Kyd's *Spanish tragedy*—ascended to the heights of works such as *Hamlet* and *Othello*, and then descended via various problematic plays and awkward collaborations to a low point marked by *Pericles* and *Timon of Athens*. To be sure, this age function is not a perfect predictor of aesthetic success as he wrote *Romeo and Juliet*, *Richard III*, and *Taming of the Shrew* early in his career, *Tempest* at the end, and mediocre works such as *Merry wives of Windsor* and *Troilus and Cressida* during his peak creative years. Despite these exceptions, the broad agewise achievement tendency survives: more than one quarter of the contrasts in dramatic success can be ascribed to Shakespeare's age.

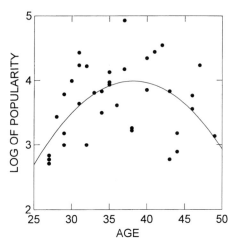

Fig. 8.1 Scatterplot depicting log-transformed popularity as a function of chronological age. The quadratic curve fit to the data accounts for 27% of the variation in the relative merit of the 37 plays.

Historical background

There are excellent sources on the events of the Elizabethan and Jacobean eras from which to devise indicators of the historical milieu in which Shakespeare created his lines, characters, and plots (e.g. Cook and Wroughton 1980; Powell and Cook 1977). Simonton (1986*b*) counted the frequency of numerous context indicators in an effort to set the historical context of each play. Using a five-year accumulation of specific events before and during the year each play is believed to have been written has a distinct advantage over yearly tabulations. It reflects the belief that dramatic creativity is affected by events over a course of years, allowing a literary idea time to germinate and grow (Simonton 1984). Five-year counts also are more reliable (Allison 1977). War, riots, rebellion, conspiracies, and other political events were counted as one set of indicators, while dramatic activity, general creativity, and other cultural events were counted as a second set of indicators. After introducing statistical controls for play type and composition date, the following findings can be reported (Simonton 1986*b*):

1. Grand conspiracies against the throne had a tremendous impact on Shakespeare's writing. His concerns for the life and rule of his sovereign and fascination with internal plots were voiced in his attention to 'the duties of command and obedience in life', 'patterns of friendship in the family', 'patterns of love and friendship in the family', 'the ages of man', 'myth of the royal personage', and 'the natural and the unnatural or monstrous'. Given how much hereditary monarchy is rooted in familial relationships, the presumed natural order of the universe, and the human life cycle as applied to a sitting monarch and his or her children, these thematic responses to conspiracies are understandable.

2. Themes concerned with 'conquest, empire, political expansion as ends of war'

emerged in the Bard's dramas during times when England was under attack by foreign powers. An important example of a political topic that sensitized the playwright into portraying England as a victim of aggression is the Spanish Armada of 1588. His treatment of the subject certainly drew patriotic cheers from his audience members who remembered these threatening events.

3. Rebellions in Ireland (rather common during this time) and other home-front political conflicts had their repercussions in Shakespeare's thematic repertoire. Such events stimulated increased attention to the theme of 'conflict in human life: opposed types of men and modes of life'.

Although we have adequate evidence that the context of a Shakespeare play is responsive to the milieu in which it was written, not one of these thematic consequences is germane to a play's popularity. None the less, data analysis revealed that the political climate may have had a more immediate effect on popularity. Plays created following a conspiracy or a rebellion are more popular than those conceived during quieter political times. In the absence of additional research, of course, we cannot know whether or not this tendency is an idiographic characteristic of Shakespeare.

Regressive imagery dictionary

We now discuss one final set of studies concerned with the relationship between the context and content of Shakespeare's plays. This pair of studies took advantage of a sophisticated computerized system that Martindale (1975, 1990) developed and validated for the content analysis of literary text. A key part of this system is the Regressive Imagery Dictionary (RID), which Derks (1994) decided to apply to the Shakespeare canon. In particular, the plays were assessed on three attributes: incongruous juxtapositions, primary process imagery, and secondary process imagery.

1. The indicator of *incongruous juxtapositions* (or oxymorons) gauges the co-occurrence of words that score highly on opposite poles on the Semantic Differential measure (Osgood *et al.* 1957). Examples include expressions like 'sweet sorrow' or 'valiant flea'.

2. *Primary process imagery*, on the other hand, is assessed by words that convey basic drives, sensations, regressive cognition, defensive symbolization, and something called Icarian imagery. For instance, drive is gauged by the presence of words like breast, kiss, naked, and caress, regressive cognition by words such as sun, sky, sea, fly, and fall.

3. *Secondary process imagery*, finally, is indicated by words denoting moral imperatives, temporal references, order, restraint, instrumental behaviour, social behaviour, and abstraction. For example, words like when, now, and then indicate temporal references, whereas such words as should, virtue, and law are taken as indicative of moral imperatives.

It is important to note that despite the obvious affinities between the measures of primary and secondary process imagery and the corresponding ideas in psychoanalytic theory, Martindale conceives these concepts in far more cognitive terms. In fact, recently Martindale (1990) has replaced these old terms with primordial and conceptual content, respectively. Derks (1994) followed this practice as well, but in reporting his results, we will retain these terms to avoid confusion later in this chapter.

In any event, Derks (1994) found that these three content analytical measures correlated with other features of the plays. In the first place, the scores on the indicators varied according to the type of play—tragedy, history, or comedy. For instance, tragedies contained more incongruous juxtapositions and primary process imagery, whereas the comedies had more secondary process imagery. More interesting still were the results of the trend analyses. For example, a curvilinear, inverted-U relationship was found between Shakespeare's age and the presence of incongruous juxtapositions, suggesting that he was most willing to exploit this literary device around the peak of his career. This curve is shown in Fig. 8.2.

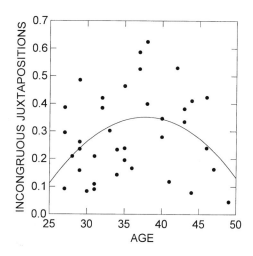

Fig. 8.2 Scatterplot depicting the prominence of incongruous juxtapositions as a function of chronological age. The quadratic curve fit to the data accounts for 13% of the variation across the 37 plays.

A sequel to Derks' (1994) pioneering investigation isolated some additional correlates of these content analytical measures (Simonton 1997). Primary process imagery was found to be positively associated with the proportion of lines in rhymed verse and negatively associated with the proportion of lines in prose. An even more intriguing result concerned the relationship between incongruous juxtapositions and the thematic richness of a play, where the latter is a measure of the total number of themes that Shakespeare discusses in a particular drama (Simonton 1983). This latter variable is negatively correlated with the presence of incongruous juxtapositions. It appears that

Shakespeare had at his disposal two alternative routes of stimulating his audiences: treating a large number of issues or filling his lines with semantically jolting juxtapositions. But if he used more of one literary resource, he had to hold back on the other. Otherwise, his audience would be intellectually overwhelmed. A similar creative trade-off occurs in classical music. For example, the richer the orchestral resources exploited in a composition, the less original the melodic material tends to be (Simonton 1980*b*, 1994*a*).

The application of the RID measures to Shakespeare's plays is fairly recent, and the results are thus exploratory in nature. However, the two RID measures of primary and secondary process imagery have proven valuable in enhancing our understanding of another distinctive manifestation of Shakespeare's creative genius—his poetic output.

The poetry

It has been shown that through historiometric analysis it is possible to discern which themes, historic events, and biographical factors, among others, lead to the eventual 'greatness' of a dramatic work, as with the work of Shakespeare. Despite this conclusion, drama remains an extremely elusive art form to study. The immense complexity of dramatic compositions compels us to find a clearer, simpler picture of what makes a literary creation 'great'. A literary art form that lends itself nicely to the historiometric study of literary success is poetry; poetry can address a wide variety of themes with the utmost compression, force, and economy. Shakespeare's 154 sonnets are perhaps quintessential of this sentiment. Although they cannot be used to delineate further the historical or biographical influences upon literary contribution (for they possess no chronology), the highly structured nature of the Shakespearean sonnet lends this collection of poetry to the study of theme, linguistic style, and aesthetic preferences.

The Shakespearean sonnet is a 14-line poem commonly composed of three four-line quatrains, plus a concluding two-line couplet. Each quatrain is presumed to contain a separate development of the sonnet's central idea, with the couplet providing a conclusion, climax, or resolution (Roberts and Jacobs 1989). More technically, this type of sonnet is written in iambic pentameter, with a rhyme scheme of *a b a b, c d c d, e f e f, g g*. A clear and eloquent example of this form is Shakespeare's well known eighteenth sonnet (Alexander 1951, p. 1311):

> Shall I compare thee to a summer's day?
> Thou art more lovely and more temperate:
> Rough winds do shake the darling buds of May,
> And summer's lease hath all too short a date:
> Sometime too hot the eye of heaven shines,
> And often is his gold complexion dimmed;
> And every fair from fair sometime declines,
> By chance, or nature's changing course, untrimmed;
> But thy eternal summer shall not fade,

> Nor lose possession of that fair thou owest;
> Nor shall Death brag thou wander'st in his shade,
> When in eternal lines to time thou growest:
>> So long as men can breathe, or eyes can see,
>> So long lives this, and this gives life to thee.

It is also important to note that when writing in iambic pentameter the poet is restricted to a count of 10 syllables per line (with 2 syllables per each of the 5 feet), thus restricting the number and size of words used in the composition. This apparently constrictive architecture, however, was thoroughly exploited by Shakespeare, as is evident by the sheer number, diversity, and quality of the sonnets he penned. In fact, there is reason to believe that Shakespeare sought to stake his posthumous fame more on these poetic compositions than on his dramatic output, the latter seeming in his day to constitute a far more ephemeral, even vulgar mode of literary entertainment. One need only look as far as the couplet of the above stated sonnet for evidence of this belief (further examples can be found in sonnets 55 and 65, among others). Thus, with the intricacy and importance of his works duly noted, let us turn our attention to the benefits of employing his sonnets in historiometric research.

Shakespeare's use of the sonnet form affords the historiometric researcher with three unique advantages in the study of writing style and content choice, as well as the examination of their consequent effects upon the future popularity of literary composition (Simonton 1989*a*). First, as four centuries have passed since these sonnets were written, we can be fairly certain that there has been sufficient time for a consensus to develop regarding their comparative quality. It is evident that the Bard's inspiration could wax and wane from sonnet to sonnet or quatrain to quatrain, resulting in a collection of poems of a rather uneven quality. As one scholar noted, while some sonnets 'bear the unmistakable stamp of his genius', others 'are no better than many a contemporary could have written' (Smith 1974, p. 1747). Some sonnets are simply quoted or discussed far more often than others, and some are more frequently included in anthologies of great literature. In fact, both of the following studies used 27 different measures of the relative popularity of the sonnets, including anthologies, books of quotations, and literary digests; these measures spanned over a century of critical judgement (from Hunt and Lee 1867 to Lever 1974). From these measures, a reliable composite score for aesthetic success, or 'greatness', was reached for each sonnet. This demarcation of the diversity of aesthetic success can be used to identify what lifts a poem to the realm of masterpiece or lowers it to the status of unrecognizable.

Second, since rhyme, rhythm, and length are exactly the same across the sonnets, other aspects such as theme or linguistic complexity can be isolated as factors that affect the sonnet's future success (Simonton 1989*a*). The difference in popularity, therefore, should be due to certain qualities present in some works and absent in others. However, Shakespeare sometimes strayed from certain stylistic concerns (vis. sonnets 99, 126, and 145); yet these infractions are relatively minor in light of the entire corpus of his work (see Simonton 1990*a*).

Finally, due to the relatively small number of lines in a sonnet, it is possible to analyse the content of the entire poetic composition or series of compositions; a daunting task to be undertaken upon a series of novels or full-length plays. Complex content analytic procedures have also become more accessible with the advent of various computer programs written for this very purpose. In fact, one such program was used in the following studies to content analyse the various lexical components of the poems (Mohler and Zuell 1986).

The 154 sonnets: study one

The first study considered whether content and form could account for the eventual aesthetic success of Shakespeare's sonnets and how this information could inform a discussion of general literary creativity (Simonton 1989*a*). The aforementioned computer program was used to examine all 154 sonnets, treating each as a unit of analysis. It was able to discriminate objectively the more popular sonnets according to both content and lexical diversity. To achieve a clearer picture of how this feat was achieved, let us turn to the variables probed by this study.

Content variables

Three general content-related variables were examined: the usage of primary process imagery, secondary process imagery, and thematic richness. Numerous psychological theories have accentuated the importance of primary process thought and imagery to creative production. From the psychoanalytic theories of Freud (1908/1959) and Kris (1953) that emphasize the sublimation of primary process material or regression in the service of the ego, respectively, to Martindale's (1975, 1986, 1990) evolutionary theory of artistic creativity, primary process content has been portrayed as integral to the creativity of the individual and the society. Thus, the RID was used in this study to discriminate the level of primary and secondary process imagery in each sonnet (Martindale 1975; see also Martindale 1984). This measure was then compared to each sonnet's level of popularity in an attempt to discern a relationship between the two. The results were quite clear: The more popular sonnets emerged as those rich in primary process imagery and more impoverished in secondary process imagery. In other words, the general reader prefers poetry that deals with the fundamental, psychodynamically rich experiences of life—love, sex, sensation, feeling, dreams, fears—not with abstractions and reason.

We may illustrate this contrast by comparing two sonnets that differ greatly in popularity. On the one hand, the unpopular sonnet 85 contains lines such as those found in the second quatrain (Craig and Bevington 1973, p. 485):

> I think good thoughts whilst others write good words,
> And like unlettered clerk still cry 'Amen'
> To every hymn that able spirit affords
> In polish'd form of well-refined pen.

This we may compare with the third quatrain from the popular sonnet 73 (Craig and Bevington 1973, p. 484):

> In me thou see'st the glowing of such fire
> That on the ashes of his youth doth lie,
> As the death-bed whereon it must expire
> Consum'd with that which it was nourish'd by.

Clearly, where the former contains conceptual imagery of rational, moral, and refined thinking, the latter features imagery of sensation (glowing flames), basic drives (eating), and mortality (death)—imagery far more primordial in content.

Regarding thematic content, previous research has shown that more highly esteemed creative products, including Shakespeare's plays, tend to treat a broad range of themes (Simonton 1983; see also Simonton 1976). Thus the *Syntopicon* (Adler 1952) was once again consulted to assist in the analysis of thematic content, this time with a focus upon the sonnets. Ignoring the thematic issues touched upon by all 154 sonnets, 24 themes were identified in the *Syntopicon* as occurring in two or more of the poems (see Table 1 in Simonton 1989*a*); from this set it was possible to delineate which sonnets explored more themes than other sonnets. Beyond this raw measure of thematic richness, the sonnets were also examined in light of how often the same theme was treated by Shakespeare's plays, the other sonnets, and other authors included in the *Great books* anthology (Hutchins 1952). The results were rather compelling. The most popular sonnets were found to explore a greater number of themes, as well as themes fundamental to other literary creations. Further, these successful works were most likely to discuss 'the love and hatred of change', 'honour or fame as a mode of immortality', and 'immortality through offspring: the perpetuation of the species'. The moderately successful sonnets tend to address 'the intensity and power of love', 'friendly, tender, or altruistic love: fraternal love', and 'the temporal course of passions: emotional attitudes toward time and mutability'. With these thematic findings in mind, let us turn our attention to the form variables.

Form variables

According to experimental aesthetics, for an artistic composition to be successful it must first feature the capacity to stimulate arousal via complexity, novelty, surprise, and other 'collative' properties (Berlyne 1974; Cupchik 1986). It has been postulated that variables such as the type-token ratio, unique word counts, the adjective-verb quotient, broken lines, and run-on lines can all be adopted as indicators of a sonnet's 'arousal potential' (Berlyne 1971). Accordingly, these five form variables were compared to our measure of aesthetic success to determine if a relationship exists between 'arousal' and popularity.

The type-token ratio is a straightforward assessment of the number of different words divided by the total number of words. It is a common gauge of lexical variability or verbal complexity, which in turn is an established predictor of poetry preferences (Kammann 1966). A related index is a simple count of the unique words that is, the number of words found once in that sonnet alone. In addition, the adjective-verb quotient, or the proportion of adjectives to verbs in a given sonnet, is considered as an alternative gauge of linguistic complexity (Boder 1940). Not surprisingly, all three variables were found to be good predictors of the future success of a sonnet: the more lush the vocabulary the greater the poem.

The remaining form variables concern two stylistic characteristics, namely the number of broken lines and the number of run-on lines. A broken line is an instance where a line is cut by a stop (i.e. a period, question mark, exclamation mark, colon, or semicolon) and a run-on line is one that continues to the following line without a pause (comma) or a stop. Neither of these stylistic measures, however, were found to be related to a sonnet's future renown.

Finally, with the help of a more complex statistical procedure, all of the thematic and form-related variables were thrown into an equation to examine which factors, when taken together, would be the most salient predictors of aesthetic success. Four variables emerged from the analysis, and explained between one-fifth and one-quarter of the variation in sonnet quality, a considerable amount for this type of analysis (see Simonton 1980*b*, 1986*a*, 1989*b*). The four salient predictors turned out to be (a) the thematic issue of 'the love and hatred of change', (b) thematic richness in terms of themes shared with Shakespeare's plays, (c) primary process imagery, and (d) the adjective-verb quotient.

All in all, the characteristics of the more successful sonnets tie in quite well with what we would expect on the basis of previous nomothetic research. In order to maximize aesthetic creativity, the technical details of poetry construction may be ignored so long as the poet treats a diversity of personally relevant themes in a language both intellectually arousing and psychodynamically rich (DeFonso 1986; Martindale 1986). The only complication is the predictive utility of the content measure regarding attitudes towards change. Whether this is a fruitful subject idiosyncratic to Shakespeare or one of the great themes for authors generally remains to be determined.

Something critical is lacking in this first study. The results suggest that a poet, to achieve success, must draw from a special lexicon. Shakespeare had to find, line by line, Flaubert's '*bon mot*'. This implies a rather static conception of poetry. A poem's effectiveness should depend on more than simply inserting the right words; those words must also be well arranged for maximal impact on the reader. Consequently, to acquire a greater understanding of poetic achievement, we must turn our attention to how word usage unfolds during the course of a single poem. Shakespeare's sonnets once again present an ideal opportunity for the historiometric researcher to achieve such an aim.

The 154 sonnets: study two

There are two central questions that frame this study (Simonton 1990*a*). First, how does Shakespeare's choice of words (form and content) differ across each consecutive section of a sonnet? Second, once a general pattern is established regarding the nuances of imagery or lexical changes across a particular sonnet, do these trends tend to differ for his most highly acclaimed poetic creations? Is there an optimal ordering of form and content for literary works?

The Shakespearean sonnet structure presents us with a unique opportunity to approach the above questions. These issues can be tackled by taking each quatrain and couplet as a distinct unit or mini poem to be analysed (Simonton 1990*a*). We can then examine a variety of form and content variables as they are presented in each successive unit. In this vein, Study Two examined two content and three form variables across the sonnet landscape.

Content variables

Regarding content, the RID (Martindale 1975) was once again used to identify the amount of primary and secondary process imagery in a given unit of each sonnet. These measures of content were found to change very little across the development of a sonnet. The amount of primary process content showed no changes across the quatrains; yet the concluding couplet, when compared to the quatrains, decreased in this type of imagery. Secondary process imagery displayed no changes across the entirety of the sonnet. And both measures were also found to have no relationship with the future success of the sonnets themselves. Thus, although in the previous study the sonnet's overall use of primary process content was found to predict its future renown, the use of such content across the development of the poem itself neither piques nor repels the interest of future generations.

Form variables

The three form-related variables tackled by this study were the number of words, different words, and unique words. A simple word count per unit may appear at first blush to be a rather uninformative indicator of Shakespeare's approach to writing. Yet one must keep in mind that when composing in iambic pentameter, a poet counts syllables rather than words (vis. 10 syllables per line). Thus, an increase or decrease in word count across successive units of the poem actually informs us as to Shakespeare's usage of monosyllabic or polysyllabic words. In this study the word count proportions were found to be a relatively important factor in the development of the sonnet. The analysis uncovered that the first and third quatrains were essentially the same, with only the middle quatrain displaying an increase in polysyllabic words. As expected, the couplets showed a large decrease in word count when compared to the quatrains. Yet if the word count for the couplet is doubled, essentially equalizing each unit's number of lines, we find a dramatic increase in word count (i.e. monosyllabic words) as compared to the quatrains. The word count variable, however, was unrelated to the eventual success or failure of the sonnet. Thus, no matter what their effectiveness, Shakespeare's second quatrains show a modest gain in polysyllabic words and the couplets display a dramatic increase in their use of monosyllabic words. Since the monosyllabic words are more primitive in meaning, this finding suggests that Shakespeare dipped into the fundamentals of expression when attempting to resolve his sonnets' central ideas.

As with the first sonnet study, both the number of different words and unique words were examined for each unit (in this case, the quatrains and couplets). These two variables can be taken as measures of linguistic style, especially the novelty of the vocabulary from which a given quatrain or couplet was built (Holsti 1969). In the case of the different words variable, a steady increase in this quality was found from the first to the final quatrain; yet, a precipitous drop in this characteristic typified the concluding couplet. A similar picture emerges for the number of unique words. Compared to the first and third quatrain, which were somewhat indistinguishable on this count, the second quatrain displayed a greater number of unique words, and the couplet was found to contain relatively few, if any, rare words at all. This general pattern of increasing lexical diversity, followed by the sharp decline in the couplet is intriguing, yet becomes much more so when related to each sonnet's aesthetic success.

A clear understanding of Shakespeare's successful writing style emerges when we look at the relationship between these two style variables and the 'greatness' of his poetic works.

Regarding his usage of unique words, Shakespeare sharply decreased their number in the concluding couplet for both the popular and mediocre works. Yet the decrease in unique words becomes even more dramatic for the most popular sonnets, with the contrast between best and worst sonnet around four words for the couplet. In the unpopular sonnet 11, for example, the concluding sonnet goes

> She carv'd thee for her seal, and meant thereby
> Thou shouldst print more, not let that copy die
>
> (Craig and Bevington 1973, p. 473)

which contains four words not used in any other Shakespeare sonnet. The far more popular sonnet 73, in contrast, concludes with

> 'This thou preceiv'st, which makes thy love more strong,
> To love that well which thou must leave ere long'
>
> (Craig and Bevington 1973, p. 484).

This contains not a single word unique to the sonnet.

Even more compelling are the findings for the usage of different words. Once again the difference between the greater and lesser sonnets is displayed in the couplet. For Shakespeare's 'great' works, the number of different words in the mix was dramatically increased, yet greatly decreased for the also-rans. Compare the couplet of the unpopular seventy-fifth sonnet

> Thus do I pine and surfeit day by day,
> Or gluttoning on all, or all away'
>
> (Craig and Bevington 1973, p. 484),

which repeats the words 'day' and 'all,' with the ending of the popular 30th sonnet

> But if the while I think on thee, dear friend,
> All losses are restor'd and sorrows end'
>
> (Craig and Bevington 1973, p. 476),

which manages not to repeat a single word!

In summary, Shakespeare's greatest sonnets contained couplets rich in their use of the lexicon, yet reluctant to introduce peculiar words into the fray. As Shakespeare moved from quatrain to quatrain he wrote with a richer, more suggestive vocabulary, slowly building a chain of associations in the reader's mind. Then, within the couplet, Shakespeare constricted his lexicon while concurrently optimizing the wealth of associations that the increase in different words could produce. The last two lines of his greatest sonnets were designed to tie into one tight package all the loose ends tossed about in the preceding dozen lines. In Macaulay's (1825/1900, p. 14) essay on Milton we find the following provocative observation: 'The most striking characteristic of the poetry of Milton is the extreme remoteness of the associations by means of which it acts on the reader. Its effect is produced, not so much by what it expresses, as by what it suggests; not so much by the ideas which it directly conveys as by other ideas which are connected with them. He electrifies the mind through conductors'. The same compositional device evidently characterizes William Shakespeare's greatest sonnets as well.

These results, in conjunction with the findings from Study One, have helped unveil the often subtle role of word choice, content, and compositional development in the eventual canonization of these literary works. Moreover, these historiometric techniques have helped to reveal that the exceptional sonnets among the 154 are those that treat an impressive diversity of universal themes, use extensive primary-process imagery, and convey this content in an arousing, increasingly rich, yet cohesive language. The Bard truly mirrored the intricacies of the human condition through his delicate mastery of the art of poetry.

Conclusion

Shakespeare scholarship is an extremely rich enterprise that has been going on for centuries. Entire scholarly journals are devoted to this single author, not only in English but also in languages as diverse as Russian and Hungarian. The number of books and articles concerning Shakespeare is very, very large. For example, the libraries of the University of California alone contain over 10 000 volumes. Despite the immensity of all this collective knowledge, it is really amazing how little all of this scholarship tells us about the creativity of this exemplary genius. The explanation for this ignorance is simple: virtually all work on Shakespeare has favoured humanistic rather than scientific methods. Quantitative studies are relatively rare, and nomothetic inquiries are rarer still. Therefore, the field was wide open for historiometric investigations into Shakespeare's life and work. These historiometric studies reveal many things about his dramatic and poetic output that could not have been discovered any other way.

Of course, the results and methods reported in this chapter are not free from potential criticisms. Indeed, because these investigations occupy the gap between two rival forms of knowledge—the humanistic and scientific—they can be criticized from more than one point of view. For example, humanists may wonder what happens to all the results reported in this paper should it happen that some dissenting scholars are indeed correct in claiming that Shakespeare was not the author of the plays and poems analysed here. The answer is surprising: it makes little difference. Not a single finding concerning the sonnets is predicated on Shakespeare actually being the author of these poems. Furthermore, the only results concerning the plays that involve the dramatist's age would seem vulnerable to the possibility of rival claimants to authorship. None the less, this vulnerability is minimal, because all that we have really assumed is that the true author of these plays is one of Shakespeare's near contemporaries, if not Shakespeare himself. We must recall that the age curve showing how the popularity of the plays varied across time is most consistent with what we would expect for a playwright born around Shakespeare's birth year (cf. Lehman 1953; Quetelet 1835/1968). Thus, if it were actually, say, Francis Bacon who wrote all the plays, our interpretations would alter very little, given that he was born just three years earlier.

In contrast, scientists may question the utility of single-case investigations. After all, we are not studying all plays and sonnets ever written, nor even all plays and sonnets in the English language. How do we know that what we have learned from these 37 plays and 154 sonnets has any generalizability beyond the person who composed these works? Still, it is essential to observe that many of the data analyses were actually guided by a larger body of previous research on creativity, both literary and otherwise. For example, there exists a sizable literature on the relationship between the complexity or richness of an artistic product and its ultimate aesthetic impact (e.g. Berlyne 1971, 1974; DeFonso 1986; Simonton 1994b). Hence, the fact that the most successful of his sonnets exhibit linguistic complexity cannot be considered idiosyncratic to this particular poet. This single-case replication of multiple-case principles echoes what has been found in other historiometric inquiries. For instance, the military genius of Napoleon is in many respects representative of military leaders generally (Simonton 1979), and the musical genius of Beethoven can be considered indicative of what holds for composers at large (Simonton 1987, 1994a). Hence, the nomothetic and the idiographic modes of analysis reveal considerable overlap (see also Simonton 1993).

Yet the ultimate justification for Shakespearean historiometry is as much humanistic as scientific. Shakespeare is not merely a single individual, comparable to one subject run in a laboratory experiment or one respondent to a survey. He is not interchangeable with any other person, nor even with any other literary creator. Shakespeare was a literary genius *par excellence*. As an exemplary representative of the phenomenon, then, Shakespeare is most worthy of scientific investigation. At the very minimum such inquiries may provide us with useful hypotheses that may later be tested on larger samples of literary creators. But more importantly, the historiometric examination of this single great mind may help validate the scientific perspective. If Shakespeare's genius cannot be fathomed by quantitative and nomothetic methods, we can never hope to claim that we have a complete understanding of creativity. It may even be an optimal strategy to begin with the highest peak, from which we can best survey the hills and valleys below. In English literature, at least, Shakespeare *is* that Mount Everest.

References

Adler, M. J. (ed.) (1952). *The great ideas: a syntopicon of great books of the Western World* (2 vols). Encyclopaedia Britannica, Chicago.

Alexander, P. (ed.) (1951). *William Shakespeare: the complete works.* Collins, London, England.

Allison, P. D. (1977). The reliability of variables measured as the number of events in an interval of time. In *Sociological methodology 1978* (ed. K. F. Schuessler), pp. 238–53. Jossey-Bass, San Francisco.

Berlyne, D. (1971). *Aesthetics and psychobiology.* Appleton-Century-Crofts, New York.

——(ed.) (1974). *Studies in the new experimental aesthetics.* Hemisphere, Washington, DC.

Boder, D. P. (1940). The adjective-verb quotient: a contribution to the psychology of language. *Psychological Record*, **3**, 310–43.

Brainerd, B. (1980). The chronology of Shakespeare's plays: a statistical study. *Computers and the Humanities*, **14**, 221–30.

Campbell, O. J. (ed.) (1966). *The reader's encyclopedia of Shakespeare.* Crowell, New York.

Cattell, J. M. (1903). A statistical study of eminent men. *Popular Science Monthly*, **62**, 359–77.

Cohen, J. M., and Cohen, M. J. (ed.) (1960). *The Penguin dictionary of quotations.* Penguin, New York.

Cook, C., and Wroughton, J. (1980). *English historical facts 1603–1688.* Rowman and Littlefield, Totowa, NJ.

Cox, C. (1926). *The early mental traits of three hundred geniuses,* Stanford University Press, Stanford, California.

Craig, H., and Bevington, D. (ed.) (1973). *The complete works of Shakespeare* (revised edn). Scott, Foresman, Glenview, Illinois.

Cupchik, G. C. (1986). A decade after Berlyne: new directions in experimental aesthetics. *Poetics*, **15**, 345–69.

DeFonso, L. E. (1986). The state of the art in arts research: directions and problems. *Poetics*, **15**, 371–400.

Derks, P. L. (1989). Pun frequency and popularity of Shakespeare's plays. *Empirical Studies of the Arts*, **7**, 23–31.

——(1994). Clockwork Shakespeare: the Bard meets the Regressive Imagery Dictionary. *Empirical Studies of the Arts*, **12**, 131–9.

Elms, A. C. (1994). *Uncovering lives: the uneasy alliance of biography and psychology,* Oxford University Press, New York.

Freud, S. (1959). Creative writers and day-dreaming. In *Creativity* (ed. P. E. Vernon), pp. 126–35. Penguin, Baltimore, Maryland. (Original work published 1908.)

Giles, H. A. (ed.) (1965). *Gems of Chinese literature,* Dover, New York. (Originally published 1923.)

Hart, M. H. (1987). *The 100: a ranking of the most influential persons in history.* Citadel Press, Secaucus, New Jersey.

Holsti, O. R. (1969). *Content analysis for the social sciences and humanities.* Addison-Wesley, Reading, Mass.

Hunt, L., and Lee, S. A. (ed.) (1867). *The book of the sonnet.* Roberts Brothers, Boston, Mass.

Hutchins, R. M. (1952). (ed.) *Great books of the Western World.* Encyclopaedia Britannica, Chicago.

Kammann, R. (1966). Verbal complexity and preferences in poetry. *Journal of Verbal Learning and Verbal Behavior*, **5**, 536–40.

Kris, E. (1953). Psychoanalysis and the study of creative imagination. *Bulletin of the New York Academy of Medicine*, **29**, 334–51.

Lehman, H. C. (1953). *Age and achievement*. Princeton University Press, Princeton, New Jersey.

Lever, J. W. (ed.) (1974). *Sonnets of the English Renaissance*. Athlone Press, London.

Macaulay, T. B. (1900). Milton. In *Critical historical essays* Vol 1 (ed. I. Gollancz), pp. 3–66. Dent, London. (Originally published 1825.)

Macrone, M. (1990). *Brush up your Shakespeare!* Harper and Row, New York.

Martindale, C. (1975). *Romantic progression: the psychology of literary history*. Hemisphere, Washington, DC.

——(1984). Evolutionary trends in poetic style: the case of English metaphysical poetry. *Computers and the Humanities*, **18**, 3–21.

——(1986). Aesthetic evolution. *Poetics*, **15**, 439–73.

——(1990). *The clockwork muse: the predictability of artistic styles*. Basic Books, New York.

McCurdy, H. G. (1953). *The personality of Shakespeare*. Yale University Press, New Haven, Connecticut.

Mohler, P. P., and Zuell, C. (1986). *TEXTPACK V*. ZUMA, Mannheim, Federal Republic of Germany.

Moreley, C. (ed.) (1953). *The shorter Barlett's familiar quotations*. Doubleday, New York.

Osgood, C. E., Suci, G., and Tannenbaum, P. (1957). *The measurement of meaning*. University of Illinois Press, Urbana, IL.

Peckham, M. (1967). *Man's rage for chaos: biology, behavior, and the arts*. Schocken Books, New York.

Powell, K. G., and Cook, C. (1977). *English historical facts 1485–1603*. Rowman and Littlefield, Totowa, NJ.

Quennell, P. (ed.) (1971). *Quotations from Shakespeare*. Plays, Boston.

Quetelet, A. (1968). *A treatise on man and the development of his faculties*. Franklin, New York. (Reprint of 1842 Edinburgh translation of 1835 French original.)

Roberts, E. V., and Jacobs, H. E. (1989). *Literature: an introduction to reading and writing*. Prentice-Hall, New Jersey.

Runyan, W. M. (1982). *Life histories and psychobiography*. Oxford University Press, New York.

——(1988). *Psychology and historical interpretation*. Oxford University Press, New York.

Sears, R. R., Lapidus, D., and Cozzens, C. (1978). Content analysis of Mark Twain's novels and letters as a biographical method. *Poetics*, **7**, 155–75.

Simonton, D. K. (1976). Philosophical eminence, beliefs, and zeitgeist: an individual generational analysis. *Journal of Personality and Social Psychology*, **34**, 630–40.

——(1977). Creative productivity, age, and stress: a biographical time-series analysis of 10 classical composers. *Journal of Personality and Social Psychology*, **35**, 791–804.

——(1979). Was Napoleon a military genius? Score: Carlyle 1, Tolstoy 1. *Psychological Reports*, **44**, 21–2.

——(1980*a*). Thematic fame and melodic originality in classical music: a multivariate computer-content analysis. *Journal of Personality*, **48**, 206–19.

——(1980*b*). Thematic fame, melodic originality, and musical zeitgeist: a biographical and transhistorical content analysis. *Journal of Personality and Social Psychology*, **39**, 972–83.

——(1983). Dramatic greatness and content: a quantitative study of eighty-one Athenian and Shakespearean plays. *Empirical Studies of the Arts*, **1**, 109–23.

——(1984). *Genius, creativity, and leadership: historiometric inquiries*. Harvard University Press, Cambridge, MA.

Simonton, D. K. (1986a). Aesthetic success in classical music: a computer analysis of 1,935 compositions. *Empirical Studies of the Arts*, **4**, 1–17.

——(1986b). Popularity, content, and context in 37 Shakespeare plays. *Poetics*, **15**, 493–510.

——(1987). Musical aesthetics and creativity in Beethoven: a computer analysis of 105 compositions. *Empirical Studies of the Arts*, **5**, 87–104.

——(1989a). Shakespeare's sonnets: a case of and for single-case historiometry. *Journal of Personality*, **57**, 695–721.

——(1989b). The swan-song phenomenon: last works effects for 172 classical composers. *Psychology and Aging*, **4**, 42–7.

——(1990a). Lexical choices and aesthetic success: a computer content analysis of 154 Shakespeare sonnets. *Computers and the Humanities*, **24**, 251–64.

——(1990b). *Psychology, science, and history: an introduction to historiometry*, Yale University Press, New Haven, Connecticut.

——(1991). Latent-variable models of posthumous reputation: a quest for Galton's G. *Journal of Personality and Social Psychology*, **60**, 607–19.

——(1993). Creative genius in music: Mozart and other composers. In *The pleasures and perils of genius: mostly Mozart* (ed. P. F. Ostwald and L. S. Zegans), pp. 1–28. International Universities Press, New York.

——(1994a). Computer content analysis of melodic structure: classical composers and their compositions. *Psychology of Music*, **22**, 31–43.

——(1994b). *Greatness: who makes history and why*, Guilford Press, New York.

——(1997). Imagery, style, and content in 37 Shakespeare plays. *Empirical Studies of the Arts*, **15**, 15–20.

Smith, H. (1974). Sonnets. In *The riverside Shakespeare* (ed. Evans, G. B.), pp. 1745–80. Houghton Mifflin, Boston, Mass.

Solomon, R. L. (1980). The opponent-process theory of acquired motivation: The costs of pleasure and the benefits of pain. *American Psychologist*, **35**, 691–712.

LORD BYRON

CHAPTER 9

Lord Byron: the apostle of affliction

Kay Redfield Jamison

'LORD BYRON', declared the poet's tutor at Cambridge, 'is a young man of *tumultuous passions*' (Marchand 1957*a*, p. 131), thus summing up succinctly the views of Byron's friends, enemies, and Byron himself. Fiery, fitful, and often high-spirited, with a temperament he described as 'naturally burning', (BLJ, vol. 9, p. 37),[1] Byron was by all means inflammable, his bold and expansive moods yoked to a restless, pervasive, and virulent melancholy. Notoriously a study in contrasts, Byron, with his divided and mercurial temperament, resembled less a cohesive personality than tectonic plates colliding and grating against one another. 'There is a war', he wrote, 'a chaos of the mind,/When all its elements convulsed—combined—/Lie dark and jarring with perturbed force' (BCPW, vol. 3, p. 182).[2] For virtually all his life, Byron engaged in such a war—a consuming civil war within his own mind, which, then convulsing outward, at times was waged as an anything but civil war on the people and world around him. From these wars came much of what made Byron who he was. 'His very defects', observed his close friend and fellow poet Moore, 'were among the elements of his greatness', and it was 'out of the struggle between the good and evil principles of his nature that his mighty genius drew its strength' (Moore 1832, vol. 13, p. 24). Byron was the first to recognize the importance of his unsettled, impetuous, and romantic temperament. In 1813 he wrote to his future wife, Annabella Milbanke: '—You don't like my 'restless' doctrines—I should be very sorry if *you* did—but I can't *stagnate* nevertheless—if I must sail let it be on the ocean no matter how stormy—anything but a dull cruise on a level lake without ever losing sight of the same insipid shores by which it is surrounded—(BLJ, vol. 3, p. 119).

The conflicting factions of his temperament, interlaced with and beholden to his constantly shifting moods, gave rise to the sense that Byron housed within himself a veritable city of selves. One of his physicians described this mutability:

Those only, who lived for some time with him, could believe that a man's temper, Proteus like, was capable of assuming so many shapes. It may literally be said, that at different hours of the

This chapter was first published as '*The mind's canker in its savage mood*', in K. R. Jamison (1993) *Touched with fire: manic-depressive illness and the artistic temperament*, Free Press, New York. Copyright © 1993 by Kay Redfield Jamison. It is modified with the permission of The Free Press, a division of Simon and Schuster.

[1] BLJ: Marchand, L. A. (ed.) (1973–82). Byron's letters and journals, John Murray, London.
[2] BCPW: McGann, J. J. (ed.) (1980–93). Lord Byron: the complete poetical works. Oxford University Press.

day he metamorphosed himself into four or more individuals, each possessed of the most opposite qualities; for, in every change, his natural impetuosity made him fly into the furthermost extremes. In the course of the day he might become the most morose, and the most gay; the most melancholy, and the most frolicsome . . . the most gentle being in existence, and the most irascible (Millengen 1831, p. 16).

Byron himself, who had written in *Don Juan* that 'I almost think that the same skin/For one without—has two or three within,' (BCPW, vol. 5, p. 660), remarked to his friend Lady Blessington, 'I am so changeable, being every thing by turns and nothing long,—I am such a strange *mélange* of good and evil, that it would be difficult to describe me' (Lovell 1969, p. 220). She clearly concurred:

I am sure, that if ten individuals undertook the task of describing Byron, no two, of the ten, would agree in their verdict respecting him, or convey any portrait that resembled the other, and yet the description of each might be correct, according to his or her received opinion; but the truth is, the chameleon-like character or manner of Byron renders it difficult to portray him. (Lovell 1969, p. 72)

Byron's chameleon-like qualities, along with the widely disparate aspects of his personality, were critical to the moody, contrasting, and Romantic casting of his poetry: Man was 'half dust, deity, alike unfit/To sink or soar', (BCPW, vol. 4, p. 63), a 'mix'd essence' (BCPW, vol. 4, p. 63), a 'conflict of elements' (BCPW, vol. 4, p. 63). Melancholic, although often sardonic, mixtures of emotions—foreboding, aloneness, regret, and a dark sense of lost destiny and ill-used passions—are woven throughout Byron's most autobiographical poems, especially *Childe Harold's Pilgrimage*, *Lara*, and *Manfred*. Perturbed and constant motion, coupled with a brooding awareness of life's impermanence, also mark the transient and often bleak nature of Byron's work.

The emphasis on shifting essences, uncertainty, and fiercely contrasting opposite states was, of course, neither new nor unique to Byron. He and the other Romantic poets, however, took these ideas and emotions to a particularly intense extreme. Shelley's belief that poetry 'marries exultation and horror, grief and pleasure, eternity and change' (Clark 1988, p. 295), and that it 'subdues to union, under its light yoke, all irreconcilable things' (Clark 1988, p. 295), was in sympathy not only with the views of Byron but those of Keats as well. '*Negative capability*', wrote Keats, exists 'when a man is capable of being in uncertainties, Mysteries, doubts, without any irritable reaching out after fact and reason' (Keats 1817 in Rollins 1958, p. 193). The 'poetical Character', he said:

has no self—it is every thing and nothing—It has no character—it enjoys light and shade; it lives in gusto, be it foul or fair, high or low, rich or poor, mean or elevated—It has as much delight in conceiving an Iago as an Imogen. What shocks the virtuous philosopher, delights the camelion Poet. It does no harm from its relish of the dark side of things any more than from its taste for the bright one; because they both end in speculation. (Keats 1818 in Rollins 1958, p. 386)

This mobility and mutability of temperament is often tied to the creative process, but here our focus is on the intensity, changeability, and complexity of Byron's temperament, its relationship to his manic-depressive illness, and Byron's quite extraordinary ability to harness and then transform the 'storms whereon he rode' (BCPW, vol. 2,

p. 92). Many of Byron's critics have assumed that much of what he wrote about—especially his tortured emotional states—was melodramatic, self-dramatizing, and posturing. It is the contention here that Byron in fact exerted a quite remarkable degree of control over a troubled, often painful existence, and that he showed an uncommonly expressive style, wit, and courage in playing out the constitutional cards he had been dealt.

'There are some natures that have a predisposition to grief, as others have to disease,' remarked Byron:

The causes that have made me wretched would probably not have discomposed, or, at least, more than discomposed, another. We are all differently organized; and that I feel *acutely* is no more my fault (though it is my misfortune) than that another feels not, is his. We did not make ourselves, and if the elements of unhappiness abound more in the nature of one man than another, he is but the more entitled to our pity and our forebearance (Lovell 1969, p. 179).

Byron suffered greatly from his 'predisposition to grief,' and often feared that he was going mad. He wrote and talked about suicide and actively engaged in a life-style likely to bring about an early death; from a medical point of view, his symptoms, family psychiatric history, and the course of his illness clearly fit the pattern of manic-depressive illness.

Symptoms and course of illness

Symptoms consistent with mania, depression, and mixed states are evident in the descriptions of Byron given by his physicians, friends, and Byron himself. His mood fluctuations were extreme, ranging from the suicidally melancholic to the irritable, volatile, violent, and expansive. Symptoms of depression included ennui, despair, lethargy, and sleeplessness. He thought of suicide and discussed it with others, to the extent that his friends and wife were at times concerned that he would take his own life. To a degree he saw his involvement with the Greek independence cause as a probable road to death, and it is likely that had he not died in Greece he would have killed himself in another way. His erratic financial behaviour was in a class by itself, and—taken together with his episodic promiscuity, violent rages, impetuousness, restlessness, risk taking, poor judgement, and extreme irritability—it constitutes a classic presentation of manic behaviour. Although there is no clear evidence that Byron suffered from either hallucinations or delusions, these are not a necessary component for the diagnosis of mania. Byron's irritability and rage often existed within the context of a melancholic mood, which is consistent with the diagnosis of mixed states (coexisting symptoms of mania and depression).

The clinical hallmark of manic-depressive illness is its recurrent, episodic nature (Kraepelin 1921/1976; Goodwin and Jamison 1990). Byron had this in an almost textbook manner, showing frequent and pronounced fluctuations in mood, energy, sleep patterns, sexual behaviour, alcohol and other drug use, and weight (Byron also exhibited extremes in dieting, obsession with his weight, eccentric eating patterns, and excessive use of epsom salts). Although these changes in mood and behaviour were dramatic and disruptive when they occurred, Byron was clinically normal most of the time; this, too, is highly characteristic of manic-depressive illness. An inordinate amount of confusion about whether someone does or does not have manic-depressive illness stems from the popular misconception that irrationality of mood and reason are stable rather than fluctuating features of the disease. Some assume that because an individual such as Byron was sane and in impressive control of his reason most of the time, that he could not have been 'mad' or have suffered from a major mental illness. Lucidity and normal functioning are, however, perfectly consistent with—indeed, characteristic of—the phasic nature of manic-depressive illness. This is in contrast to schizophrenia, which is usually a chronic and relatively unrelenting illness characterized by, among other things, an inability to reason clearly.

The diagnosis of manic-depressive illness in Lord Byron is given further support by other aspects of the natural course of his illness. Byron first wrote about his melancholic moods while still a schoolboy at Harrow; this is consistent with what is well known about manic-depressive illness, that its first symptoms tend to occur in adolescence or early adulthood (Goodwin and Jamison 1990). It is not uncommon for the underlying mobility of temperament to be apparent even earlier, and this also was the case with Byron. Manic-depressive illness is frequently seasonal as well, with depressive episodes more common in the winter months and around the time of the vernal and autumnal equinoxes, and mania more common in the summer (Eastwood and Peacocke 1976; Symonds and Williams 1976; Kasper *et al.* 1989; Goodwin and Jamison 1990). In addition to experiencing 'September melancholias', which he described to his mistress Teresa Guiccioli, Byron appears to have had a tendency toward both winter depressions and mixed states. August, for Byron, was often a time of extreme irritability, wrathfulness, and irrationality. In manic-depressive illness such states frequently are followed by depressive ones, and this would be consistent with Byron's observations that Septembers 'kill with their sadness'. Mood disorders, in addition to exhibiting seasonal patterns, frequently show pronounced diurnal rhythms as well. Byron described the most common form of this, being depressed in the morning and showing improved mood and increased energy as the day progressed. Yet another feature of the natural course of the disease, and probably the most important, is that manic-depressive and recurrent depressive illness, left untreated (or inadequately treated), often worsen over time; that is, the episodes of mania, depression, and mixed states tend to occur more frequently, be more severe, or last longer (Kraepelin 1921/1976; Angst 1981; Post *et al.* 1984; Roy-Byrne *et al.* 1985; Goodwin and Jamison 1990). This was true for Byron.

Family history

Byron had a family history remarkable for its suicide (in itself more likely to be associated with manic-depressive illness than with any other condition), violence, irrationality, financial extravagance, and recurrent melancholia. All these are common features of manic-depressive illness. Byron himself was the first to believe in the constitutional basis of his illness and temperament: 'It is ridiculous', he remarked to Lady Blessington, 'to say that we do not inherit our passions, as well as . . . any other disorder' (Lovell 1969, p. 55), and to Teresa Guiccioli he wrote, 'My melancholy is something tempera-mental, inherited' (BLJ, vol. 7, p. 189). To his publisher John Murray, he stated, 'I am not sure that long life is desirable for one of my temper and constitutional depression of Spirits' (BLJ, vol. 8, p. 216). Lady Byron, who ultimately sued Byron for separation on the grounds that he was insane, wrote: 'The day after my marriage he said, "You were determined not to marry a man in whose family there was insanity." . . . "You have done very well indeed," or some ironical expression to that effect, followed by the informa-tion that his maternal grandfather had committed suicide and a Cousin . . . had been mad and set fire to a house' (Elwin 1962, p. 252).

Lord Byron's morbidly excitable temperament was indeed an almost inevitable inheritance, far more so than that of his title and properties. For the latter he was obliged to the quirk of the early death of more probable heirs; for the former, he was the recipient of genes passed down inexorably by generations of violent, reckless, suicidal, and occasionally insane ancestors. In 1880 one of Byron's biographers noted: 'Never was poet born to so much illustrious, and to so much bad blood' (Nichol 1880, p. 12), a sentiment shared by Byron scholar Leslie Marchand. 'The Byrons', declared Marc-hand, 'seem to have grown more irresponsible with each generation, until the summit of social irregularity is reached in the character and conduct of the great-uncle and the father of the poet, if not indeed in the poet himself' (Marchand 1957, p. 3). He wrote that Byron's maternal side, the Gordons of Gight, displayed, 'a startling record of vio-lence rare even in the annals of Scottish lairds', presenting 'a spectacle of unrestrained barbarity' (Marchand 1957, p. 3).

Certainly, the Byrons were an ancient and notorious family in England—among other things, by the mid-seventeenth century, it was being written, 'Is't not enough the Byrons all excell,/As much in loving, as in fighting well?' (Walker 1988, p. 113). In the late seventeenth century, Margaret Fitzwilliam, wife of Sir John Byron and mother of the first and second Lords Byron, 'went out of her mind and never recovered her rea-son' (Walker 1988, p. 45). Lady Margaret was described as a woman of 'rare talent and beauty, skilled in the composition of music and poetry,' (Walker 1988, p. 44) and it was said that 'her ravings were more delightful then [*sic*] other women's most rational con-versations' (Walker 1988, p. 45). From its description, and because the breakdown occurred following childbirth, it is possible that what she experienced was manic-depressive psychosis. The genes, however, do not appear to have been passed on down through the branch of the family tree leading directly to George Gordon Byron, the poet. The true dissipation, eccentricity, financial chaos, and wildness of temperament appear to have been brought into the bloodlines at a quite specific point in the eight-eenth century. In 1720 William, the fourth Lord Byron, and amateur artist who had studied under the Flemish painter Peter Tillemans, married for a third time. It was this wife, Frances, daughter of Lord Berkeley and great-grandmother of the poet, who seems to have been largely responsible for bringing the 'taint of blood' into the Byron line (Nichol 1880, p. 5). She and the fourth Lord Byron had five children who survived into adulthood. The eldest, Isabella who showed strong interests in art and literature, had 'many money difficulties' (Walker 1988, p. 170), was 'distinguished for eccentricity of manners' (Nichol 1880, p. 7), and exhibited 'peculiar conduct' which 'excited comment even in that golden age of eccentrics' (Walker 1988, p. 118). The youngest child, George, showed 'neither marked eccentricity nor blameless respectability' (Walker 1988, p. 174), and Richard, the next youngest, was a clergyman and amateur artist hallmarked by his 'undeviating respectability' (Walker 1988, p. 172). In striking contrast to the younger Byrons, however, was the eldest son and heir to the title, William, who became the fifth Lord Byron. Known as the 'Wicked Lord', he was renowned for his extravagances, strange behaviour, and violent temper. In 1795, after a relatively minor dispute, Byron killed his cousin and was brought to trial in the House of Lords. He was found guilty of manslaughter but acquitted of murder and allowed to return to Newstead Abbey, the Byron family seat in Nottinghamshire. Like his grandnephew the poet, the fifth Lord Byron was easily inflamed. Enraged at his son, who—having inherited his father's financial irresponsibility but not his willingness to marry for money—eloped with his cousin (he, like several other Byrons, married first cousins, thus hopelessly muddling the attribution of inheritance patterns, or acquired traits), the Wicked Lord did everything possible to ensure that little of worth passed on to his heirs. His singularity of purpose and peculiarity of style were described by biographer André Maurois:

He paid his gambling debts with the oaks of the park, felling five thousand pounds' worth and stripping his marvelous forest nearly bare of timber . . . As a finishing touch in the spoliation of his son, Lord Byron killed two thousand seven hundred head of deer in the park, and granted a twenty-one years' lease of the Rochdale estate, where coal-seams had just been discovered, at the ridiculous rental of sixty pounds a year. His pleasures were those of a mischievous child. He would go down in the dark and open sluice-gates on the streams in order to damage the cotton mills; he emptied his neighbours' ponds; and on the edge of his own lake he had two small stone forts constructed, with a fleet of toy ships which he used sometimes to launch. He would spend whole days directing naval battles between the vessels and the forts; they fired on each other with miniature cannon. Lord Byron crouched in one of the forts, while his manservant, Joe Murray, lay stretched in a boat commanding the fleet. Sometimes, again, his lordship would lie on the stone flags of the Abbey kitchen and amuse himself by staging races of cockroaches up and down his own body, flipping the insects with straws when they were sluggish (Maurois 1984, pp. 23–4).

The Wicked Lord, in fact, outlived both his son and his grandson; when he died in 1798 he passed on not only his title to his grandnephew, the future poet, but his financial shambles as well.

John ('Foulweather Jack') Byron, the fifth lord's brother and George Gordon's grandfather, became a vice admiral in the British Navy and wrote one of the classic books about shipwreck; portions of his adventures, in altered form, found their way years later into Byron's great poem *Don Juan*. Although little has been written about any psychological difficulties Admiral Byron might have experienced, a suggestive comment about a possible 'breakdown' has been made by Byron genealogist Violet Walker. She notes that Byron declined, for 'health reasons', an appointment as second in command in North America during the War of Independence, and a few years later was the subject of a concerned letter written by a fellow officer; included in the latter's report was the observation: 'Since I wrote to your Lordship concerning Mr. Byron, I learn that this unfortunate man was struck with disorder and disease that deprived him of his reason' (Walker 1988, p. 158). Admiral Byron, like his nephew, had married a first cousin; of particular interest here, she was the daughter of the sister of Frances, Lady Byron, the wife of the fourth Lord Byron and the one thought responsible for inserting the 'family madness' into the Byron line. Sophia Trevanion, Admiral Byron's wife and therefore the poet's paternal grandmother, appears to have had a rather vivacious and mercurial temperament herself. Dr Johnson wrote, after meeting her, 'Poor Mrs. Byron is a feeler' (Rowse 1978, p. 138), and her friends 'all agreed that she had too much sensibility, was very much up and down' (Rowse 1978, p. 139); she was, as A. L. Rowse said about both her and her famous grandson, a 'true Celt' (Rowse 1978, p. 139).

In 1756 the first son of these two cousins (Sophia Trevanion and Admiral Byron), Byron's father, was born. John ('Mad Jack') Byron soon made the gambling debts, financial mayhem, and overall level of dissipation of his uncle the Wicked Lord seem subdued by comparison. Charming, good-looking, and ebullient, he served briefly in America with the Coldstream Guards before returning to the social whirl of London. There he met the wife of the future Duke of Leeds, and an heiress in her own right. After a scandalous affair and her subsequent divorce, they married, moved to France, and had several children. The only child to survive infancy, Augusta, was the poet's half-sister and great love. (In the Byron tradition, Augusta married their first cousin, George Leigh, who went on to have massive financial problems and gambling debts of his own; two of their three sons and two of their daughters had severe financial difficulties as well (Moore 1974, p. 16). (In addition, at least one of their children, described as 'mentally unbalanced,' had to be removed from their home and taken care of elsewhere.) When his wife died, Mad Jack, after accumulating even more debts, returned to England and married yet another heiress—this one Scottish—Catherine Gordon of Gight. He made rapid headway in spending this second fortune as well; eventually, a few years after the birth of their son, George Gordon, he moved back to France to avoid his creditors. He died young, dissolute, alcoholic, a victim of 'his restless moods, his sensual appetites, his wild gaieties and glooms' (Moore 1974, p. 29), and a probable suicide (Maurois 1984, p. 33; Moore 1961, p. 82; Kiernan 1898).

Byron's heritage from his mother's family was far more fierce, colourful, and dangerously unstable than the one from the spendthrift, now and again rather eccentric Byrons:

The first laird of Gight, Sir William Gordon, had been the son of the Earl of Huntly and Annabella Stuart, sister of King James the Second. But although the family history opened thus royally, a more tragic sequence of events could hardly be imagined. William Gordon was drowned, Alexander Gordon murdered. John Gordon hanged for the killing of Lord Moray in

1592, another John Gordon hanged in 1634 for the assassination of Wallenstein—it seemed as if a Gordon of Gight had been strung up on every branch of their family tree . . . The sixth laird, a conscious evildoer, used to say: 'I can tak' no rest. I know I will die upon a scaffold. There is an evil turn in my hand' (Maurois 1984, pp. 26–7).

Several generations later, Alexander Gordon, the eleventh laird and great-grandfather of Byron, died in a midwinter drowning that was almost certainly a suicide. Marchand quotes one sceptical response to a contemporary newspaper article (which had reported that the death was due to drowning while bathing): 'Scotsmen in 1760 had not become slaves to the tub so much as to induce them to bathe in ice-covered rivers in the depths of winter' (Marchand 1957a, p. 18). Alexander Gordon's son, the twelfth laird, George Gordon, also drowned; his death was probably a suicide as well (BLJ, vol. 8, p. 217; Maurois 1984, p. 27). Years later his grandson the poet in describing the constitutional basis for his own melancholy, wrote:

You know—or you do *not* know—that my maternal Grandfather (a very clever man and amiable I am told) was strongly suspected of Suicide (he was found drowned in the Avon at Bath) and that another very near relative of the same branch—took poison—and was merely saved by antidotes.—For the first of these events—there was no apparent cause—as he was rich, respected,—and of considerable intellectual resources—hardly forty years of age—and not at all addicted to any unhinging vice.—It was however but a strong suspicion—owing to the manner of his death—and to his melancholy temper (BLJ, vol. 8, p. 217).

Predictably, Byron's mother was left not altogether untouched by the Gordon inheritance; described as a woman 'full of the most passionate extremes' (Moore 1832, vol. 12) she was easily excited to rage and subject to wildly swinging changes of mood. During his adolescence Byron often confided in his half-sister Augusta about his mother's violent moods and unpredictable behaviour: 'My mother has lately behaved to me in such an eccentric manner' (BLJ, vol. 1, p. 54), he wrote while still a student at Harrow, adding several days later, 'Her temper is so variable, and when inflamed, so furious, that I dread our meeting . . . she flies into a fit of phrenzy' (BLJ, vol. 1, pp. 55–6). 'Her method is so violent, so capricious', he continued, with traces of the wit that was to characterize so much of his writing and speech as he grew older, 'that the patience of Job, the versatility of a member of the House of Commons could not support it' (BLJ, vol. 1, p. 56). The following year brought a continuation of Byron's outcries about his mother's behaviour and temperament: 'She is as I have before declared certainly mad . . . her conduct is a . . . compound of derangement and Folly' (BLJ, vol. 1, p. 68); she was, he complained, his 'tormentor' whose *diabolical* disposition . . . seems to increase with age, and to acquire new force with Time' (BLJ, vol. 1, p. 75). The combination of Byron's temperament with his mother's must have been an incendiary one, and Thomas Moore recounts: 'It is told, as a curious proof of their opinion of each other's violence, that, after parting one evening in a tempest . . . they were known each to go privately that night to the apothecary's inquiring anxiously whether the one had been to purchase poison, and cautioning the vender of drugs not to attend to such an application, if made' (Moore 1832, vol. 12, pp. 99–100).

Byron's children

The mingling of the Byron and Gordon bloodlines was bound to raise the temperature of the already fiery gene pools. As we shall see, Byron was the most immediate beneficiary of this coalescence but inevitably the effects extended to Byron's descendants as well. Allegra, his illegitimate daughter with Claire Clairmont (stepsister of Mary Shelley), died when she was only five years old and was therefore far too young to show definitive signs of either the Gordon-Byron temperament or any kind of serious mood disorder. It is suggestive, however, that Shelley quoted Byron as saying that his daughter's temper was 'violent and imperious' (Marchand 1957a, p. 920) and Shelley himself noted that 'she has a contemplative seriousness which mixed with her excessive vivacity . . . has a very peculiar effect in a child' (Marchand 1957a, p. 923). In a letter to his sister, Byron observed that Allegra had 'a devil of a spirit but that is Papa's' (BLJ, vol. 6, p. 62). Assessments of Allegra's temperament must, due to her early death, remain highly speculative. Much more is known about Byron's one legitimate child, however. Ada Byron, later to become Ada, Countess of Lovelace, inherited from her mother— whom Byron early in their relationship had dubbed the 'Princess of Parallelograms'— remarkable mathematical abilities. Described by eminent mathematician Augustus De Morgan as having the potential to become 'an original mathematical investigator, perhaps of first rate eminence' (Baum 1986, p. 40), Ada worked on Charles Babbage's calculating machine and earned for herself the designation of being the first computer programmer. In 1980 the United States Department of Defense honoured her contributions by naming its computer programming language ADA (Baum 1986, p. 40).

From her father Ada inherited a mercurial temperament that swung precipitously from the ecstatic and grandiose to the melancholic. She also acquired the Byron proclivities for gambling and financial chaos; at one point, convinced she had invented an infallible system for betting on horses, she suffered such severe losses that she was forced to pawn the Lovelace family jewels. It was her temperament, however, by which she was most particularly her father's daughter. Indeed, Byron, who although in exile followed her childhood as closely as he could, noted not long before he died that a description he had received of her disposition and tendencies 'very nearly resembles that of my *own* at a similar age except that I was much more impetuous' (BLJ, vol. 11, p. 121). Earlier, in his inimitable manner he had summed up his notion of the more diversified headwaters of Ada's temperament:

Her temper is said to be extremely violent.—Is it so.—It is not unlikely considering her parentage.—My temper is what it is—as you may perhaps divine—and my Lady's was a nice little sullen nucleus of concentrated Savageness to mould my daughter upon,—to say nothing of her two Grandmothers—both of whom, to my knowledge were as pretty specimens of female Spirit—as you might wish to see on a Summer's day. (BLJ, vol. 9, p. 77)

Ada, like her father, was episodically charged with an '*awful* energy and power' and a vastly confident 'exhilaration of spirit' (Baum 1986, p. 65); her grandiosity, occasionally delusional in degree, rivalled the cosmic sweep of Poe and Melville. One of her biographers quotes Ada, who had outlined her plans for taking on 'the mysteries of the universe, in a way no purely mortal lips or brains could do' (Baum 1986, p. 57):

I intended to incorporate with one department of *my* labours a complete reduction to a system, of the principles and methods of *discovery*, elucidating the same with examples. I am already noting down a list of discoveries hitherto made, in order myself to examine into their *history, origin, and progress*. One first and main point, *whenever and wherever I introduce the subject, will be to define and to classify* all that is to be legitimately included under the term *discovery*. Here will be a fine field for my *clear, logical and accurate*, mind, to work its powers upon; and to develop its *metaphysical* genius, which is not least amongst its qualifications and characteristics. (Baum 1986, p. 65)

No wonder that Ada wrote elsewhere that 'there is in my nervous system such utter want of *all* ballast and steadiness that I cannot regard my life or powers as other than precarious' (Baum 1986, p. 65). The lack of ballast was reflected also in her grandiose belief that she was 'simply the *instrument* for the divine purpose to act *on and thro*. . .' Like the Prophets of old, I shall *speak the voice I* am inspired with. I may be the Deborah, the Elijah of Science' (Moore 1977, p. 154). Doris Langley Moore points out that Ada's swings from 'transcendent elation' to 'despair' were often only weeks, rather than months or years apart (Moore 1977, p. 219). These rapid cycling mood swings were quite similar, in many respects, to those experienced by her father. Her writing during her melancholic moods occasionally bears an uncanny resemblance to his as well. In a letter to her mother she wrote:

I must refer you to Dr. Locock as to my present condition, for I am WHOLLY *unable* to write . . . He will tell you how shattered and done for I at length am. Pray don't be angry with me for *what I can't do* . As long as I had *fever* I could *write*, and had almost preternatural power. *Now*, this is all over . . .

The least exertion, either mental or bodily, has effects now that I never knew before. And *repose* is absolutely necessary. . . . Every power, mental and bodily, seems worn out (Moore 1977, p. 217).

Ada, like her father and his father before him, died at the age of thirty-six:

> The child of love,—though born in bitterness,
> And nurtured in convulsion,—of thy sire
> These were the elements,—and thine no less
>
> From *Childe Harold's Pilgrimage*, Canto III

Manic-depressive illness is the only medical diagnosis that could reasonably account for Byron's singular family history of suicide, tempestuous moods, violent melancholy, and erratic behaviour—to say nothing of Byron's own symptoms and the worsening course of his depressions and rages. A few months before he died Byron had a convulsive attack of some kind ('Epileptic—Paralytic—or Apoplectic is not yet decided by the two medical men who attend me') (BLJ, vol. 11, p. 113), and this, in conjunction with

Byron's violent rages, has been used as an argument that he may have suffered from an epileptic or seizure disorder (Abeshouse 1965). The attack was, however, the first in his life ('This is the first attack that I have had of this kind to the best of my belief. I never heard that any of my family were liable to the same—though my mother was subject to *hysterical* affections') (BLJ, vol. 11, p. 113) and almost certainly related to the final illness that caused his death. The diagnosis of a seizure disorder, such as temporal lobe epilepsy (or, complex partial seizures), would not account for Byron's pronounced family history of suicide and psychiatric illness, nor would it be the most explanatory diagnosis for his history of mood swings and the other symptoms so characteristic of manic-depressive illness.

The severity and pattern of Byron's moods and their devastating effect upon his life, form part of the argument for a diagnosis of manic-depressive illness rather than cyclothymic temperament alone. Yet Byron's temperament, coupled with his poetic genius, made him who he was. Byron is perhaps alone among English writers in having a particular kind of temperament and personal style named for him. The 'Byronic' has come to mean the theatrical, Romantic, brooding, mock heroic, posturing, cynical, passionate, or sardonic. Unfortunately, these epithets suggest an exaggerated or even insincere quality, and in doing so tend to minimize the degree of genuine suffering that Byron experienced; such a characterization also overlooks the extraordinary intellectual and emotional discipline he exerted over a kind of pain that brings most who experience it to their knees.

Byron's fiery and melancholic temperament at times crossed over the fine line that separates illness from health. (This is analogous to many other medical conditions—for example, diabetes, thyroid disease, and hypertension—in which the underlying predisposition flares up, from time to time, into acute disease. Such exacerbations of ongoing metabolic and other states may be temporary and ultimately self-correcting, representing only short-term discomfort and possible danger, or they may be progressive and life threatening. But they can also be both, and manic-depressive illness tends to fit the latter description). In Byron's case aspects of his underlying temperament often worsened into periods of painful melancholia and disruptive, perturbed mental states; by the end of his life these periods of emotional distress began to outweigh periods of health. His temperament also, however, made him exquisitely responsive to virtually everything in his physical and psychological world; it gave to him much of his great capacity for passion and understanding, as well as for suffering.

Childhood

George Gordon Byron was born in London in 1788, shortly after his parents' return from France, where 'Mad Jack' Byron had taken refuge from his creditors. Before young Byron was two, the family moved to Aberdeen, where he and his mother stayed until he inherited his great-uncle's title and properties at the age of ten. 'Mad Jack', in the meantime, had returned to France and died before Byron was three. It seems clear that

Byron's temperament as a child was father to his temperament as a man. His friend Moore wrote that 'as a child his temper was violent, or rather sullenly passionate'; his was, he said, an 'uncontrollable spirit' (Moore 1832, vol. 12, p. 11). His schoolmasters in Aberdeen described him as 'lively, warmhearted, and high-spirited . . . passionate and resentful, but affectionate and companionable . . . to a remarkable degree venturous and fearless' (Moore 1832, vol. 12, p. 18).

Byron wrote later in his life: 'I differed not at all from other children, being neither tall nor short, dull nor witty . . . but rather lively except in my sullen moods, and then I was always a devil' (BLJ, vol. 8, p. 258). Describing himself when he was about ten years old, he said: 'They once (in one of my silent rages) wrenched a knife from me, which I had snatched from [the] table . . . and applied to my breast' (BLJ, vol. 8, p. 258). By all accounts Byron also manifested early a desire and ability for deeply held friendships. Moore said: 'Of all the qualities, indeed, of his nature, affectionateness seems to have been the most ardent and deep,' (Moore 1832, vol. 12, p. 255) and his closest friend, John Cam Hobhouse, wrote in his journal:

No man ever lived who had such devoted friends. His power of attaching those about him to his person was such as no one I ever knew possessed. No human being could approach him without being sensible of this magical influence. There was something commanding, but not overawing in his manner. He was neither grave nor gay out of place, and he seemed always made for that company in which he happened to find himself. There was a mildness and yet a decision in his mode of conversing, and even in his address, which are seldom united in the same person. He appeared exceedingly free, open, and unreserved to everybody. (quoted in Moore 1961, p. 15)

Most of the qualities in his temperament that made Byron who he was—volatility, contradictoriness, and intensity of emotions; generosity of impulse and money; caustic and occasionally bitter wit usually followed by regret and softened by compassion; and a straightforwardness and honesty in dealing with emotional matters—had been set in place by the time he was sixteen years old. He possessed, through his experience and understanding, a piercing insight into the human condition and a broad understanding of the things that make human nature so especially human—love, envy, disappointment, aspiration, sex, revenge, vulnerability, and man's uneasy awareness of his own mortality.

Byron's proneness to melancholy was evident even when he was a schoolboy; while at Harrow, for example, he wrote to his sister of being 'peevish and fretful,' (BLJ, vol. 1, p. 48) thanking her for a letter that 'acted as a cordial on my drooping spirits and for a while dispelled the gloom' (BLJ, vol. 1, p. 48). A year later he described his 'idle disposition', 'very bad spirits', and then continued, 'I never was in such low spirits in my life' (BLJ, vol. 1, pp. 62–63). His constitutional melancholy was joined by painful self-consciousness about having been born lame. To Byron, taunted about it as a child in Scotland and then as a student in England, his deformity remained a source of bitterness and unhappiness throughout his life. Two examples of this, given by his friend Moore, are particularly poignant:

Seeing an unfortunate woman lying on the steps of a door, Lord Byron, with some expression of compassion, offered her a few shillings; but, instead of accepting them, she violently pushed away his hand, and, starting up with a yell of laughter, began to mimic the lameness of his gait. He did not utter a word; but 'I could feel,' said Mr. Bailey, 'his arm trembling within mine, as we left her'. (Moore 1832, vol. 13, p. 447)

In coming out, one night, from a hall, with Mr. Rogers, as they were on their way to the carriage, one of the link-boys ran on before Lord Byron, crying, 'This way, my lord'. 'He seems to know you,' said Mr. Rogers. 'Know me!' answered Lord Byron, with some degree of bitterness in his tone; 'every one knows me—I am deformed'. (Moore 1832, vol. 13, p. 447)

Byron took on and transformed his personal anguish; the following passage from his drama *The deformed transformed* captures the belief that disadvantage and pain—both psychological and physical—often fuel action and drive excellence:

> . . . Deformity is daring.
> It is its essence to o'ertake mankind
> By heart and soul, and make itself the equal—
> Aye, the superior of the rest. There is
> A spur in its halt movements, to become
> All that others cannot.
>
> (BCPW, vol. 6, p. 531)

Cambridge and early years

In October 1805 Byron arrived at Trinity College, Cambridge, where, if he 'ever attended a lecture,' wrote one biographer, 'he found it too dull to mention' (Marchand 1957*a*, p. 113). He did, however, read a great deal, write poetry, make friends, and lead an intermittently dissolute life. 'I have been extravagant,' (BLJ, vol. 1, p. 86) he wrote to Augusta in December of his first year, an understated confession if ever there was one. His personal generosity, as well as his other intemperate financial ways, led him inevitably to moneylenders and an ever-increasing indebtedness (by January 1808 he had accrued debts of £3000; by the end of that year he owed £12000; and by the time of his marriage in 1815 he was at least £30000 in debt) (Moore 1832; Marchand 1957*a*). During the following years at Cambridge and in London these extravagances fitted into a larger pattern of frenzied activity and excesses of all kinds; this pattern, skeined with melancholy, was particularly pronounced in the winter and spring. In January 1806 he wrote to Augusta that her attempts to 'reanimate' his spirits would 'I am afraid, fail in their effort' (BLJ, vol. 1, p. 87), and by the end of that year and into the beginning of 1807, Byron was in the throes of 'alternate moods of depression, ambition, and reckless indulgence' (Marchand 1957*a*, p. 125). His letters to his sister and friends throughout his Cambridge and early London years confirm this. In February he wrote to a close friend from Harrow days, 'I have recovered every thing but my spirits, which are subject to depression' (BLJ, vol. 1, p. 106); two months later he wrote to another friend, 'Nature stampt me in the Die of *Indifference*. I consider myself as destined never to be happy, although in some instances fortunate. I am an isolated Being on the Earth, without a Tie to attach me to life' (BLJ, vol. 1, p. 114).

Life never remained entirely bleak for Byron, however. In autumn 1807, having been told that regulations would not allow him to keep his dog at Cambridge, he acquired a tame bear— there being no rule forbidding bears—and housed it in the turret of his college rooms. His pleasure in the bear, which he walked through the streets of Cambridge, was obvious: 'I have got a new friend, the finest in the world, a *tame bear*, when I brought him here, they asked me what I meant to do with him, and my reply was "he should *sit for a Fellowship* . . ." This answer delighted them not' (BLJ, vol. 1, pp. 135–6). Byron and the bear, when later reunited at Newstead Abbey, would occasionally swim together in a vault leading to the graves of the monks who had previously inhabited the Byron ancestral home; along with other animals, the bear was kept in the family chapel, a thirteenth-century converted Chapter House. Byron had inherited his father's love for animals—in addition to their shared capacity for incurring debt, as well as probable incest with their respective sisters (Moore 1974)—and eventually developed a menagerie that, by the time he went into exile years later, was the subject of Shelley's bemused comments:

Lord B's establishment consists, besides servants of ten horses, eight enormous dogs, three monkeys, five cats, an eagle, a crow, and a falcon; and all these, except the horses, walk about the house, which every now and then resounds with their unarbitrated quarrels, as if they were the masters of it . . . [later] I find that my enumeration of the animals in this Circean Palace was defective, and that in a material point. I have just met on the grand staircase five peacocks, two guinea hens, and an Egyptian crane. (quoted in Marchand 1957a, p. 923)

By January 1808 Byron was living in London and writing to a friend that others thought of him as 'the votary of Licentiousness, and the Disciple of Infidelity' (BLJ, vol. 1, p. 146); typically, however, the rest of the letter was filled with discussion about poetry and literary critics. Just after his twentieth birthday in the same month, Byron wrote that he was 'buried in an abyss of Sensuality', 'given to Harlots', and in a 'state of Concubinage' (BLJ, vol. 1, p. 158). His immersion in drinking, gambling, and women was not without its expected toll:

My dear Hobhouse,—The Game is almost up, for these last five days I have been confined to my room, Laudanum is my sole support, and even Pearson wears a woeful visage as he prescribes, however I am now *better* and I trust my hour is not yet arrived.—I began to apprehend a complete Bankruptcy of Constitution, and on disclosing the mode of my Life for these last two years (of which my residence at Cambridge constituted the most sober part) my [Surgeon] pronounced another quarter would have settled my earthly accounts, and left the worms but a scant repast—(BLJ, vol. 1, p. 160).

In July 1809, Byron left England for a two-year 'Grand Tour' of Portugal, Spain, Gibraltar, Malta, Greece, and Turkey. His high spirits and aggressive enjoyment of life continued to be mixed with periods of melancholy. In May 1810 he resolved to adopt a new life: 'I am tolerably sick of vice which I have tried in its agreeable varieties, and mean on my return to cut all dissolute acquaintance, leave off wine and "carnal company"; he meant, he said, to keep to 'politics and Decorum' (BLJ, vol. 1, p. 241). Intermittently he was 'vastly happy and childish' (BLJ, vol. 2, p. 13), having a 'most social and fantastical' (BLJ, vol. 2, p. 48) winter in Athens, and enjoying excellent health. His inevitable melancholy caught up with him again in late 1810, however, and he wrote from Greece with blackish humour: 'I have nothing more to hope, and may begin to consider the most eligible way of walking out of it [life], probably I may find in England somebody inclined to save me the trouble . . . I wish I could find some of Socrates' Hemlock' (BLJ, vol. 2, p. 29). In May of the following year he wrote: 'At twenty three the best of life is over and its bitters double . . . I am sick at heart . . . I have outlived all my appetites and most of my vanities' (BLJ, vol. 2, pp. 47–8), and the next month he explained to a friend the morbidity at the heart of his seeming levity: 'I am so out of Spirits, and hopes, and humour, and pocket, and health, that you must bear with my merriment, my only resource against a Calenture' (BLJ, vol. 2, p. 51). As usual the low spirits were preceded and followed by high ones, for Byron's enthusiasms and excesses were part breeding ground for, and part distraction from, his brooding seasons; ultimately, of course, the ennui and vivacity were inextricably bound to one another, not entirely opposite sides to the same temperamental coin.

When Byron returned to England in July 1811 he brought with him the first two cantos of *Childe Harold's Pilgrimage*, the largely autobiographical (Moore 1832) poem that was to make him famous, as well as a typically intriguing collection of acquisitions, including additions to his menagerie. He catalogued a few of these purchases: 'Four ancient Athenian skulls, dug out of Sarcophagi—a phial of Attic Hemlock—four live Tortoises—a Greyhound . . . two live Greek Servants' (BLJ, vol. 2, p. 59). Already depressed prior to his return to England, within a few months of being back, Byron experienced the deaths of his mother, two close friends, and his 'violent, though *pure*' (BLJ, vol. 8, p. 24) love from his Cambridge days, John Edleston. The combination of his naturally melancholic temperament with the losses of these deaths sent him into a deep depression; he drafted a will, adding twice for emphasis that he wished neither ceremony nor burial service and desired to be buried with his 'faithful dog,' who was not to be removed from their shared vault. His dark mood was strangely mixed, however, 'for though I feel tolerably miserable, yet I am at the same time subject to a kind of hysterical merriment, or rather laughter without merriment, which I can neither account for nor conquer' (BLJ, vol. 2, p. 75). He remained depressed for several months and wrote to a friend about his state of mind:

I am growing *nervous* (how you will laugh!)—but it is true,—really, wretchedly, ridiculously, fine-ladically *nervous* . . . I can neither read, write, or amuse myself, or any one else. My days are listless, and my nights restless . . . I don't know that I sha'n't end with insanity, for I find a want of method in arranging my thoughts that perplexes me strangely (BLJ, vol. 2, pp. 111–12).

To another friend he wrote a few days later, 'I am very low-spirited on many accounts . . . I am indeed very wretched . . . all places are alike, I cannot live under my present feelings, I have lost my appetite, my rest, and can neither read write or act in comfort—(BLJ, vol. 2, pp. 117–18).

Rise to fame

Byron's spirits revived gradually, and in February 1812 he delivered his maiden speech, the first of three speeches he was to give, in the House of Lords. It was fiery—'perhaps a little theatrical' (BLJ, vol. 2, p. 167) by his own account—and one that reportedly 'kept the House in a roar of laughter' (Marchand 1957a, p. 345). A few days later his brooding poem *Childe Harold's Pilgrimage* was published; he awoke one morning, he reported drolly, and found himself famous. Byron became, almost overnight, the focus of London society. The Duchess of Devonshire wrote that *Childe Harold* 'is on every table, and himself courted, visited, flattered and praised whenever he appears . . . He is really the only topic of conversation—the men jealous of him, the women of each other' (Marchand 1957a, p. 335). Lady Caroline Lamb, wife of the future prime minister (Lord Melbourne), dashed in her journal after meeting him that Byron was 'mad—bad—and dangerous to know' (Marchand 1957a, p. 328), giving credence to the notion that the similar are inclined toward their own. Although their temperaments were likewise overwrought and volatile, their characters were in fact quite different. Byron was ultimately a highly disciplined if yet emotional man, and he was used to keeping his tempestuous moods under relatively tight control; Lady Caroline Lamb either would not or could not do the same, and after several turbulent months of passionate attraction on both sides, and then dreadful, acrimonious public scenes—including knife slashing (on her part) and verbal slashing (on his) Byron ended the relationship. He had written to her that:

People talk as if there were no other pair of absurdities in London.—It is hard to bear all this without cause, but worse to give cause for it.—Our folly has had the effect of a fault.—I conformed and could conform, if you would lend your aid, but I can't bear to see you look unhappy . . . we must make an effort, this dream this delirium of two months must pass away (BLJ, vol. 2, p. 177).

Although there continued to be some contact and correspondence, the affair was, for all intents and purposes, over; she continued to request time, meetings, and commitment but Byron remained resolute that the damage was long past repairing. Despite the public embarrassment, he held himself singularly accountable for his own actions, as he was to do years later following the far greater hurts and damages he experienced due to his wife's behaviour. In a letter to his closest confidante, Lady Melbourne (who was also Caroline Lamb's mother-in-law and the aunt of Byron's wife-to-be), he wrote that Caroline 'never did nor can deserve a single reproach which must fall hot with double justice and truth upon myself, who am much much more to blame in every respect, nor shall I in the least hesitate in declaring this to any of her family' (BLJ, vol. 2, p. 188).

Byron's spirits continued to fluctuate over the months that followed. January 1813 found him 'exceedingly wearied' (Marchand 1957a, p. 382) and irritable, November with a 'mind in fermentation' (BLJ, vol. 3, p. 157) and by the end of the year he was again feeling depressed and aimless:

I am *ennuyé* beyond my usual tense of that yawning verb, which I am always conjugating; and I don't find that society much mends the matter. I am too lazy to shoot myself—and it would annoy Augusta . . . but it would be a good thing for George [Byron's first cousin and successor to his title], on the other side, and no bad one for me; but I won't be tempted (BLJ, vol. 3, p. 236).

By the end of the same month, however, he was working at breakneck speed on a new poem, *The Corsair*, writing more than two hundred lines a day; when published a few months later, it sold ten thousand copies on the first day of publication and twenty-five thousand copies within one month. Yet he wrote on February 27, 'I am not well; and yet I look in good health. At times, I fear, "I am not in my perfect mind;"—and yet my heart and head have stood many a crash, and what should ail them now? They prey upon themselves, and I am sick—sick—. . . "why should a cat, a rat, a dog have life and *thou* no life at all?" ' (BLJ, vol. 3, p. 246). Although the quality of his life may have been in question to Byron, it was not strictly the case that he had no life at all: In addition to affairs with Lady Oxford and Lady Frances Webster, he had become involved in the most emotionally binding and scandalous relationship of his life, an affair with his half-sister Augusta:

> I say 'tis blood—my blood! the pure warm stream
> Which ran in the veins of my fathers, and in ours
>
> When we were in our youth, and had one heart,
> And loved each other as we should not love . . .
>
> .   .   .   .
>
> She was like me in lineaments—her eyes,
> Her hair, her features, all, to the very tone
> Even of her voice, they said were like to mine;
> But soften'd all, and temper'd into beauty;
> She had the same lone thoughts and wanderings.

(BCPW, vol. 4, pp. 68, 74)
From Manfred, Act II

They travelled together in the summer and autumn of 1813 and then spent part of the early winter of 1814 together in Newstead Abbey. She became pregnant, but it remains unclear whether Byron or Augusta's husband was the father of the child (in any event Byron was godfather).

Marriage and separation

In April 1814 Byron wrote to Lady Melbourne that he had called in a physician for himself and that he 'puts so many questions to me about *my mind* and the state of it—that I begin to think he half suspects my senses—he asked me how I felt "when anything weighed upon my mind—" and I answered him by a question why he should suppose that anything did?—I was laughing and sitting quietly in my chair the whole time of his visit—and yet he thinks me horribly restless—and irritable and talks about my having lived *excessively* "out of all compass" ' (BLJ, vol. 4, p. 105). The following month Byron described feeling a deep indifference to life and most sensations, 'the same indifference which has frozen over the "Black Sea" of almost all my passions' (BLJ, vol. 4, p. 121). Continuing in the same letter to Moore, he wrote, 'It is that very indifference which makes me so uncertain and apparently capricious. It is not eagerness of new pursuits, but that nothing impresses me sufficiently to *fix*; neither do I feel disgusted, but simply indifferent to almost all excitements' (BLJ, vol. 4 p. 121). He was again reporting to Moore in August that he felt 'quite enervated and indifferent' (BLJ, vol. 4, p. 153); during the same period of time, in a rage, he threw a bottle of ink out the window. Increasingly convinced that his only 'salvation' in life was to marry, he proposed late that summer to Annabella Milbanke, an unlikely and unfortunate choice: Prophetically, Byron was to write of his 'Princess of Parallelograms' that 'Her proceedings are quite rectangular, or rather we are two parallel lines prolonged to infinity side by side but never to meet' (BLJ, vol. 2, p. 231). To all intents and purposes humourless, she was also cool, cerebral, morally superior, and in almost every possible respect opposite in temperament from her husband-to-be. She was, as biographer Doris Langley Moore has pointed out, 'a conspicuously frigid type . . . perhaps no young woman ever lived whose writings show so intense a preoccupation with her own rectitude' (Moore 1961, p. 251). Annabella had, however, shown not inconsiderable, if somewhat smug, insight into Byron's character and temperament in her 'Character of Lord Byron,' written not long after she first met him. 'The passions have been his guide from childhood,' she wrote, 'and have exercised a tyrannical power over his very superior Intellect'; there was, however, 'a chivalrous generosity in his ideas of love and friendship, and selfishness is totally absent from his character'. She then went on to describe his mercurial temperament and his inconsistency of mind and mood:

When indignation takes possession of his mind—and it is easily excited—his disposition becomes malevolent. He hates with the bitterest contempt. But as soon as he has indulged those feelings, he regains the humanity which he had lost—from the immediate impulse of provocation—and repents deeply. So that his mind is continually making the most sudden transitions—from good to evil, from evil to good. A state of such perpetual tumult must be attended with the misery of restless inconsistency. He laments his want of tranquillity and speaks of the power of application to composing studies, as a blessing placed beyond his attainment, which he regrets. (quoted in Elwin 1962, p. 328)

She concluded, with unintended irony, 'He is inclined to open his heart unreservedly to those whom he believes *good*'.

In the midst of much melancholy and ambivalence, Byron—in part 'to repair the ravages of myself and prodigal ancestry' (BLJ, vol. 2, p. 85)—married Annabella Milbanke in January 1815. Despite his resentments, reservations, and savage mood, Byron was able to maintain some of his customary wit. His friend John Cam Hobhouse, serving as best man and well aware that Byron was at least thirty thousand pounds in debt, described the marriage ceremony: 'Miss M. was as firm as a rock and during the whole ceremony looked steadily at Byron—she repeated the words audibly and well. B[yron] hitched at first when he said, "I George Gordon" and when he came to the words, "with all my worldly goods I thee endow" looked at me with half a smile' (Hobhouse 1909, vol. 1, p. 196). By every account available the year of married life to follow was a nightmare for both parties, seared with the absolute ferocity of Byron's moods and Lady Byron's inability to deal with them (Professor Marchand notes that 'Byron's valet, Fletcher, who had seen his master in all of his moods and had by then been witness to his relations with dozens of women of all kinds, remarked with naïve wisdom: "It is very odd, but I never yet knew a lady that could not manage my Lord, *except* my Lady." ' (quoted in Marchand 1957a, p. 547). Byron's rages and periods of morbid depression were clearly frightening to Lady Byron, and excessive drinking and discussions of other women only exacerbated the situation:

He had for many months professed his intention of giving himself up either to women or drinking, and had asked me to sanction these courses, adding however that he should pursue them whether I gave him leave or not. Accordingly for about three months before my confinement he was accustomed to drink Brandy and other liquors to intoxication, which caused him to commit many outrageous acts, as breaking and burning several valuable articles, and brought on paroxysms of rage or frenzy—not only terrifying but dangerous to me in my then situation [her pregnancy]—(quoted in Elwin 1962, p. 328).

Lady Byron also reported her concerns that Byron might kill himself: 'He used to get up almost every night, and walk up and down the long Gallery in a state of horror and agitation which led me to apprehend he would realize his repeated threats of Suicide' (quoted in Elwin 1962, p. 256). On another occasion she noted, 'He then had his loaded pistols and dagger (which are always by his bedside at night) on the table through the day, and frequently intimated a design of Suicide. Once he seized the dagger, and ran with it to his own room, the door of which I heard him lock' (quoted in Elwin 1962, p. 344). Not only Annabella was concerned that Byron might take his own life. Augusta, in a letter to Annabella, wrote:

I have before told you of *his hints* of self destruction. The night before last, I went as usual to his room to light his Candles and seeing a Draught on the chimney piece which looked fermenting, I said 'What is this'. 'My Draught, to be sure—what did you think it was? Laudanum?' I replied jokingly that I was not even *thinking* of Laudanum and the truth—that I thought the Draught spoilt, which caused my inquiry. He immediately looked very dark and black (in the old way) and said 'I have plenty of Laudanum—and shall use it.' Upon my laughing and trying to turn off the subject he only repeated in the most awful manner *his most solemn determination* on the subject (Elwin 1962, p. 413).

The winter of 1815 appears to have been filled with violent rages and dark moods, but the spring and summer brought some relief, despite unremitting financial problems. By August, however, Byron's moods again had become wild and unpredictable, and in October 'he became the victim again of sleepless nights and nervous fears' (Marchand 1957a, p. 543). His drinking and rages became even worse, his behaviour 'increasingly erratic,' and by the end of the year Lady Byron was convinced that he was insane. She called in a consulting physician who could not give a 'decided opinion'; neither he nor Lady Byron's own doctor could agree that Byron was definitely insane (he had 'nothing like a settled lunacy') (Marchand 1957*a*, p. 569) and so Lady Byron was left to conclude that, if not the first part of Lady Caroline's jottings—that is, mad—then Byron must instead be bad (the 'dangerous to know' was a given). Later Byron was to write to this point in *Don Juan*:

> Don Jóse and the Donna Inez led
> For some time an unhappy sort of life,
> Wishing each other, not divorced, but dead.
> They lived respectably as man and wife,
> Their conduct was exceedingly well-bred,
> And gave no outward signs of inward strife,
> Until at length the smother'd fire broke out,
> And put the business past all kind of doubt.
> For Inez called some druggists and physicians,
> And tried to prove her loving lord was *mad*,
> But as he had some lucid intermissions,
> She next decided he was only *bad;*
> Yet when they ask'd her for her depositions,
> No sort of explanation could be had,
> Save that her duty both to man and God
> Required this conduct—which seem'd very odd

(BCPW, vol. 5, pp. 16–17).

In December 1815 their daughter was born; in January of the following year Byron and his wife separated. He never saw Lady Byron or his daughter again. Augusta described her brother's demeanour shortly after the separation:

He staid at home last night and was tolerably quiet, tho singing wildly and irritable. He gave me an opportunity of saying much more of *derangement,* and took it very quietly. He said 'Oh don't say so or talk of it because of my Will'—told me about Grandfather's end and his Mother always perceiving a resemblance between them—talked quietly and rationally abt it, but seemed rather alarmed at the thought (quoted in Elwin 1962, p. 382).

Byron's depression grew worse, deepening to the extent that his friend Hobhouse thought it worse than at any time since he had known Byron. In a letter to his father-in-law, written early in February, Byron discussed his own perspective on his temperament and marriage:

During the last year I have had to contend with distress without—and disease within:—upon the former I have little to say—except that I have endeavoured to remove it by every sacrifice in my power—and the latter I should not mention if I had not recent and professional authority for saying—that the disorder which I have to combat—without much impairing my apparent health—is such as to induce a morbid irritability of temper—which—without recurring to external causes—may have rendered me little less disagreeable to others than I am to myself.— I am however ignorant of any particular ill treatment which your daughter has encountered:— she may have seen me gloomy—and at times violent—but she knows the causes too well to attribute such inequalities of disposition to herself—or even to me—if all things be fairly considered (BLJ, vol. 5, p. 20).

Exile

It soon became clear that there was to be no reconciliation with his wife, and that the thickening rumours of incest, insanity, perversion, and violence were to provide no opportunity for even a semblance of a livable existence in England. Accordingly, Byron made plans to go abroad. Before doing so, however—and despite staggering debts requiring the forced auction even of his books—he ordered an inordinately lavish travelling coach modelled on Napoleon's; it cost five hundred pounds and was furnished with dining and sleeping facilities as well as a library. It turned out to be, in its own way, a bit like Byron: grand, Romantic, and liable to breakdowns. Byron and his companions, including his physician (the youngest graduate in the history of the University of Edinburgh medical school, he was himself no bastion of sanity and eventually went on to commit suicide), left London in April 1816. Byron left with bitterness and never saw England again:

I was accused of every monstrous vice by public rumour and private rancour; my name, which had been a knightly or a noble one since my fathers helped to conquer the kingdom for William the Norman, was tainted. I felt that, if what was whispered, and muttered, and murmured, was true, I was unfit for England; if false, England was unfit for me . . . I recollect, some time after, Madame de Staël said to me in Switzerland, 'You should not have warred with the world—it will not do—it is too strong always for any individual.' . . . I perfectly acquiesce in the truth of this remark; but the world has done me the honour to begin the war. (Moore 1832, vol. 15, pp. 105–8)

Shortly after arriving in Europe, during repairs to the carriage which had broken down for the third time, Byron began writing the third canto (his favorite, and the most personally revealing) of *Childe Harold's Pilgrimage*. When published later in the year, it caused Byron's great friend and supporter, Sir Walter Scott, to write:

I have just received *Childe Harold*, part 3rd. Lord Byron has more avowedly identified himself with his personage than upon former occasions, and in truth does not affect to separate them. It is wilder and less sweet, I think, than the first part, but contains even darker and more powerful pourings forth of the spirit which boils within him. I question whether there ever lived a man who, without looking abroad for subjects excepting as they produced an effect on himself, has contrived to render long poems turning almost entirely upon the feelings, character, and emotions of the author, so deeply interesting. We gaze on the powerful and ruined mind which he presents us, as on a shattered castle, within whose walls, once intended for nobler guests, sorcerers and wild demons are supposed to hold their Sabbaths. There is something dreadful in reflecting that one gifted so much above his fellow-creatures, should thus labour under some strange mental malady that destroys his peace of mind and happiness, altho' it cannot quench the fire of his genius. I fear the termination will be fatal in one way or other, for it seems impossible that human nature can support the constant working of an imagination so dark and so strong. Suicide or utter insanity is not unlikely to close the scene. (Scott 1816, p. 297)

A few weeks after beginning the third canto, in late May 1816, Byron met Percy Bysshe Shelley for the first time. The two poets rented villas near one another, not far from Geneva, and spent long days and evenings together talking, sailing, reading, and critiquing each other's poetry. Byron was 'an exceedingly interesting person,' wrote Shelley, but 'mad as the winds' (Shelley 1816, p. 181). Claire Clairmont, Mary Godwin's stepsister, with whom Byron had begun an affair just before leaving England, was also living with the Shelleys; when they returned to England in August she left with them, pregnant with Byron's child. The rest of 1816 passed uneventfully, at least by Byron standards. His friend Hobhouse, who visited in September, reported than Byron was 'free from all offense, either to God, or man, or woman; no brandy; no very late hours . . . Neither passion nor perverseness' (quoted in Prothero 1899, vol. 3, pp. 347–8). In the same month Byron began *Manfred*, in November he fell in love, and in December he described his recent times as among the 'pleasantest' and 'quietest' of any in his life (BLJ, vol. 5, p. 141). To Augusta he wrote, in high spirits and humour, 'At present I am better—thank Heaven above and woman beneath' (BLJ, vol. 5, p. 141).

Moderation, of course, could last only so long, and by January and February 1817 Byron was ill from the dissipations of an increasingly reckless and promiscuous lifestyle. In March he wrote to Moore that he had been plagued by sleeplessness and 'half-delirium' for a week (BLJ, vol. 5, p. 187). June and July found him again in good spirits, living near Venice and writing furiously (including the completion of more than 125 stanzas of the fourth canto of *Childe Harold*). Hobhouse, in October, noted that Byron was 'well, and merry and happy' (quoted in Page 1985, p. 54). Byron, never one to be paralysed by convention, sent for his horses so that he could gallop them along the water. Marchand writes that 'Byron's horses on the Lido became a byword in the city.' When Henry Matthews, brother of Byron's Cambridge friend, visited Venice in 1819, he recorded: "There are eight horses in Venice: four are of brass, over the gate of the cathedral; and the other four are alive in Lord Byron's stable" '(Marchand 1957*a*, p. 717).

January and February 1818 brought with them the early-winter dissolution that had become an almost predictable pattern, dating back to his Cambridge and London days. In May he described 'a world of other harlotry,' (BLJ, vol. 6, p. 40), and in June he moved into the Palazzo Mocenigo on the Grand Canal, where he was joined—rather improbably given the circumstances—by his infant daughter Allegra and her nurse. The following month Byron began writing *Don Juan*, and by August, according to Shelley, he had 'changed into the liveliest and happiest looking man I ever met' (Shelley 1818, vol. 9, p. 334); by December, however, Shelley had altered his view somewhat and, with clear disapproval, wrote that Byron 'allows fathers and mothers to bargain with him for their daughters . . . He associates with wretches . . . who do not scruple to avow practices which are not only not named, but I believe seldom even conceived in England' (Shelley 1818, vol. 9, p. 12). Perhaps. In any event, Mary Shelley added her concerns to those of her husband by April of the following year (Byron, it must be admitted, had written to his publisher in February that his involvement in the dissipations of Carnival had resulted in his not going to bed until 7:00 or 8:00 am. for ten days in a row): 'All goes on as badly with the noble poet as ever I fear—he is a lost man if he does not escape soon' (M. Shelley 1819, vol. 1, p. 92). Byron, in the meantime, was in the midst of falling in love again—this time with the Countess Guiccioli, a nineteen-year-old girl married to a man in his late fifties. The relationship with Teresa Guiccioli was to prove a long and stable one, certainly as measured against the chaos of the rest of Byron's life. His moods, however, were becoming increasingly melancholic and disturbing to him. Writing to his publisher in London, Byron said, 'I am out of sorts—out of nerves—and now and then (I begin to fear) out of my senses' (BLJ, vol. 6, p. 216), and in August he wrote to Hobhouse that he was writing 'with ill health and worse nerves'. He continued:

I am so bilious—that I nearly lose my head—and so nervous that I cry for nothing—at least today I burst into tears all alone by myself over a cistern of Gold fishes—which are not pathetic animals . . . I have been excited—and agitated and exhausted mentally and bodily all this sum-mer—till I really sometimes begin to think not only 'that I shall die at top first'—but that the moment is not very remote.—I have had no particular cause of grief—except the usual accom-paniments of all unlawful passions (BLJ, vol. 6, p. 214).

Byron's melancholy returned in January 1820 and January 1821, as well as intermit-tently throughout the year. In September he wrote to Teresa describing his depression and its seasonal turns: 'This season kills me with sadness every year. You know my last year's melancholy—and when I have that disease of the Spirit—it is better for others that I should keep away . . . Love me. My soul is like the leaves that fall in autumn—all yellow—A *cantata*!' (BLJ, vol. 7, p. 185). The next day he wrote her again: 'As to my sad-ness—you know that it is in my character—particularly in certain seasons. It is truly a temperamental illness—which sometimes makes me fear the approach of madness—and for this reason, and at these times, I keep away from everyone' (BLJ, vol. 7, p. 186).

In January 1821 Byron wrote in his journal:

What is the reason that I have been, all my lifetime, more or less *ennuyé* . . . [I] presume that it is constitutional,—as well as the waking in low spirits, which I have invariably done for many years. Temperance and exercise, which I have practised at times, and for a long time together vigorously and violently, made little or no difference. Violent passions did;—when under their immediate influence—it is odd, but—I was in agitated, but *not* in depressed spirits (BLJ, vol. 8, p. 15).

The following month he noted again the tendency for his mood to be more despond-ent in the morning: 'I have been considering what can be the reason why I always wake, at a certain hour in the morning, and always in very bad spirits—I may say, in actual despair and despondency, in all respects even of that which pleased me over night. In about an hour or two, this goes off, and I compose either to sleep again, or, at least, to quiet' (BLJ, vol. 8, p. 42). In September, as in the preceding year, he was again despairing, describing 'a mountain of lead upon my heart' (BLJ, vol. 8, p. 230); he also noted the worsening nature of his illness, writing that 'I have found increasing upon me (without sufficient cause at times) the depression of Spirits (with few intervals) which I have some reason to believe constitutional or inherited' (BLJ, vol. 9, p. 47). In April 1822, Byron's young daughter Allegra died; he again wrote in his journal that his melancholy was becoming worse. In July Shelley drowned. Byron, who had for a long time been involved in various political causes, became deeply caught up in the Greek independence movement. Always an activist, and one who believed that 'a man ought to do something more for mankind than write verses' (quoted in Marchand 1957*a*, p. 1052), he gave freely of his money, his efforts, and ultimately his life. The winter before Byron sailed for Greece, an English physician observed the poet's melancholy and reported that Byron had asked him, 'Which is the best and quickest poison?' (quoted in Marchand 1957*a*, p. 1052). His sudden and ungovernable rages, which had been part of his emotional make-up since childhood, and which had been especially pronounced during his year with Lady Byron, became more frequent and more furiously irrational. Moore noted that one of the grounds for the charges of insanity brought by Lady Byron against her husband, in addition to fears for her own safety, was the fact that Byron had taken an old watch that he loved and had had for years, and in 'a fit of vexation and rage . . . furiously dashed this watch upon the hearth, and ground it to pieces among the ashes with the poker' (Moore 1832, vol. 14, p. 464). In the spring of 1823, not long before he sailed for Greece, Lady Blessington described a scene in which Byron had 'betrayed such ungovernable rage, as to astonish all who were present'. His appearance and conduct, she wrote:

forcibly reminded me of the description of Rousseau: he declared himself the victim of perse-cution wherever he went; said that there was a confederacy to pursue and molest him, and uttered a thousand extravagances, which proved that he was no longer master of himself. I now understood how likely his manner was, under any violent excitement, to give rise to the idea that he was deranged in his intellects . . . The next day, when we met, Byron . . . asked me if I had not thought him mad the night before: 'I assure you,' said he, 'I often think myself not in my right senses, and this is perhaps the only opinion I have in common with Lady Byron'. (Lovell 1969, p. 80)

Byron had earlier commented to her:

As long as I can remember anything, I recollect being subject to violent paroxysms of rage, so disproportioned to the cause, as to surprise me when they were over, and this still continues. I cannot coolly view anything that excites my feelings; and once the lurking devil in me is roused, I lose all command of myself. I do not recover a good fit of rage for days after: mind, I do not by this mean that the ill-humour continues, as, on the contrary, that quickly subsides, exhausted by its own violence; but it shakes me terribly, and leaves me low and nervous after (Lovell 1969, p. 80).

Final months

Byron sailed for Greece in July 1823, and in the following month he experienced an even more violent attack of irrationality and rage. One of his companions at the time described the onset of the episode: 'He now vented his anger in sundry anathemata and imprecations, until he gradually lashed himself into one of those furious and ungovern-able torrents of rage, to which at times he was liable; the paroxysm increased so as almost to divest him of reason' (quoted in Marchand 1957a, p. 1111). Byron escaped into another room; the resulting scene is described by Marchand:

First the abbot [host for the evening's activity] and then Dr. Bruno attempted to soothe the angry lord, but both were forcibly ejected. 'It appeared,' Smith wrote, 'that Lord Byron was seized with violent spasms in the stomach and liver, and his brain was excited to dangerous excess, so that he would not tolerate the presence of any person in his room. He refused all medicine, and stamped and tore all his clothes and bedding like a maniac. . .' Trelawny entered next, 'but soon returned, saying that it would require ten such as he to hold his lordship for a minute, adding that Lord Byron would not leave an unbroken article in the room.' The Doctor asked Smith to get Byron to take a pill. Pushing past a barricade, Smith found Byron 'half-undressed, standing in a far corner like a hunted animal at bay. As I looked determined to advance in spite of his imprecations of "Baih! out, out of my sight! fiends, can I have no peace, no relief from this hell! Leave me, I say!" and he simply lifted the chair nearest to him, and hurled it direct at my head; I escaped as best I could' (quoted in Marchand 1957a, p. 1112).

The remainder of 1823 and the beginning of 1824 were filled with political and military planning focused on the Greek freedom cause. On his birthday, January 22, 1824, Byron wrote one of his last poems:

> On This Day I Complete My Thirty-Sixth Year
> Missolonghi, Jan. 22nd, 1824
>
> 'Tis time this heart should be unmoved,
>   Since others it hath ceased to move:
> Yet though I cannot be beloved,
>   Still let me love!
>
> My days are in the yellow leaf;
>   The flowers and fruits of Love are gone;
> The worm—the canker, and the grief
>   Are mine alone!
>
>   . . . .
>
> If thou regret'st thy Youth, *why live?*
>   The land of honourable Death
> Is here:—up to the Field, and give
>   Away thy Breath!
>
> Seek out—less often sought than found—
>   A Soldier's Grave, for thee the best;
> Then look around, and choose thy Ground,
>   And take thy Rest!

(BCPW, vol. 7, pp. 79–81)

Byron contracted a fever and died in April 1824, almost certainly a result not only of the illness but the medical treatment he received for it. He expressed repeatedly during the final days of his life a fear of going mad. To both his physician and servant he said: 'I know that without sleep one must either die or go mad. I would sooner die a thousand times' (Page 1985, p. 152), and it was only by using his fear that he might lose his reason that his doctors were able to persuade Byron to be bled. 'Do you suppose that I wish for life?' Byron asked his physician, 'I have grown heartily sick of it, and shall welcome the hour I depart from it' (Millengen 1831, p. 119). At another point he said, 'Your efforts to preserve my life will be vain. Die I must: I feel it. Its loss I do not lament; for to terminate my wearisome existence I came to Greece' (Millengen 1831, p. 141). Byron briefly recovered his mordant wit, however. A servant, told that his master was dying, said: 'The Lord's will be done'. 'Yes,' Byron replied, 'not mine' (Gamba 1825, p. 263).

Byron's body was returned to England. The scandal attached to Byron's life was such that the Dean of Westminster Abbey refused him burial there (he was buried near Newstead Abbey instead), and the aristocracy was unwilling to participate directly in the funeral procession. Instead they sent their carriages, a 'very long train of splendid carriages [more than forty], all of which . . . were empty' (Marchand 1957a, p. 1260). Finally, as recently as 1969, nearly a century and a half after Byron's death, C. Day Lewis, England's poet laureate, put a wreath of laurel and red roses on the white marble tablet newly laid for Byron in the floor of Westminster Abbey. No doubt Byron would have been gratified, as he would have been vastly amused by the absurd delay and attendant moral outrages. It is also likely, however, that he would have appreciated the two lines chosen for his epitaph, taken from a stanza in *Childe Harold*:

> But I have lived, and have not lived in vain:
> My mind may lose its force, my blood its fire,
> And my frame perish even in conquering pain,
> *But there is that within me which shall tire*
> *Torture and Time, and breathe when I expire;*
> Something unearthly, which they deem not of,
> Like the remembered tone of a mute lyre,
> Shall on their softened spirits sink, and move
> In hearts all rocky now the late remorse of love
>
> (BCPW, vol. 2, p. 170).

The apostle of affliction

Byron's work was inextricably bound to his life. He has become truly mythic, and his life's story, like a Greek tragedy or a requiem mass, is written and rewritten, within a given form and with a certain ordering of elements: set pieces to be arranged, anecdotes to tell, fragments of poetry from which to choose and then to recite. Upon this framework the thoughts, theories, and speculations of each writer are woven, and into this framework each writer's feelings about Byron—and the human condition— are projected. Byron seems often to command in death what he commanded in life: love, hate, respect, contempt, loyalty, and disdain—in short, controversy. Seldom, however, does Byron elicit indifference. In his own time, for example, *Blackwood's*

Edinburgh Magazine published an article stating that he was 'one of the most remarkable men to whom [England] has had the honour and disgrace of giving birth.' 'It appears', the authors wrote, 'as if *this miserable man*, having exhausted every species of sensual gratification—having drained the cup of sin even to its bitterest dregs, were resolved to shew us that he is no longer a human being, even in his frailties; but *a cool unconcerned fiend*' (quoted in Calder 1985, p. 66). Byron fared even less well at the hands of William Hazlitt, a contemporary critic and essayist, who, while admitting that Byron was 'never dull, or tedious' (quoted in Perkins 1967, p. 697), vehemently objected to the shadow Byron's temperament cast over his work, as well as his bent for making 'man in his own image, woman after his own heart' (Perkins 1967, p. 696). These criticisms were captured in a particularly good description of extreme Byronism:

He hangs the cloud, the film of his existence over all outward things—sits in the centre of his thoughts, and enjoys dark night, bright day, the glitter and the gloom "in cell monastic"—we see the mournful pall, the crucifix, the death's heads, the faded chaplet of flowers, the gleaming tapers, the agonized growl of genius, the wasted form of beauty—but we are still imprisoned in a dungeon, a curtain intercepts our view, we do not breathe freely the air of nature or of our own thoughts (quoted in Perkins 1967, p. 696).

His influence on other writers and artists, however, was profoundly different. Tennyson related to William Allingham: 'When I heard of his death . . . I went out to the back of the house and cut on a wall with my knife, "Lord Byron is dead" ' (Allingham p. 324) and Goethe acknowledged that 'Byron alone I admit to a place by my side' (quoted in Steffan 1968, p. 324). To John Ruskin 'Byron wrote, as easily as a hawk flies'; 'Byron', he said, 'was to be my master in verse, as Turner in colour'. 'Here at last', he continued, 'I have found a man who spoke only of what he had seen, and known; and spoke without exaggeration, without mystery, without enmity, and without mercy' (Ruskin 1978, p. 134). More recently W. H. Auden stated his belief that, 'Whatever its faults, *Don Juan* is the most original poem in English' (Auden 1966), and Byron was the only poet singled out for a separate chapter in Bertrand Russell's *History of Western Philosophy*. The list of writers, artists, and composers who were directly inspired by Byron's life and poetry is almost without peer; it includes Hector Berlioz, Alexander Pushkin, J. M. W. Turner, Robert Schumann, Victor Hugo, Alfred Victor de Vigny, Alfred de Musset, Giuseppe Verdi, Gaetano Donizetti, Franz Liszt, Peter Ilich Tchaikovsky, Arnold Schoenberg, Gioacchino Rossini, Charles Baudelaire, and Virgil Thomson (Stephenson 1983; Coote 1988). Not surprisingly, most of those influenced by Byron were themselves intensely emotional and inclined toward the Romantic. Byron, for all his Romanticism, thought and wrote with remarkable clarity, maintaining an unrelenting grasp on the realities of both his own and human nature. His biographers have made this point repeatedly. Moore, who was also a close friend, noted: 'Born with strong affections and ardent passions, the world had, from first to last, too firm a hold on his sympathies to let imagination altogether usurp the place of reason' (Moore 1832, pp. 385–6) and Leslie Marchand wrote that Byron was the 'most completely realistic of all the romantics' because 'he accepted the romantic urge as a part of human nature without pretending it was more than a dream' (Marchand 1957*b*, p. 164). In a related vein, but with a more interpersonal emphasis, Doris Langley Moore has made the point that Byron's 'was a singularly reasonable mind' (Moore 1961, p. 4); this comes through again and again in his journals, what is known of his conversations, and most especially in his letters. A particularly impressive example is contained in a letter written by Byron to his wife several years after their separation. In it he asked that she review what he had written about her in his memoirs (which, unfortunately, were burned by his publisher and friends after he died):

I could wish you to see, read and mark any part or parts that do not appear to coincide with the truth.—The truth I have always stated—but there are *two* ways of looking at it—and your way may not be mine.—*I* have never revised the papers since they were written.—You may read them—and mark what you please. . . You will find nothing to flatter you—nothing to lead you to the most remote supposition that we could ever have been—or be happy together.—But I do not choose to give to another generation statements which we cannot arise from the dust to prove or disprove—without letting you see fairly and fully what I look upon you to have been—and what I depict you as being.—If seeing this—you can detect what is false—or answer what is charged—do so—*your mark* shall not be erased (BLJ, vol. 6, p. 261).

One of the many things that makes Byron so interesting is the sheer power of his life and emotions. To focus exclusively, or even largely, on his psychopathology—other than to use it to understand him and his work—would be to make a mockery of his complexity, imagination, and vast energies. His personal discipline was extraordinary; his technical discipline, although overshadowed by the more Romantic notion of effortless poetry written 'as easily as the hawk flies' (and not helped by the fact that he seems to have published, with little discrimination, virtually everything he ever wrote) was also impressive. 'His reason was punctuated, even disturbed, by passion' wrote Alan Bold. 'But whatever he was in person he was not, as an artist, passion's slave. In the poetry Byron masks his passion and makes it into endurable art' (Bold 1983, p. 13). Byron himself wrote: 'Yet, see, he mastereth himself, and makes/His torture tributary to his will' (BCPW, vol. 4, p. 86).

In the end Byron brought a deeply redemptive spirit to the problems of despair, ennui, uncertainty, and disillusionment. In writing about another, he more finally described himself:

> The apostle of affliction, he who threw
> Enchantment over passion, and from woe
> Wrung overwhelming eloquence, first drew
> The breath which made him wretched; yet he knew
> How to make madness beautiful, and cast
> O'er erring deeds and thoughts, a heavenly hue
> Of words.

From *Childe Harold's Pilgrimage*, Canto III

References

Abeshouse, B. S. (1965). *A medical history of Lord Byron*. Eaton Laboratories, Norwich, New York.

Allingham, W. (1990). *The diaries*. (ed. H.Allingham and D. Radford). Folio Society, 1990.

Angst, J. (1981). Course of affective disorders. In *Handbook of biological psychiatry* (ed. H. M. van Praag, M. H. Lader, O. J. Rafaelsen, and E. J. Sachar), pp. 225–42. Marcel Dekker, New York.

Auden, W. H. (ed.) (1966). *Byron: selected poetry and prose*. New American Library, New York.

Baum, J. (1986). *The calculating passion of Ada Byron*. Shoe String Press, Hamden, Connecticut.

Bold, A. (ed.) (1983). *Byron: wrath and rhyme*. Vision Press Ltd, London.

Calder, A. (1985). *Byron*. Open University Press, Milton Keynes, England.

Clark, D. L. (ed.) (1988). *Shelley's prose*. New Amsterdam, New York.

Coote, S. (1988). *Byron: the making of a myth*. Bodley Head, London.

Eastwood, M. R., and Peacocke, J. (1976). Seasonal patterns of suicide, depression and electro-convulsive therapy. *British Journal of Psychiatry*, **129**, 472–5.

Elwin, M. (1962). *Lord Byron's wife*. Harcourt, Brace and World, New York.

Gamba, P. (1825). A narrative of Lord Byron's last Journey to Greece. John Murray, London.

Goodwin, F. K., and Jamison K. R. (1990). *Manic-depressive illness*. Oxford University Press, New York.

Hobhouse, J. C. (1909–1911). *Recollections of a long life*, 6 vols. John Murray, London.

Kasper, S., Wehr, T. A., Bartko, J. J., Gaist, P. A., and Rosenthal, N. E. (1989). Epidemiological findings of seasonal changes in mood and behavior. *Archives of General Psychiatry*, **46**, 823–33.

Kiernan, J. G. (1898). Degeneracy stigmata. *Alienist Neurologist*, **22**, 50–7.

Kraepelin, E. (1976) *Manic-depressive insanity and paranoia*. (Trans. R. M. Barclay; ed. G. M. Robertson). Originally published in 1921 by E and S Livingstone, Edinburgh. Reprinted by Arno Press, New York.

Lovell, E. U. (ed.) (1969). *Lady Blessington's conversations*. (Originally published in 1834 as the *Journal of the conversations of Lord Byron* by the Countess of Blessington). Princeton University Press, Princeton, New Jersey.

McGann, J. J. (ed.) (1980–1993). *Lord Byron: the complete poetical works*, 7 vols. Oxford University Press, Oxford. (Cited in text as BCPW)

Marchand, L. A. (1957*a*). *Byron: a biography*, 3 vols. Alfred A. Knopf, New York.

——(1957*b*). Byron and the modern spirit. In *The major English Romantic poets: a symposium in reappraisal*. Southern Illinois University Press, Carbondale, Illinois.

——(ed.) (1973–1982). *Byron's letters and journals*, 12 vols. John Murray, London. (Cited in text as BLJ)

Maurois, A. (1984). *Byron* (trans. H. Miles). Originally published in 1930. Reprinted by Constable, London.

Millingen, J. (1831). *Memoirs of the affairs of Greece*. John Rodwell, London.

Moore, D. L. (1961). *The late Lord Byron: posthumous dramas*. J. B. Lippinicott, Philadelphia.

——(1974). *Lord Byron: accounts rendered*. Harper and Row, New York.

——(1977). *Ada, Countess of Lovelace: Byron's legitimate* daughter. John Murray, London.

Moore, T. (1832; reprint 1900). *The works of Lord Byron: with his letters and journals and his life*, 14 vols. (ed. R. H. Stoddard). Frances A. Nicholls, London.

Nichol, J. (1880). *Byron*. Harcourt, Brace and World, New York.

Page, N. (1985). *Byron: interviews and recollections*. Humanities Press, Atlantic Highlands, New Jersey.

Perkins, D. (1967). *English Romantic writers*. Harcourt Brace Jovanovich, San Diego.

Post, R. M., Rubinow, D. R., and Ballenger, J. C. (1984). Conditioning, sensitization, and kindling: implications for the course of affective illness. In *The neurobiology of mood disorders* (ed. R. M. Post and J. C. Ballenger), pp. 432–66. Williams and Wilkins, Baltimore.

Prothero, R. E. (ed.) (1899). *The works of Lord Byron, letters and journals*, 6 vols. John Murray, London.

Rollins, H. E. (ed.) (1958). *The letters of John Keats*, 2 vols. Harvard University Press, Cambridge, Ma.

Rowse, A. L. (1978). *The Byrons and the Trevanions*. Weidenfeld and Nicholson, London.

Roy-Byrne, P., Post, R. M., Uhde, T. W., Porcu, T., and Davis, D. (1985). The longitudinal course of recurrent affective illness: life chart data from research patients at the NIMH. *Acta Psychiatrica Scandinavica*, **71**, Suppl. 317, 1–34.

Ruskin, J. (1978). *Praeterita: the autobiography of John Ruskin*. Oxford University Press, Oxford.

Scott, W. (1816) *The letters of Sir Walter Scott* (ed. H. J. C. Grierson 1933). Constable, London.

Shelley, M. (1819). *The letters of Mary Wollstonecraft Shelley*. (ed. B. T. Bennett) 1980, Johns Hopkins University Press, Baltimore.

Shelley, P. B. (1965). *The complete works of Percy Bysshe Shelley*, 10 vols. (ed. R. Ingpen). Gordian Press, New York.

Steffan, T. G. (1968). *Lord Byron's Cain: twelve essays and text with variants and annotations*. University of Texas, Austin.

Stephenson, R. (1983) *Byron as lyricist: the poet among the musicians*. In *Byron: wrath and rhyme* (ed. A. Bold) pp. 78–9. Vision Press Ltd., London.

Symonds, R. L., and Williams, P. (1976). Seasonal variation in the incidence of mania. *British Journal of Psychiatry*, **129**, 45–8.

Walker, V. (1988). *The house of Byron: a history of the family from the Norman Conquest, 1066–1988*. Quiller Press, London.

VIRGINIA WOOLF

CHAPTER 10

Creativity and madness: clues from modern psychiatric diagnosis

Gordon Claridge

Introduction to questions at issue

AT first glance, a connection of creativity to madness is both difficult and easy to make. On the one hand, especially in the current climate of psychiatric opinion about serious mental disorder as frank neurological disease, it is hard to see how possession of the intellectual qualities necessary for original thought can be associated in any way with the degraded cognitive functioning generally ascribed to psychosis. On the other hand, intuitively the notion has, to use a piece of psychometric jargon, a certain ecological validity, for several reasons. The meandering thoughts and images of the clinically insane are definitely novel; they are sometimes difficult to distinguish from others judged genuinely creative; and, even when recognized on closer scrutiny as more chaotic than that, they can nevertheless often convey the feel of an insight achieved, if not properly articulated. Awareness of this fact undoubtedly accounts for the centuries-old folklore belief about the topic—as well as the numerous quotable epigrams of the 'great wits and madness' variety to which it has given rise. These in turn have been inspired by the repeated observation that there is a raised incidence of mental illness among individuals of genius, a phenomenon that has generated a long stream of biographical and other descriptive literature (Lombroso 1891; Tsanoff 1949; Juda 1949; Grant 1968; Storr 1976; Becker 1978; Claridge *et al.* 1990; Jamison 1993; Post 1994).

These psychiatric and semi-psychiatric accounts of the creative personality have been supplemented by more systematic study, using psychometric and other test procedures to examine the question as part of normal differential psychology (Cattell and Butcher 1968; Barron 1971; Woody and Claridge 1977; Poreh *et al.* 1994; Merten 1995). An important, relatively recent, development here, influencing the choice of personality measures, has been the emergence of dimensional views of the psychotic disorders: the notion that the latter represent pathological variants of normal personality dispositions of a psychotic or 'schizotypal' kind (Claridge 1997; Eysenck and Eysenck 1976; Eysenck 1992).

The recognition that such traits exist as a healthy individual difference has two crucial implications for creativity research. First, it establishes a more explicit theoretical and empirical framework than hitherto for conceptualizing and investigating how creativity and psychosis might be related. Well-validated questionnaires for measuring psychotic characteristics are readily available (Mason *et al.* 1997) and conclusions no longer have to rely on inferences from less focused personality data. Also, the accompanying theories and experimental paradigms open up a wide range of possibilities for explaining the psychosis/creativity connection, a potential that has already been exploited in various guises (Prentky 1980; Eysenck 1995; see also Brod 1997, for a recent evaluation).

The second implication of the dimensional view of psychosis is that it helps to resolve the dilemma, referred to at the beginning of this chapter, of how to reconcile the superior qualities of creativity with the disabilities of madness. It does so by allowing the argument that it is not, of course, the psychotic *state* that mediates the connection, for that surely is inimical to creative production: as Plath put it, 'When you are insane you are busy being insane . . .'. Instead, the association, if it exists, needs to be sought in the underlying personality and cognitive *traits* that creativity and madness might have in common and which can, so the argument goes, have either a positive or a negative outcome, depending on interactions with situational and other individual differences characteristics, such as intelligence (Claridge and Beech 1995). As discussed later, this state/trait dichotomy may actually be too sharp a separation to make; for, in practice, particular creative acts, in so far as they do relate to psychosis, presumably reflect both transient and permanent features. However, distinguishing between the two, serves to clear up one confusion, the resolution of which, as Brod (1997) rather impatiently points out, should be obvious but which does not yet '. . . seem to have permeated the comprehension of many researchers, both within the field of creativity research and outside it'.

Although there appears to be satisfactory evidence that *something* about madness can inform our understanding of creativity, it has not proved easy to go beyond that and to agree on the detail of where the connection actually lies. Some reasons for this are familiar: the definition of creativity; possible differences among its various forms of expression (e.g. arts versus science); the poor reliability and validity of so-called 'creativity tests'; the latters' inability, perhaps, to tap true genius, as distinct from talent; the likelihood that originality filtered through madness is of a special kind; and so on. Important as they are, these questions mostly cannot be considered here: the present chapter has the more modest aim of examining some specific issues closer to the madness/creativity debate itself.

The issues referred to all stem from emerging differences of opinion that are apparent in the field, concerning the precise aspects or forms of psychosis with which heightened creativeness might be held to be associated. In the current psychological literature on personality and creativity, this is revealed in the way differing interpretations of 'psychoticism' are applied to the problem. In psychiatry the matter has been articulated more as a question about diagnosis, in the form: is it schizophrenia or is it affective psychosis that relates to creativity? Older biographical writings about the mental illnesses of the famously creative usually left the answer obscure, either because the distinction was not clearly drawn or, if it was, unreliably. Modern interpretations of such evidence have addressed the point, but have disagreed about the answer. Some recent reviewers, notably Jamison (1993), have strongly rejected any association of creativity to schizophrenia, preferring a connection to affective psychosis, especially bipolar (manic-depressive) disorder. As an illustration of this argument, Jamison in Chapter 9 describes the ways in which Byron's life and actions might be said to fit the manic-depressive description. On the other hand, earlier compilations (e.g. Prentky 1980) refer extensively to both, the schizophrenia diagnosis being applied to many of the eminent individuals considered; famous examples include Strindberg, Baudelaire, Faraday, and Newton.

Ambiguity in the use of diagnostic labels in creativity research has paralleled psychiatry's general, and long standing, confusion about the nosology (and aetiology) of the major psychoses. The problem has been eased somewhat by a series of revisions to the psychiatric glossaries, which state diagnostic criteria for defining different disorders: the international (ICD) system of the World Health Organisation (1992) and, in North America, the Diagnostic and Statistical Manual (DSM), currently the DSM-IV (American Psychiatric Association 1994). Interestingly, using an earlier version, the DSM-IIIR, to assess the psychiatric status of nearly 300 world-famous men, Post (1994) concluded that schizophrenia was not a significant factor. In a later study focused specifically on writers, the same author (Post 1996) does not even mention schizophrenia; instead he starts from the assumption, and concludes, that affective disorder predominates. In this he joins others reporting on similar data (Jamison 1989; Andreasen 1987; Ludwig 1994).

On the face of it, the studies just quoted (as the most recently conducted) might be held to have already answered the question posed earlier about diagnostic specificity in relation to creativity. However, glossaries such as ICD and DSM, even in their revised forms, do not represent the last word in psychiatric nosology. They are largely atheoretic systems of description and classification, arrived at by committee consensus; practical manuals designed to facilitate diagnostic decision-making. As such, they are based on categorical divisions of mental illness that may or may not be valid and merely reflect the latest psychiatric *Zeitgeist*. The psychoses are especially problematical in this respect, because of difficulties in defining their exact boundaries and, in ignorance of aetiology, of finding a rational way of dealing with their evident heterogeneity. This leaves considerable room for disagreement and debate, which ICD and DSM do not address.

There are two, somewhat related, issues pertinent to the topic. One, concerning schizophrenia, stems from the varied ways in which different classificatory systems define the disorder. The other concerns the separateness or otherwise of schizophrenia and affective psychosis, some authorities arguing that they constitute distinct types of disease, others that they simply represent different expressions of a single disorder. The next section will consider this question of definition; after which, to see how it impacts upon creativity research, I will present some illustrative data from our own studies of eminent writers. Finally, I will offer suggestions about how, in the light of such evidence, one might best construe the association between madness and creativity.

One psychosis or more?

The psychiatric perspective

The observation that insanity can take various forms—differentially affecting perception, thinking, and the emotions—has a long history in psychiatry. But so, too, does the idea of there being only a *single* form of insanity, or unitary psychosis (*Einheitpsychose* in the German). Indeed, during the nineteenth century the latter theory was very prominent, but later receded as psychiatry gradually tried to arrive at a classification of mental diseases (Berrios 1995). The credit for finally doing so is usually ascribed jointly to Emil Kraepelin (1919) and Eugen Bleuler (1911). Kraepelin's contribution was the distinguishing of two major varieties of insanity: an affective, manic-depressive, type and the heterogeneous set, *dementia praecox* (renamed 'the schizophrenias' by Bleuler). This binary view of psychosis laid the groundwork for modern psychiatric nosology and has shaped most psychiatric theory and practice during the twentieth century.

In recent years, however, there has been something of a revival of *Einheitpsychose* theory; centring partly on observations that bipolar (manic-depressive) psychosis and schizophrenia do not appear to be as distinguishable as was once thought. One sign of this is to be found in the latest versions of ICD and DSM themselves—as the listing of a mixed, 'schizoaffective', form of disorder, of which depressive, manic, and bipolar types are recognized. Yet two points are worth noting about the way in which the psychiatric glossaries actually handle this overlap between schizophrenia and affective illness. First schizoaffective disorder is firmly bundled in with schizophrenia, in DSM-IV in the section headed 'Schizophrenia and other psychotic disorders', and therefore as primarily schizophrenia, complicated by significant mood disturbance. Secondly, in both DSM-IV and ICD-10 the mood disorders themselves occupy an entirely separate section in which the term 'psychotic' is scarcely referred to. Where it is, it is used only to denote a 'specifier', viz. a feature (like hallucinations and delusions) that identifies a variant on the major mood diagnosis. Deliberate or otherwise, there appears to be a subtle move in the DSM (and ICD) terminology to distance the concept of manic-depression from its traditional roots as a *psychotic* disorder. The current psychiatric glossaries therefore tend, if anything, to strengthen, rather than weaken, the idea of a separation of schizophrenia from other types of psychosis. But this has been challenged on a number of fronts (see Taylor (1992) for a useful review).

Most obviously, at the symptom level it has been claimed that statistical analyses fail to show any clear point of disunity between schizophrenia and affective psychosis (Brockington *et al.* 1979; Kendell and Brockington, 1980); leading Kendell (1991) to comment that 'it is time we questioned Kraepelin's paradigm of distinct disease entities and of two discrete types of functional psychosis'. Further support for this view comes from the interchangeability of treatments between the two forms of psychosis (Klein and Fink 1963; Overall *et al.* 1964; Delva and Letemendia 1982; Abraham and Kulhara 1987). Then, on a more scientific front, there are observations that many experimentally established differences claimed for schizophrenia can often be found in affective disorder. Kendell (1991) also comments on this phenomenon, as follows:

Time after time research workers have compared groups of schizophrenics and normal controls and found some difference between the two which they assumed to be a clue to the aetiology of schizophrenia, only for someone else, years later, to find the same abnormality in patients with affective disorders. Of all the dozens of biological abnormalities reported in schizophrenics in the last 50 years, none has yet proved to be specific to that syndrome. All have been found, although often less frequently, in patients with affective psychoses, and none has been demonstrated in more than a minority of schizophrenics.

An example of the overlap in experimental data that is especially relevant here is overinclusive thinking, a form of psychotic thought disorder that can be considered a pathological equivalent of the 'divergent' thinking implicated in creativity. The phenomenon of overinclusion has its origins very firmly rooted in schizophrenia research—as a classically described feature of *schizophrenic* cognition (Cameron 1938; Payne *et al.* 1959). Yet it also occurs in mania (Andreasen and Powers 1974).

Adherents of the unitary model also quote genetic findings (e.g. Baron and Gruen 1991) on the intermingling of familial liabilities to schizophrenia and affective disorders; coupled to the failure to establish, among the schizophrenias, what McGuffin *et al.* (1987) have called natural 'lines of cleavage' that might be traceable back to the gene. The most strongly stated psychiatric interpretation of such evidence is that offered by Crow (1986, 1991). He has argued for a continuum of psychosis, running from normality, through affective disorder, to schizophrenia, and biologically mediated by genetic influences on the neurodevelopment of brain asymmetry (Crow 1990). It remains to be seen whether such a sweeping and explicit version of *Einheitpsychose* theory is helpful. Certainly some commentators (e.g. Strömgren 1994; LaPierre 1994) have been more cautious, finding the genetic evidence in particular difficult to reconcile with an outright rejection of the binary model. Nevertheless, the very existence of the debate puts down a strong marker that the traditional Kraepelinian division of serious mental illness might benefit from some revision which takes account of continuities and overlap between the two classic forms.

The psychological perspective

An early theoretical bridge between psychiatric and psychological formulations of psychosis is to be found in the writings of Ernst Kretschmer (1925). His notion of a personality dimension of schizothymia-cyclothymia, anchored at the far ends by schizophrenia and manic-depression, incorporated the twin features expected of a unitary model of psychosis; namely, defining characteristics that distinguished two different types of insanity, but connected on a continuum so that mixed forms were possible. Eysenck's (1952*a*, *b*) later adaptation of Kretschmer stated the *Einheitpsychose* view even more explicitly, by proposing, on the basis of factor analysis of psychological test data, a single dimension of psychoticism; this allowed for variations *within* the unitary psychosis being due to differences along a second, orthogonal, dimension of introversion-extraversion. Thus, Eysenck anticipated by many years psychiatry's own rediscovery of *Einheitpsychose* theory. Neglect of his contribution, especially by psychiatrists, is perhaps due to the way in which he subsequently developed the psychoticism concept as toughmindedness or aggressiveness (Eysenck and Eysenck 1976). This tended to focus his interpretation of psychoticism rather narrowly and idiosyncratically and to take it outside a mainstream of clinical thinking about psychosis (Claridge 1981, 1983). On the other hand, it did draw particular attention to an important part of the dimensionality of psychosis—the latter's connections to the personality disorders (Eysenck 1992).

A construct having, historically and in contemporary research, more clinical influence is 'schizotypy'. Unlike Eysenck's theory, its origins lie firmly in a binary view of psychosis; it was developed by Meehl (1962, 1990) and his followers as a highly specific (in its more extreme form single gene) explanation of the schizophrenia spectrum. This slant continues in the North American development of the concept (for a comprehensive coverage see Raine *et al.* 1995). However, some workers elsewhere, partly influenced by Eysenck, have pursued a more broadly-based approach (see Claridge 1997 for reviews). This has tended to draw schizotypy into the normal personality sphere and to link it to more general psychotic traits. Underlining the point, an important recent development, based on factor analyses of questionnaire measures, has been the observation that schizotypy breaks down into four distinct components: tendency to unusual experiences, attentional dysfunction, negative affect, and impulsive behaviour. Evaluation of such findings (reviewed by Mason *et al.* 1997) has mostly concentrated on the *schizophrenia* connection; e.g. in the close parallel that can be seen to exist between the factors found in normal schizotypy and those isolated in clinical symptom data collected on schizophrenic patient samples. Yet there is every indication that this is too restrictive a view: the domain tapped by so-called 'schizotypy' measures actually seems much wider. It appears to include, on the clinical side, the whole of psychosis and in personality a 'broad psychoticism', i.e. more extensive than that covered by Eysenck's P-scale, which measures only one component.

There are three reasons for believing this to be the case. First, the symptom clusters found in schizophrenia—on to which the schizotypal components referred to above have been mapped—have also been demonstrated in bipolar disorder (Maziade *et al.* 1995). Secondly, where a scale of Hypomanic Personality was included in a large factor analysis of 'schizotypy' questionnaires, it loaded highly on the leading component, alongside more manifestly schizophrenic-like measures, such as magical ideation, perceptual aberration, and schizotypal personality (Claridge *et al.* 1996). Thirdly, it has been claimed (Eysenck and Barrett 1993) that, in analyses of test batteries made up of these same 'schizotypy' scales, an alternative factor solution can be found that corresponds to Eysenck's three dimensions of E, N, and P. In other words, an Eysenckian *Einheitpsychose* view and a more conventional 'schizotypy' description of the same correlation matrix appear to be completely interchangeable, making the alternative unitary theory perfectly feasible.

Summary

One of the striking things about psychotic illness is its great variety of clinical presentation. This is true even for what have classically been called the schizophrenias; it becomes even more evident if one includes the affective disorders. The point at issue for psychiatric nosology is whether, in trying to deal with such heterogeneity, it is better to seek distinct entities of disorder; or whether it is more sensible to recognize certain commonalities in all serious (functional) mental illness, with variable modes of expression accounting for the different clinical forms. The evidence reviewed above suggests that the latter solution is certainly a strong contender; whether judged from studies of the disorders themselves or from work on the underlying (dimensional) dispositions.

It might be argued that the above debate has little relevance to the association between creativity and mental illness. For it should make no difference whether one uses a unitary or a binary classification of psychosis: relationships with schizophrenic or affective forms should show up either way. This is probably true at a purely descriptive level. But one's choice of an overall model for mental illness does make a difference when it comes to causal explanation; for the latter may vary substantially depending on whether or not it is derived from a view of psychiatric disorders as distinct entities with discrete aetiologies. As an example, consider an observation that pure schizophrenia is rare, but affective disorder is common, among creative individuals. If one adopts a binary view of psychosis, this would tend to dissuade any attempt to seek an explanation in theories, paradigms, or experimental findings drawn from the schizophrenia literature. A unitary psychosis perspective, on the other hand, would consider these to be very pertinent sources of information and inspiration.

I will elaborate further on that point at the end of the chapter. But first, as additional background, the following section considers some particular examples of using psychiatric diagnosis to examine the creativity/madness question. It involved reassessing the psychiatric status of a small group of (deceased) writers whose psychoses had already been documented. The exercise is unusual because it made use, for the first time as far as I am aware, of a polydiagnostic computer program system applied to biographical material on such individuals. Diagnoses available in the program cover both the schizophrenias and affective disorder, arrived at according to different sets of criteria. The method therefore allowed us to check the results against previous diagnoses made on the same subjects, as well as discover how much diagnostic variation there is across the psychosis spectrum and what diagnoses, if any, predominate.

A polydiagnostic investigation of writers

Method of diagnostic evaluation

The procedure used for assessing our subjects was version 3.3 of the OPCRIT (OPerationalCRITeria) diagnostic system (McGuffin *et al.* 1991; Farmer *et al.* 1992). OPCRIT consists of a suite of computer programs that allow multiple operational criteria of schizophrenia and affective disorder to be applied to data coded from a 90-item checklist. It is currently in use in a number of biological, epidemiological, and clinical research settings and has recently been shown to have good concurrent validity when judged against consensual diagnoses arrived at by the more conventional method of rater agreement (Craddock *et al.* 1996).

OPCRIT uses 12 classificatory systems, as follows:

Diagnostic and Statistical Manual (DSM-III) (American Psychiatric Association 1980): Ten categories covering major affective and psychotic disorders, including schizophrenic, paranoid, atypical, and mixed states.

DSM-IIIR (American Psychiatric Association 1987): as for DSM-III, but in 17 categories.

Research Diagnostic Criteria (RDC) (Spitzer *et al.* 1978): nine categories, including three mixed variants of schizoaffective disorder and 'broad' and 'narrow' definitions of schizophrenia.

St Louis criteria (Feighner *et al.* 1972): eight categories for affective and schizophrenic disorders, and variants.

'Flexible' system (Carpenter *et al.* 1973): two categories allowing for 'broad' and 'narrow' definitions of schizophrenia.

First rank symptoms (Schneider 1959): schizophrenia diagnosed according to the presence or absence of symptoms considered to be cardinal or 'first rank'. These consist of certain bizarre experiences, such as auditory hallucinations in which the person hears a running commentary of voices on his or her thoughts and behaviour, or delusions that ideas are being inserted, removed, or controlled by an outside force.

French criteria (Pull *et al.* 1987): four categories of non-affective psychosis.

Taylor and Abrams criteria (1978): four categories, one for schizophrenia and three for affective disorder.

Tsuang and Winokur subtypes (1974): three categories of schizophrenia: paranoid, undifferentiated, hebephrenic. The last of these, labelled with a term that originates in the earliest attempts to subdivide schizophrenia, describes a particularly 'malignant' form of the illness. Hebephrenia typically starts in late adolescence, and is characterized by disorganized, incoherent thought and speech, silly, inappropriate affect, and unpredictable behaviour that rapidly progress into the apathy, self-absorption, and loss of volition that define 'negative' symptoms (see below).

Crow subtypes (1980): three categories of schizophrenia: Type I (positive symptoms); Type II (negative symptoms); and mixed. Here positive symptoms refer to 'active' features of illness, such as delusions, hallucinations, and disorganized thought and speech; negative symptoms consist of the 'absence' of behaviours: apathy, paucity of speech, blunting of emotion, and so on.

Farmer subtypes (Farmer *et al.* 1983; Williams *et al.* 1993): two categories of schizophrenia-paranoid-like (P-type) and hebephrenic-like (H-type).

International Classification of Disease (ICD-10) (World Health Organisation 1992): a total of 20 categories covering the whole range of psychotic disorders, including affective, schizophrenic, and mixed forms.

The clinical information entered into the OPCRIT program is divided into five sections: appearance and behaviour; speech and form of thought; affect and associated features; abnormal beliefs and ideas; and abnormal perceptions. Additional data entered consists of personal details, family background, and other medical history, including drug dependence and brain disease. A glossary and set of definitions provide guidelines for completing the checklist.

OPCRIT is intended to be usable over a choice of time frames—from lifetime to a single episode of illness—and with a wide range of information, including personal interview with the client, hospital case notes, or a combination of other sources of data, with or without interview. Since the subjects in the present application of the method were not available for inverview, in making our assessments we drew upon as much lifetime biographical information as possible, following a procedure described below.

There is one further point to be made, about the interpretation of our results obtained with OPCRIT. Should we demand consensus across all 12 of the OPCRIT diagnostic systems before we accept that a particular author was, say, schizophrenic rather than suffering from manic-depression? Or can we be content with a majority opinion? And what do we do about the presence in OPCRIT of intermediate diagnostic classes, such as schizoaffective psychosis? In a sense, of course, these dilemmas literally beg the questions that OPCRIT was designed to answer, part of the purpose of current 'professional' research with it being to try to settle the debate about different psychotic disorders as distinct, and definable disease entities. The interim use of OPCRIT in the present, more applied, context can therefore only be expected to work within the continuing uncertainty on that matter. In practice, this means hoping that a pattern of results emerges from OPCRIT that is unambiguous enough to allow conclusions to be drawn about the main point at issue here: the relative importance of schizophrenic, as compared, with affective elements in the psychopathology of our authors. Ideally, we would hope for this to be revealed in consensus across the diagnostic systems contained in OPCRIT: we can anticipate that in general that will not be the case and that conclusions will need to be based on a combination of majority verdict and evidence from other sources.

Ten psychotic authors revisited

In an earlier book (Claridge *et al.* 1990) two literary scholars and I examined in detail the lives of ten authors who, we suggested, illustrate some important themes in current thinking about psychosis, creativity, and their association. The subjects of our investigation, who covered a lengthy time period from the Middle Ages to the present day, were chosen for three main reasons. First, they had all clearly suffered from what in contemporary terminology would be regarded as psychotic illness. Secondly, there was abundant evidence of this in their own writings. Thirdly, my two collaborators were sufficiently familiar with the authors' works and biographical detail to be able to provide the information necessary to arrive at a psychiatric diagnosis.

Several of the authors had already been given psychiatric labels, either formally or informally, but it was considered of interest to try to arrive at a diagnosis for each according to a standard procedure. The classificatory system adopted was one of those included in OPCRIT: the Research Diagnostic Criteria (RDC). But in our original study judgements were based on manual scoring of a slightly reworded form of the protocol accompanying the RDC; viz. the *Schedule for affective disorders and schizophrenia—lifetime version* or SADS-L (Spitzer and Endicott 1977). This was applied in such a way that one or other of my co-authors drew upon her knowledge of the subject being evaluated, so as to respond to probe questions precisely enough to decide whether particular symptom/sign criteria had been met. In doing so, she was asked to refer wherever possible to the subject's own words. In one instance the information was supplemented by data from the subject's hospital case-notes.

A similar procedure was followed for the subsequent OPCRIT evaluations to be reported here. Before describing the results of this later exercise, some brief notes will be presented about each of the ten authors.

Margery Kempe (d.o.b. *c.*1373). A mediaeval mystic who, though not strictly an author (she was illiterate), dictated to scribes her famous *Book of Margery Kempe*. A remarkable mixture of madness and religious fervour, it is probably the first long prose autobiography of a psychotic person in the English language. Even her contemporaries thought her insane. Our own SADS-L diagnosis was 'schizoaffective disorder'.

Thomas Hoccleve (d.o.b. 1368/9). A contemporary of Chaucer who, like Kempe, also wrote autobiographically—in verse—about his mental state. The best example is his poem, *Complaint*, in which Hoccleve expresses thoughts and feelings clearly recognizable to the modern clinician as psychotic in quality. He has been judged by others as, alternatively, 'bordering on insanity' (Mitchell 1968) and suffering from a manic form of affective disorder (Medcalf 1981). Our own diagnosis was 'depressive psychosis'.

Christopher Smart (d.o.b. 1722). A poet whose tendency to insanity is beyond doubt; as evidenced in his behaviour, his confinement in asylums, and his writings. Sir William Russell Brain (1960) considered Smart to have been manic-depressive. Our SADS-L diagnosis—in the contemporary form, 'bipolar disorder'—agreed with that, though we did note some schizophrenic features. An example of the latter, to be found in Smart's poetry, is his *Jubilate Agno*, written in a linguistic style that is strongly reminiscent of schizophrenic language.

William Cowper (d.o.b. 1731). Another poet who, like Smart, had well-documented recurrent breakdowns with a religious content; in Cowper's case featuring delusions of eternal damnation, sustained by visions and auditory hallucinations. If these are considered 'mood congruent' (and therefore not schizophrenic) SADS-L indicates a diagnosis of 'psychotic depression'; though 'atypical psychosis' was preferred by Meyer and Meyer (1987), applying DSM-III criteria.

John Clare (d.o.b. 1793). Clare's lifelong struggle with himself, his tendency to mood swings, his delusions (e.g. that he was married to his long-dead first sweetheart), his withdrawal from life, and his eventual death in the Northampton Asylum, where he was confined for many years, has provided considerable material for biographers and modern clinicians to mull over and disagree about when trying to label his psychiatric state. Some observers, among them Jamison (1993), have opted for 'bipolar disorder'; whereas our preference, guided by SADS-L, was for 'schizophrenia' (chronic).

John Ruskin (d.o.b. 1819). Art critic, social commentator, and Slade Professor of Fine Art at Oxford—a position whose duties he was often unable to fulfil and from which he ultimately had to resign through ill health. Ruskin was beset by bouts of serious mental illness. Even in well periods he was irrational, grandiose, paranoid, and driven to bizarre extremes of 'lateral thinking'—clearly seen, for example, in many disorganized passages in his *Brantwood diary*. A SADS-L diagnosis of 'bipolar disorder' was not difficult to reach although, as with some of the other authors, we found that Ruskin also met some of the criteria for schizophrenia.

Arthur Benson (d.o.b. 1862). Son of an Archbishop of Canterbury and himself eventually Master of Magdalene College, Cambridge, Arthur Benson belonged to a famous Victorian family in which madness and literary creativity (and prolific output) were inextricably intertwined. Arthur's own affliction was severe persistent depression, for which there is ample evidence in his life and writings, not least in his diary of over four million words!

Virginia Woolf (d.o.b. 1882). Leonard Woolf considered that his wife's undoubted 'madness' was of a manic-depressive form and our SADS-L diagnosis certainly supported that. But in reporting it we also noted that some signs of schizophrenia were recordable, even if not sufficient to offer an alternative, or additional, diagnosis. In support, we noted Woolf's probably accurate autobiographical portrayal of the schizophrenic Septimus in her novel *Mrs Dalloway*.

Antonia White (d.o.b. 1899). An autobiographical novelist in the complete sense, much of White's fictional writing stayed close to her own life experience, including that of mental illness. How close was uncovered in her original hospital case-notes (from the 1920s) which we were given permission to examine and which we partly drew upon in completing the SADS-L. The notes referred to a single episode of illness—possibly acute manic episode—but over a lifetime we were confident of a diagnosis of 'schizoaffective disorder/bipolar type'.

Sylvia Plath (d.o.b. 1932). As a doyenne of feminism, Plath has proved difficult to discuss objectively from a psychiatric viewpoint. Her emotional problems are not in dispute—they are clearly described, among other sources, in her own autobiographical novel, *The bell jar*. More at issue are their psychotic quality and whether they were influenced by life factors (as though these two factors are incompatible). Assessed 'objectively', Plath certainly seemed to meet the criteria for major depression, including of course her final suicide. Yet Holbrook (1988) also points to her existential angst as a sign of her schizoid, if not schizophrenic, personality; he bases the whole of his analysis of her work on this point. Taking all of the evidence together, we judged that nowadays Plath would probably be diagnosed as 'schizoaffective with predominantly depressive features'.

The OPCRIT diagnoses for our ten authors are presented in Table 10.1. Before examining these, it is worth noting that there was a reasonable amount of agreement between the two RDC diagnoses: our original, based on SADS-L, and that subsequently assigned to the subjects by OPCRIT. The main discrepancy was in the consistent tendency for the computer program to use the diagnosis 'schizoaffective', together with a qualifier, e.g. 'manic'. Our manual SADS-L scoring, on the other hand, tended more often to lead to a major psychotic category diagnosis; though there were exceptions, viz. Kempe, White, and Plath. Notably, where two major categories were considered as possibilities, or one as a qualifier for the other, the 'flavour' of the mix across the two RDC evaluations was mostly consistent. For example, Virginia Woolf was judged by us as meeting the criteria for both schizophrenia and bipolar disorder; RDC in OPCRIT considered her 'schizoaffective/bipolar'.

Returning to Table 10.1, the first point to note is the relatively small number of failures by OPCRIT to arrive at a diagnosis: 21 instances, or 17.5% of the total. A disproportionate number of these involved just one of the classificatory schemes (Feighner) which returned no diagnosis in nine of the authors. The null returns were otherwise fairly randomly scattered, with the exception of Sylvia Plath for whom four of the classifications assigned no diagnosis.

Looking within subjects, it can be seen that individual authors had a range of diagnoses assigned to them by OPCRIT. This was more straightforwardly consensual for some than for others. Both Kempe and Clare, for example, were labelled 'schizophrenic' in almost all instances. Ruskin, on the other hand, covered the whole gamut of diagnoses: schizophrenia (with various specifiers), major affective illness, and schizoaffective disorder. However, even in cases where there was more variation, the mixture of schizophrenic and affective features was again, as with our RDC SADS-L comparison, consistent across classifications. For Ruskin, where mood disorder was identified, it was always 'bipolar', for Hoccleve and Benson 'depression', and so on. Even for Plath there was some agreement, if only about her ambiguous diagnostic status: four failures to reach a conclusion and two labels of 'atypical psychosis'. Interestingly, where a clear decision was made for Plath it was predominantly 'schizophrenia'.

Comparing across subjects, it is clear from the table that 'schizophrenia' is fairly commonly found, whether unqualified or qualified (e.g. 'narrow', 'Type I', etc.). The number of occasions on which the diagnosis appeared ranged from three to ten times per

Table 10.1 OPCRIT diagnoses for *Sounds from the bell jar* authors

	DSM-III	DSM-IIIR	RDC	Feighner	Carpenter 'Flexible'	Schneider
Kempe	Schizophrenia	Schizophrenia	Schizoaffective - bipolar	No diagnosis	No diagnosis	Schizophrenia
Hoccleve	Depression with psychosis	Depression with psychosis	Schizoaffective - depressive	No diagnosis	No diagnosis	No diagnosis
Smart	Atypical psychosis	Schizoaffective - manic	Schizoaffective - manic	No diagnosis	Schizophrenia (narrow)	Schizophrenia
Cowper	Bipolar with psychosis	Bipolar with psychosis	Schizoaffective - bipolar	No diagnosis	Schizophrenia (narrow)	No diagnosis
Clare	Schizophrenia	Schizophrenia	Schizoaffective - bipolar	Schizophrenia with aff. dis.	Schizophrenia (narrow)	Schizophrenia
Ruskin	Atypical psychosis	Schizoaffective - bipolar	Schizoaffective - bipolar	No diagnosis	Schizophrenia (narrow)	Schizophrenia
Benson	Depression with psychosis	Depression with psychosis	Schizoaffective - depressive	No diagnosis	No diagnosis	Schizophrenia
Woolf	Atypical psychosis	Schizoaffective - bipolar	Schizoaffective - bipolar	No diagnosis	Schizophrenia (narrow)	Schizophrenia
White	Atypical psychosis	Schizophrenia	Schizoaffective - bipolar	No diagnosis	No diagnosis	Schizophrenia
Plath	Atypical psychosis	Atypical psychosis	Schizoaffective - bipolar	No diagnosis	No diagnosis	No diagnosis

	French	Taylor and Abrams	Tsuang and Winokur	Crow	Farmer	ICD-10
Kempe	Chronic schizophrenia	Schizophrenia	Undifferentiated schizophrenia	Type I schizophrenia	H-type schizophrenia	Hebephrenic schizophrenia
Hoccleve	No diagnosis	depression	Hebephrenic schizophrenia	Type II schizophrenia	P-type schizophrenia	Other non-organic psychosis
Smart	Chronic schizophrenia	Mania	Hebephrenic schizophrenia	Type I schizophrenia	H-type schizophrenia	Schizoaffective - manic
Cowper	Chronic schizophrenia	Depression	Paranoid schizophrenia	Mixed type schizophrenia	H-type schizophrenia	Other non-organic psychosis
Clare	Chronic schizophrenia	Schizophrenia	Hebephrenic schizophrenia	Mixed type schizophrenia	H-type schizophrenia	Hebephrenic schizophrenia
Ruskin	Chronic schizophrenia	Bipolar disorder	Hebephrenic schizophrenia	Type I schizophrenia	P-type schizophrenia	Schizoaffective - bipolar
Benson	No diagnosis	Depression	Undifferentiated schizophrenia	Type I schizophrenia	P-type schizophrenia	Depression with moodcongruent delusions
Woolf	Chronic schizophrenia	Bipolar disorder	Hebephrenic schizophrenia	Type I schizophrenia	H-type schizophrenia	Schizoaffective -bipolar
White	No diagnosis	Schizophrenia	Hebephrenic schizophrenia	Mixed type schizophrenia	H-type schizophrenia	Hebephrenic schizophrenia
Plath	No diagnosis	Schizophrenia	Undifferentiated schizophrenia	Type I schizophrenia	P-type schizophrenia	Undifferentiated schizophrenia

author (mean = 6.1); this included, for seven of the authors, meeting Schneiderian first-rank criteria, defined according to what can be considered the most bizarre of the symptoms found in schizophrenia. Of course, such figures are slightly misleading because in six of the classifications no alternative to the schizophrenia diagnosis is offered. Where an alternative was available, 'schizophrenia' was chosen much less frequently: on average 1.3 times per subject (range 0–4). On the other hand, in the (three) classifications where '*schizoaffective*' was available as an alternative, it was assigned to all of the subjects on at least one occasion (mean 1.6; range 1–3). Confining ourselves to these classifications—DSM-IIIR, RDC, and ICD-10—'schizophrenia' and 'schizoaffective' together accounted for 77% of all diagnoses; by comparison, only 13% involved a major affective disorder category, whether alone or with 'psychosis' as a specifier.

The sample used in this study was, of course, very small. The subjects are also non-representative in being deliberately selected for having shown clear signs—even by non-professional standards—of severe mental illness; though they can all be judged highly creative. For this group, at least, two observations can be made. First, a diagnosis of schizophrenia could frequently be applied, much more commonly than that of major affective disorder. Secondly, where an author's clinical state showed a strong affective component, this was usually reflected diagnostically in the label, 'schizoaffective disorder'. As a general conclusion, and contrary to some current opinion, a schizophrenic element seems to account for a substantial proportion of the variance in the link between creativity and madness. This is illustrated even more explicitly in another example, where again we applied the OPCRIT program to the retrospective data of a creative person: the English poet, Ivor Gurney.

The case of Ivor Gurney (1890–1937)

The inclusion of Ivor Gurney here arose from a continuing interest in the content and style of psychotics' poetry, within the context of a comparison between schizophrenic language and poetic style in general (Rhodes *et al.* 1995). The study of Gurney was an extension of this, undertaken by Choudhury (1994), whose report I draw upon here. As a method of comparing examples of psychotic and non-psychotic poetry, Choudhury adopted a neat strategy which enabled her to control some of the major secondary variables that could otherwise have influenced her data. She did this by looking at the works of two distinguished First World War poets: Ivor Gurney and Siegfried Sassoon.[1]

Gurney, who was gassed at Passchendaele, and Sassoon, who was invalided home twice in the first two years, were comparable not just because they both experienced the horrors of some of the worst battles of the war. They were also similar because, in curiously different ways, they both found themselves in mental hospitals. In Sassoon's

[1] Ms Choudhury and I are extremely grateful to the late Professor Sir William Trethowan for his interest in and help with the project. This included not only drawing our attention to his own detailed article on Gurney's mental state and medical history (Trethowan 1981), but also assisting us with the completion of the OPCRIT entries. When researching his own article, Professor Trethowan had received permission to inspect Gurney's hospital case-notes and his summary of this material was invaluable in completing the OPCRIT analysis.

case it followed his famous protest against the war, resulting in him being sent to Craiglockhart Hospital near Edinburgh. The move was largely a device by the officer class to cover the 'shame' of Sassoon's perceived (though of course totally unfounded) cowardice, and he was never actually diagnosed as having a mental illness.

Gurney, on the other hand, was invalided home with shell shock after Passchendaele and a year later discharged from the Army. After the war his behaviour deteriorated, he was suicidal, and he was eventually admitted—with 'delusional insanity'—to the City of London Mental Hospital at Dartford, where he remained for the rest of his life. Trethowan (1981 and personal communications) leaves us in no doubt that Gurney suffered from what he considered clinicians would now label severe 'paranoid schizophrenia'. This was characterized by hallucinations and florid delusions—mostly of 'electrical torture' from the wireless, which Gurney claimed, among other effects, bruised his body and his brain and forced him to eat food he did not want and which at one point caused him to stuff up the cracks in the ward windows to keep the electricity out.

Gurney's OPCRIT diagnoses are shown in Table 10.2. It can be seen that, although only one classification—Farmer—refers to the specifically paranoid element, the schizophrenia diagnosis predominates. The single exception is RDC, which returned 'schizoaffective/bipolar'. (As may be recalled from Table 10.1 in the previous section, the RDC classification seems particularly biased towards the schizoaffective diagnosis.) The picture otherwise is quite clear: Gurney's long-standing illness was of a severely schizophrenic type.

Although not strictly the remit of this chapter, it is worth noting briefly some conclusions that Choudhury reached from her study of Gurney's poetry, in comparison with Sassoon's. In fact, there was little difference between them on the features she anticipated: degree of self-reference and expressions of loneliness in the content, or the way analogies were used as poetic devices. However, Gurney did make less use of rhyme, showed more word omissions, and wrote less comprehensible poems, particularly after the war. The last of these, especially, could merely reflect the progressive

Table 10.2 OPCRIT diagnoses for Ivor Gurney

Diagnostic criteria	Diagnosis
DSM-III	Schizophrenia
DSM-IIIR	Schizophrenia
RDC	Schizoaffective-bipolar
Feighner	Schizophrenia with secondary depression
Carpenter	Schizophrenia (narrow)
Schneider	Schizophrenia
French	Chronic schizophrenia
Taylor and Abrams	Schizophrenia
Tsuang and Winokur	Undifferentiated schizophrenia
Crow	Type I schizophrenia
Farmer	P-type schizophrenia
ICD-10	Undifferentiated schizophrenia

impact of his psychosis. The early failure of his musical talent—which was considerable and for which in some quarters he is better known—has been ascribed to this (Hurd 1978). Yet Choudhury sensibly warns us against too dismissive an interpretation. Much poetry *does* border on the incomprehensible and Gurney's written from the depth of his psychosis deserves attention in its own right, she suggests, as an attempt to express feelings beyond those experienced by most of us.

Creativity and (unitary) psychosis

Earlier in this chapter I noted that the unitary/binary debate about psychosis only matters in creativity research to the extent that it puts constraints upon or, alternatively, opens our minds to varieties of explanation. In this regard, given the evidence reviewed, it could be claimed that the *Einheitpsychose* view has more to recommend it and perhaps should be the default position, forming the starting-point for choosing theoretical models to account for an association between creativity and madness. But even that only becomes relevant if it can first be shown that creativity has significant connections to the full range of psychotic symptomatology. One way to do that is to conduct the kind of diagnostic exercise described in the previous section. Admittedly, the sample reported on was small in size; but this limitation was offset by the use of a relatively sophisticated, 'objective', method of achieving diagnoses, sampling a wide range of alternative classification systems for the psychotic disorders.

The value of evidence using this methodology should not be underestimated. The literary debate about the connection between madness and creativity has mostly been founded on anecdotes about eccentricities and peculiarities of behaviour, plucked more or less arbitrarily from biography and historical records. This contrasts markedly with the more systematic approach adopted here, in which individual life data could be evaluated according to standardized, well-defined criteria, and translated into modern diagnostic terminology. The fact that consensus diagnoses were rarely possible for the authors studied does not weaken this conclusion: it merely reflects contemporary uncertainties about the precise boundaries of different expressions of insanity—and is of interest in its own right in showing how literary creativity can be associated with a wide range of psychotic symptomatology.

The results certainly suggest that the 'schizophrenic' components of psychosis are likely to be very common in highly creative individuals. But, in addition, there will often be accompanying affective features; with the result that in a clinical context the composite diagnosis, 'schizoaffective', can frequently be applied. Recognizing this could be important when attempting to disentangle the underlying processes connecting creativity to madness.

As indicated elsewhere (Claridge *et al.* 1990), the primary causal mechanisms are most probably those that can be referred to the schizophrenic (cognitive) element, given the nature and end-product of much creative activity. Indeed, appropriately it is the *schizophrenic* form of psychosis that has generated most of the research and almost all of the theoretical models upon which we can so far usefully draw, in our search for explanatory mechanisms. Huge amounts of data have accumulated and a plethora of theories generated about schizophrenic cognition (Hemsley 1993); now spilling over into an increasing research effort on the dimensional aspects (reviewed in Raine *et al.* 1995 and Claridge *et al.* 1997). Correspondingly, the literature on schizophrenic thought and language have long been an inspiration for writers about creativity (e.g. Arieti 1976), with notions like overinclusive thinking commonly providing a bridge, as mentioned earlier, to similar constructs—divergent and lateral thinking—in normal cognitive psychology. Furthermore, recent developments on the experimental side of schizotypy and schizophrenia research now offer the possibility of firming up these connections. I am thinking here of work being carried out under several theoretically similar experimental paradigms, such as latent inhibition (Cassaday 1997), negative priming (Williams and Beech 1997), and semantic activation without conscious identification, or SAWCI (Evans 1997). All of these can be contained within a general model of 'cognitive inhibition'—assumed to be weaker than average in schizotypal and schizophrenic individuals—which could contribute to the mechanism through which the associative products of consciousness are filtered, to provide the raw material of creative activity (see Eysenck (1995) for a recent use of this idea as a way of theorizing about creativity). The point hardly needs to be laboured: although much detail remains to be filled in, there is in place a well-established body of knowledge, highly relevant to creativity research, that derives from study of the schizophrenic form of psychosis.

The contribution from the affective side of psychosis surely derives more from its acting as a motivational and emotional source for creativity: providing manic energy, revealing insights uncovered in depressive mood, or adding colour and tone to the associative links in thought or imagery. This addition of 'affective' to 'schizophrenic' elements might be crucial in ensuring actual creative output: for the avolitional, anhedonic individual, while assailed with original ideas, will be disinclined or unable to express them in an overt form. There might also here be a way of addressing the question raised right at the beginning of this chapter, about the relative influence on creativity of trait, as compared with state, aspects of personality and psychopathology. Logically, stable trait effects are to be expected across the whole gamut of psychosis: as schizoid and schizotypal personality dispositions on the schizophrenic side and as cyclothymic temperament extending into normality from affective disorder. The argument still stands, therefore, that creativity is mostly connected to psychosis through its association, not with illness but with relevant personality characteristics. But the latter, in the case of the affective forms of psychosis, are much more mood related: it is this element that can help us understand the fluctuating nature of creative output in some individuals.

The distinctions implied above—between 'schizophrenic' and 'affective', 'trait' and 'state', and 'cognitive' and 'motivational'—are of course simplistic in the extreme; but they—and further subdivisions of them—might provide a useful, albeit rough and ready, framework for identifying themes in the topic, preparatory to formulating causal hypotheses about process. One such application arises from the fact that various types of creativity almost certainly map on to different aspects of psychosis, inviting us to call upon different theoretical models in psychology to explain the connections. Thus, writing abuts closely on to schizophrenia because of the affinity with those linguistic aspects of cognitive functioning in which the illness predominantly manifests itself— as thought and language disorder. Painting, and musical composition, on the other hand, rest more upon other, sensory and perceptual, modalities where theories about psychotic and normal imagery, rather than language, will be more applicable. Cutting across these comparisons, and within each form of creative expression, there will then be effects ascribable to more emotionally based traits in the personality, accounting for different stylistic forms: stream of consciousness writing, representational versus impressionist art, and so on.

The same idea can be pursued into other types of originality not considered in this chapter, where our emphasis has been entirely on artistic, relatively open-ended, forms. Although the latter certainly share some common underlying mechanisms, creativeness of a more goal-directed, scientific kind seems to reflect a somewhat different mix of qualities. In so far as these, too, can be judged 'psychotic', they point us towards yet other theoretical models. A particular example is the possible similarity between scientific theory-building and delusional thought. This can be understood using Bentall's (1990) analysis of how normal—and by extrapolation pathological—belief systems develop (see Fig. 10.1). Most beliefs can be said to be established as a result of drawing inferences from some perceived data in the outside world; the belief is then normally subjected to a further stage of information search in which additional data collection might refute or confirm it. According to Bentall, in the deluded psychotic there can be abnormalities at one or more of these stages: for example, the patient misperceives the data in the first place or forms the wrong inference. Either way, he or she gets caught in a self-fulfilling cognitive loop of confirmation bias: the person only attends to, selects out for notice, those data that corroborate, and hence progressively strengthen, the belief.

As Chadwick (1992) observes, scientific thinking could be said to proceed in the

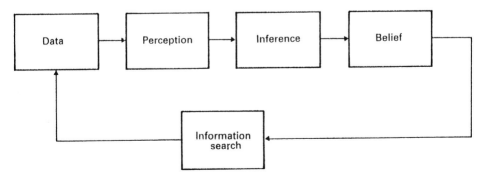

Fig. 10.1 Model of stages involved in the acquisition and maintenance of beliefs, whether normal normal. (From Bentall (1990). Reproduced by permission of the author and publishers.)

same way! Chadwick lists a number of similarities: the thought is held with great conviction and the person can hardly ever be argued out of it; talking about it causes considerable emotion to be expressed, especially anger at others' failure to accept the ideas proposed; there are often 'paranoid' reactions, like grandiosity and tenacious hold on the theory (delusion), despite evidential disconfirmation; and so on. Of course, there are, as Chadwick admits, many differences, among which are the fact that the scientific hypothesis generally does have a more plausible, less person-centred, referent in the outside world. Nevertheless the comparison is a striking one and opens up interesting avenues for extending the creativity/madness connection beyond the more usually studied domain of artistic expression.

Our general point here is that both creativity and psychosis are extremely diverse forms of human expression—and there seem to be several meeting points between them. In exploring these connections further, it would seem unwise to foreclose prematurely on a single explanatory model, driven by a too narrow focus on one form, or one aspect, of psychotic disorder. Even the small diagnostic exercise reported in the present chapter underlines that conclusion. It also illustrates the value of the method we used as a research tool for investigating the creativity/madness issue from a clinical biographical point of view.

References

Abraham, K. R. and Kulhara, P. (1987). The efficacy of electroconvulsive therapy in the treatment of schizophrenia: a comparative study. *British Journal of Psychiatry*, **151**, 152–5.

American Psychiatric Association (1980). *Diagnostic and Statistical Manual* (3rd edn). APA, Washington, DC.

——(1987). *Diagnostic and Statistical Manual* (3rd edn, revised). APA, Washington, DC.

——(1994). *Diagnostic and Statistical Manual* (4th edn). APA, Washington, DC.

Andreasen, N. C. (1987). Creativity and mental illness: prevalence rates in writers and their first-degree relatives. *American Journal of Psychiatry*, **144**, 1288–92.

Andreasen, N. J. C., and Powers, P. S. (1974). Overinclusive thinking in mania and schizophrenia. *British Journal of Psychiatry*, **125**, 452–6.

Arieti, S. (1976). *Creativity*. Basic Books, New York.

Baron, M., and Gruen, R. S. (1991). Schizophrenia and affective disorder: are they genetically linked? *British Journal of Psychiatry*, **159**, 267–70.

Barron, F. (1971). Some studies of creativity at the Institute of Personality Assessment and Research. In *The creative organisation* (ed. G. A. Steiner), pp. 5–36. University of Chicago Press.

Becker, G. (1978). *The mad genius controversy*. Sage Publications, Beverley Hills.

Bentall, R. P. (1990). The syndromes and symptoms of psychosis. In *Reconstructing schizophrenia* (ed. R. P. Bentall), pp. 23–60. Routledge, London.

Berrios, G. E. (1995). Conceptual problems in diagnosing schizophrenic disorders. In *Advances in the neurobiology of schizophrenia* (ed. J. A. Den Boer, H. G. M. Westenberg, and H. M. van Praag), pp. 7–25. Wiley, Chichester.

Bleuler, E. (1911). *Dementia praecox or the group of schizophrenias* (trans. J. Zinkin 1950). International Universities Press, New York.

Brain, R. (1960). *Sane reflections on genius*. Pitman, London.

Brockington, I. F., Kendell, R. E., Wainwright, S., Hillier, V. F., and Walker, J. (1979). The distinction between the affective psychoses and schizophrenia. *British Journal of Psychiatry*, **135**, 243–8.

Brod, J. H. (1997). Creativity and schizotypy. In *Schizotypy: implications for illness and health* (ed. G. Claridge), pp. 274–98. Oxford University Press.

Cameron, N. (1938). Reasoning, regression and communication in schizophrenics. *Psychological Monographs*, **50**, 1–34.

Carpenter, W. T., Strauss, J. S., and Bartko, J. J. (1973). Flexible system for the diagnosis of schizophrenia: report from the WHO international Pilot Study of Schizophrenia. *Science*, **182**, 1275–8.

Cassaday, H. (1997). Latent inhibition: relevance to the neural substrates of schizophrenia and schizotypy? In *Schizotypy: implications for illness and health* (ed. G. Claridge), pp. 124–44. Oxford University Press.

Cattell, R. B., and Butcher, H. J. (1968). *The prediction of achievement and creativity*. Bobbs-Merrill, Indianapolis.

Chadwick, P. (1992). *Borderline. A psychological study of paranoia and delusional thinking*. Routledge, London.

Choudhury, V. (1994). Schizophrenic and non-schizophrenic poetry compared: an analysis of the work of two World War 1 poets. B. A. dissertation. University of Oxford.

Claridge, G. S. (1981). Psychoticism. In *Dimensions of personality. Papers in honour of H. J. Eysenck* (ed. R. Lynn), pp. 79–109. Pergamon, Oxford.

——(1983). The Eysenck psychoticism scale. In *Advances in personality* assessment (Vol. 2) (ed. J. N. Butcher and C. D. Spielberger). Lawrence Erlbaum, New Jersey.

Claridge, G. (ed.) (1997). *Schizotypy: implications for illness and health*. Oxford University Press.

——, and Beech, A. (1995). Fully and quasi-dimensional constructions of schizotypy. In *Schizotypal personality* (ed. A. Raine, T. Lencz, and S. A. Mednick), pp. 192–216. Cambridge University Press.

——, Pryor, R., and Watkins, G. (1990). *Sounds from the bell jar. Ten psychotic authors*. Macmillan, London.

——, McCreery, C., Mason, O., Bentall, R., Boyle, G., Slade, P., and Popplewell, D. (1996). The factor structure of 'schizotypal' traits: a large replication study. *British Journal of Clinical Psychology*, **35**, 103–15.

Craddock, N., Asherson, P., Owen, M. J., Williams, J., McGuffin, P., and Farmer, A. (1996). Concurrent validity of the OPCRIT diagnostic system. Comparison of OPCRIT diagnoses with consensus best-estimate lifetime diagnoses. *British Journal of Psychiatry*, **169**, 58–63.

Crow, T. J. (1980). The molecular pathology of schizophrenia: more than one disease process? *British Medical Journal*, **280**, 66–8.

——(1986). The continuum of psychosis and its implication for the structure of the gene. *British Journal of Psychiatry*, **149**, 419–29.

——(1990). Temporal lobe asymmetries as the key to the etiology of schizophrenia. *Schizophrenia Bulletin*, **16**, 434–43.

——(1991). The failure of the Kraepelinian binary concept and the search for the psychosis gene. In *Concepts of mental disorder. A continuing debate* (ed. A. Kerr and H. McClelland), pp. 31–47. Gaskell, London.

Delva, N. J., and Letemendia, F. J. J. (1982). Lithium treatment in schizophrenia and schizoaffective disorders. *British Journal of Psychiatry*, **141**, 387–400.

Evans, J. L. (1997). Semantic activation and preconscious processing in schizotypy and schizophrenia. In *Schizotypy: implications for illness and health* (ed. G. Claridge), pp. 80–97. Oxford University Press.

Eysenck, H. J. (1952*a*). Schizothymia-cyclothymia as a dimension of personality. II. Experimental. *Journal of Personality*, **20**, 345–84.

——(1952*b*). *The scientific study of personality*. Routledge and Kegan Paul, London.

——(1992). The definition and measurement of psychoticism. *Personality and individual Differences*, **13**, 757–85.

——(1995). *Genius: the natural history of creativity*. Cambridge University Press.

——, and Barrett, P. (1993). The nature of schizotypy. *Psychological Reports*, **73**, 59–63.

——, and Eysenck, S. B. G. (1976). *Psychoticism as a dimension of personality*. Hodder and Stoughton, London.

Farmer, A., McGuffin, P., and Spitznagel, L. (1983). Heterogeneity in schizophrenia: a cluster analytic approach. *Psychiatry Research*, **8**, 1–12.

——Wessely, S., Castle, D., and McGuffin, P. (1992). Methodological issues using a polydiagnostic approach to define psychotic illness. *British Journal of Psychiatry*, **161**, 824–30.

Feighner, J. P., Robins, E., Guze, S. B., Woodruff, R. A., and Munoz, R. (1972). Diagnostic criteria for use in psychiatric research. *Archives of General Psychiatry*, **26**, 57–63.

Grant, V. W. (1968). *Great abnormals*. Hawthorn Books, New York.

Hemsley, D. R. (1993). A simple (or simplistic?) cognitive model for schizophrenia. *Behaviour Research and Therapy*, **31**, 633–45.

Holbrook, D. (1988). *Sylvia Plath. Poetry of existence*. The Athlone Press, London.

Hurd, M. (1978). *The ordeal of Ivor Gurney*. Oxford University Press.

Jamison, K. R. (1989). Mood disorders and patterns of creativity in British writers and artists. *Psychiatry*, **52**, 125–34.

——(1993). *Touched with fire. Manic-depressive illness and the artistic temperament*. The Free Press, New York.

Juda, A. (1949). The relationship between highest mental capacity and psychic abnormalities. *American Journal of Psychiatry*, **106**, 296–304.

Kendell, R. E. (1991). The major functional psychoses: are they independent entities or part of a continuum? Philosophical and conceptual issues underlying the debate. In *Concepts of mental disorder. A continuing debate* (ed. A. Kerr and H. McClelland), pp. 1–16. Gaskell, London.

Kendell, R. E., and Brockington, I. F. (1980). The identification of disease entities and the relationship between schizophrenic and affective psychoses. *British Journal of Psychiatry*, **135**, 243–8.

Klein, D. F., and Fink, M. (1963). Multiple item factors as change measures in psychopharmacology. *Psychopharmacologia*, **4**, 43–52.

Kraepelin, E. (1919). *Dementia praecox and paraphrenia* (trans. R. M. Barclay). Churchill Livingstone, Edinburgh.

Kretschmer, E. (1925). *Physique and character* (trans. W. J. H. Sprott). Kegan, Trench, and Trubner, London.

LaPierre, Y. D. (1994). Schizophrenia and manic-depression: separate illnesses or a continuum? *Canadian Journal of Psychiatry*, **39**, 559–64.

Ludwig, A. M. (1994). Mental illness and creative activity in female writers. *American Journal of Psychiatry*, **151**, 1650–6.

Lombroso, C. (1891). *The man of genius*. Walter Scott, London.

McGuffin, P., Farmer, A., and Gottesman, I. I. (1987). Is there really a split in schizophrenia? The genetic evidence. *British Journal of Psychiatry*, **150**, 581–92.

——, ——, and Harvey, I. (1991). A polydiagnostic application of operational criteria in studies of psychotic illness. Development and reliability of the OPCRIT system. *Archives of General Psychiatry*, **48**, 764–70.

Mason, M., Claridge, G., and Williams, L. (1997). Questionnaire measurement. In *Schizotypy: implications for illness and health* (ed. G. Claridge), pp. 19–37. Oxford University Press.

Maziade, M., Roy, M.-A., Martinez, M., Cliche, D., Fournier, J.-P., Garneau, Y. *et al.* (1995). Negative, psychoticism, and disorganised dimensions in patients with familial schizophrenia or bipolar disorder: continuity and discontinuity between the major psychoses. *American Journal of Psychiatry*, **152**, 1458–63.

Medcalf, S. (1981). Inner and outer. In *The later Middle Ages* (ed. S. Medcalf), pp. 122–68. Methuen, London.

Meehl, P. E. (1962). Schizotaxia, schizotypy, schizophrenia. *American Psychologist*, **17**, 827–38.

—— (1990). Toward an integrated theory of schizotaxia, schizotypy, and schizophrenia. *Journal of Personality Disorders*, **4**, 1–99.

Merten, T. (1995). Factors influencing word-association responses: a reanalysis. *Creativity Research Journal*, **8**, 249–63.

Meyer, J. E. and Meyer, R. (1987). Self-portrayal by a depressed poet: a contribution to the clinical biography of William Cowper. *American Journal of Psychiatry*, **144**, 127–32.

Mitchell, J. (1968). *Thomas Hoccleve. A study in early fifteenth-century poetic*. University of Illinois Press, Urbana.

Overall, J. E., Hollister, L. E., and Meyer, F. (1964). Imipramine and thioridazine in depressed and schizophrenic patients. *Journal of the American Medical Association*, **189**, 605–8.

Payne, R. W., Mattusek, P., and George, E. I. (1959). An experimental study of schizophrenia thought disorder. *Journal of Mental Science*, **105**, 627–52.

Poreh, A. M., Whitman, D. R., and Ross, T. P. (1994). Creative thinking abilities and hemisphere asymmetry in schizotypal college students. *Current Psychology*, **12**, 344–52.

Post, F. (1994). Creativity and psychopathology. A study of 291 world-famous men. *British Journal of Psychiatry*, **165**, 22–34.

—— (1996). Verbal creativity, depression and alcoholism. An investigation of one hundred American and British writers. *British Journal of Psychiatry*, **168**, 545–55.

Prentky, R. A. (1980). *Creativity and psychopathology: a neurocognitive perspective*. Praeger, New York.

Pull, M. C., Pull, C. B., and Pichot, P. (1987). Des critères empiriques français pour les psychoses. II. Consensus des psychiatres français et definitions provisoires. *L'Encephale*, **XIII**, 53–57.

Raine, A., Lencz, T., and Mednick, S. A. (ed.) (1995). *Schizotypal personality*. Cambridge University Press.

Rhodes, N., Dowker, A., and Claridge, G. (1995). Subject matter and poetic devices in psychotics' poetry. *British Journal of Medical Psychology*, **68**, 311–21.

Schneider, K. (1959). *Clinical psychopathology* (trans. M. Hamilton). Grune and Stratton, New York.

Spitzer, R. L., and Endicott, J. (1977). *Schedule for affective disorders and schizophrenia—lifetime version (SADS-L)*. New York State Psychiatric Institute, New York.

——, and Robins, E. (1978). Research diagnostic criteria: rationale and reliability. *Archives of General Psychiatry*, **35**, 773–82.

Storr, A. (1976). *The dynamics of creation*. Penguin Books, Harmondsworth.

Strömgren, E. (1994). The unitary psychosis (*Einheitpsychose*) concept: past and present. *Neurology, Psychiatry and Brain Research*, **2**, 201–5.

Taylor, M. A. (1992). Are schizophrenia and affective disorder related? A selective literature review. *American Journal of Psychiatry*, **149**, 22–32.

Taylor, M. A., and Abrams, R. (1978). The prevalence of schizophrenia: a reassessment using modern diagnostic criteria. *American Journal of Psychiatry*, **135**, 945–8.

Tsanoff, R. A. (1949). *The ways of genius*. Harper and Brothers, New York.

Trethowan, W. H. (1981). Ivor Gurney's mental illness. *Music and Letters*, **62**, 300–9.

Tsuang, M. T., and Winokur, G. (1974). Criteria for subtyping schizophrenia. *Archives of General Psychiatry*, **31**, 43.

Williams, J., Farmer, A. E., Wessely, S., Castle, D. J., and McGuffin, P. (1993). Heterogeneity in schizophrenia: an extended replication of the hebephrenic-like and paranoid-like subtypes. *Psychiatry Research*, **49**, 199–210.

Williams, L., and Beech, A. (1997). Investigations of cognitive inhibitory processes in schizotypy and schizophrenia. In *Schizotypy: implications for illness and health* (ed. G. Claridge), pp. 63–79. Oxford University Press.

Woody, E., and Claridge, G. (1977). Psychoticism and thinking. *British Journal of Social and Clinical Psychology*, **16**, 241–8.

World Health Organisation (1992). *ICD: the ICD-10 classification of mental and behavioural disorders—clinical descriptions and diagnostic guidelines*. WHO, Geneva.

MICHELANGELO BUONARROTI

CHAPTER 11

Artistic temperament in the Italian Renaissance: a study of Giorgio Vasari's Lives

Andrew Steptoe

THE image of the artist as a turbulent and troubled individual is firmly established in popular consciousness. Since the Romantic era, we have been accustomed to viewing artistic creations as emerging from conflict and turmoil, and artists as tempestuous and alienated. Nowhere is this more apparent than in the colourful era of the Italian Renaissance, and it is no accident that the arch-romantic Hector Berlioz chose the sixteenth century sculptor Benvenuto Cellini as the hero of an opera. Freudian thought has reinforced the notion that artistic expression is a product of unrealized psychic conflict, and of dark forces that defy logical analysis. Modern creativity researchers have described the artistic personality as hypersensitive, aggressive, autonomous, and independent, preoccupied with work to the exclusion of social activity, intolerant of order and seeking novelty and change, suffused with intense but chaotic emotions, and opposed to the conventional and banal (Dudek *et al.* 1991). Artistic creativity has also been allied with a melancholic temperament and periods of despair close to madness. This perspective was elaborated by Klibansky *et al.* (1964) in their influential *Saturn and melancholy*, but some commentators have gone further to pathologize the artist. In a recent study of nineteenth and twentieth century artists, Post (Post 1994) argued that 56.3% exhibited 'severe' or 'marked' psychopathology. Perhaps the most extreme view of all was that of the Italian criminologist Cesare Lombroso, who described genius as a 'degenerative psychosis', and as 'moral degeneracy' not far removed from criminality (Lombroso 1890).

At the same time, there has been a long tradition of highly creative but worldly and well-balanced artists who do not fit these stereotypes. Some successful artists appear almost to have been establishment figures, without this in any way diminishing their creative stature. They include such individuals as Titian, Rubens, Tintoretto and the charming Anthony van Dyck. In 1715, the portrait painter Jonathan Richardson wrote: 'The way to be an excellent painter is to be an excellent man . . . A painter ought to have a sweet, and happy turn of mind, that great, and lovely ideas may have a reception there'.

Another eighteenth century example is the English painter Sir Joshua Reynolds, who lived comfortably and was described by his pupil John Northcote in the following terms:

He had none of the those eccentric bursts of action, those fiery impetuousities which are supposed by the vulgar to characterise genius, and which frequently are found to accompany a secondary rank of talent, but are never conjoined with the first. His incessant industry was never wearied into despondency by miscarriage, nor elated into negligence by success . . . His general manner, deportment, and behaviour were amiable and prepossessing; his disposition was naturally courtly. He always evinced a desire to pay due respect to persons in superior stations . . . (Northcote 1813).

Even in the eighteenth century, it was recognized that a moody temperament was sometimes feigned by artists who cultivated a nonconformist and natural image. Some creative individuals may exaggerate their distinctiveness either out of affectation, or in order to conform to popular stereotypes (Richards 1981). The greatest artists were not above some massaging of their personal histories at times. Michelangelo, for example, liked to see himself as a natural genius with untutored talent. Through his amanuensis Ascanio Condivi, he therefore presented himself as having undergone no formal training, even though by doing this, he denied the years of his apprenticeship in the workshop of the Florentine painter Domenico Ghirlandaio (Murray 1984). To complicate matters further, the stigma of supposed mental disorder may be imposed by an envious public, eager to explain exceptional beings as aberrations (Kessel 1989). Oliver Sacks (1995) has warned that 'we may go overboard in medicalizing our predecessors, reducing their complexity to expressions of neurological or psychiatric disorder'.

The question that arises is whether the moody and mercurial image of the artist is an accurate representation of a temperament conducive to creativity. An alternative is that it is a social construct, and that artists actually range across the spectrum of personality and temperaments in just the same way as the rest of the population. There are many approaches to this problem, from biographical analyses of exceptional individuals to studies of mental health among the more able sectors of the general population (Richards 1990; Ludwig 1995). The chapters by Kay Jamison and Gordon Claridge in this book illustrate how detailed investigations can uncover intimate associations between mental state and creativity. In the present chapter, I address the issue of artistic temperament through a content analysis of the first major extended biography in the history of art, and the principal source of much of our information about the artists of the Italian Renaissance. This is Giorgio Vasari's *Lives of the painters, sculptors and architects*, written in the middle decades of the sixteenth century.

The significance of Vasari

Giorgio Vasari (1511–1574) was a prolific painter and architect, notable for his vast decorative schemes in Florence and Rome, and for his design of buildings such as the Uffizi Palace. However, his reputation chiefly rests on the *Lives*, or *Le Vite de più eccellenti pittori, scultori, et archittori*. This is a collection of more than 150 biographies of painters, sculptors, and architects ranging from Giotto's supposed teacher Cimabue in the thirteenth century, to Vasari's contemporaries 250 years later. The first edition was published in 1550, and the second much revised edition in 1568. Vasari was not the first commentator to write about artists, since the great ancient Greek artists such as Apelles and Lysippus were mentioned in contemporary tracts. At the dawn of the Renaissance, Giotto was praised by Boccaccio and Petrarch. But Vasari provided the first systematic treatment, taking a historical approach and founding his narrative on a theory of artistic development. Equally importantly, he supplied personal information about the artists and their lives, and his picturesque anecdotes have added colour to our image of this extraordinary period of creativity, war, economic and social development.

Vasari's *Lives* are therefore deeply embedded within the history of Renaissance art, and in the work of art historians such as Heinrich Wölfflin, Jacob Burckhardt, and Martin Wackernagel. Cole (1983) has described Vasari's book as 'the single most influential work on Italian painting', while Rudolf and Margaret Wittkower (1965) regard Vasari's work to be 'the cornerstone of art historical literature'. Several writers and artists had copies of Vasari, including El Greco, Inigo Jones, Velazquez, Constable, and Thomas Jefferson (Cast 1993). Vasari's errors and embellishments have long been known, leading scholars such as Barolsky (1990, 1992) to argue that he was more of a historical novelist than art historian. Nevertheless, the *Lives* are uniquely useful in studying artistic temperament, since they cover such a wide range of individuals. The book allows us to enquire about the characteristics Vasari identified in the great artists of his own time and the recent past. Did he see the most creative individuals as disturbed, melancholic, and unconventional, or in other terms? These issues call for statistical treatment of Vasari's writing, since it is all too easy to use selective quotations to identify eccentricities and foibles.

The image of the artist in the Renaissance

Cultivated people in Renaissance Italy were fascinated by the ancient world, so classical authors' views on creativity were eagerly studied. Some of the characteristics we associate with creativity had already been identified in ancient Greece (Murray 1989). For example, Plutarch attributed Archimedes's powers to natural endowments coupled with hard labour, while describing him as absent-minded, neglectful of external circumstances, and impractical. Plato emphasized the role of inspiration from the gods, arguing that poetic composition occurs in a frenzy of 'divine madness'. Pindar proclaimed the importance of inborn ability, although the ancient Greeks do not appear to have had any notion of ability being passed between generations. Rather, talent was endowed at birth, a gift of the gods bestowed on favoured individuals.

However, these traits were discussed by classical authors in relation to poetry and philosophy, and not the visual arts. In a world in which manual labour was carried out by slaves, there was considerable ambivalence about mechanical crafts such as painting and sculpture. Exceptional artists were recognized, but even the most celebrated had a socially fragile status. A distinction was also drawn between the artist and the product, for if technical ability was a divine gift, it was possible to admire the work without revering its maker.

Information about the identity of artists was all but lost during the Dark Ages. At this time there appeared to be little recognition of a link between a melancholic or depressive temperament and creativity. Indeed, melancholy tended to be denigrated, and melancholics were regarded as avaricious and miserly, given to deceit and stealth (Klibansky *et al.* 1964). But the Renaissance saw the growth of the cult of the artist, and the elevation of painters and sculptors out of the anonymous world of craft guilds and stone masons' lodges. This was associated with a transformation in attitudes towards melancholy, founded intellectually on the interpretation of a text attributed (falsely) to Aristotle. In *Problem 30.1*, the question is posed 'Why is it that all those who are outstanding in philosophy, politics, poetry or arts are melancholic?' Murray (1989) has argued that this statement is quite outside the mainstream of classical thought on creativity, not only in its glorification of melancholia, but also in aligning the manual crafts with the study of elevated subjects such as philosophy and poetry. Nevertheless, it was a view that was championed by Marsilio Ficino (1433–1499), the influential neoplatonist scholar who worked under the patronage of the Medici in Florence. He developed a doctrine of melancholy as divine inspiration, and of genius arising in the souls of divided beings balanced dangerously between the animal and the divine. In his book *De vita triplici*, Ficino allied poetic inspiration with melancholy, arguing that melancholy is a divine gift, enabling its possessors to delve into the core of problems with insight forbidden to others. At the same time, he recognized that the negative forces of a depressive temperament could be overwhelming and destructive.

This work signalled a reappraisal of creative gifts, and traits such as eccentricity, moodiness and solitariness came to be seen as essential attributes of the talented painter (Wittkower and Wittkower 1965). But at the same time, the conceptualization of the artist as a marginalized and alienated being was not compatible with another cultural force of the era. This was the drive towards the professionalization of the artist, and the recognition of painting and sculpture as legitimate activities of cultivated people. This theme is central to an understanding of Vasari's perspective on his fellow artists.

The social status of painters and sculptors

At the beginning of the Renaissance, there was a range of crafts devoted to the creation of objects designed to decorate buildings, to enhance the splendour of secular and religious centres, and to give pleasure to their owners. Apart from painters and sculptors, there were goldsmiths, metal-workers, carvers of bone and ivory, fabric manufacturers, jewellers and workers in mosaic, tapestry and embroidery, stained glass, and marquetry. None stood out in terms of prestige, and although goldsmiths were more likely to become wealthy, they remained relatively anonymous. Yet over the next 100 years, painters and sculptors left workers in other crafts behind, becoming individuals of stature widely known outside their local area, and revered even today.

This was not a uniform trend across Europe, but was for several reasons particularly prominent in the Italian Peninsula (Kempers 1987). Painting had the advantage over many other crafts in that the raw materials were relatively inexpensive, and the work was less labour-intensive than mosaic, tapestry, or metal work. The thirteenth century saw the rapid rise of the mendicant orders of friars, and by 1316 there was some 1400 churches belonging to the Franciscans alone. The mendicant orders were particularly attracted to painting, since large areas could be decorated attractively with images designed to educate and inspire the population, but without the taint of luxury associated with other crafts. Merchant clans emerged in the cities of Tuscany, and competed with each other in commissioning works of art and self-engrandising monuments. As artists gravitated to centres such as Florence and Sienna, their pooling of knowledge and experience led to improvements in professional skills. Thus the fourteenth century saw innovations in fresco technique, and in the introduction of panel painting. A century later, these centres pioneered the application of perspective and the use of oil-based paints.

The change in the status of painters and sculptors in relation to other crafts can be seen as an example of professionalization. The key elements in the development of a profession are generally held to be the identification of specialist skills, the establishment of organizations to regulate the training and use of these skills, the control of access to clientele, and the creation of a historiography and theoretical framework. Painting and sculpture went through these stages, with an apprenticeship system in which experienced practitioners taught the next generation, and the banding together of individual artists into associations or guilds that supervised training and practice and assured quality control. The beginnings of a historiography emerged with the publication of commentaries. Successful practitioners such as Cennino Cennini and Lorenzo Ghiberti (1378–1455) wrote treatises that emphasized technical skills and developed notions about the appropriate conduct of artists. Talented predecessors were admired, with the achievements of Giotto being given pride of place.

The social status of painters and sculptors was enhanced by these developments. However, in order to break from the ranks of craftsmen and artisans and be accepted into higher circles, it was necessary to distinguish painting and sculpture from manual labour. The ideal therefore emerged of the artist as a learned and dignified individual, well-educated and familiar with the liberal arts. Classical texts were scoured for any mention of artists receiving favour from rulers, and instances of painting actually being practised by great men were sought (Blunt 1962). Leon Battista Alberti (1404–1472), himself a man of noble descent, argued that the arts of painting, sculpture, and architecture were legitimate objects of study by 'noble intellects'. Mathematics was one of the liberal arts, so its role in painting and design was increasingly emphasized. In his treatise *Della pittura* of about 1435, Alberti discussed the importance of mathematical constructs in the depiction of proportion, perspective, and the treatment of colour and shade.

Another central issue in establishing the social status of artists was control over the work. At the beginning of the Renaissance, contracts detailed the raw materials (gold-leaf, lapis lazuli) and their costs, rather than the makers; what mattered to the commission was not the artist, but the quality of the physical ingredients of the product. Progressively, the skills of artists came to be more admired than their materials, and contracts might stipulate that the master carry out all the work unaided, without the involvement of assistants and apprentices. Nevertheless, in the fifteenth century, artists only rarely decided on the subjects of their work. There was a constant pressure to increase autonomy, so that artists might exert as much influence as the sponsor over the subject of the work. In the early sixteenth century, Isabella d'Este, the wife of Francesco Gonzaga of Mantua, sought works from a number of the leading artists of the period including Perugino, Titian, and Giovanni Bellini. From her negotiations, it is clear that she was more concerned to have paintings from these masters than about the specific subject of the compositions (Goffen 1989). Perhaps the defining moment in the emergence of artistic autonomy was when Michelangelo was working for Pope Julius II in Rome in 1506 (Murray 1984). Michelangelo returned to Rome from selecting marble in Carrara, but was blocked from seeing the Pope by pressing political business. Incensed, he abruptly left Rome and returned to Florence. His departure caused a diplomatic furore, with couriers being sent and the Governor of Florence being threatened if he failed to return. He eventually complied, but his arrogant treatment of the Pope came to be seen as a mark of the power that could be wielded by the supremely talented artist.

Vasari's background

Giorgio Vasari grew up in an artistic world in which status and independence were live issues. He was born in Arezzo in 1511 into a family of craftsmen, and showed an early inclination to paint. He received humanist instruction in Arezzo, and when he was 13 years old he recited in Latin to Cardinal Silvio Passerini. Passerini encouraged Vasari's father to send him to Florence, and under the Cardinal's patronage he was taught along with Alessandro and Ippolito de'Medici, direct descendants of Lorenzo the Magnificent. This turn of events allowed him to acquire more of an education and a knowledge of the upper echelons of society than he might have expected. His artistic ambitions came to be coupled with the values of loyalty and service (Boase 1979).

Vasari was trained by Andrea del Sarto, then one of the leading painters in Florence, and formed friendships with artists such as Agnolo Bronzino, Francesco Salviati, and Jacopo da Pontormo. There was a Republican revolt in Florence in 1527, and Cardinal Passerini and the young Medici fled. Vasari returned to Arezzo, where he made a modest living as a painter, and avoided the horrors of the sack of Rome and the depredations of the Imperial army in Italy. He subsequently moved to Rome under the patronage of Ippolito de'Medici (now a cardinal), and achieved more success. He became a student of followers of Raphael such as Perino del Vaga and Giulio Romano, admiring their speed of work and bravura. He soon moved back to Florence in the entourage of Alessandro de'Medici, who had now become Duke of Florence. Here he began to develop his entrepreneurial talent for organizing other artists and workers in decorative enterprises, notably in the celebrations marking the visit of Emperor Charles V to Florence in 1536. But Duke Alessandro was assassinated in 1537, and this event lead Vasari to avoid relying too much on a single patron in his future career. Over the next few years, he therefore worked in various parts of central Italy and Venice, spending most of his time in Rome, Florence, and Arezzo (Kleinman 1996).

Vasari began his research on the *Lives* in Rome in the 1540s, where he also became friendly with Michelangelo. The book attracted widespread interest when it appeared in 1550, and over the years preceding the publication of the second edition in 1568, Vasari's position became increasingly assured as he established a dominant role in the court of Duke Cosimo I in Florence.

Vasari's set of biographies is divided into three phases beginning with the rebirth of art after the Dark Ages. He saw the first phase as spearheaded by Cimabue and Giotto, and lasting from about 1250–1420. The artists of this period developed new skills, increasing the elegance of painting and the faithfulness of art to life. The second phase began in 1420 with the Florentines Masaccio and Brunelleschi applying perspective so as to produce greater verisimilitude. Oil painting was introduced during this phase, which was dominated by commissions from great merchant families. Mendicant orders and communes also played their part, as did the various courts of Italy. The third phase began around 1500, when according to Vasari painting began to reach the highest levels, as artists solved all the technical problems that confronted them. He believed that perfection in art would be reached through mastery of the principles of ancient art coupled with observation of the real world, with the ultimate goal being the imitation of nature. He regarded Michelangelo as the pinnacle of artistic development, the goal towards which the progress of the past three centuries had been directed.

Hypotheses about artistic temperament

I suggest that Vasari had a complex agenda in writing the *Lives*. Firstly, he wished to present a history of painting, sculpture, and architecture, glorifying the achievements of the past and presenting the works of masters as enduring monuments. In doing this, he had an investment in veracity, and in describing people as they really were. Secondly, he detailed a view of art as progressing from limited skills to perfection, an ascent accompanied by increasing knowledge and technical facility. Finally, I propose that he was interested in establishing a status for artists that placed the most successful in the higher echelons of Renaissance society. Since many artists were born into humble circumstances, this status was not endorsed by family background or education. He therefore hoped to show that artists possessed the appropriate personal characteristics by virtue of their own natural temperaments and endowments.

The analyses described in this chapter are intended to assess Vasari's descriptions of the personalities of the artists of the Renaissance in a systematic fashion. Assuming the method is successful, there are a number of possible outcomes. The first is that these painters, sculptors, and architects, widely recognized as among the greatest in Western art, conformed to the modern view of artistic temperament. If this was the case, then the analysis of the *Lives* should show that many of his subjects were tempestuous, depressive, anti-establishment individuals. Secondly, it is possible that the great artists had characteristics which were socially acceptable within the constraints of the era, in which case traits such as courteousness, modesty, and nobility would emerge as predominant. Thirdly, it is possible that the personalities of the artists discussed by Vasari have no commonalities, in which case descriptions would be distributed randomly across socially desirable and less acceptable idiosyncratic characteristics.

Analysing Vasari's writings

The standard modern edition of Vasari's *Lives* is edited by Bettarini and Barocci, and was published in Florence between 1966 and 1987 (Vasari 1966–1987). There is no complete modern translation into English, although many selections have been published. The analyses described here used the translations by Mrs Jonathan Foster published in 1850, and the translation by Gaston de Vere published in 1912 and recently reprinted (Vasari 1996). The *Lives* contains biographies of more than 150 artists of the Italian Renaissance. Most are allocated an entire chapter, but there are also a number of compendium chapters that discuss groups, such as the painters of Lombardy surrounding Benvenuto Garofalo, and the Bellini family of Venice. Some chapters mention artists without providing any information on their personal characteristics, so were excluded from the analysis.

I also decided to exclude the artists discussed in the 30 chapters of Part 1 of the *Lives*, beginning with Cimabue and finishing with Lorenzo di Bicci. Vasari was writing at a time before documentary records were available. He relied on hearsay and word of mouth, and this inevitably limited accuracy. He was also writing about artists who were not necessarily revered by their immediate contemporaries, so there was little reason to retain information about them. The material he had available about the lives of the artists of the thirteenth and fourteenth centuries was negligible and unreliable. Indeed, he was reduced to inventing lives for some early subjects, adapting stories from classical authors of the ancient world. For example, he describes how Giotto was a humble shepherd boy who drew while tending his flock, using the rude materials available to him. One day, the Florentine artist Cimabue passed by, and was so impressed by Giotto's natural ability that he gave the boy formal training. The same story is told of the great classical artist Lysippus, and is known in tales about the early lives of Japanese masters as well (Kris and Kurz 1979). Giotto was also said to have painted a spider so life-like that his master mistook it for the real thing and tried to flick it off the picture; this tale is also told of the Flemish master Quentin Massys, the Siennese painter Beccafumi and various Chinese artists. Part 1 of the *Lives* is full of these stereotyped formulae designed to celebrate the artists, and it is generally accepted that Vasari's information about the period up to 1400 was very unreliable (White 1966).

The analysis was therefore confined to the artists discussed in the 53 chapters of Part II, and the 75 chapters of Part III. It covers the 123 artists for whom Vasari provided at least some information about their lives and experience rather than just their works. It therefore includes all the better known Renaissance figures—Michelangelo, Raphael,

Leonardo da Vinci, Titian, Masaccio, Donatello and Brunelleschi—as well as minor masters such as Giuliano di Maiano and Nanni di Banco. The method used for evaluating the narratives is content analysis, which is a technique for abstracting systematic information from written or spoken narratives. It is a procedure that generates quantitative information from qualitative sources, and has a long tradition in the social sciences (Weber 1990). The analysis involved defining categories of interest, then scanning the sources to identify the occurrence of reference to these types of information. The categories used were a series of temperamental and character traits.

Initially, the content of the biographies was scrutinized for reference to each of 42 different characteristics, including general traits such as honesty and pride, together with features of the artistic temperament such as melancholy and eccentricity. Many of these traits were mentioned rather infrequently in the *Lives*, so they were subsequently grouped into broader categories for the purposes of analysis. The following set of descriptors was used:

High ability:	references to exceptional talent, natural ability, inventiveness and genius, excellence and originality (terms like ingegno, divino, virtù, invenzione).
Studiousness:	references to a deep knowledge of art, and to study of other artists, nature, and the ancients.
Hard work:	comments on the exceptional hard working attitude of the artist.
Critical remarks:	negative comments about the artist, such as complaints about a lack of inventiveness or excessive reliance on study.
Sociability:	descriptions of the artist as socially adept, charming, gregarious, and amusing.
Courteousness:	honourable, obliging, generous, and kind to others (terms like gentilezza).
Sophisticated:	comments on the artist being cultivated, graceful, and at home in educated circles.
Moderate:	moderate and temperate in habits.
Unworldly:	absent minded, saintly, careless about material things.
Depressive:	references to melancholy, gloom, reclusiveness, and social withdrawal.
Oddities of character:	features such as eccentricity, bizarre actions, and descriptions of highly temperamental behaviour.
Unworthy:	reference to a range of undesirable characteristics including licentiousness, villainy, jealousy, and fecklessness.
Conceit:	descriptions of the artist as proud or jealous of others.

The characteristics of artists in general

The 123 artists in this analysis include 83 painters, 38 sculptors, and 22 architects, many individuals having more than one craft. All were Italian or worked predominantly in Italy, with a large majority being Tuscan. The distribution of psychological traits in the complete sample is illustrated in Fig. 11.1. This shows the proportion of artists in whom each of the traits was described by Vasari. The error bars are 95% confidence intervals, estimates of the reliability of the proportions. It is apparent from Fig. 11.1 that studiousness was the most frequently cited trait; 48 of the artists (39%)

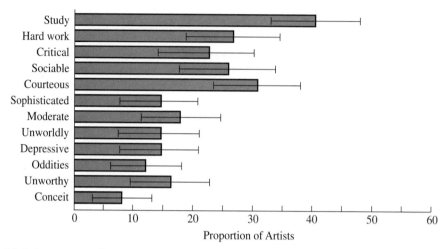

Fig. 11.1 Proportion of artists in percent who were described by Vasari as having each of twelve traits or temperamental characteristics. The error bars represent 95% confidence intervals.

were praised by Vasari for their knowledge of art or dedication to the study of past masters and nature. Interestingly, courteousness emerged as the second most common characteristic. The proportion of artists described as courteous (or honourable and obliging) was significantly greater than the number said to be unworldly, depressive, sophisticated, or temperamentally odd. Sociability and an affable nature were factors that were also frequently cited. Vasari made critical comments about the artistic achievements of 28 (22.8%) of individuals.

The overall impression from the enumeration of these traits is that courteousness and sociability were common characteristics among Renaissance artists. Depressive tendencies and other temperamental oddities were comparatively rare, and were no more likely to be described than were unworldiness, sophistication, or unworthy traits such as licentiousness and pride. There is little here to endorse the presence either of a melancholic temperament, or of the hypersensitive alienated creature of modern conceptualizations. Nevertheless, it is possible that these latter traits are present in the truly great artists, and are swamped in this analysis by the characteristics of the less able.

Artistic traits in the elite

I have used two methods to examine this question. The first was to compare those artists described by Vasari as having high ability with the remainder. Thirty eight of the painters, sculptors, and architects discussed in the *Lives* were described as having exceptionally high ability by virtue of specific reference to their talent, inventiveness, and creativity. They include most of the great Renaissance artists, from the Siennese sculptor Jacopo della Quercia (1374–1438) and other early masters such as Ghiberti and Uccello, to Vasari's contemporaries Titian, Pordenone, and the architect Jacopo Sansovino. The characteristics of this group were compared with the remainder, and the results are summarized in Fig. 11.2.

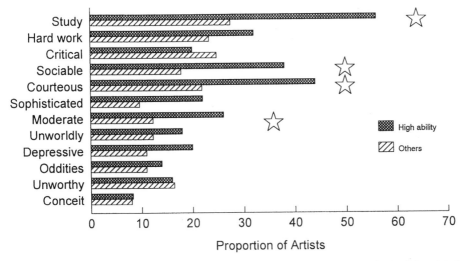

Fig. 11.2 Proportion of artists who were regarded by Vasari as having high ability (dark bars) and the remainder (hatched bars) displaying each of the twelve traits or temperamental characteristics. The stars indicate significant differences between groups at *p* < 0.05.

There were statistically significant differences (*p* < .05) between the artists of high ability and others in four traits. The high ability group were more likely to be described as studious, sociable, courteous, and moderate in their habits, than were others. None of the remaining differences between groups were statistically reliable. This result is interesting, in that it suggests that the traits of courteousness and sociability were accentuated among the artists of high ability and achievement. There is no sign that this élite group was more likely to be described as depressive or eccentric in their habits than was the remainder of the artists meriting inclusion in the *Lives*. This analysis therefore provides no support for the argument that the greatest artists of the Renaissance were particularly unconventional or temperamental.

A second approach to this issue refined the comparison still further. Vasari rented a house in the Borgo Santa Croce in Florence, and in June 1561 this was given to him by Duke Cosimo de'Medici. He and his assistants decorated the house with frescos of allegories and scenes from the history of painting. He also inserted portraits of 13 artists, 11 of whom were included in Parts II and III of *The Lives*. The prominence given to these individuals suggests that they were Vasari's favourites, and he considered them to be the most important of all. They are Masaccio, Brunelleschi, Donatello, Leonardo da Vinci, Raphael, Andrea del Sarto, Rosso Fiorentino, Giulio Romano, Perino del Vaga, Francesco Salviati, and Michelangelo.

A further analysis was therefore carried out comparing these eleven with the other 112 artists included in the *Lives*, and the results are shown in Fig. 11.3. This special élite vastly outstrips the remainder in descriptions of studiousness and diligence (as might

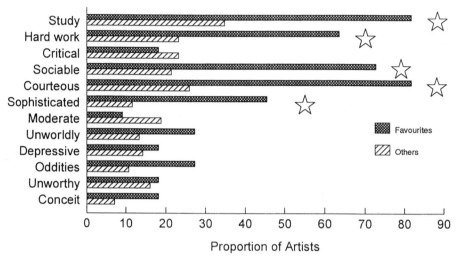

Fig. 11.3 Proportion of Vasari's favourite artists (dark bars) and the remainder (hatched bars) displaying each of the twelve traits or temperamental characteristics. The stars indicate significant differences between groups at $p < 0.05$.

be expected). However, they were also very likely to be described as sociable and courteous, and the differences were statistically significant. More than 80% were said to be courteous, generous, and helpful to others, while eight of the eleven (72.7%) were noted for being agreeable company. Interestingly, this group was also more likely than others to be described as sophisticated and cultivated ($p < 0.005$). There were no differences in depressive traits or temperamental oddities.

It might be argued that these characteristics were recorded by Vasari in the élite because they were the subjects of longer biographies. Perhaps Vasari knew more about these men since they were famous, and so was able to provide greater detail of their personalities. This explanation is improbable for the following reasons. Firstly, if length of biography or Vasari's familiarity with the subjects were the causes of these traits being mentioned, then this élite would also have been described more frequently as having the other traits summarized in Fig. 11.3. This is not the case. Secondly, if Vasari was trying to present this small group in a glowing light, he might have been tempted to describe them as moderate in habits, or holy and unworldly. There are no differences in these aspects between the two sets of artists. Moreover, Vasari's favourite artists were just as likely to have been tarred with negative attributes such as pride or fecklessness as the other artists. Consequently, the depiction by Vasari of his favourite artists as courteous, sociable, and sophisticated is not simply an artefact of the way he wrote their biographies, or of the way in which the data were analysed.

Errors and evasions

How much confidence can we place on the profile of the artist that emerges from Vasari's biographies? Not surprisingly, the *Lives* contain many errors that have been exposed by art historians. Vasari misdated works, attributed them to the wrong artists, and sometimes confused the lives of different painters (Boase 1979). His style of writing was rhetorical, and used classical forms of argument and interpretation (Carrier 1987). Part of this style involved exaggeration of praise and of blame, with the consequence that artists were criticized more strongly than their limitations might warrant (Goldstein 1991). Moreover, at times, Vasari was misled by his sources. For example, his long biography of Michelangelo gives an impression of bitter rivalry between Michelangelo and Raphael. Michelangelo was at work on the vast project for a grandiose tomb for Pope Julius II in the early years of the sixteenth century. Vasari describes how the jealous Raphael teamed up with the architect Bramante to jeopardize this work, by persuading the Pope to order Michelangelo to paint the ceiling of the Sistine Chapel instead. They hoped this would divert Michelangelo from sculpture, a domain in which he was undisputed master, on to fresco painting with which he was less familiar. In fact, Raphael had not even arrived in Rome by the time that Michelangelo was commissioned to work on the Chapel. The notion of a conspiracy probably emerged in Michelangelo's suspicious mind, and was relayed from him to Vasari.

Important though these errors are, they are less interesting in the present context than the deliberate evasions of the truth in which Vasari engaged. These deliberate evasions are rather infrequent, but are significant in that they sustain a particular image of the great artist. The sculptor Donatello (1386–1466) was one of his great heroes, an early genius of the Renaissance whose works were unsurpassed. Vasari's sources described Donatello as proud and arrogant, a man of sharp and bitter wit (Rubin 1995). Vasari suppressed this, and portrayed the sculptor as considerate, gracious, and courteous. His life is a panegyric to friendship and goodness of character, and eulogizes the virtues of kindness to others. Donatello was said to be so generous that he kept his money in a basket in his workshop, so that his assistants and friends could help themselves to what they needed. This virtue had its reward with Donatello living to a happy old age surrounded by friends and grateful patrons.

Vasari's intention was to emphasize the serene and generous personalities of the greatest artists, and not to present them as difficult or vainglorious. Perhaps the biggest challenge in this respect was Michelangelo. There seems no doubt that Michelangelo was a deeply troubled man whose melancholy was abundantly documented in his own writings. He viewed himself as fated for ecstasy and discontent in equal measure, and often despaired at being able to bring his transcendental ideas to fruition because of his own physical inadequacies (Kemp 1989). His letters to his family bespeak of persistent anxieties and unhappiness, while also having a self-pitying tone. Many of his projects were frustrated by intrigue or the fickleness of patrons, and his work was frequently greeted with incomprehension. However, he was not helped by an arrogant temperament, and some of his plans were so grandiose as to verge on the megalomaniacal.

Only glimpses of these traits emerge in Vasari's biography. He chose to portray Michelangelo as the saviour of art, presenting his birth as a second coming:

The most benign Ruler of Heaven in His clemency turned His eyes to the earth and . . . became minded to send down to earth a spirit with universal ability in every art and every profession, who might be able, working by himself alone, to show what manner of thing is the perfection of the art of design . . . and what it is to work with correct judgement in sculpture, and how in architecture it is possible to render habitations secure and commodious, healthy and cheerful, well-proportioned, and rich with varied ornaments. He was pleased, in addition, to endow him with the true moral philosophy and with the ornament of sweet poesy, to the end that the world might choose him and admire him as its highest exemplar in the life, works, saintliness of character, and every action of human creatures, and that he might be acclaimed by us as being rather divine than human. (Vasari 1996, p. 642)

The hyperbole continues, with Michelangelo being described as shrewd and observant, a man of sublime intellect coupled with a natural inborn grace. He was respected and admired by popes and sovereigns, and enjoyed the friendship of learned men as well as fellow artists and sculptors. He was always ready with friendly advice and support, and led a sober and decent life. In a final piece of idealization, Vasari claims that when Michelangelo died and his body was transferred from Rome to Florence, it was found to be uncorrupted and sweet smelling even after 25 days.

Vasari's portrayal of Renaissance artists

The results of this content analysis of Vasari's biographies are consistent with the idea that he was stimulated in part by a wish to establish painters and sculptors as respectable citizens fit for cultured society. His social construction of genius was intended to widen the social gulf that had emerged between artists and the ranks of unnamed decorative craftsmen. Vasari capitalized on this distinction in his own career, since he was not only successful as an artist, but also acquired a position of wealth and respect. He achieved this not by being temperamental and unpredictable, but through being reliable, efficient and willing to serve. Ironically, the virtues that he extolled are not the one for which the *Lives* are now read. Instead, his biographies are trawled for the eccentric, melancholic, and picaresque, characteristics that fulfil the popular image of the artist.

The model to which Vasari aspired for artists was that of the courtier, epitomized by Baldassare Castiglione in his celebrated *Il Cortegiano* of 1528. Castiglione described the true courtier as possessing charm, grace, and facility in conversation, dance, fighting, hunting, and other noble pursuits. The underlying principle was that these accomplishments should show an unforced ease (*sprezzatura*), an effortless superiority that came in later generations to be seen as the mark of the gentleman. Castiglione considered then that noble birth was a fundamental attribute of the true courtier:

Noble birth is like a bright lamp that makes clear and visible both good deeds and bad . . . As a general rule, both in arms and in other worthy activities, those who are most distinguished are of noble birth, because Nature has implanted in everything a hidden seed which has a certain way of influencing and passing on its own essential characteristics to all that grows from it making it similar to itself. (Castiglione 1976, p. 54)

The problem for Vasari was that some of the greatest artists came from modest backgrounds; Uccello's father was a barber, Botticelli's a tanner, Mantegna's a shepherd, and Fra Bartolomeo's a muleteer. Michelangelo's family was more distinguished, but was shamed by his ambition to become a sculptor. It is said that his father refused to recognize any distinction between a sculptor and plebeian stone mason. So in the absence of noble birth, Vasari's artists were portrayed as noble and gracious by nature. Charm and facility were coupled with natural ability. The model in life as well as art was Raphael, who was presented by Vasari as a gentleman painter, socially assured and graceful, possessing a sophistication and cultivation that allowed him to converse easily with intellectuals and rulers. Raphael came from a worthy family and studied diligently in his youth, so was later able to practise his art without apparent effort. Vasari loved the idea that Raphael lived like a prince, and admired artists who dressed richly and had opulent lifestyles.

Implications for understanding artistic temperament

One clear consequence of the analysis described in this chapter is that it raises once again the status of biographies as sources of objective data for psychological investigations. This is not a problem that is confined to Vasari's work, since all biographers have opinions about their subjects, and are influenced by the cultural and social mores of their times. All biographers make selections from the material that is available to them, filtering the information and its presentation. Vasari may be more extreme than many, since he had fewer facts to work on, and so was obliged to fall back on his own resources. However, inferences about creative people that go beyond verified facts must always be treated with great caution (e.g. Post 1994; Ludwig 1995; Sulloway 1996).

What conclusions can be drawn about the temperament and personality of artists? The investigation described here provides no support for the idea that the great painters, sculptors, and architects of the Renaissance conformed to the modern concept of the artistic personality. Across the entire group, unconventional behaviours or signs of psychological disturbance were less frequently described than many other characteristics. This pattern was even more marked among the artists especially admired by Vasari and by posterity.

One possibility is that Vasari's descriptions of personalities were entirely fictitious, and that no weight can be placed upon them at all. I have already described how he edited the information about certain artists so they emerged in a positive and socially acceptable light. However, I think it is unlikely that the profiles which emerge are without foundation for the following reasons. Firstly, he clearly relished the eccentricities that he did describe in some individuals. The peculiar traits of Piero di Cosimo and Pontormo, or the irascible nature of Andrea del Castagno, were emphasized in the *Lives*. It is improbable that Vasari would have suppressed other choice tales if they had been known to him. Secondly, he was writing about contemporaries and recently deceased artists. If his descriptions had been far from the mark, this would almost certainly have been noticed at the time. But there are no indications that his biographies were received with scepticism in this respect.

The alternative possibility is that the characteristics of sociability, courtesy, and generosity were genuinely common among the successful artists of fifteenth and sixteenth century Italy. If this was the case, then psychological disturbance, unconventionality or other aspects of the 'artistic personality' cannot be intrinsic to creativity. Indeed, there are many examples from later centuries of artists or other exceptionally creative people being sociable together and with others, including the Impressionists, the Bloomsbury group, and the Imagist poets such as William Carlos Williams and Ezra Pound. Ludwig (1995) has noted in his recent systematic analysis of twentieth century notables that some 45% of artistic individuals were gregarious and sociable. I have also remarked on Mozart's sociability in Chapter 7.

One might go further, and suggest that the 'artistic personality' may be an invention that has little bearing on artistic ability or achievement. They may indeed be modern accretions or stereotypes. The notion that creative individuals are impulsive, nonconformist, and emotional is part of society's implicit theory of creativity (Sternberg 1985). MacKinnon (1964), for example, collected ratings from architects of varying degrees of eminence concerning their own personalities and their ideal selves. The features that most typified creative architects were inventiveness, independence, and individualism, while the least creative were responsible, reliable, tolerant, and good-natured. Students at art colleges, only a minority of whom are likely to emerge as very talented, also appear higher than other students in traits such as autonomy and aggression and lower in self-control, nurturance, and deference (Dudek *et al.* 1991).

There are several reasons why these profiles may emerge. Kasof (1995) has presented a detailed argument suggesting that the coincidence between unconventional or disturbed behaviour and creativity may be illusory, and result from our tendency to attribute creative outputs to dispositional rather than situational factors. Nonconformist behaviour is by definition exceptional in society, so it strikes people as particularly salient when it does occur. If successful creators behave in an eccentric fashion, there may be a tendency to relate their productivity to this disposition. Salience heuristics may also account for some of the associations observed between mental instability and artistic creativity. Because mental instability is present in only a minority, co-occurrence with exceptional talent (another rare event) may lead people to assume there is a greater correlation than is actually present. Another possibility is that unusual behaviour may increase the chances that a talent is recognized by society. People who behave outrageously tend to be noticed more than conventional types, and so in the competitive art market their products may be noticed as well. Richards and Kinney (1990) have argued that the behaviours associated with mania—drive, energy, high work level, ability to think in large and even grandiose terms—may bring artists and their work to public awareness more effectively that reticent behaviours. Claridge makes a similar point in Chapter 10.

Whatever the explanation, temperamental and individualistic behaviour is probably adaptive among artists in the present day. It is the stuff of racy biographies, and may help to maintain interest in the works of artists at a higher pitch than might otherwise be expected. In the twentieth century, artists such as Eric Gill and Augustus John are as renowned for their behaviour and way of living as for their creations, while less colourful individuals are all but forgotten. It might be argued that in the sixteenth century, the sociable and cultivated traits highlighted by Vasari were equally adaptive, and ensured artists of the time a reliable income and respected place in society.

References

Barolsky, P. (1990). *Michelangelo's nose*. Pennsylvania State University Press, University Park.
——(1992). *Giotto's father and the family of Vasari's Lives*. Pennsylvania State University Press, University Park.
Blunt, A. (1962). *Artistic theory in Italy 1450–1600*. Oxford University Press, Oxford.
Boase, T. S. R. (1979). *Giorgio Vasari, the man and the book*. Princeton University Press, Princeton.
Carrier, D. (1987). Ekphrasis and interpretation: two modes of art history writing. *British Journal of Aesthetics*, **27**, 20–31.
Cast, D. (1993). Reading Vasari again: history, philosophy. *Word and Image*, **9**, 29–38.
Castiglione, B. (1976). *The book of the courtier* (trans. G. Bull). Harmondsworth, Penguin Books.
Cole, B. (1983). *The Renaissance artist at work*. John Murray, London.
Dudek, S. Z., Berneche, R., Berube, H., and Royer, S. (1991). Personality determinants of the commitment to the profession of art. *Creativity Research Journal*, **4**, 367–98.
Goffen, R. (1989). *Giovanni Bellini*. Yale University Press, New Haven.
Goldstein, C. (1991). Rhetoric and art history in the Italian Renaissance. *Art Bulletin* **73**, 641–52.
Kasof, J. (1995). Explaining creativity: the attributional perspective. *Creativity Research Journal*, **8**, 311–66.
Kemp, M. (1989). The 'super-artist' as genius: the sixteenth century view. In *Genius: the history of an idea* (ed. P. Murray), pp. 32–53. Basil Blackwell, Oxford.
Kempers, B. (1987). *Painting, power and patronage* (trans. B. Jackson). Allen Lane, London.
Kessel, N. (1989). Genius and mental disorder: a history of ideas concerning their conjuction. In *Genius: the history of an idea* (ed. P. Murray), pp. 196–212. Blackwell, Oxford.
Kleinman, J. (1996). Giorgio Vasari, In *The dictionary of art*, Vol. 32 (ed. J. Turner), pp. 10–25. Macmillan, London.
Klibansky, R., E. Panofsky, and Saxl, F. (1964). *Saturn and melancholy: studies in the history of natural philosophy, religion and art*. Nelson, London.

Kris, E., and Kurz, O. (1979). *Legend, myth, and magic in the image of the artist* (trans. A. Laing and L. M. Newman). Yale University Press, New Haven.

Lombroso, C. (1890). *The man of genius*. Scott, London.

Ludwig, A. M. (1995). *The price of greatness*. Guilford Press, New York.

MacKinnon, D. W. (1964). *The study of lives*. Atherton Press, New York.

Murray, L. (1984). *Michelangelo: his life, work and times*. Thames and Hudson, London.

Murray, P. (1989). Poetic genius and its classical origins. In *Genius: the history of an idea* (ed. P. Murray), pp. 9–31. Blackwell, Oxford.

Northcote, J. (1813). *Memoirs of Sir Joshua Reynolds*. London.

Post, F. (1994). Creativity and psychopathology: a study of 291 world-famous men. *British Journal of Psychiatry*, **305**, 1198–202.

Richards, R. (1981). Relationships between creativity and psychopathology: an evaluation and interpretation of the evidence. *Genetic Psychology Monographs*, **103**, 261–324.

——(1990). Everyday creativity, eminent creativity, and health. *Creativity Research Journal*, **3**, 300–26.

Richards, R., and Kinney, D. K. (1990). Mood swings and creativity. *Creativity Research Journal*, **3**, 203–18.

Rubin, P. L. (1995). *Giorgio Vasari: art and history*. Yale University Press, New Haven.

Sacks, O. (1995). *An anthropologist on Mars*. Picador, London.

Sternberg, R. J. (1985). Implicit theories of intelligence, creativity, and wisdom. *Journal of Personality and Social Psychology*, **49**, 607–27.

Sulloway, F. J. (1996). *Born to rebel*. Little, Brown and Co., London.

Vasari, G. (1966–1987). *Le vite de'piu eccellenti pittori scultori e architettore nelle redazione del 1550 e 1568*. Sansoni, Florence.

——(1996). *Lives of the painters, sculptors and architects* (trans. Gaston de Vere). Everyman's Library, London.

Weber, R. B. (1990). *Basic content analysis*. Sage Publications, Newbury Park, CA.

White, J. (1966). *Art and architecture in Italy 1250–1400*. Yale University Press, New Haven.

Wittkower, R., and Wittkower, M. (1965). *Born under Saturn*. Weidenfeld, London.

Index

social support 153–5
specialization in music 72
Stadler, Anton 83
Stephenson, George 6, 106–8
Stigler, George 59, 106–8
stress
    and creativity 152
    and health 7, 151
suicide 198, 204, 213, 238, 242
systems perspective 39–64

temperament
    artistic 6, 10, 59, 253, 259–65, 267–8
    genetics and 33, 199
    scientific 120, 125
    see also Lord Byron
Thalburg, Sigismund 83–4, 87

theatre 5, 171–81
twin studies 3, 22, 24–8

Van Gogh, Vincent 48
Vasari, Giorgio 101
    biography 258–9
    errors of 255, 265–6
    Lives 254–5, 260
    significance 254–5
    view of progress in art 259
verse forms 175, 176
violin 72, 82
Vivaldi, Antonio 83, 87

Weber, Aloisia 148
White, Antonia 237
Woolf, Virginia 9, 237–9